Study Guide

Essentials of Economics

Seventh Edition

N. Gregory Mankiw
Harvard University

Preparer

David R. Hakes
University of Northern Iowa

D1316063

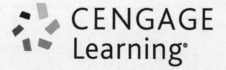

Australia • Brazil • Japan • Korea • Mexico • Singapore • Spain • United Kingdom • United States

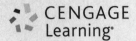

ISBN-13: 978-1-285-86428-0
ISBN-10: 1-285-86428-X

Cengage Learning
200 First Stamford Place, 4th Floor
Stamford, CT 06902
USA

Cengage Learning is a leading provider of customized learning solutions with office locations around the globe, including Singapore, the United Kingdom, Australia, Mexico, Brazil, and Japan. Locate your local office at: **international.cengage.com/region**.

Cengage Learning products are represented in Canada by Nelson Education, Ltd.

For your course and learning solutions, visit **www.cengage.com**.

Purchase any of our products at your local college store or at our preferred online store **www.CengageBrain.com**.

Printed in the United States of America
1 2 3 4 5 6 7   17 16 15 14 13

One must learn by doing the thing;
For though you think you know it
You have no certainty, until you try.

Sophocles, c. 496–406 b.c.
Greek playwright
Trachiniae

Preface

This *Study Guide* accompanies N. Gregory Mankiw's *Essentials of Economics*, Seventh Edition. It was written with only one audience in mind—you, the student.

Your time is scarce. To help you use it efficiently, this *Study Guide* focuses strictly on the material presented in Mankiw's *Essentials of Economics*, Seventh Edition. It does not introduce extraneous material.

Objectives of the Study Guide

There are three broad objectives to the *Study Guide*. First, the *Study Guide* reinforces the text and improves your understanding of the material presented in the text. Second, it provides you with experience in using economic theories and tools to solve actual economic problems. That is, this *Study Guide* bridges the gap between economic concepts and economic problem solving. This may be the most important objective of the *Study Guide* because those students who find economics inherently logical often think that they are prepared for exams just by reading the text or attending lectures. However, it is one thing to watch an economist solve a problem in class and another thing altogether to solve a problem alone. There is simply no substitute for hands-on experience. Third, the *Study Guide* includes a self-test to validate areas of successful learning and to highlight areas needing improvement.

It is unlikely that you will truly enjoy any area of study if you fail to understand the material or if you lack confidence when taking tests over the material. It is my hope that this *Study Guide* improves your understanding of economics and improves your test performance so that you are able to enjoy economics as much as I do.

Organization of the Study Guide

Each chapter in the *Study Guide* corresponds to a chapter in Mankiw's *Essentials of Economics.* Each chapter is divided into the following sections:

* The Chapter Overview begins with a description of the purpose of the chapter and how it fits into the larger framework of the text. Following this context and purpose section are learning objectives, a section-by-section Chapter Review, and some helpful hints for understanding the material. The Chapter Overview ends with terms and definitions. This part is particularly important because it is impossible for the text to communicate information to you or for you to communicate information to your instructor on your exams without the use of a common economic vocabulary.

* Problems and Short-Answer Questions provide hands-on experience with problems based on the material presented in the text. The practice problems are generally multiple-step problems while the short-answer questions are generally based on a single issue.

* The Self-Test is composed of 15 True/False questions and 20 Multiple-Choice questions.

* The Advanced Critical Thinking section is a real-world problem that employs the economic reasoning and tools developed in the chapter. It is an applied story problem.

* Solutions are provided for all questions in the *Study Guide.* Explanations are also provided for false responses to True/False questions in the Self-Test.

Use of the Study Guide

I hesitate to suggest a method for using this *Study Guide* because how one best uses a study guide is largely a personal matter. It depends on your preferences and talents and on your instructor's approach to the material. I will, however, discuss a few possible approaches, and trial and error may help you sort out an approach that best suits you.

Some students prefer to read an entire chapter in the text prior to reading the *Study Guide.* Others prefer to read a section in the text and then read the corresponding section in the Chapter Overview portion of the *Study Guide.* This second method may help you focus your attention on the most important aspects of each section in the text. Some students who feel particularly confident after reading the text may choose to take the Self-Test immediately. I do not generally support this approach. I suggest that you complete all of the Practice Problems and Short-Answer Questions before you attempt the Self-Test. You will receive more accurate feedback from the Self-Test if you are well prepared prior to taking it.

A study guide is not a substitute for a text any more than *Cliff Notes* is a substitute for a classic novel. Use this *Study Guide* in conjunction with Mankiw's *Essentials of Economics,* not in place of it.

Final Thoughts

All of the problems and questions in this *Study Guide* have been checked by a number of accuracy reviewers. However, if you find a mistake, or if you have comments or suggestions for future editions, please feel free to contact me via email at hakes@uni.edu.

Acknowledgments

I would like to thank Greg Mankiw for having written such a well thought-out text that it made writing the *Study Guide* a truly enjoyable task. I thank Jennifer Thomas, the Product Development Manager, for keeping things on schedule. I thank OffCenter Concept House for designing the layout and editing the manuscript. Ken McCormick, a friend and colleague, provided constructive counsel throughout the project.

Finally, I would like to thank my family for being patient and understanding during the time I spent working on this *Study Guide*.

David R. Hakes
University of Northern Iowa

Comparative Table of Contents

Contents

Chapter 1

Ten Principles of Economics

Goals
In this chapter you will

- Learn that economics is about the allocation of scarce resources

- Examine some of the trade-offs that people face

- Learn the meaning of opportunity cost

- See how to use marginal reasoning when making decisions

- Discuss how incentives affect people's behavior

- Consider why trade among people or nations can be good for everyone

- Discuss why markets are a good, but not perfect, way to allocate resources

- Learn what determines some trends in the overall economy

Outcomes
After accomplishing these goals, you should be able to

- Define scarcity

- Explain the classic trade-off between "guns and butter"

- Add up your particular opportunity cost of attending college

- Compare the marginal costs and marginal benefits of continuing to attend school indefinitely

- Consider how a quadrupling of your tuition payments would affect your decision to educate yourself

- Explain why specialization and trade improve people's choices

- Give an example of an externality

- Explain the source of large and persistent inflation

Chapter Overview

Context and Purpose

Chapter 1 is the first chapter in a three-chapter section that serves as the introduction to the text. Chapter 1 introduces ten fundamental principles on which the study of economics is based. In a broad sense, the rest of the text is an elaboration on these ten principles. Chapter 2 will develop how economists approach problems, while Chapter 3 will explain how individuals and countries gain from trade.

The purpose of Chapter 1 is to lay out ten economic principles that will serve as building blocks for the rest of the text. The ten principles can be grouped into three categories: how people make decisions, how people interact, and how the economy works as a whole. Throughout the text, references will be made repeatedly to these ten principles.

Chapter Review

Introduction   Households and society face decisions about how to allocate scarce resources. Resources are scarce in that we have fewer resources than we wish. Economics is the study of how society manages its scarce resources. Economists study how people make decisions about buying and selling, and saving and investing. We study how people interact with one another in markets where prices are determined and quantities are exchanged. We also study the economy as a whole when we concern ourselves with total income, unemployment, and inflation.

This chapter addresses ten principles of economics. The text will refer to these principles throughout. The ten principles are grouped into three categories: how people make decisions, how people interact, and how the economy works as a whole.

How People Make Decisions

- **Principle 1: People face trade-offs**   Economists often say, "There ain't no such thing as a free lunch." This means that there are always trade-offs—to get more of something we like, we have to give up something else that we like. For example, if you spend money on dinner and a movie, you won't be able to spend it on new clothes. Socially, we face trade-offs as a group. For example, there is the classic trade-off between "guns and butter." That is, if society spends more on national defense (guns), then it will have less to spend on social programs (butter). There is also a social trade-off between efficiency (getting the most from our scarce resources) and equality (benefits being distributed uniformly across society). Policies such as taxes and welfare make incomes more equal, but these policies reduce returns to hard work, and thus, the economy doesn't produce as much. As a result, when the government tries to cut the pie into more equal pieces, the pie gets smaller.

- **Principle 2: The cost of something is what you give up to get it**   The opportunity cost of an item is what you give up to get that item. It is the true cost of the item. The opportunity cost of going to college obviously includes your tuition payment. It also includes the value of your time that you could have spent working, valued at your potential earnings. It would exclude your room and board payment because you have to eat and sleep whether you are in school or not.

- **Principle 3: Rational people think at the margin**   Rational people systematically do the best they can to achieve their objectives. A marginal change is an incremental change to an existing plan. Rational decision makers only proceed with an action if the marginal benefit exceeds the marginal cost. For example, you should only attend school for another year if the benefits from that year of schooling exceed the cost of attending that year. A farmer should produce another bushel of corn only if the benefit (price received) exceeds the cost of producing it.

- **Principle 4: People respond to incentives**   An incentive is something that induces a person to act. Because rational people weigh marginal costs and marginal benefits of activities, they will respond when these costs or benefits change. For example, when the price of automobiles rises, buyers have an incentive to buy fewer cars while automobile producers have an incentive to hire more workers and produce more autos. An increase in the price of gasoline causes people to buy smaller cars, ride mass transit, and ride bicycles. Public policy can alter the costs or benefits of activities. For example, a tax on gasoline raises the price and discourages the purchase of gasoline. Some policies have unintended consequences because they alter behavior in a manner that was not predicted.

How People Interact

- **Principle 5: Trade can make everyone better off**   Trade is not a contest in which one wins and one loses. Trade can make each trader better off. Trade allows each trader to specialize in what he or she does best, whether it be farming, building, or manufacturing, and trade their output for the output of other efficient producers. This is as true for countries as it is for individuals.

- **Principle 6: Markets are usually a good way to organize economic activity**   In a market economy, the decisions about what goods and services to produce, how much to produce, and who gets to consume them are made by millions of firms and households. Firms and households, guided by self-interest, interact in the marketplace where prices and quantities are determined. Although this may appear to be chaos, Adam Smith made the famous observation in the *Wealth of Nations* in 1776 that self-interested households and firms interact in markets and generate desirable social outcomes as if guided by an "invisible hand." These optimal social outcomes were not their original intent. The prices generated by their competitive activity signal the value of costs and benefits to producers and consumers, whose activities usually maximize the well-being of society. Alternatively, the prices dictated by central planners contain no information on costs and benefits, and therefore, these prices fail to guide economic activity efficiently. Prices also fail to guide economic activity efficiently when governments distort prices with taxes or restrict price movements with price controls.

- **Principle 7: Governments can sometimes improve market outcomes**   Government must first protect property rights in order for markets to work. In addition, government can sometimes intervene in the market to improve efficiency or equality. When markets fail to allocate resources efficiently, there has been market failure. There are many different sources of market failure. An externality is when the actions of one person affect the well-being of a bystander. Pollution is a standard example. Market power is when a single person or group can influence the price. In these cases, the government may be able to intervene and improve economic efficiency. The government may also intervene to improve equality with income taxes and welfare. Sometimes well-intentioned policy intervention has unintended consequences.

How the Economy as a Whole Works

- **Principle 8: A country's standard of living depends on its ability to produce goods and services**   There is great variation in average incomes across countries at a point in time and within the same country over time. These differences in incomes and standards of living are largely attributable to differences in productivity. Productivity is the amount of goods and services produced by each unit of labor input. As a result, public policy intended to improve standards of living should improve education, generate more and better tools, and improve access to current technology.

- **Principle 9: Prices rise when the government prints too much money**   Inflation is an increase in the overall level of prices in the economy. High inflation is costly to the economy. Large and persistent inflation is caused by rapid growth in the quantity of money. Policymakers who wish to keep inflation low should maintain slow growth in the quantity of money.

- **Principle 10: Society faces a short-run trade-off between inflation and unemployment**
In the short run, an increase in the quantity of money stimulates spending, which raises both prices and production. The increase in production requires more hiring, which reduces unemployment. Thus, in the short run, an increase in inflation tends to reduce unemployment, causing a trade-off between inflation and unemployment. The trade-off is temporary but can last for a year or two. Understanding this trade-off is important for understanding the fluctuations in economic activity, known as the business cycle. In the short run, policymakers may be able to affect the mix of inflation and unemployment by changing government spending, taxes, and the quantity of money. Some economists are concerned that President Obama's stimulus package, which is intended to reduce unemployment, may lead to inflation.

Helpful Hints

1. Place yourself in the story. Throughout the text, most economic situations will be composed of economic actors—buyers and sellers, borrowers and lenders, firms and workers, and so on. When you are asked to address how any economic actor would respond to economic incentives, place yourself in the story as the buyer or the seller, the borrower or the lender, the producer or the consumer. Don't think of yourself always as the buyer (a natural tendency) or always as the seller. You will find that your role-playing will usually produce the right response once you learn to think like an economist—which is the topic of the next chapter.

2. Trade is not a zero-sum game. Some people see an exchange in terms of winners and losers. Their reaction to trade is that, after the sale, if the seller is happy, the buyer must be sad because the seller must have taken something from the buyer. That is, they view trade as a zero-sum game where what one gains the other must have lost. They fail to see that both parties to a voluntary transaction gain because each party is allowed to specialize in what it can produce most efficiently and then trade for items that are produced more efficiently by others. Nobody loses because trade is voluntary. Therefore, a government policy that limits trade reduces the potential gains from trade.

3. An externality can be positive. Because the classic example of an externality is pollution, it is easy to think of an externality as a cost that lands on a bystander. However, an externality can be positive in that it can be a benefit that lands on a bystander. For example, education is often cited as a product that emits a positive externality because when your neighbor educates herself, she is likely to be more reasonable, responsible, productive, and politically astute. In short, she is a better neighbor. Positive externalities, just as much as negative externalities, may be a reason for the government to intervene to promote efficiency.

Terms and Definitions

Choose a definition for each key term.

Key Terms	
_3_	Scarcity
_13_	Economics
_7_	Efficiency
_1_	Equality
_14_	Opportunity cost
_18_	Rational
_12_	Marginal change
_16_	Incentive
_8_	Market economy
_17_	Property rights
_6_	"Invisible hand"
_2_	Market failure
_10_	Externality
_15_	Market power
_5_	Monopoly
_4_	Productivity
_11_	Inflation
_9_	Business cycle

Definitions

1. The property of distributing economic prosperity uniformly among society's members
2. A situation in which the market fails to allocate resources efficiently
3. Limited resources and unlimited wants
4. The amount of goods and services produced from each unit of labor input
5. The case in which there is only one seller in the market
6. The principle that self-interested market participants may unknowingly maximize the welfare of society as a whole
7. The property of society getting the most from its scarce resources
8. An economic system where interaction of households and firms in markets determines the allocation of resources
9. Fluctuations in economic activity
10. When one person's actions have an impact on a bystander
11. An increase in the overall level of prices
12. An incremental adjustment to an existing plan
13. Study of how society manages its scarce resources
14. Whatever is given up to get something else
15. The ability of an individual or group to substantially influence market prices
16. Something that induces a person to act
17. The ability of an individual to own and exercise control over scarce resources
18. Systematically and purposefully doing the best you can to achieve your objectives

Problems and Short-Answer Questions

Practice Problems

1. People respond to incentives. Governments can alter incentives and, hence, behavior with public policy. However, sometimes public policy generates unintended consequences by producing results that were not anticipated. For each of the following public policies, determine which result was likely the intended result and which was the unintended consequence.
   a. The government raises the minimum wage to $10 per hour. Some workers find jobs at the higher wage making these workers better off. Some workers find no job at all because few firms want to hire low-productivity workers at this high wage.

   intended: gets people to work harder
   unintended: unemployment

b. The government places rent controls on apartments restricting rent to $300 per month. Few landlords are willing to produce an apartment at this price causing more homelessness. Some low-income renters are able to rent an apartment more cheaply.

intended: restricting low income renters

unintended: homelessness

c. The government raises the tax on gasoline by $2 per gallon. The deficit is reduced, and people economize on their use of gasoline. There is a boom in bicycle sales.

_____

_____

d. The government declares marijuana and cocaine illegal. The price of illegal drugs increases, creating more gangs and gang warfare. Due to the high price of illegal drugs, fewer street drugs are consumed.

_____

_____

e. The government prohibits the killing of wolves. The wolf population increases. Sheep and cattle herds suffer losses.

_____

_____

f. The government bans imports of sugar from South America. South American sugar beet growers can't repay their loans to U.S. banks and turn to more profitable crops such as coca leaves and marijuana. U.S. sugar beet growers avoid a financial crisis.

_____

_____

2. Opportunity cost is what you give up to get an item. Because there is no such thing as a free lunch, what would likely be given up to obtain each of the items listed below?
   a. Susan can work full time or go to college. She chooses college.

   _____

   b. Susan can work full time or go to college. She chooses work.

   _____

   c. Farmer Jones has 100 acres of land. He can plant corn, which yields 100 bushels per acre, or he can plant beans, which yield 40 bushels per acre. He chooses to plant corn.

   _____

   d. Farmer Jones has 100 acres of land. He can plant corn, which yields 100 bushels per acre, or he can plant beans, which yield 40 bushels per acre. He chooses to plant beans.

   100 bushels

   e. In *a* and *b* above and *c* and *d* above, which is the opportunity cost of which—college for work or work for college? corn for beans or beans for corn?

   _____

Short-Answer Questions

1. Is air scarce? Is clean air scarce?

   no air is an unlimited resource
   clean air is maybe if pollution increases

2. What is the opportunity cost of saving some of your paycheck?

   not being able to buy something with it

3. Why is there a trade-off between equality and efficiency?

   cant always ~~equally~~ distribute the most out
   of scares resources equally

4. Water is necessary for life. Diamonds are not. Is the marginal benefit of an additional glass of water greater or lesser than an additional one-carat diamond? Why?

   less. Diamonds are more expensive/rare.
   Not giving up anything for water.

5. Your car needs to be repaired. You have already paid $500 to have the transmission fixed, but it still doesn't work properly. You can sell your car "as is" for $2,000. If your car were fixed, you could sell it for $2,500. Your car can be fixed with a guarantee for another $300. Should you repair your car? Why?

   No you would be paying more to fix it than
   to just sell it

6. Why do you think air bags have reduced deaths from auto crashes less than we had hoped?

7. Suppose one country is better at producing agricultural products (because they have land that is more fertile), while another country is better at producing manufactured goods (because they have a better educational system and more engineers). If each country produced their specialty and traded, would there be more or less total output than if each country produced all of their agricultural and manufacturing needs? Why?

8. In the *Wealth of Nations*, Adam Smith said, "It is not from the benevolence of the butcher, the brewer, or the baker that we expect our dinner, but from their regard to their own interest." What do you think he meant?

_____

_____

_____

9. If we save more and use it to build more physical capital, productivity will rise and we will have rising standards of living in the future. What is the opportunity cost of future growth?

_____

10. If the government printed twice as much money, what do you think would happen to prices and output if the economy were already producing at maximum capacity?

_____

_____

_____

11. A goal for a society is to distribute resources more equally and fairly. How might you distribute resources if everyone were equally talented and worked equally hard? What if people had different talents and some people worked hard, while others did not?

_____

_____

_____

_____

12. Who is more self-interested, the buyer or the seller?

_____

_____

_____

_____

Self-Test

True/False Questions

____ 1.   When the government redistributes income with taxes and welfare, the economy becomes more efficient.

____ 2.   When economists say, "There ain't no such thing as a free lunch," they mean that all economic decisions involve trade-offs.

____ 3.   Adam Smith's "invisible hand" concept describes how corporate business reaches into the pockets of consumers like an "invisible hand."

_____ 4. Rational people act only when the marginal benefit of the action exceeds the marginal cost.

_____ 5. The United States will benefit economically if we eliminate trade with Asian countries because we will be forced to produce more of our own cars and clothes.

_____ 6. When a jet flies overhead, the noise it generates is an externality.

_____ 7. A tax on liquor raises the price of liquor and provides an incentive for consumers to drink more.

_____ 8. An unintended consequence of public support for higher education is that low tuition provides an incentive for many people to attend state universities even if they have no desire to learn anything.

_____ 9. Sue is better at cleaning, and Bob is better at cooking. It will take fewer hours to eat and clean if Bob specializes in cooking and Sue specializes in cleaning than if they share the household duties evenly.

_____ 10. High and persistent inflation is caused by excessive growth in the quantity of money in the economy.

_____ 11. In the short run, a reduction in inflation tends to cause a reduction in unemployment.

_____ 12. An auto manufacturer should continue to produce additional autos as long as the firm is profitable, even if the cost of the additional units exceeds the price received.

_____ 13. An individual farmer is likely to have market power in the market for wheat.

_____ 14. To a student, the opportunity cost of going to a basketball game would include the price of the ticket and the value of the time that could have been spent studying.

_____ 15. Workers in the United States have a relatively high standard of living because the United States has a relatively high minimum wage.

Multiple-Choice Questions

1. Which of the following involve a trade-off?
   a. buying a new car
   b. going to college
   c. watching a football game on Saturday afternoon
   d. taking a nap
   e. All of the above involve trade-offs.

2. Trade-offs are required because wants are unlimited and resources are
   a. efficient.
   b. economical.
   c. scarce.
   d. unlimited.
   e. marginal.

3. Economics is the study of how
   a. to fully satisfy our unlimited wants.
   b. society manages its scarce resources.
   c. to reduce our wants until we are satisfied.
   d. to avoid having to make trade-offs.
   e. society manages its unlimited resources.

4. A rational person does not act unless
   a. the action makes money for the person.
   b. the action is ethical.
   c. the action produces marginal costs that exceed marginal benefits.
   d. the action produces marginal benefits that exceed marginal costs.
   e. None of the above is true.

5. Raising taxes and increasing welfare payments
   a. proves that there is such a thing as a free lunch.
   b. reduces market power.
   c. improves efficiency at the expense of equality.
   d. improves equality at the expense of efficiency.
   e. does none of the above.

6. Suppose you find $20. If you choose to use the $20 to go to the football game, your opportunity cost of going to the game is
   a. nothing, because you found the money.
   b. $20 (because you could have used the $20 to buy other things).
   c. $20 (because you could have used the $20 to buy other things) plus the value of your time spent at the game.
   d. $20 (because you could have used the $20 to buy other things) plus the value of your time spent at the game plus the cost of the dinner you purchased at the game.
   e. none of the above.

7. Foreign trade
   a. allows a country to have a greater variety of products at a lower cost than if it tried to produce everything at home.
   b. allows a country to avoid trade-offs.
   c. makes the members of a country more equal.
   d. increases the scarcity of resources.
   e. is none of the above.

8. Because people respond to incentives, we would expect that if the average salary of accountants increases by 50 percent while the average salary of teachers increases by 20 percent,
   a. students will shift majors from education to accounting.
   b. students will shift majors from accounting to education.
   c. fewer students will attend college.
   d. None of the above is true.

9. Which of the following activities is most likely to produce an externality?
   a. A student sits at home and watches television.
   b. A student has a party in her dorm room.
   c. A student reads a novel for pleasure.
   d. A student eats a hamburger in the student union.

10. Which of the following products would be least capable of producing an externality?
    a. cigarettes
    b. stereo equipment
    c. inoculations against disease
    d. education
    e. food

11. Which of the following situations describes the greatest market power?
    a. a farmer's impact on the price of corn
    b. Volvo's impact on the price of autos
    c. Microsoft's impact on the price of desktop operating systems
    d. a student's impact on college tuition

12. Which of the following statements is true about a market economy?
    a. Market participants act as if guided by an "invisible hand" to produce outcomes that promote general economic well-being.
    b. Taxes help prices communicate costs and benefits to producers and consumers.
    c. With a large enough computer, central planners could guide production more efficiently than markets.
    d. The strength of a market system is that it tends to distribute resources evenly across consumers.

13. Workers in the United States enjoy a high standard of living because
    a. unions in the United States keep the wage high.
    b. we have protected our industry from foreign competition.
    c. the United States has a high minimum wage.
    d. workers in the United States are highly productive.
    e. None of the above is true.

14. High and persistent inflation is caused by
    a. unions increasing wages too much.
    b. OPEC raising the price of oil too much.
    c. governments increasing the quantity of money too much.
    d. regulations raising the cost of production too much.

15. In the short run,
    a. an increase in inflation temporarily increases unemployment.
    b. a decrease in inflation temporarily increases unemployment.
    c. inflation and unemployment are unrelated.
    d. the business cycle has been eliminated.
    e. None of the above is true.

16. An increase in the price of beef provides
    a. information that tells consumers to buy more beef.
    b. information that tells consumers to buy less pork.
    c. information that tells producers to produce more beef.
    d. no information because prices in a market system are managed by planning boards.

17. You have spent $1,000 building a hot-dog stand based on estimates of sales of $2,000. The hot-dog stand is nearly completed, but now you estimate total sales to be only $800. You can complete the hot-dog stand for another $300. Should you complete the hot-dog stand? (Assume that the hot dogs cost you nothing.)
    a. Yes.
    b. No.
    c. There is not enough information to answer this question.

18. Referring to question 17, your decision rule should be to complete the hot-dog stand as long as the cost to complete the stand is less than
    a. $100.
    b. $300.
    c. $500.
    d. $800.
    e. none of the above.

19. Which of the following is not part of the opportunity cost of going on vacation?
    a. the money you could have made if you had stayed home and worked
    b. the money you spent on food
    c. the money you spent on airline tickets
    d. the money you spent on a Broadway show

20. Productivity can be increased by
    a. raising minimum wages.
    b. raising union wages.
    c. improving the education of workers.
    d. restricting trade with foreign countries.

Advanced Critical Thinking

Suppose your university decides to lower the cost of parking on campus by reducing the price of a parking permit from $200 per semester to $5 per semester.

1. What do you think would happen to the number of students desiring to park their cars on campus?

   Everyone would be more willing to park

2. What do you think would happen to the amount of time it would take to find a parking place?

   Time would increase

3. Thinking in terms of opportunity cost, would the lower price of a parking permit necessarily lower the true cost of parking?

4. Would the opportunity cost of parking be the same for students with no outside employment and students with jobs earning $15 per hour?

Solutions

Terms and Definitions

_3_ Scarcity

_13_ Economics

_7_ Efficiency

_1_ Equality

_14_ Opportunity cost

_18_ Rational

_12_ Marginal change

_16_ Incentive

_8_ Market economy

_17_ Property rights

_6_ "Invisible hand"

_2_ Market failure

_10_ Externality

_15_ Market power

_5_ Monopoly

_4_ Productivity

_11_ Inflation

_9_ Business cycle

Practice Problems

1. a. Intended: Raise the wage of low-productivity workers. Unintended: Some workers are unemployed at the higher wage.
   b. Intended: Low-income renters get a cheap apartment. Unintended: Some people find no apartment at all causing more homelessness.
   c. Intended: Reduce the deficit and use less gasoline. Unintended: Bicycle sales increase.
   d. Intended: Fewer street drugs are consumed. Unintended: More gangs and gang warfare.
   e. Intended: Increase the wolf population. Unintended: Damage to sheep and cattle herds.
   f. Intended: Improve the financial condition of U.S. sugar beet growers. Unintended: Cause South American growers to grow marijuana and coca leaves.

2. a. Susan gives up income from work (and must pay tuition).
   b. Susan gives up a college degree and the increase in income through life that it would have brought her (but doesn't have to pay tuition).
   c. Farmer Jones gives up 4,000 bushels of beans.
   d. Farmer Jones gives up 10,000 bushels of corn.
   e. Each is the opportunity cost of the other because each decision requires giving something up.

Short-Answer Questions

1. No, you don't have to give up anything to get air. Yes, you can't have as much clean air as you want without giving up something to get it (pollution equipment on cars, etc.).

2. The items you could have enjoyed had you spent that portion of your paycheck (current consumption).

3. Taxes and welfare make us more equal but reduce incentives for hard work, lowering total output.

4. The marginal benefit of another glass of water is generally lower because we have so much water that one more glass is of little value. The opposite is true for diamonds.

5. Yes, because the marginal benefit of fixing the car is $2,500 – $2,000 = $500, and the marginal cost is $300. The original repair payment is not relevant.

6. The cost of an accident was lowered. This changed incentives, so people drive faster and have more accidents.

7. There would be more total output if the two countries specialize and trade because each is doing what it does most efficiently.

8. The butcher, brewer, and baker produce the best food possible, not out of kindness, but because it is in their best interest to do so. Self-interest can maximize general economic well-being.

9. We must give up consumption today.

10. Spending would double, but since the quantity of output would remain the same, prices would double.

11. Fairness might require that everyone get an equal share because they were equally talented and worked equally hard. Fairness might require that people not get an equal share because they were not equally talented and did not work equally hard.

12. They are equally self-interested. The seller will sell to the highest bidder, and the buyer will buy from the lowest offer.

True/False Questions

1. F; the economy becomes less efficient because it decreases the incentive to work hard.
2. T
3. F; the "invisible hand" refers to how markets guide self-interested people to create desirable social outcomes.
4. T
5. F; all countries gain from voluntary trade.
6. T
7. F; higher prices reduce the quantity demanded.
8. T
9. T
10. T
11. F; a reduction in inflation tends to raise unemployment.
12. F; a manufacturer should produce as long as the marginal benefit exceeds the marginal cost.

13. F; a single farmer is too small to influence the market.
14. T
15. F; workers in the United States have a high standard of living because they are productive.

Multiple-Choice Questions

1. e
2. c
3. b
4. d
5. d
6. c
7. a
8. a
9. b
10. e
11. c
12. a
13. d
14. c
15. b
16. c
17. a
18. d
19. b
20. c

Advanced Critical Thinking

1. More students would wish to park on campus.
2. It would take much longer to find a parking place.
3. No, because we would have to factor in the value of our time spent looking for a parking place.
4. No. Students who could be earning money working are giving up more while looking for a parking place. Therefore, their opportunity cost is higher.

Chapter 2
Thinking Like an Economist

Goals
In this chapter you will

- See how economists apply the methods of science
- Consider how assumptions and models can shed light on the world
- Learn two simple models—the circular-flow diagram and the production possibilities frontier
- Distinguish between microeconomics and macroeconomics
- Learn the difference between positive and normative statements
- Examine the role of economists in making policy
- Consider why economists sometimes disagree with one another

Outcomes
After accomplishing these goals, you should be able to

- Describe the scientific method
- Understand the art of making useful assumptions
- Explain the slope of a production possibilities frontier
- Place economic issues into the categories of microeconomics or macroeconomics
- Place economic statements into the categories of normative or positive
- See the link between policymaking and normative statements
- List two reasons why economists disagree

Chapter Overview

Context and Purpose

Chapter 2 is the second chapter in a three-chapter section that serves as the introduction of the text. Chapter 1 introduced ten principles of economics that will be revisited throughout the text. Chapter 2 develops how economists approach problems, while Chapter 3 will explain how individuals and countries gain from trade.

The purpose of Chapter 2 is to familiarize you with how economists approach economic problems. With practice, you will learn how to approach similar problems in this dispassionate, systematic way. You will see how economists employ the scientific method, the role of assumptions in model building, and the application of two specific economic models. You will also learn the important distinction between two roles economists can play: as scientists when we try to explain the economic world, and as policymakers when we try to improve it.

Chapter Review

Introduction   Like other fields of study, economics has its own jargon and way of thinking. It is necessary to learn the special language of economics because knowledge of the economic vocabulary will help you communicate with precision to others about economic issues. This chapter will also provide an overview of how economists look at the world.

The Economist as Scientist

Although economists don't use test tubes or telescopes, they are scientists because they employ the scientific method—the dispassionate and objective development and testing of theories.

- **The Scientific Method: Observation, Theory, and More Observation**   Just as in other sciences, an economist observes an event, develops a theory, and collects data to test the theory. An economist observes inflation, creates a theory that excessive growth in money causes inflation, and then collects data on money growth and inflation to see if there is a relationship. Collecting data to test economic theories is difficult, however, because economists usually cannot create data from experiments. That is, economists cannot manipulate the economy just to test a theory. Therefore, economists often use data gathered from historical economic events.

- **The Role of Assumptions**   Assumptions are made to make the world easier to understand. A physicist assumes an object is falling in a vacuum when measuring acceleration due to gravity. This assumption is reasonably accurate for a marble but not for a beach ball. An economist may assume that prices are fixed (can't be changed) or may assume that prices are flexible (can move up or down in response to market pressures). Because prices often cannot be changed quickly (the menu in a restaurant is expensive to change) but can be changed easily over time, it is reasonable for economists to assume that prices are fixed in the short run but flexible in the long run. The art of scientific thinking is deciding which assumptions to make.

- **Economic Models**   Biology teachers employ plastic models of the human body. They are simpler than the actual human body but that is what makes them useful. Economists use economic models that are composed of diagrams and equations. Economic models are based on assumptions and are simplifications of economic reality.

- **Our First Model: The Circular-Flow Diagram**   The circular-flow diagram shows the flow of goods and services, factors of production, and monetary payments between households and firms. Households sell the factors of production, such as land, labor, and capital to firms, in the market for factors of production. In exchange, the households receive wages, rent, and profit. Households use these dollars to buy goods and services from firms in the market for goods and services. The firms use this revenue to pay for the factors of production, and so on. This is a simplified model of the entire economy. This version of the circular-flow diagram has been simplified because it excludes international trade and the government.

- **Our Second Model: The Production Possibilities Frontier**   A production possibilities frontier is a graph that shows the combinations of output the economy can possibly produce given the available factors of production and the available production technology. It is drawn assuming the economy produces only two goods. This model demonstrates the following economic principles:

  - If the economy is operating on the production possibilities frontier, it is operating *efficiently* because it is producing a mix of output that is the maximum possible from the resources available.

  - Points inside the curve are, therefore, *inefficient*. Points outside the curve are currently unattainable.

  - If the economy is operating on the production possibilities frontier, we can see the *trade-offs* society faces. To produce more of one good, it must produce less of the other. The amount of one good given up when producing more of another good is the *opportunity cost* of the additional production.

  - The production possibilities frontier is bowed outward because the opportunity cost of producing more of a good increases as we near maximum production of that good. This is because we use resources better suited toward production of the other good in order to continue to expand production of the first good.

  - A technological advance in production shifts the production possibilities frontier outward. This is a demonstration of *economic growth*.

- **Microeconomics and Macroeconomics**   Economics is studied on various levels. Microeconomics is the study of how households and firms make decisions and how they interact in specific markets. Macroeconomics is the study of economy-wide phenomena such as the federal deficit, the rate of unemployment, and policies to improve our standard of living. Microeconomics and macroeconomics are related because changes in the overall economy arise from decisions of millions of individuals. Although related, the methods employed in microeconomics and macroeconomics differ enough that they are often taught in separate courses.

The Economist as Policy Adviser

When economists attempt to explain the world as it is, they act as scientists. When economists attempt to improve the world, they act as policy advisers. Correspondingly, positive statements describe the world *as it is,* while normative statements prescribe how the world *ought to be.* Positive statements can be confirmed or refuted with evidence. Normative statements involve values (ethics, religion, political philosophy) as well as facts.

For example, "Money growth causes inflation" is a positive statement (of a scientist). "The government ought to reduce inflation" is a normative statement (of a policy adviser). The two statements are related because evidence about whether money causes inflation might help us decide what tool the government should use if it chooses to reduce inflation.

Economists act as policy advisers to the government in many different areas. The president is advised by economists on the Council of Economic Advisers, the Department of the Treasury, the Department of Labor, and the Department of Justice. Congress is advised by economists from the Congressional Budget Office and the Federal Reserve. For a variety of reasons, presidents (and other politicians) do not necessarily advance policies that economists advocate.

Why Economists Disagree

There are two reasons why economists have a reputation for giving conflicting advice to policymakers.

- Economists may have different scientific judgments. That is, economists may disagree about the validity of alternative positive theories regarding how the world works. For example, economists differ in their views of the sensitivity of household saving to changes in the after-tax return to saving.

- Economists may have different values. That is, economists may have different normative views about what policy should try to accomplish. For example, economists differ in their views of whether taxes should be used to redistribute income.

In reality, although there are legitimate disagreements among economists on many issues, there is tremendous agreement on many basic principles of economics.

Let's Get Going

In the next chapter, we will begin to apply the ideas and methods of economics. As you begin to think like an economist, you will use a variety of skills—mathematics, history, politics, philosophy—with the objectivity of a scientist.

Helpful Hints

1. Opportunity costs are usually not constant along a production possibilities frontier. Notice that the production possibilities frontier shown in Exhibit 1 is bowed outward. It shows the production trade-offs for an economy that produces only paper and pencils.

   If we start at the point where the economy is using all of its resources to produce paper, producing 100 units of pencils only requires a trade-off or an opportunity cost of 25 units of paper (point A to point B). This is because when we move resources from paper to pencil production, we first move those resources best suited for pencil production and poorly suited for paper production.

   Therefore, pencil production increases with very little decrease in paper production. However, if the economy were operating at point C, the opportunity cost of an additional 100 pencils (point C to D) is 200 units of paper. This is because we now move resources toward pencil production that were extremely well suited for paper production and are poorly suited for pencil production. Therefore, as we produce more and more of any particular good, the opportunity cost per unit tends

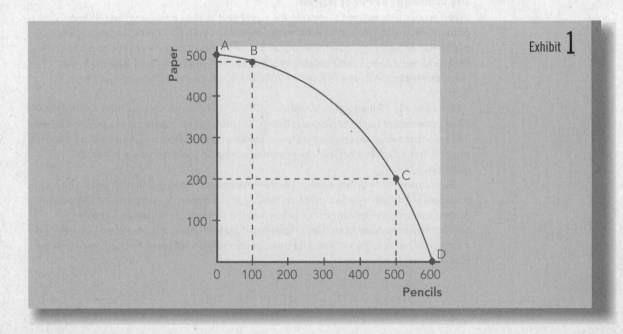

Exhibit **1**

to rise because resources are specialized. That is, resources are not equally well suited for producing each output.

The argument here applies when moving either direction on the production possibilities frontier. For example, if we start at point D (maximum production of pencils), a small reduction in pencil production (100 units) releases enough resources to increase production of paper by a large amount (200 units). However, moving from point B to point A only increases paper production by 25 units.

2. A production possibilities frontier only shows the choices available—not which point of production is best. A common mistake made by students when using production possibilities frontiers is to look at a production possibilities frontier and suggest that a point somewhere near the middle "looks best." Students make this subjective judgment because the middle point appears to provide the biggest total number of units of production of the two goods. However, ask yourself the following question. Using the production possibilities frontier in Exhibit 1, what production point would be best if paper were worth $10 per sheet and pencils were worth 1 cent per dozen? We would move our resources toward paper production. What if paper were worth 1 cent per sheet and pencils were worth $50 each? We would move our resources toward pencil production. Clearly, what we actually choose to produce depends on the price of each good. Therefore, a production possibilities frontier only provides the choices available; it alone cannot determine which choice is best.

3. Economic disagreement is interesting, but economic consensus is more important. Economists have a reputation for disagreeing with one another because we tend to highlight our differences. While our disagreements are interesting to us, the matters on which we agree are more important to you. There are a great number of economic principles for which there is near unanimous support within the economics profession. The aim of this text is to concentrate on the areas of agreement within the profession as opposed to the areas of disagreement.

Terms and Definitions

Choose a definition for each key term.

Key Terms

3 Scientific method

8 Economic models

11 Circular-flow diagram

1 Factors of production

9 Production possibilities frontier

4 Opportunity cost

6 Efficiency

10 Microeconomics

2 Macroeconomics

7 Positive statements

5 Normative statements

Definitions

1. Inputs such as land, labor, and capital

2. The study of economy-wide phenomena

3. Objective development and testing of theories

4. Whatever is given up to get something else

5. Prescription for how the world ought to be

6. Getting maximum output from the resources available

7. Descriptions of the world as it is

8. Simplifications of reality based on assumptions

9. A graph that shows the combinations of output the economy can possibly produce given the available factors of production and the available production technology

10. The study of how households and firms make decisions and how they interact in markets

11. A diagram of the economy that shows the flow of goods and services, factors of production, and monetary payments between households and firms

Problems and Short-Answer Questions

Practice Problems

1. Identify the parts of the circular-flow diagram immediately involved in the following transactions.
    a. Mary buys a car from General Motors for $20,000.

        _____

        _____

        _____

        _____

    b. General Motors pays Joe $5,000 per month for work on the assembly line.

        _____

        _____

        _____

        _____

    c. Joe gets a $15 haircut.

        _____

        _____

        _____

        _____

    d. Mary receives $10,000 of dividends on her General Motors stock.

        _____

        _____

        _____

        _____

2. The following table provides information about the production possibilities frontier of Athletic Country.

Bats	Rackets
0	420
100	400
200	360
300	300
400	200
500	0

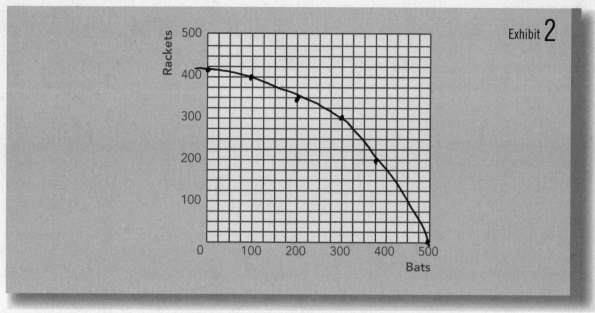

a. In Exhibit 2, plot and connect these points to create Athletic Country's production possibilities frontier.

b. If Athletic Country currently produces 100 bats and 400 rackets, what is the opportunity cost of an additional 100 bats?

 norm. 8 _____   4. _____

c. If Athletic Country currently produces 300 bats and 300 rackets, what is the opportunity cost of an additional 100 bats?

_____

d. Why does the additional production of 100 bats in part *c* cause a greater trade-off than the additional production of 100 bats in part *b*?

_____

_____

e. Suppose Athletic Country is currently producing 200 bats and 200 rackets. How many additional bats could they produce without giving up any rackets? How many additional rackets could they produce without giving up any bats?

_____

f. Is the production of 200 bats and 200 rackets efficient? Explain.

_____

_____

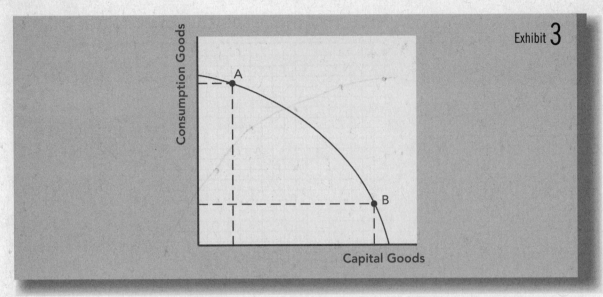

Exhibit 3

3. The production possibilities frontier in Exhibit 3 shows the available trade-offs between consumption goods and capital goods. Suppose two countries face this identical production possibilities frontier.

a. Suppose Party Country chooses to produce at point A, while Parsimonious Country chooses to produce at point B. Which country will experience more growth in the future? Why?

_____

_____

b. In this model, what is the opportunity cost of future growth?

_____

_____

c. Demonstrate in Exhibit 4 the impact of growth on a production possibilities frontier such as the one shown here. Would the production possibilities frontier for Parsimonious Country shift more or less than that for Party Country? Why?

_____

_____

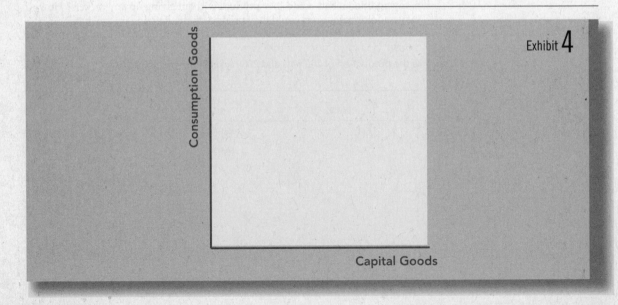

Exhibit 4

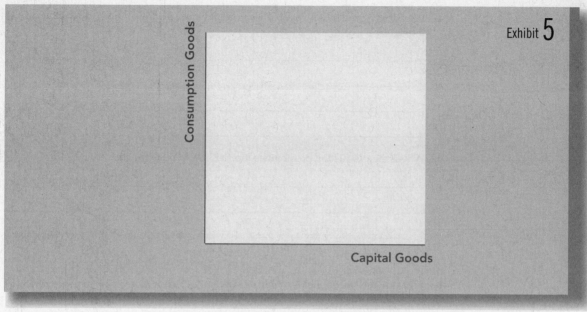

Consumption Goods

Capital Goods

Exhibit 5

d. On the graph in Exhibit 5, show the shift in the production possibilities curve if there was an increase in technology that only affected the production of capital goods.

e. Does the shift in part *d* imply that all additional production must be in the form of capital goods? Why?

_____

_____

Short-Answer Questions

1. Describe the scientific method.

_____

_____

_____

2. What is the role of assumptions in any science?

_____

_____

_____

3. Is a more realistic model always better?

_____

_____

_____

_____

4. Why does a production possibilities frontier have a negative slope (slope down and to the right)?

_____

_____

_____

_____

5. Why is the production possibilities frontier bowed outward?

_____

_____

_____

_____

6. What are the two subfields within economics? Which is more likely to be a building block of the other? Why?

_____

_____

_____

_____

7. When an economist makes a normative statement, is she more likely to be acting as a scientist or a policy adviser? Why?

_____

_____

_____

_____

8. Which statements are testable: positive statements or normative statements? Why?

_____

_____

_____

9. Name two reasons why economists disagree.

_____

_____

10. Name two economic propositions for which more than 90 percent of economists agree.

_____

_____

_____

Self-Test

True/False Questions

_____ 1. Economic models must mirror reality or they are of no value.

_____ 2. Assumptions make the world easier to understand because they simplify reality and focus our attention.

_____ 3. It is reasonable to assume that the world is composed of only one person when modeling international trade.

_____ 4. When people act as scientists, they must try to be objective.

_____ 5. If an economy is operating on its production possibilities frontier, it must be using its resources efficiently.

_____ 6. If an economy is operating on its production possibilities frontier, it must produce less of one good if it produces more of another.

_____ 7. Points outside the production possibilities frontier are attainable but inefficient.

_____ 8. If an economy were experiencing substantial unemployment, the economy is producing inside the production possibilities frontier.

_____ 9. The production possibilities frontier is bowed outward because the trade-off between the production of any two goods is constant.

_____ 10. An advance in production technology would cause the production possibilities curve to shift outward.

_____ 11. Macroeconomics is concerned with the study of how households and firms make decisions and how they interact in specific markets.

_____ 12. The statement, "An increase in inflation tends to cause unemployment to fall in the short run" is normative.

_____ 13. When economists make positive statements, they are more likely to be acting as scientists.

_____ 14. Normative statements can be refuted with evidence.

_____ 15. Most economists believe that tariffs and import quotas usually reduce general economic welfare.

Multiple-Choice Questions

1. The scientific method requires that
   a. scientists use test tubes and have clean labs.
   b. scientists be objective.
   c. scientists use precision equipment.
   d. only incorrect theories are tested.
   e. only correct theories are tested.

2. Which of the following is most likely to produce scientific evidence about a theory?
   a. an economist employed by the AFL/CIO doing research on the impact of trade restrictions on workers' wages
   b. a radio talk show host collecting data on how capital markets respond to taxation
   c. a tenured economist employed at a leading university analyzing the impact of bank regulations on rural lending
   d. a lawyer employed by General Motors addressing the impact of air bags on passenger safety

3. Which of the following statements regarding the circular-flow diagram is true?
    a. The factors of production are owned by households.
    b. If Susan works for IBM and receives a paycheck, the transaction takes place in the market for goods and services.
    c. If IBM sells a computer, the transaction takes place in the market for factors of production.
    d. The factors of production are owned by firms.
    e. None of the above is true.

4. In which of the following cases is the assumption most reasonable?
    a. To estimate the speed at which a beach ball falls, a physicist assumes that it falls in a vacuum.
    b. To address the impact of money growth on inflation, an economist assumes that money is strictly coins.
    c. To address the impact of taxes on income distribution, an economist assumes that everyone earns the same income.
    d. To address the benefits of trade, an economist assumes that there are two people and two goods.

5. Economic models are
    a. created to duplicate reality.
    b. built with assumptions.
    c. usually made of wood and plastic.
    d. useless if they are simple.

6. Which of the following is *not* a factor of production?
    a. land
    b. labor
    c. capital
    d. money
    e. All of the above are factors of production.

7. Points on the production possibilities frontier are
    a. efficient.
    b. inefficient.
    c. unattainable.
    d. normative.
    e. none of the above.

8. Which of the following will not shift a country's production possibilities frontier outward?
    a. an increase in the capital stock
    b. an advance in technology
    c. a reduction in unemployment
    d. an increase in the labor force

9. Economic growth is depicted by
    a. a movement along a production possibilities frontier toward capital goods.
    b. a shift in the production possibilities frontier outward.
    c. a shift in the production possibilities frontier inward.
    d. a movement from inside the curve toward the curve.

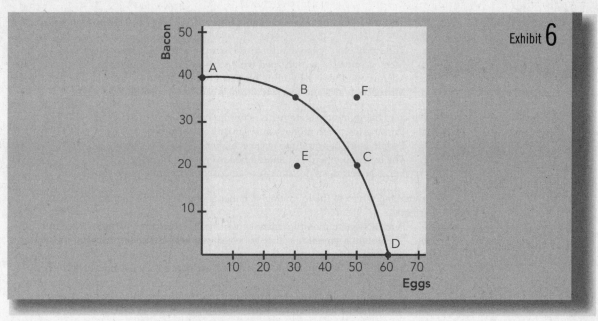

Use Exhibit 6 to answer questions 10 through 13.

10. If the economy is operating at point C, the opportunity cost of producing an additional 15 units of bacon is
    a. 10 units of eggs.
    b. 20 units of eggs.
    c. 30 units of eggs.
    d. 40 units of eggs.
    e. 50 units of eggs.

11. If the economy were operating at point E,
    a. the opportunity cost of 20 additional units of eggs is 10 units of bacon.
    b. the opportunity cost of 20 additional units of eggs is 20 units of bacon.
    c. the opportunity cost of 20 additional units of eggs is 30 units of bacon.
    d. 20 additional units of eggs can be produced with no impact on bacon production.

12. Point F represents
    a. a combination of production that can be reached if we reduce the production of eggs by 20 units.
    b. a combination of production that is inefficient because there are unemployed resources.
    c. a combination of production that can be reached if there is a sufficient advance in technology.
    d. none of the above.

13. As we move from point A to point D,
    a. the opportunity cost of eggs in terms of bacon is constant.
    b. the opportunity cost of eggs in terms of bacon falls.
    c. the opportunity cost of eggs in terms of bacon rises.
    d. the economy becomes more efficient.
    e. the economy becomes less efficient.

14. Which of the following issues is related to microeconomics?
    a. the impact of money on inflation
    b. the impact of technology on economic growth
    c. the impact of the deficit on saving
    d. the impact of oil prices on auto production

15. Which of the following statements about microeconomics and macroeconomics is *not* true?
    a. The study of very large industries is a topic within macroeconomics.
    b. Macroeconomics is concerned with economy-wide phenomena.
    c. Microeconomics is a building block for macroeconomics.
    d. Microeconomics and macroeconomics cannot be entirely separated.

16. Which of the following statements is normative?
    a. Printing too much money causes inflation.
    b. People work harder if the wage is higher.
    c. The unemployment rate should be lower.
    d. Large government deficits cause an economy to grow more slowly.

17. In making which of the following statements is an economist acting more like a scientist?
    a. A reduction in unemployment benefits will reduce the unemployment rate.
    b. The unemployment rate should be reduced because unemployment robs individuals of their dignity.
    c. The rate of inflation should be reduced because it robs the elderly of their savings.
    d. The state should increase subsidies to universities because the future of our country depends on education.

18. Positive statements are
    a. microeconomic.
    b. macroeconomic.
    c. statements of prescription that involve value judgments.
    d. statements of description that can be tested.

19. Suppose two economists are arguing about policies that deal with unemployment. One economist says, "The government should fight unemployment because it is the greatest social evil." The other economist responds, "Hogwash. Inflation is the greatest social evil." These economists
    a. disagree because they have different scientific judgments.
    b. disagree because they have different values.
    c. really don't disagree at all. It just looks that way.
    d. do none of the above.

20. Suppose two economists are arguing about policies that deal with unemployment. One economist says, "The government could lower unemployment by one percentage point if it would just increase government spending by 50 billion dollars." The other economist responds, "Hogwash. If the government spent an additional 50 billion dollars, it would reduce unemployment by only one-tenth of 1 percent, and that effect would only be temporary!" These economists
    a. disagree because they have different scientific judgments.
    b. disagree because they have different values.
    c. really don't disagree at all. It just looks that way.
    d. do none of the above.

Advanced Critical Thinking

You are watching the *PBS NewsHour* on public television. The first focus segment is a discussion of the pros and cons of free trade (lack of obstructions to international trade). For balance, there are two economists present—one in support of free trade and one opposed. Your roommate says, "Those economists have no idea what's going on. They can't agree on anything. One says free trade makes us rich. The other says it will drive us into poverty. If the experts don't know, how is the average person ever going to know whether free trade is best?"

1. Can you give your roommate any insight into why economists might disagree on this issue?

   _____

   _____

   _____

   _____

2. Suppose you discover that 93 percent of economists believe that free trade is generally best (which is the greatest agreement on any single issue). Could you now give a more precise answer as to why economists might disagree on this issue?

   _____

   _____

   _____

   _____

3. What if you later discovered that the economist opposed to free trade worked for a labor union. Would that help you explain why there appears to be a difference of opinion on this issue?

   _____

   _____

   _____

   _____

Solutions

Terms and Definitions

  _3_ Scientific method

  _8_ Economic models

_11_ Circular-flow diagram

  _1_ Factors of production

  _9_ Production possibilities frontier

  _4_ Opportunity cost

  _6_ Efficiency

_10_ Microeconomics

  _2_ Macroeconomics

  _7_ Positive statements

  _5_ Normative statements

Practice Problems

1. a. $20,000 of spending from households to market for goods and services. $20,000 of revenue from market for goods and services to firms. Car moves from firm to market for goods and services. Car moves from market for goods and services to household.

   b. $5,000 of wages from firms to market for factors of production. $5,000 of income from market for factors of production to households. Labor from households to market for factors of production. Inputs from market for factors of production to firms.

   c. $15 of spending from households to market for goods and services. $15 of revenue from market for goods and services to firms. Services from firms to market for goods and services. Services from market for goods and services to households.

   d. $10,000 of profit from firms to market for factors of production. $10,000 income from market for factors of production to households. Capital services from households to market for factors of production. Inputs from market for factors of production to firms.

2. a. See Exhibit 7.

Exhibit 7

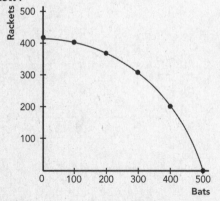

b. 40 rackets

c. 100 rackets

d. Because as we produce more bats, the resources best suited for making bats are already being used. Therefore, it takes even more resources to produce 100 bats and greater reductions in racket production.

e. 200 bats; 160 rackets

f. No. Resources were not used efficiently if production can be increased with no opportunity cost.

3. a. Parsimonious Country. Capital (plant and equipment) is a factor of production and producing more of it now will increase future production.

   b. Fewer consumption goods are produced now.

   c. See Exhibit 8. The production possibilities curve will shift more for Parsimonious Country because they have experienced a greater increase in factors of production (capital).

Exhibit 8

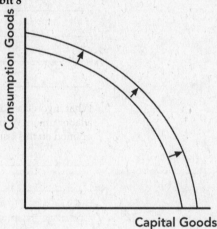

d. See Exhibit 9.

Exhibit 9

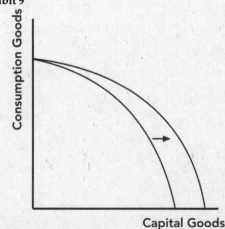

e. No, the outward shift improves choices available for both consumption and capital goods.

Short-Answer Questions

1. The dispassionate development and testing of theory by observing, testing, and observing again.

2. To simplify reality so that we can focus our thinking on what is actually important.

3. Not necessarily. Realistic models are more complex. They may be confusing, and they may fail to focus on what is important.

4. Because if an economy is operating efficiently, production choices have opportunity costs. If we want more of one thing, we must have less of another.

5. Because resources are specialized and, thus, are not equally well suited for producing different outputs.

6. Microeconomics and macroeconomics. Microeconomics is more of a building block of macro because when we address macro issues (for example, unemployment) we have to consider how individuals respond to work incentives such as wages and welfare.

7. As a policy adviser because normative statements are prescriptions about what ought to be and are somewhat based on value judgments.

8. Positive statements are statements of fact and are refutable by examining evidence.

9. Economists may have different scientific judgments. Economists may have different values.

10. A ceiling on rents reduces the quantity and quality of housing available. Tariffs and import quotas usually reduce general economic welfare.

True/False Questions

1. F; economic models are simplifications of reality.
2. T
3. F; there must be at least two individuals for trade.
4. T
5. T
6. T
7. F; points outside the production possibilities frontier cannot yet be attained.
8. T
9. F; it is bowed outward because the trade-offs are not constant.
10. T
11. F; macroeconomics is the study of economy-wide phenomena.
12. F; this statement is positive.
13. T
14. F; normative statements cannot be refuted.
15. T

Multiple-Choice Questions

1. b
2. c
3. a
4. d
5. b
6. d
7. a
8. c
9. b
10. b
11. d
12. c
13. c
14. d
15. a
16. c
17. a
18. d
19. b
20. a

Advanced Critical Thinking

1. Economists may have different scientific judgments. Economists may have different values. There may not really be any real disagreement because the majority of economists may actually agree.

2. Those opposed to free trade are likely to have different values than the majority of economists. There is not much disagreement on this issue among the mainstream economics profession.

3. Yes. It suggests that impediments to international trade may benefit some groups (organized labor), but these impediments are unlikely to benefit the public in general. Supporters of these policies are promoting their own interests.

Appendix

Practice Problems

1. The following ordered pairs of price and quantity demanded describe Joe's demand for cups of gourmet coffee.

Price per cup of coffee	Quantity demanded of coffee
$5	2 cups
4	4 cups
3	6 cups
2	8 cups
1	10 cups

   a. Plot and connect the ordered pairs on the graph in Exhibit 10.

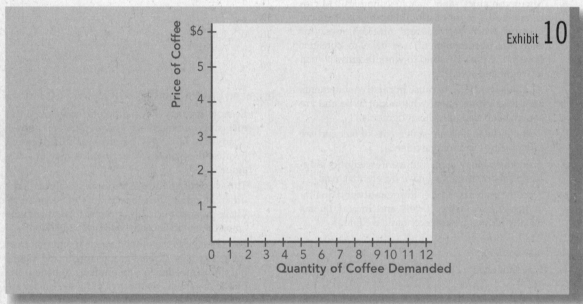

   b. What is the slope of Joe's demand curve for coffee in the price range of $5 and $4?

   _____

   c. What is the slope of Joe's demand curve for coffee in the price range of $2 and $1?

   _____

   d. Are the price of coffee and Joe's quantity demanded of coffee positively correlated or negatively correlated? How can you tell?

   _____

   _____

   e. If the price of coffee moves from $2 per cup to $4 per cup, what happens to the quantity demanded? Is this a movement along a curve or a shift in the curve?

   _____

f.   Suppose Joe's income doubles from $20,000 per year to $40,000 per year. Now the following ordered pairs describe Joe's demand for gourmet coffee. Plot these ordered pairs on the graph provided in part *a* above.

Price per cup of coffee	Quantity demanded of coffee
$5	4 cups
4	6 cups
3	8 cups
2	10 cups
1	12 cups

g.   Did the doubling of Joe's income cause a movement along his demand curve or a shift in his demand curve? Why?

_____

_____

2.   An alien lands on earth and observes the following: on mornings when people carry umbrellas, it tends to rain later in the day. The alien concludes that umbrellas cause rain.

a.   What error has the alien committed?

b.   What role did expectations play in the alien's error?

_____

_____

c.   If rain is truly caused by humidity, temperature, wind currents, and so on, what additional type of error has the alien committed when it decided that umbrellas cause rain?

_____

_____

True/False Questions

_____   1.   When graphing in the coordinate system, the *x*-coordinate tells us the horizontal location while the *y*-coordinate tells us the vertical location of the point.

_____   2.   When a line slopes upward in the *x*-, *y*-coordinate system, the two variables measured on each axis are positively correlated.

_____   3.   Price and quantity demanded for most goods are positively related.

_____   4.   If three variables are related, one of them must be held constant when graphing the other two in the *x*-, *y*-coordinate system.

_____   5.   If three variables are related, a change in the variable not represented on the *x*-, *y*-coordinate system will cause a movement along the curve drawn in the *x*-, *y*-coordinate system.

_____   6.   The slope of a line is equal to the change in *y* divided by the change in *x* along the line.

_____   7.   When a line has negative slope, the two variables measured on each axis are positively correlated.

_____ 8. There is a positive correlation between lying down and death. If we conclude from this evidence that it is unsafe to lie down, we have an omitted variable problem because critically ill people tend to lie down.

_____ 9. Reverse causality means that while we think A causes B, B may actually cause A.

_____ 10. Because people carry umbrellas to work in the morning and it rains later in the afternoon, carrying umbrellas must cause rain.

Solutions

Practice Problems

1. a. See Exhibit 11.

Exhibit 11

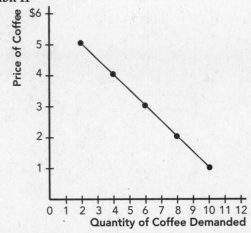

b. –1/2

c. –1/2

d. Negatively correlated, because an increase in price is associated with a decrease in quantity demanded. That is, the demand curve slopes negatively.

e. Decrease by four cups. Movement along curve.

f. See Exhibit 12.

Exhibit 12

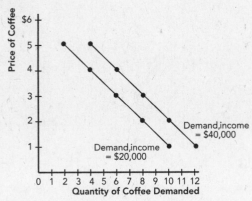

g. Shift in curve because a variable changed (income) that is not measured on either axis.

2. a. Reverse causality.

b. Because rain can be predicted, people's expectation of rain causes them to carry umbrellas before it rains, making it appear as if umbrellas cause rain.

c. Omitted variables.

True/False Questions

1. T
2. T
3. F; they are negatively correlated.
4. T
5. F; a change in a variable not represented on the graph will cause a shift in the curve.
6. T
7. F; negative slope implies negative correlation.
8. T
9. T
10. F; this is an example of reverse causation.

Chapter 3

Interdependence and the Gains from Trade

Goals
In this chapter you will

- Consider how everyone can benefit when people trade with one another

- Learn the meaning of absolute advantage and comparative advantage

- See how comparative advantage explains the gains from trade

- Apply the theory of comparative advantage to everyday life and national policy

Outcomes
After accomplishing these goals, you should be able to

- Show how total production rises when individuals specialize in the production of goods for which they have a comparative advantage

- Explain why all people have a comparative advantage even if they have no absolute advantage

- Demonstrate the link between comparative advantage and opportunity cost

- Explain why people who are good at everything still tend to specialize

Chapter Overview

Context and Purpose

Chapter 3 is the third chapter in the three-chapter section that serves as the introduction of the text. The first chapter introduced ten fundamental principles of economics. The second chapter developed how economists approach problems. This chapter shows how people and countries gain from trade (which is one of the ten principles discussed in Chapter 1).

The purpose of Chapter 3 is to demonstrate how everyone can gain from trade. Trade allows people to specialize in the production of goods for which they have a comparative advantage and then trade for goods that other people produce. Because of specialization, total output rises, and through trade, we are all able to share in the bounty. This is as true for countries as it is for individuals. Because everyone can gain from trade, restrictions on trade tend to reduce welfare.

Chapter Review

Introduction   Each of us consumes products every day that were produced in a number of different countries. Complex products contain components that were produced in many different countries, therefore these products have no single country of origin. Those who produce are neither generous nor ordered by government to produce. People produce because they wish to trade and get something in return. Hence, trade makes us interdependent.

A Parable for the Modern Economy

Imagine a simple economy. There are two people—a cattle rancher and a potato farmer. There are two goods—meat and potatoes.

- If each can produce only one product (the rancher can produce only meat and the farmer potatoes), they will trade just to increase the variety of products they consume. Each benefits because of increased variety.

- If each can produce both goods, but each is more efficient than the other at producing one good, then each will specialize in what he or she does best (again the rancher produces meat, and the farmer produces potatoes), total output will rise, and they will trade. Trade allows each to benefit because trade allows for specialization, and specialization increases the total production available to share.

- If one producer is better than the other at producing both meat and potatoes, there are the same advantages to trade but it is more difficult to see. Again, trade allows each to benefit because trade allows for specialization, and specialization increases the total production available to share. To understand the source of the gains from trade when one producer is better at producing both products, we must understand the concept of comparative advantage.

Comparative Advantage: The Driving Force of Specialization

To understand comparative advantage, we begin with the concept of absolute advantage. Absolute advantage compares the quantity of inputs required to produce a good. The producer who requires fewer resources (say fewer hours worked) to produce a good is said to have an absolute advantage in the production of that good. That is, the most efficient producer (the one with the highest productivity) has an absolute advantage.

While absolute advantage compares the actual cost of production for each producer, comparative advantage compares opportunity costs of production for each producer. The producer with the lower opportunity cost of production is said to have a comparative advantage. Regardless of absolute advantage, if producers have different opportunity costs of production for each good, each should specialize in the production of the good for which their opportunity cost of production is lower. That is, each producer should produce the item for which he or she has a comparative advantage. They can then trade some of their output for the other good. Trade makes both producers better off because trade allows for specialization, and specialization increases the total production available to be shared. Both producers gain when they trade at a price that lies between their domestic opportunity costs.

The decision to specialize and the resulting gains from trade are based on comparative advantage, not absolute advantage. Although a single producer can have an absolute advantage in the production of both goods, he cannot have a comparative advantage in the production of both goods because a low opportunity cost of producing one good implies a high opportunity cost of producing the other good.

In summary, trade allows producers to exploit the differences in their opportunity costs of production. Each specializes in the production of the good for which they have the lower opportunity cost of production and, thus, a comparative advantage. This increases total production and makes the economic pie larger. Everyone can benefit. The additional production generated by specialization is the gain from trade.

Adam Smith in his 1776 book *An Inquiry into the Nature and Causes of the Wealth of Nations* and David Ricardo in his 1817 book *Principles of Political Economy and Taxation* both recognized the gains from trade through specialization and the principle of comparative advantage. Current arguments for free trade are still based on their work.

Applications of Comparative Advantage

The principle of comparative advantage applies to individuals as well as countries. Absolute advantage does not determine specialization in production. For example, suppose Tom Brady is the best football player and the best lawn mower in the world, and thus he has an absolute advantage in the production of both goods. If he can earn $20,000 filming a commercial in the time it takes him to mow his own lawn, he gains from trade as long as he pays a lawn service less than $20,000 to mow his lawn. This is because the opportunity cost of mowing for Brady is $20,000. Brady will likely specialize in football and trade for other services. He does this because he has a comparative advantage in football and a comparative disadvantage in lawn mowing (his opportunity cost of mowing is very high) even though he has an absolute advantage in both.

Trade between countries is subject to the same principle of comparative advantage. Goods produced abroad and sold domestically are called imports. Goods produced domestically and sold abroad are called exports. Even if the United States has an absolute advantage in the production of both cars and food, it should specialize in the production of the item for which it has a comparative advantage. Because the opportunity cost of food is low in the United States (better land) and high in Japan, the United States should produce more food and export it to Japan in exchange for imports of autos from Japan. Although the United States gains from trade, the impact of trade on U.S. autoworkers is different from the impact of trade on U.S. farmers.

A reduction in barriers to free trade improves the welfare of the importing country as a whole, but it does not improve the welfare of the domestic producers in the importing country. For this reason, domestic producers lobby their governments to maintain (or increase) barriers to free trade.

Helpful Hints

1. A step-by-step example of comparative advantage will demonstrate most of the concepts discussed in Chapter 3. It will give you a pattern to follow when answering questions at the end of the chapter in your text and for the problems that follow in this Study Guide.

    Suppose we have the following information about the productivity of industry in Japan and Korea. The data are the units of output per hour of work.

	Steel	Televisions
Japan	6	3
Korea	8	2

    A Japanese worker can produce 6 units of steel or 3 televisions per hour. A Korean worker can produce 8 units of steel or 2 televisions per hour.

    We can plot the production possibilities frontier for each country, assuming each country has only one worker and the worker works only one hour. To plot the frontier, plot the end points and connect them with a line. For example, Japan can produce 6 units of steel with its worker or 3 televisions. It can also allocate 1/2

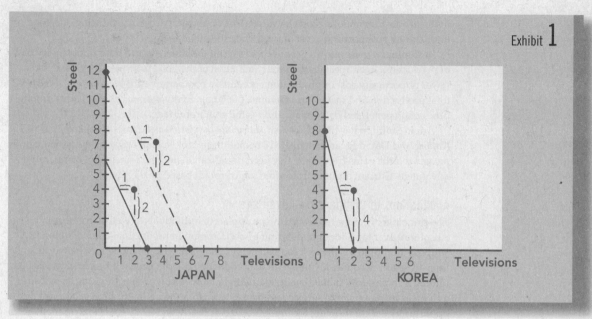

Exhibit 1

hour to the production of each and get 3 units of steel and 1 1/2 televisions. Any other proportion of the hour can be allocated to the two productive activities. The production possibilities frontier is linear in these cases because the labor resource can be moved from the production of one good to the other at a constant rate. We can do the same for Korea. Without trade, the production possibilities frontier is also the consumption possibilities frontier.

Comparative advantage determines specialization and trade. The opportunity cost of a television in Japan is 2 units of steel, which is shown by the slope of the production possibilities frontier in Exhibit 1. Alternatively, the opportunity cost of 1 unit of steel in Japan is 1/2 of a television. In Korea, the opportunity cost of a television is 4 units of steel and the cost of a unit of steel is 1/4 of a television. Because the opportunity cost of a television is lower in Japan, Japan has a comparative advantage in television production and should specialize in televisions. Because the opportunity cost of steel is lower in Korea, Korea has a comparative advantage in steel production and should specialize in steel.

What is the range of prices at which each country would be willing to exchange? If Japan specializes in television production, it would be willing to trade televisions for steel as long as it receives at least 2 units of steel for 1 television because that was the rate at which it could convert televisions into steel prior to trade. Korea would be willing to specialize in steel production and trade for televisions as long as it gives less than 4 units of steel for 1 television because that was the Korean trade-off prior to trade. In short, the final price must be between the original trade-offs each faced in the absence of trade. One television will cost between 2 and 4 units of steel, and therefore, 1 unit of steel will cost between 1/2 and 1/4 of a television.

2. Trade allows countries to consume outside their original production possibilities frontier. Suppose that Japan and Korea settle on a trading price of 3 units of steel for 1 television (or 1/3 of a television for 1 unit of steel). (I am giving you this price. There is nothing in the problem that would let you calculate the final trading price. You can only calculate the range in which it must lie.) This price is halfway between the two prices that each faces in the absence of trade. The range for the trading price is 4 units of steel for 1 television to 2 units of steel for 1 television.

    If Japan specializes in television production, produces 3 televisions, and exports 1 television for 3 units of steel, Japan will be able to consume 2 televisions and 3 units of steel. If we plot this point (2 televisions and 3 steel) on Japan's graph, we see that it lies outside its production possibilities frontier. If Korea specializes, produces 8 units of steel, and exports 3 units for 1 television, Korea will be able to consume 5 units of steel and 1 television. If we plot this point (5 steel and 1 television) on Korea's graph, we see that it also lies outside its production possibilities frontier.

This is the gain from trade. Trade allows countries (and people) to specialize. Specialization increases world output. After trading, countries consume outside their individual production possibilities frontiers. In this way, trade is like an improvement in technology. It allows countries to move beyond their current production possibilities frontiers.

3. Only comparative advantage matters—absolute advantage is irrelevant. In the previous example, Japan had an absolute advantage in the production of televisions because it could produce 3 per hour whereas Korea could only produce 2. Korea had an absolute advantage in the production of steel because it could produce 8 units per hour compared to 6 for Japan.

To demonstrate that comparative advantage, not absolute advantage, determines specialization and trade, we alter the previous example so that Japan has an absolute advantage in the production of both goods. To this end, suppose Japan becomes twice as productive as in the previous table. That is, a worker can now produce 12 units of steel or 6 televisions per hour.

	Steel	Televisions
Japan	12	6
Korea	8	2

Now Japan has an absolute advantage in the production of both goods. Japan's new production possibilities frontier is the dashed line in Exhibit 1. Will this change the analysis? Not at all. The opportunity cost of each good within Japan is the same—2 units of steel per television or 1/2 television per unit of steel (and Korea is unaffected). For this reason, Japan still has the identical comparative advantage as before, and it will specialize in television production while Korea will specialize in steel. However, because productivity has doubled in Japan, its entire set of choices has improved, and thus, its material welfare has improved.

Terms and Definitions

Choose a definition for each key term.

Key Terms

 5 Absolute advantage

 1 Opportunity cost

 2 Comparative advantage

 6 Gains from trade

 4 Imports

 3 Exports

Definitions

1. Whatever is given up to obtain some item
2. The ability to produce a good at a lower opportunity cost than another producer
3. Goods produced domestically and sold abroad
4. Goods produced abroad and sold domestically
5. The ability to produce a good using fewer inputs than another producer
6. The increase in total production due to specialization allowed by trade

Problems and Short-Answer Questions

Practice Problems

1. Angela is a college student. She takes a full load of classes and has only 5 hours per week for her hobby. Angela is artistic and can make 2 clay pots per hour or 4 coffee mugs per hour.

    a. Draw Angela's production possibilities frontier for pots and mugs in Exhibit 2.

    b. What is Angela's opportunity cost of 1 pot? 10 pots?

    _____

    c. What is Angela's opportunity cost of 1 mug? 10 mugs?

    _____

    d. Why is her production possibilities frontier a straight line instead of bowed out like those presented in Chapter 2?

    _____

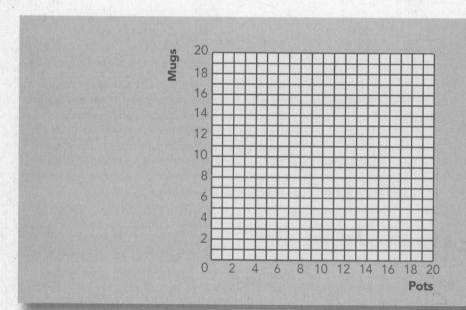

Exhibit 2

2. Suppose a worker in Germany can produce 15 computers or 5 tons of grain per month. Suppose a worker in Poland can produce 4 computers or 4 tons of grain per month. For simplicity, assume that each country has only one worker.

    a. Fill out the following table:

	Computers	Grain
Germany	_____	_____
Poland	_____	_____

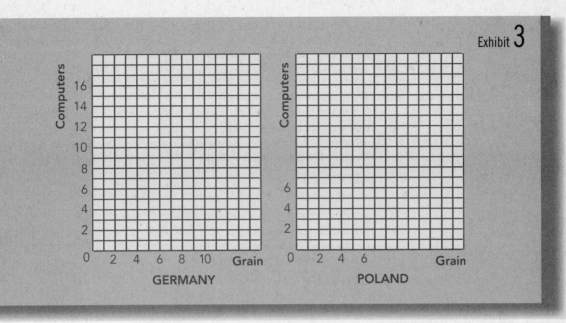

b. Graph the production possibilities frontier for each country in Exhibit 3.

c. What is the opportunity cost of 1 computer in Germany? What is the opportunity cost of 1 ton of grain in Germany?

_____

d. What is the opportunity cost of 1 computer in Poland? What is the opportunity cost of 1 ton of grain in Poland?

_____

e. Which country has the absolute advantage in producing computers? grain?

_____

_____

f. Which country has the comparative advantage in producing computers? grain?

_____

_____

g. Each country should tend toward specialization in the production of which good? Why?

_____

_____

h. What is the range of prices for computers and grain for which both countries would benefit?

_____

_____

i. Suppose Germany and Poland settle on a price of 2 computers for 1 ton of grain or 1/2 ton of grain for a computer. Suppose each country specializes in production and they trade 4 computers for 2 tons of grain. Plot the final consumption points on the graphs you made in part *b* above. Are these countries consuming inside or outside of their production possibilities frontier?

_____

j. Suppose the productivity of a worker in Poland doubles so that a worker can produce 8 computers or 8 tons of grain per month. Which country has the absolute advantage in producing computers? grain?

_____

_____

k. After the doubling of productivity in Poland, which country has a comparative advantage in producing computers? grain? Has the comparative advantage changed? Has the material welfare of either country changed?

_____

_____

l. How would your analysis change if you assumed, more realistically, that each country had 10 million workers?

_____

_____

3. Suppose a worker in the United States can produce 4 cars or 20 computers per month whereas a worker in Russia can produce 1 car or 5 computers per month. Again, for simplicity, assume each country has only one worker.
    a. Fill out the following table:

	Cars	Computers
United States	_____	_____
Russia	_____	_____

b. Which country has the absolute advantage in the production of cars? computers?

_____

_____

c. Which country has the comparative advantage in the production of cars? computers?

_____

_____

d. Are there any gains to be made from trade? Why?

_____

_____

e. Does your answer in part *d* above help you pinpoint a source for gains from trade?

_____

_____

f. What might make two countries have different opportunity costs of production? (Use your imagination. This was not directly discussed in Chapter 3.)

_____

_____

Short-Answer Questions

1. Why do people choose to become interdependent as opposed to self-sufficient?

_____

_____

_____

2. Why is comparative advantage important in determining trade instead of absolute advantage?

_____

_____

_____

3. What are the gains from trade?

_____

_____

_____

_____

4. Why is a restriction of trade likely to reduce material welfare?

_____

_____

5. Suppose a lawyer who earns $200 per hour can also type 200 words per minute. Should the lawyer hire a secretary who can only type 50 words per minute? Why?

_____

_____

6. Evaluate this statement: A technologically advanced country, which is better than its neighbor at producing everything, would be better off if it closed its borders to trade because the less productive country is a burden to the advanced country.

_____

_____

_____

_____

Self-Test

True/False Questions

_____ 1. If Japan has an absolute advantage in the production of an item, it must also have a comparative advantage in the production of that item.

_____ 2. Comparative advantage, not absolute advantage, determines the decision to specialize in production.

_____ 3. Absolute advantage is a comparison among producers based on productivity.

_____ 4. Self-sufficiency is the best way to increase one's material welfare.

_____ 5. Comparative advantage is a comparison among producers based on opportunity cost.

_____ 6. If a producer is self-sufficient, the production possibilities frontier is also the consumption possibilities frontier.

_____ 7. If a country's workers can produce 5 hamburgers per hour or 10 bags of French fries per hour, absent trade, the price of 1 bag of fries is 2 hamburgers.

_____ 8. If producers have different opportunity costs of production, trade will allow them to consume outside their production possibilities frontiers.

_____ 9. If trade benefits one country, its trading partner must be worse off due to trade.

_____ 10. Talented people who are the best at everything have a comparative advantage in the production of everything.

_____ 11. The gains from trade can be measured by the increase in total production that comes from specialization.

_____ 12. When a country removes a specific import restriction, it always benefits every worker in that country.

_____ 13. If Germany's productivity doubles for everything it produces, this will not alter its prior pattern of specialization because it has not altered its comparative advantage.

_____ 14. If an advanced country has an absolute advantage in the production of everything, it will benefit if it eliminates trade with less-developed countries and becomes completely self-sufficient.

_____ 15. If gains from trade are based solely on comparative advantage, and if all countries have the same opportunity costs of production, then there are no gains from trade.

Multiple-Choice Questions

1. If a nation has an absolute advantage in the production of a good,
   a. it can produce that good at a lower opportunity cost than its trading partner.
   b. it can produce that good using fewer resources than its trading partner.
   c. it can benefit by restricting imports of that good.
   d. it will specialize in the production of that good and export it.
   e. none of the above is true.

2. If a nation has a comparative advantage in the production of a good,
   a. it can produce that good at a lower opportunity cost than its trading partner.
   b. it can produce that good using fewer resources than its trading partner.
   c. it can benefit by restricting imports of that good.
   d. it must be the only country with the ability to produce that good.
   e. none of the above is true.

3. Which of the following statements about trade is true?
    a. Unrestricted international trade benefits every person in a country equally.
    b. People who are skilled at all activities cannot benefit from trade.
    c. Trade can benefit everyone in society because it allows people to specialize in activities in which they have an absolute advantage.
    d. Trade can benefit everyone in society because it allows people to specialize in activities in which they have a comparative advantage.

4. According to the principle of comparative advantage,
    a. countries with a comparative advantage in the production of every good need not specialize.
    b. countries should specialize in the production of goods that they enjoy consuming.
    c. countries should specialize in the production of goods for which they use fewer resources in production than their trading partners.
    d. countries should specialize in the production of goods for which they have a lower opportunity cost of production than their trading partners.

5. Which of the following statements is true?
    a. Self-sufficiency is the road to prosperity for most countries.
    b. A self-sufficient country consumes outside its production possibilities frontier.
    c. A self-sufficient country at best can consume on its production possibilities frontier.
    d. Only countries with an absolute advantage in the production of every good should strive to be self-sufficient.

6. Suppose a country's workers can produce 4 watches per hour or 12 rings per hour. If there is no trade,
    a. the domestic price of 1 ring is 3 watches.
    b. the domestic price of 1 ring is 1/3 of a watch.
    c. the domestic price of 1 ring is 4 watches.
    d. the domestic price of 1 ring is 1/4 of a watch.
    e. the domestic price of 1 ring is 12 watches.

7. Suppose a country's workers can produce 4 watches per hour or 12 rings per hour. If there is no trade,
    a. the opportunity cost of 1 watch is 3 rings.
    b. the opportunity cost of 1 watch is 1/3 of a ring.
    c. the opportunity cost of 1 watch is 4 rings.
    d. the opportunity cost of 1 watch is 1/4 of a ring.
    e. the opportunity cost of 1 watch is 12 rings.

The following table shows the units of output a worker can produce per month in Australia and Korea. Use this table to answer questions 8 through 15.

	Food	Electronics
Australia	20	5
Korea	8	4

8. Which of the following statements about absolute advantage is true?
    a. Australia has an absolute advantage in the production of food while Korea has an absolute advantage in the production of electronics.
    b. Korea has an absolute advantage in the production of food while Australia has an absolute advantage in the production of electronics.
    c. Australia has an absolute advantage in the production of both food and electronics.
    d. Korea has an absolute advantage in the production of both food and electronics.

9. The opportunity cost of 1 unit of electronics in Australia is
   a. 5 units of food.
   b. 1/5 of a unit of food.
   c. 4 units of food.
   d. 1/4 of a unit of food.

10. The opportunity cost of 1 unit of electronics in Korea is
    a. 2 units of food.
    b. 1/2 of a unit of food.
    c. 4 units of food.
    d. 1/4 of a unit of food.

11. The opportunity cost of 1 unit of food in Australia is
    a. 5 units of electronics.
    b. 1/5 of a unit of electronics.
    c. 4 units of electronics.
    d. 1/4 of a unit of electronics.

12. The opportunity cost of 1 unit of food in Korea is
    a. 2 units of electronics.
    b. 1/2 of a unit of electronics.
    c. 4 units of electronics.
    d. 1/4 of a unit of electronics.

13. Which of the following statements about comparative advantage is true?
    a. Australia has a comparative advantage in the production of food while Korea has a comparative advantage in the production of electronics.
    b. Korea has a comparative advantage in the production of food while Australia has a comparative advantage in the production of electronics.
    c. Australia has a comparative advantage in the production of both food and electronics.
    d. Korea has a comparative advantage in the production of both food and electronics.
    e. Neither country has a comparative advantage.

14. Korea should
    a. specialize in food production, export food, and import electronics.
    b. specialize in electronics production, export electronics, and import food.
    c. produce both goods because neither country has a comparative advantage.
    d. produce neither good because it has an absolute disadvantage in the production of both goods.

15. Prices of electronics can be stated in terms of units of food. What is the range of prices of electronics for which both countries could gain from trade?
    a. The price must be greater than 1/5 of a unit of food but less than 1/4 of a unit of food.
    b. The price must be greater than 4 units of food but less than 5 units of food.
    c. The price must be greater than 1/4 of a unit of food but less than 1/2 of a unit of food.
    d. The price must be greater than 2 units of food but less than 4 units of food.

16. Suppose the world consists of two countries—the United States and Mexico. Furthermore, suppose there are only two goods—food and clothing. Which of the following statements is true?
    a. If the United States has an absolute advantage in the production of food, then Mexico must have an absolute advantage in the production of clothing.
    b. If the United States has a comparative advantage in the production of food, then Mexico must have a comparative advantage in the production of clothing.
    c. If the United States has a comparative advantage in the production of food, it must also have a comparative advantage in the production of clothing.
    d. If the United States has a comparative advantage in the production of food, Mexico might also have a comparative advantage in the production of food.
    e. None of the above is true.

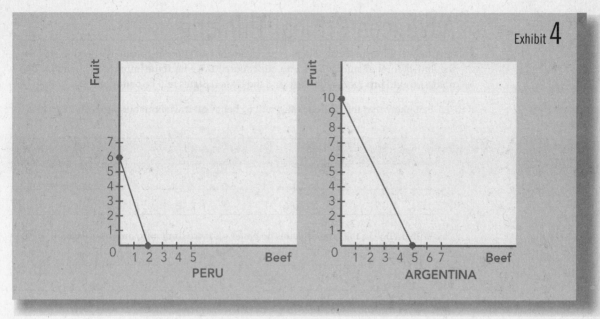

Use the production possibilities frontiers in Exhibit 4 to answer questions 17 through 19. Assume each country has the same number of workers, say 20 million, and that each axis is measured in metric tons per month.

17. Argentina has a comparative advantage in the production of
    a.   both fruit and beef.
    b.   fruit.
    c.   beef.
    d.   neither fruit nor beef.

18. Peru will export
    a.   both fruit and beef.
    b.   fruit.
    c.   beef.
    d.   neither fruit nor beef.

19. The opportunity cost of producing 1 metric ton of beef in Peru is
    a.   1/3 ton of fruit.
    b.   1 ton of fruit.
    c.   2 tons of fruit.
    d.   3 tons of fruit.
    e.   6 tons of fruit.

20. Joe is a tax accountant. He receives $100 per hour doing tax returns. He can type 10,000 characters per hour into spreadsheets. He can hire an assistant who types 2,500 characters per hour into spreadsheets. Which of the following statements is true?
    a.   Joe should not hire an assistant because the assistant cannot type as fast as he can.
    b.   Joe should hire the assistant as long as he pays the assistant less than $100 per hour.
    c.   Joe should hire the assistant as long as he pays the assistant less than $25 per hour.
    d.   None of the above is true.

Advanced Critical Thinking

You are watching an election debate on television. A candidate says, "We need to stop the flow of foreign automobiles into our country. If we limit the importation of autos, our domestic auto production will rise and the United States will be better off."

1. Is it likely that the United States will be better off if we limit auto imports? Explain.

    _____

    _____

    _____

    _____

2. Will anyone in the United States be better off if we limit auto imports? Explain.

    _____

    _____

    _____

    _____

3. In the real world, does every person in the country gain when restrictions on imports are reduced? Explain.

    _____

    _____

    _____

    _____

Solutions

Terms and Definitions

_5_ Absolute advantage

_1_ Opportunity cost

_2_ Comparative advantage

_6_ Gains from trade

_4_ Imports

_3_ Exports

Practice Problems

1. a. See Exhibit 5.

Exhibit 5

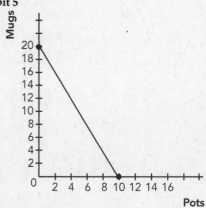

b. 2 mugs. 20 mugs.

c. 1/2 pot. 5 pots.

d. Because here resources can be moved from the production of one good to another at a constant rate.

2. a.

	Computers	Grain
Germany	15	5
Poland	4	4

b. See Exhibit 6.

Exhibit 6

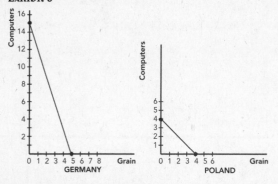

c. 1/3 ton grain. 3 computers.

d. 1 ton grain. 1 computer.

e. Germany because one worker can produce 15 computers compared to 4. Germany because one worker can produce 5 tons of grain compared to 4.

f. Germany because a computer has the opportunity cost of only 1/3 ton of grain compared to 1 ton of grain in Poland. Poland because a ton of grain has the opportunity cost of only 1 computer compared to 3 computers in Germany.

g. Germany should produce computers while Poland should produce grain because the opportunity cost of computers is lower in Germany and the opportunity cost of grain is lower in Poland. That is, each has a comparative advantage in those goods.

h. Grain must cost less than 3 computers to Germany. Computers must cost less than 1 ton of grain to Poland.

i. See Exhibit 7. They are consuming outside their production possibilities frontier.

Exhibit 7

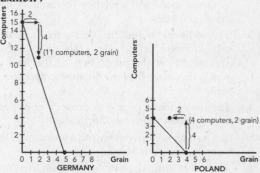

j. Germany because one worker can produce 15 compared to 8. Poland because one worker can produce 8 compared to 5.

k. Germany has comparative advantage in computers. Poland has comparative advantage in grain. No change in comparative advantage. Poland is better off, however, because it now has a larger set of choices.

l. It would not change absolute advantage or comparative advantage. It would change the scale in the previous two graphs by a factor of 10 million.

3. a.

	Cars	Computers
United States	4	20
Russia	1	5

b. United States because one worker can produce 4 cars compared to 1. The United States because one worker can produce 20 computers compared to 5.

c. In both, the opportunity cost of 1 car is 5 computers. In both, the opportunity cost of 1 computer is 1/5 of a car. Therefore, neither has a comparative advantage in either good.

d. No. Each can get the same trade-off between goods domestically.

e. Yes. There needs to be differences in opportunity costs of producing goods across countries for there to be gains from trade.

f. The availability of resources or technology might be different across countries. That is, workers could have different levels of education, land could be of different quality, capital could be of different quality, or the available technology might be different.

Short-Answer Questions

1. Because a consumer gets a greater variety of goods at a much lower cost than they could produce by themselves. That is, there are gains from trade.

2. What is important in trade is how a country's costs without trade differ from each other. This is determined by the relative opportunity costs across countries.

3. The additional output that comes from countries with different opportunity costs of production specializing in the production of the item for which they have the lower domestic opportunity cost.

4. Because it forces people to produce at a higher cost than they pay when they trade.

5. Yes, as long as the secretary earns less than $50 per hour, the lawyer is ahead.

6. This is not true. All countries can gain from trade if their opportunity costs of production differ. Even the least productive country will have a comparative advantage at producing something, and it can trade this good to the advanced country for less than the advanced country's opportunity cost.

True/False Questions

1. F; absolute advantage compares the quantities of inputs used in production while comparative advantage compares the opportunity costs.

2. T

3. T

4. F; restricting trade eliminates gains from trade.

5. T

6. T

7. F; the price of 1 bag of fries is 1/2 of a hamburger.

8. T

9. F; voluntary trade benefits both traders.

10. F; a low opportunity cost of producing one good implies a high opportunity cost of producing the other good.

11. T

12. F; it may harm those involved in that industry.

13. T

14. F; voluntary trade benefits all traders.

15. T

Multiple-Choice Questions

1. b
2. a
3. d
4. d
5. c
6. b
7. a
8. c
9. c
10. a
11. d
12. b
13. a
14. b
15. d
16. b
17. c
18. b
19. d
20. c

Advanced Critical Thinking

1. No. If we import autos, it is because the opportunity cost of producing them elsewhere is lower than in the United States.

2. Yes. Those associated with the domestic auto industry—stockholders of domestic auto producers and autoworkers.

3. No. When we reduce restrictions on imports, the country gains from the increased trade but individuals in the affected domestic industry may lose.

Chapter 4

The Market Forces of Supply and Demand

Goals
In this chapter you will

- Learn what a competitive market is
- Examine what determines the demand for a good in a competitive market
- Examine what determines the supply of a good in a competitive market
- See how supply and demand together set the price of a good and the quantity sold
- Consider the key role of prices in allocating scarce resources in market economies

Outcomes
After accomplishing these goals, you should be able to

- List the two characteristics of a competitive market
- List the factors that affect the amount that consumers wish to buy in a market
- List the factors that affect the amount that producers wish to sell in a market
- Draw a graph of supply and demand in a market and find the equilibrium price and quantity
- Shift supply and demand in response to an economic event and find the new equilibrium price and quantity

Chapter Overview

Context and Purpose

Chapter 4 is the first chapter in a three-chapter sequence that deals with supply and demand and how markets work. Chapter 4 shows how supply and demand for a good determine both the quantity produced and the price at which the good sells. Chapter 5 will add precision to our discussion of supply and demand by addressing the concept of elasticity—the sensitivity of the quantity supplied and quantity demanded to changes in economic variables. Chapter 6 will address the impact of government policies on prices and quantities in markets.

The purpose of Chapter 4 is to establish the model of supply and demand. The model of supply and demand is the foundation for our discussion for the remainder of this text. For this reason, time spent studying the concepts in this chapter will return benefits to you throughout your study of economics. Many instructors would argue that this chapter is the most important chapter in the text.

Chapter Review

Introduction In a market economy, supply and demand determine both the quantity of each good produced and the price at which each good is sold. In this chapter, we develop the determinants of supply and demand. We also address how changes in supply and demand alter prices and change the allocation of the economy's resources.

Markets and Competition

A market is a group of buyers and sellers of a particular good or service. It can be highly organized like a stock market or less organized like the market for ice cream. A competitive market is a market in which there are many buyers and sellers so that each has a negligible impact on the market price.

A *perfectly competitive* market has two main characteristics:

- The goods offered for sale are all exactly the same.

- The buyers and sellers are so numerous that no one buyer or seller can influence the price.

If a market is perfectly competitive, both buyers and sellers are said to be *price takers* because they cannot influence the price. The assumption of perfect competition applies well to agricultural markets because the product is similar and no individual buyer or seller can influence the price.

If a market has only one seller, the market is known as a *monopoly*. Other types of markets fall between the extremes of perfect competition and monopoly.

Demand

The behavior of buyers is captured by the concept of demand. The quantity demanded is the amount of a good that buyers are willing and able to purchase. Although many things determine the quantity demanded of a good, the *price* of the good plays a central role. The law of demand states that, other things equal, an increase in the price of a good reduces the quantity demanded of the good, while a decrease in the price of a good increases the quantity demanded of the good.

The demand schedule is a table that shows the relationship between the price of a good and the quantity demanded. The demand curve is a graph of this relationship with the price on the vertical axis and the quantity demanded on the horizontal axis. The demand curve is downward sloping due to the law of demand.

Market demand is the sum of the quantities demanded for each individual buyer at each price. That is, the market demand curve is the horizontal sum of the individual demand curves. The market demand curve shows the total quantity demanded of a good at each price, while all other factors that affect how much buyers wish to buy are held constant.

- **Shifts in the Demand Curve**   When people change how much they wish to buy at each price, the demand curve shifts. If buyers increase the quantity demanded at each price, the demand curve shifts to the right, which is called an *increase in demand*. Alternatively, if buyers decrease the quantity demanded at each price, the demand curve shifts to the left, which is called a *decrease in demand*. The most important factors that shift demand curves are:

  ◆ *Income:* A normal good is a good for which an increase in income leads to an increase in demand. An inferior good is a good for which an increase in income leads to a decrease in demand.

  ◆ *Prices of Related Goods:* If two goods can be used in place of one another, they are known as substitutes. When two goods are substitutes, an increase in the price of one good leads to an increase in the demand for the other good. If two goods are used together, they are known as complements. When two goods are complements, an increase in the price of one good leads to a decrease in the demand for the other good.

  ◆ *Tastes:* If your preferences shift toward a good, it will lead to an increase in the demand for that good.

  ◆ *Expectations:* Expectations about future income or prices will affect the demand for a good today.

  ◆ *Number of Buyers:* An increase in the number of buyers will lead to an increase in the market demand for a good because there are more individual demand curves to horizontally sum.

A demand curve is drawn with price on the vertical axis and quantity demanded on the horizontal axis while holding other things equal. Therefore, a change in the price of a good represents a movement along the demand curve while a change in income, prices of related goods, tastes, expectations, and the number of buyers causes a shift in the demand curve.

Supply

The behavior of sellers is captured by the concept of supply. The quantity supplied is the amount of a good that sellers are willing and able to sell. Although many things determine the quantity supplied of a good, the *price* of the good is central. An increase in the price of a good makes production of the good more profitable. Therefore, the law of supply states that, other things equal, an increase in the price of a good increases the quantity supplied of the good, while a decrease in the price of a good reduces the quantity supplied of the good.

The supply schedule is a table that shows the relationship between the price of a good and the quantity supplied. The supply curve is a graph of this relationship with the price on the vertical axis and the quantity supplied on the horizontal axis. The supply curve is upward sloping due to the law of supply.

Market supply is the sum of the quantity supplied for each individual seller at each price. That is, the market supply curve is the horizontal sum of the individual supply curves. The market supply curve shows the total quantity supplied of a good at each price, while all other factors that affect how much producers wish to sell are held constant.

- **Shifts in the Supply Curve**   When producers change how much they wish to sell at each price, the supply curve shifts. If producers increase the quantity supplied at each price, the supply curve shifts right, which is called an *increase in supply*. Alternatively, if producers decrease the quantity supplied at each price, the supply curve shifts left, which is called a *decrease in supply*. The most important factors that shift supply curves are:

  ◆ *Input Prices:* A decrease in the price of an input makes production more profitable and increases supply.

♦ *Technology:* An improvement in technology reduces costs, makes production more profitable, and increases supply.

♦ *Expectations:* Expectations about the future will affect the supply of a good today.

♦ *Number of Sellers:* An increase in the number of sellers will lead to an increase in the market supply for a good because there are more individual supply curves to horizontally sum.

A supply curve is drawn with price on the vertical axis and quantity supplied on the horizontal axis while holding other things equal. Therefore, a change in the price of a good represents a movement along the supply curve while a change in input prices, technology, expectations, and the number of sellers causes a shift in the supply curve.

Supply and Demand Together

When placed on the same graph, the intersection of supply and demand is called the market's equilibrium. Equilibrium is a situation in which the price has reached the level where quantity supplied equals quantity demanded. The equilibrium price, or the market-clearing price, is the price that balances the quantity demanded and the quantity supplied. When the quantity supplied equals the quantity demanded at the equilibrium price, we have determined the equilibrium quantity.

The market naturally moves toward its equilibrium. If the price is above the equilibrium price, the quantity supplied exceeds the quantity demanded, and there is a surplus, or an excess supply, of the good. A surplus causes the price to fall until it reaches equilibrium. If the price is below the equilibrium price, the quantity demanded exceeds the quantity supplied, and there is a shortage, or an excess demand for the good. A shortage causes the price to rise until it reaches equilibrium. This natural adjustment of the price to bring the quantity supplied and the quantity demanded into balance is known as the law of supply and demand.

When an economic event shifts the supply or the demand curve, the equilibrium in the market changes, resulting in a new equilibrium price and quantity. When analyzing the impact of some event on the market equilibrium, employ the following three steps:

• Decide whether the event shifts the supply curve or demand curve or both.

• Decide in which direction the curve shifts.

• Use the supply-and-demand diagram to see how the shift changes the equilibrium price and quantity.

A shift in the demand curve is called a "change in demand." It is caused by a change in a variable that affects the amount people wish to purchase of a good *other than the price of the good*. A change in the price of a good causes a movement along a given demand curve and is called a "change in the quantity demanded." Likewise, a shift in the supply curve is called a "change in supply." It is caused by a change in a variable that affects the amount producers wish to supply of a good *other than the price of the good*. A change in the price of a good causes a movement along a supply curve and is called a "change in the quantity supplied."

For example, a frost that destroys much of the orange crop causes a decrease in the supply of oranges (supply of oranges shifts to the left). This increases the price of oranges and decreases the quantity demanded of oranges. In other words, a decrease in the supply of oranges increases the price of oranges and decreases the quantity of oranges purchased.

If both supply and demand shift at the same time, there may be more than one possible outcome for the changes in the equilibrium price and quantity. For example, if demand were to increase (shift right) while supply were to decrease (shift left), the price will certainly rise but the impact on the equilibrium quantity is ambiguous. In this case, the change in the equilibrium quantity depends on the magnitudes of the shifts in supply and demand.

Conclusion: How Prices Allocate Resources

Markets generate equilibrium prices. These prices are the signals that guide the allocation of scarce resources. Prices of products rise to the level necessary to allocate the products to those who are willing to pay for them. Prices of inputs (such as labor) rise to the level necessary to induce people to do the jobs that need to be done. Prices coordinate decentralized decision making so that no jobs go undone and there is no shortage of goods and services for those willing and able to pay for them.

Helpful Hints

1. By far, the greatest difficulty students have when studying supply and demand is distinguishing between a "change in demand" and a "change in the quantity demanded" and between a "change in supply" and a "change in the quantity supplied." It helps to remember that "demand" is the entire relationship between price and quantity demanded. That is, demand is the entire demand curve, not a point on a demand curve. Therefore, a change in demand is a shift in the entire demand curve, which can only be caused by a change in a determinant of demand other than the price of the good. A change in the quantity demanded is a movement along the demand curve and is caused by a change in the price of the good. Likewise, "supply" refers to the entire supply curve, not a point on the supply curve. Therefore, a change in supply is a shift in the entire supply curve, which can only be caused by a change in a determinant of supply other than the price of the good. A change in the quantity supplied is a movement along the supply curve and is caused by a change in the price of the good.

2. If both supply and demand shift at the same time and we do not know the magnitude of each shift, then the change in either the price or the quantity must be ambiguous. For example, if there is an increase in supply (supply shifts right) and an increase in demand (demand shifts right), the equilibrium quantity must certainly rise, but the change in the equilibrium price is ambiguous. Do this for all four possible combinations of changes in supply and demand. You will find that if you know the impact on the equilibrium price with certainty, then the impact on the equilibrium quantity must be ambiguous. If you know the impact on the equilibrium quantity with certainty, then the impact on the equilibrium price must be ambiguous.

Terms and Definitions

Choose a definition for each key term.

Key Terms		Definitions

Key Terms

__5__ Market

__12__ Competitive market

__6__ Monopoly

__10__ Quantity demanded

__13__ Law of demand

__2__ Demand schedule

__14__ Demand curve

__20__ Normal good

__7__ Inferior good

__4__ Substitutes

__19__ Complements

__16__ Quantity supplied

__17__ Law of supply

__3__ Supply schedule

__21__ Supply curve

__11__ Equilibrium

__15__ Equilibrium price

__1__ Equilibrium quantity

__9__ Surplus

__8__ Shortage

__18__ Law of supply and demand

Definitions

1. The quantity supplied and the quantity demanded at the equilibrium price

2. A table that shows the relationship between the price of a good and the quantity demanded

3. A table that shows the relationship between the price of a good and the quantity supplied

4. Two goods for which an increase in the price of one leads to an increase in the demand for the other

5. A group of buyers and sellers of a particular good or service

6. Market with only one seller

7. A good for which, other things equal, an increase in income leads to a decrease in demand

8. A situation in which quantity demanded is greater than quantity supplied

9. A situation in which quantity supplied is greater than quantity demanded

10. The amount of a good that buyers are willing and able to purchase

11. A situation in which the price has reached the level where quantity supplied equals quantity demanded

12. A market in which there are many buyers and sellers so that each has a negligible impact on the market price

13. The claim that, other things equal, the quantity demanded of a good falls when the price of the good rises

14. A graph of the relationship between the price of a good and the quantity demanded

15. The price that balances quantity supplied and quantity demanded

16. The amount of a good that sellers are willing and able to sell

17. The claim that, other things equal, the quantity supplied of a good rises when the price of the good rises

18. The claim that the price of any good adjusts to bring the quantity supplied and quantity demanded for that good into balance

19. Two goods for which an increase in the price of one leads to a decrease in the demand for the other

20. A good for which, other things equal, an increase in income leads to an increase in demand

21. A graph of the relationship between the price of a good and the quantity supplied

Problems and Short-Answer Questions

Practice Problems

1. Suppose we have the following market supply and demand schedules for bicycles:

Price	Quantity Demanded	Quantity Supplied
$100	70	30
200	60	40
300	50	50
400	40	60
500	30	70
600	20	80

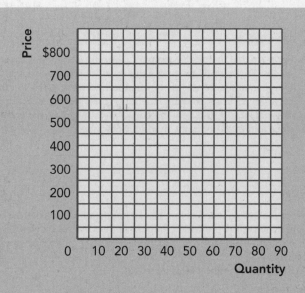

Exhibit 1

a. Plot the supply curve and the demand curve for bicycles in Exhibit 1.
b. What is the equilibrium price of bicycles?

_____

c. What is the equilibrium quantity of bicycles?

_____

d. If the price of bicycles were $100, is there a surplus or a shortage? How many units of surplus or shortage are there? Will this cause the price to rise or fall?

_____

e. If the price of bicycles were $400, is there a surplus or a shortage? How many units of surplus or shortage are there? Will this cause the price to rise or fall?

_____

_____

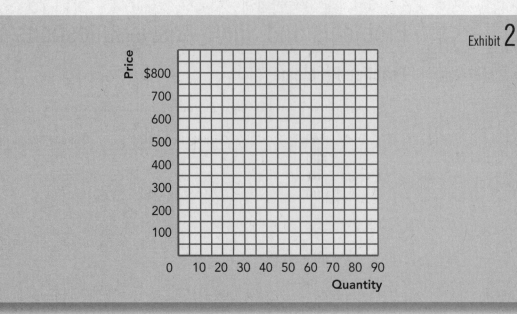

Exhibit 2

f. Suppose that the bicycle maker's labor union bargains for an increase in its wages. Furthermore, suppose this event raises the cost of production, makes bicycle manufacturing less profitable, and reduces the quantity supplied of bicycles by 20 units at each price of bicycles. Plot the new supply curve and the original supply and demand curves in Exhibit 2. What is the new equilibrium price and quantity in the market for bicycles?

_____

_____

2. Each of the events listed below has an impact on the market for bicycles. For each event, which curve is affected (supply or demand for bicycles), what direction is it shifted, and what is the resulting impact on the equilibrium price and quantity of bicycles?

a. The price of automobiles increases.

_____

b. Consumers' incomes decrease, and bicycles are a normal good.

_____

c. The price of steel used to make bicycle frames increases.

_____

d. An environmental movement shifts tastes toward bicycling.

_____

e. Consumers expect the price of bicycles to fall in the future.

_____

f. A technological advance in the manufacture of bicycles occurs.

_____

g. The prices of bicycle helmets and shoes are reduced.

_____

h. Consumers' incomes decrease, and bicycles are an inferior good.

_____

3. The following questions address a market when both supply and demand shift.
   a. What would happen to the equilibrium price and quantity in the bicycle market if there were an increase in both the supply and the demand for bicycles?

   _____

   b. What would happen to the equilibrium price and quantity in the bicycle market if the demand for bicycles increases more than the increase in the supply of bicycles?

   _____

Short-Answer Questions

1. What are the two main characteristics of a perfectly competitive market?

   _____

   _____

2. Explain the law of demand.

   _____

   _____

3. What are the variables that should affect the amount of a good that consumers wish to buy, other than its price?

   _____

   _____

4. What is the difference between a normal good and an inferior good?

   _____

   _____

5. Explain the law of supply.

   _____

   _____

6. What are the variables that should affect the amount of a good that producers wish to sell, other than its price?

   _____

   _____

7. Suppose *suppliers* of corn expect the price of corn to rise in the future. How would this affect the supply and demand for corn and the equilibrium price and quantity of corn?

   _____

   _____

   _____

   _____

8. If there is a surplus of a good, is the price above or below the equilibrium price for that good?

_____

9. Suppose there is an increase in consumers' incomes. In the market for automobiles (a normal good), does this event cause an increase in demand or an increase in quantity demanded? Does this cause an increase in supply or an increase in quantity supplied? Explain.

_____

_____

_____

_____

_____

10. Suppose there is an advance in the technology employed to produce automobiles. In the market for automobiles, does this event cause an increase in supply or an increase in the quantity supplied? Does this cause an increase in demand or an increase in the quantity demanded? Explain.

_____

_____

_____

_____

_____

Self-Test

True/False Questions

_____   1. A perfectly competitive market consists of products that are all slightly different from one another.

_____   2. A monopolistic market has only one seller.

_____   3. The law of demand states that an increase in the price of a good decreases the demand for that good.

_____   4. If apples and oranges are substitutes, an increase in the price of apples will decrease the demand for oranges.

_____   5. If golf clubs and golf balls are complements, an increase in the price of golf clubs will decrease the demand for golf balls.

_____   6. If consumers expect the price of shoes to rise, there will be an increase in the demand for shoes today.

_____   7. The law of supply states that an increase in the price of a good increases the quantity supplied of that good.

_____ 8. An increase in the price of steel will shift the supply of automobiles to the right.

_____ 9. When the price of a good is below the equilibrium price, it causes a surplus.

_____ 10. The market supply curve is the horizontal summation of the individual supply curves.

_____ 11. If there is a shortage of a good, then the price of that good tends to fall.

_____ 12. If pencils and paper are complements, an increase in the price of pencils causes the demand for paper to decrease or shift to the left.

_____ 13. If Coca-Cola and Pepsi are substitutes, an increase in the price of Coca-Cola will cause an increase in the equilibrium price and quantity in the market for Pepsi.

_____ 14. An advance in the technology employed to manufacture Rollerblades™ will result in a decrease in the equilibrium price and an increase in the equilibrium quantity in the market for Rollerblades™.

_____ 15. If there is an increase in supply accompanied by a decrease in demand for coffee, then there will be a decrease in both the equilibrium price and quantity in the market for coffee.

Multiple-Choice Questions

1. A perfectly competitive market has
   a. only one seller.
   b. at least a few sellers.
   c. many buyers and sellers.
   d. firms that set their own prices.
   e. none of the above.

2. If an increase in the price of blue jeans leads to an increase in the demand for tennis shoes, then blue jeans and tennis shoes are
   a. substitutes.
   b. complements.
   c. normal goods.
   d. inferior goods.
   e. none of the above.

3. The *law of demand* states that an increase in the price of a good
   a. decreases the demand for that good.
   b. decreases the quantity demanded for that good.
   c. increases the supply of that good.
   d. increases the quantity supplied of that good.
   e. does none of the above.

4. The *law of supply* states that an increase in the price of a good
   a. decreases the demand for that good.
   b. decreases the quantity demanded for that good.
   c. increases the supply of that good.
   d. increases the quantity supplied of that good.
   e. does none of the above.

5. If an increase in consumer incomes leads to a decrease in the demand for camping equipment, then camping equipment is
   a. a complementary good.
   b. a substitute good.
   c. a normal good.
   d. an inferior good.
   e. none of the above.

6. A monopolistic market has
   a. only one seller.
   b. at least a few sellers.
   c. many buyers and sellers.
   d. firms that are price takers.
   e. none of the above.

7. Which of the following shifts the demand for watches to the right?
   a. a decrease in the price of watches
   b. a decrease in consumer incomes if watches are a normal good
   c. a decrease in the price of watch batteries if watch batteries and watches are complements
   d. an increase in the price of watches
   e. none of the above

8. All of the following shift the supply of watches to the right except
   a. an increase in the price of watches.
   b. an advance in the technology used to manufacture watches.
   c. a decrease in the wage of workers employed to manufacture watches.
   d. manufacturers' expectations of lower watch prices in the future.
   e. All of the above cause an increase in the supply of watches.

9. If the price of a good is above the equilibrium price,
   a. there is a surplus, and the price will rise.
   b. there is a surplus, and the price will fall.
   c. there is a shortage, and the price will rise.
   d. there is a shortage, and the price will fall.
   e. the quantity demanded is equal to the quantity supplied, and the price remains unchanged.

10. If the price of a good is below the equilibrium price,
    a. there is a surplus, and the price will rise.
    b. there is a surplus, and the price will fall.
    c. there is a shortage, and the price will rise.
    d. there is a shortage, and the price will fall.
    e. the quantity demanded is equal to the quantity supplied, and the price remains unchanged.

11. If the price of a good is equal to the equilibrium price,
    a. there is a surplus, and the price will rise.
    b. there is a surplus, and the price will fall.
    c. there is a shortage, and the price will rise.
    d. there is a shortage, and the price will fall.
    e. the quantity demanded is equal to the quantity supplied, and the price remains unchanged.

12. An increase (rightward shift) in the demand for a good will tend to cause
    a. an increase in the equilibrium price and quantity.
    b. a decrease in the equilibrium price and quantity.
    c. an increase in the equilibrium price and a decrease in the equilibrium quantity.
    d. a decrease in the equilibrium price and an increase in the equilibrium quantity.
    e. none of the above.

13. A decrease (leftward shift) in the supply for a good will tend to cause
    a. an increase in the equilibrium price and quantity.
    b. a decrease in the equilibrium price and quantity.
    c. an increase in the equilibrium price and a decrease in the equilibrium quantity.
    d. a decrease in the equilibrium price and an increase in the equilibrium quantity.
    e. none of the above.

14. Suppose there is an increase in both the supply and demand for personal computers. In the market for personal computers, we would expect the
    a. equilibrium quantity to rise and the equilibrium price to rise.
    b. equilibrium quantity to rise and the equilibrium price to fall.
    c. equilibrium quantity to rise and the equilibrium price to remain constant.
    d. equilibrium quantity to rise and the change in the equilibrium price to be ambiguous.
    e. change in the equilibrium quantity to be ambiguous and the equilibrium price to rise.

15. Suppose there is an increase in both the supply and demand for personal computers. Furthermore, suppose the supply of personal computers increases more than demand for personal computers. In the market for personal computers, we would expect the
    a. equilibrium quantity to rise and the equilibrium price to rise.
    b. equilibrium quantity to rise and the equilibrium price to fall.
    c. equilibrium quantity to rise and the equilibrium price to remain constant.
    d. equilibrium quantity to rise and the change in the equilibrium price to be ambiguous.
    e. change in the equilibrium quantity to be ambiguous and the equilibrium price to fall.

16. Which of the following statements is true about the impact of an increase in the price of lettuce?
    a. The demand for lettuce will decrease.
    b. The supply of lettuce will decrease.
    c. The equilibrium price and quantity of salad dressing will rise.
    d. The equilibrium price and quantity of salad dressing will fall.
    e. Both *a* and *d* are true.

17. Suppose a frost destroys much of the Florida orange crop. At the same time, suppose consumer tastes shift toward orange juice. What would we expect to happen to the equilibrium price and quantity in the market for orange juice?
    a. Price will increase; quantity is ambiguous.
    b. Price will increase; quantity will increase.
    c. Price will increase; quantity will decrease.
    d. Price will decrease; quantity is ambiguous.
    e. The impact on both price and quantity is ambiguous.

18. Suppose consumer tastes shift toward the consumption of apples. Which of the following statements is an accurate description of the impact of this event on the market for apples?
    a. There is an increase in the demand for apples and an increase in the quantity supplied of apples.
    b. There is an increase in the demand and supply of apples.
    c. There is an increase in the quantity demanded of apples and in the supply for apples.
    d. There is an increase in the demand for apples and a decrease in the supply of apples.
    e. There is a decrease in the quantity demanded of apples and an increase in the supply for apples.

19. Suppose both buyers and sellers of wheat expect the price of wheat to rise in the near future. What would we expect to happen to the equilibrium price and quantity in the market for wheat today?
    a. The impact on both price and quantity is ambiguous.
    b. Price will increase; quantity is ambiguous.
    c. Price will increase; quantity will increase.
    d. Price will increase; quantity will decrease.
    e. Price will decrease; quantity is ambiguous.

20. An inferior good is one for which an increase in income causes a(n)
    a. increase in supply.
    b. decrease in supply.
    c. increase in demand.
    d. decrease in demand.

Advanced Critical Thinking

You are watching a national news broadcast. It is reported that an early snowstorm is heading for Washington state and that it will likely destroy much of this year's apple crop. Your roommate says, "If there are going to be fewer apples available, I'll bet that apple prices will rise. We should buy enormous quantities of apples now and put them in storage. Later we will sell them and make a killing."

1. If this information about the storm is publicly available so that all buyers and sellers in the apple market expect the price of apples to rise in the future, what will happen immediately to the supply and demand for apples and the equilibrium price and quantity of apples?

   _____

   _____

   _____

   _____

2. Can you "beat the market" with public information? That is, can you use publicly available information to help you buy something cheap and quickly sell it at a higher price? Why or why not?

   _____

   _____

   _____

   _____

3. Suppose a friend of yours works for the U.S. Weather Bureau. She calls you and provides you with inside information about the approaching storm—information not available to the public. Can you "beat the market" with inside information? Why or why not?

   _____

   _____

   _____

   _____

Solutions

Terms and Definitions

  _5_ Market

_12_ Competitive market

  _6_ Monopoly

_10_ Quantity demanded

_13_ Law of demand

  _2_ Demand schedule

_14_ Demand curve

_20_ Normal good

  _7_ Inferior good

  _4_ Substitutes

_19_ Complements

_16_ Quantity supplied

_17_ Law of supply

  _3_ Supply schedule

_21_ Supply curve

_11_ Equilibrium

_15_ Equilibrium price

  _1_ Equilibrium quantity

  _9_ Surplus

  _8_ Shortage

_18_ Law of supply and demand

Practice Problems

1. a. See Exhibit 3.

Exhibit 3

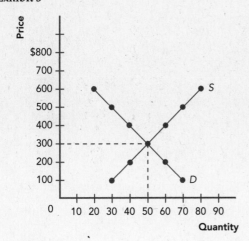

  b. \$300

  c. 50 bicycles

  d. Shortage, 70 – 30 = 40 units, the price will rise

  e. Surplus, 60 – 40 = 20 units, the price will fall

  f. See Exhibit 4. equilibrium price = \$400, equilibrium quantity = 40 bicycles

Exhibit 4

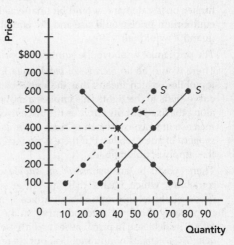

2. a. demand, shifts right, equilibrium price and quantity rise

  b. demand, shifts left, equilibrium price and quantity fall

  c. supply, shifts left, equilibrium price rises and equilibrium quantity falls

  d. demand, shifts right, equilibrium price and quantity rise

  e. demand, shifts left, equilibrium price and quantity fall

  f. supply, shifts right, equilibrium price falls and equilibrium quantity rises

  g. demand, shifts right, equilibrium price and quantity rise

  h. demand, shifts right, equilibrium price and quantity rise

3. a. equilibrium quantity will rise, equilibrium price is ambiguous

  b. equilibrium price and quantity will rise

Short-Answer Questions

1. The goods offered for sale are all the same, and the buyers and sellers are so numerous that no one buyer or seller can influence the price.

2. Other things equal, price and quantity demanded of a good are negatively related.

3. Income, prices of related goods, tastes, expectations, and number of buyers in the market.

4. When income rises, demand for a normal good increases or shifts right. When income rises, demand for an inferior good decreases or shifts left.

5. Other things equal, price and quantity supplied of a good are positively related.

6. The variables are input prices, technology, expectations, and number of sellers in the market.

7. The supply of corn in today's market would decrease (shift left) as sellers hold back their offerings in anticipation of greater profits if the price rises in the future. If only suppliers expect higher prices, demand would be unaffected. The equilibrium price would rise and the equilibrium quantity would fall.

8. The price must be above the equilibrium price.

9. There would be an *increase in the demand* for automobiles, which means that the entire demand curve shifts to the right. This implies a movement along the fixed supply curve as the price rises. The increase in price causes an *increase in the quantity supplied* of automobiles, but there is no increase in the supply of automobiles.

10. There would be an *increase in the supply* of automobiles, which means that the entire supply curve shifts to the right. This implies a movement along the fixed demand curve as the price falls. The decrease in price causes an *increase in the quantity demanded* of automobiles, but there is no increase in the demand for automobiles.

True/False Questions

1. F; a perfectly competitive market consists of goods offered for sale that are all exactly the same.
2. T
3. F; the law of demand states that an increase in the price of a good decreases the *quantity demanded* of that good (a movement along the demand curve).
4. F; it will increase the demand for oranges.
5. T
6. T
7. T
8. F; an increase in the price of an input shifts the supply curve for the output to the left.
9. F; it causes an excess demand.
10. T
11. F; an excess demand causes the price to rise.
12. T
13. T
14. T
15. F; there will be a decrease in the equilibrium price, but the impact on the equilibrium quantity is ambiguous.

Multiple-Choice Questions

1. c
2. a
3. b
4. d
5. d
6. a
7. c
8. a
9. b
10. c
11. e
12. a
13. c
14. d
15. b
16. d
17. a
18. a
19. b
20. d

Advanced Critical Thinking

1. Sellers reduce supply (supply shifts left) in the hope of selling apples later at a higher price, and buyers increase demand (demand shifts right) in the hope of buying apples now before the price goes up. The price will immediately rise, and the quantity exchanged is ambiguous.

2. No. Usually the market immediately adjusts, so that the price has already moved to its new equilibrium value before the amateur speculator can make his or her purchase.

3. Yes. In this case, you can make your purchase before the market responds to the information about the storm.

Chapter 5
Elasticity and Its Application

Goals
In this chapter you will

- Learn the meaning of the elasticity of demand

- Examine what determines the elasticity of demand

- Learn the meaning of the elasticity of supply

- Examine what determines the elasticity of supply

- Apply the concept of elasticity in three very different markets

Outcomes
After accomplishing these goals, you should be able to

- Calculate the price and income elasticity of demand

- Distinguish between the price elasticity of demand for necessities and luxuries

- Calculate the price elasticity of supply

- Distinguish between an inelastic and elastic supply curve

- Demonstrate the impact of the price elasticity of demand on total revenue

Chapter Overview

Context and Purpose

Chapter 5 is the second chapter of a three-chapter sequence that deals with supply and demand and how markets work. Chapter 4 introduced supply and demand. Chapter 5 shows how much buyers and sellers respond to changes in market conditions. Chapter 6 will address the impact of government policies on competitive markets.

The purpose of Chapter 5 is to add precision to our supply and demand model. We introduce the concept of elasticity, which measures the responsiveness of buyers and sellers to changes in

69

economic variables such as prices and income. The concept of elasticity allows us to make quantitative observations about the impact of changes in supply and demand on equilibrium prices and quantities.

Chapter Review

Introduction   In Chapter 4, we learned that an increase in price reduces the quantity demanded and increases the quantity supplied in a market. In this chapter, we will develop the concept of elasticity so that we can address how much the quantity demanded and the quantity supplied responds to changes in market conditions such as price.

The Elasticity of Demand

To measure the response of demand to changes in its determinants, we use the concept of elasticity. Price elasticity of demand measures how much the quantity demanded responds to a change in the price of that good, computed as the percentage change in quantity demanded divided by the percentage change in price.

If the quantity demanded changes substantially from a change in price, demand is *elastic*. If the quantity demanded changes little from a change in price, demand is *inelastic*. Whether a demand curve tends to be price elastic or inelastic depends on the following:

- *Availability of close substitutes:* The demand for goods with close substitutes is more sensitive to changes in prices and, thus, is more price elastic.

- *Necessities versus luxuries:* The demand for necessities is inelastic while the demand for luxuries is elastic. Because one cannot do without a necessity, an increase in the price has little impact on the quantity demanded. However, an increase in price greatly reduces the quantity demanded of a luxury.

- *Definition of the market:* The more narrowly we define the market, the more likely there are to be close substitutes and the more price elastic the demand curve.

- *Time horizon:* The longer the time period considered, the greater the availability of close substitutes and the more price elastic the demand curve.

The formula for computing the price elasticity of demand is:

$$\text{Price elasticity of demand} = \frac{\text{Percentage change in quantity demanded}}{\text{Percentage change in price}}$$

Because price elasticity of demand is always negative, it is customary to drop the negative sign.

When we compute price elasticity between any two points on a demand curve, we get a different answer depending on our chosen starting point and our chosen finishing point if we take the change in price and quantity as a percent of the starting value for each. To avoid this problem, economists often employ the *midpoint method* to calculate elasticities. With this method, the percentage changes in quantity and price are calculated by dividing the change in the variable by the *average* or midpoint value of the two points on the curve, not the starting point on the curve. Thus, the formula for the price elasticity of demand using the midpoint method is:

$$\text{Price elasticity of demand} = \frac{(Q_2 - Q_1)/\left[(Q_2 + Q_1)/2\right]}{(P_2 - P_1)/\left[(P_2 + P_1)/2\right]}.$$

If price elasticity of demand is greater than one, demand is elastic. If elasticity is less than one, demand is inelastic. If elasticity is equal to one, demand is said to have unit elasticity. If elasticity is zero, demand is perfectly inelastic (vertical). If elasticity is infinite, demand is perfectly elastic (horizontal). In general, the flatter the demand curve, the more elastic. The steeper the demand curve, the more inelastic.

Total revenue is the amount paid by buyers and received by sellers, computed simply as price times quantity. The elasticity of demand determines the impact of a change in price on total revenue:

- If demand is price inelastic (less than one), an increase in price increases total revenue because the price increase is proportionately larger than the reduction in quantity demanded.
- If demand is price elastic (greater than one), an increase in price decreases total revenue because the decrease in the quantity demanded is proportionately larger than the increase in price.
- If demand is unit price elastic (exactly equal to one), a change in price has no impact on total revenue because the increase in price is proportionately equal to the decrease in quantity.

Along a linear demand curve, price elasticity is not constant. When price is high and quantity low, price elasticity is large because a change in price causes a larger *percentage* change in quantity. When price is low and quantity high, price elasticity is small because a change in price causes a smaller *percentage* change in quantity.

There are additional demand elasticities. The income elasticity of demand is a measure of how much the quantity demanded responds to a change in consumers' income, computed as the percentage change in quantity demanded divided by the percentage change in income or:

$$\text{Income elasticity of demand} = \frac{\text{Percentage change in quantity demanded}}{\text{Percentage change in income}}$$

For *normal goods*, income elasticity is positive. For *inferior goods*, income elasticity is negative. Within the group of normal goods, necessities like food have small income elasticities because the quantity demanded changes little when income changes. Luxuries have larger income elasticities.

The cross-price elasticity of demand is a measure of the response of the quantity demanded of one good to a change in the price of another good, computed as the percentage change in the quantity demanded of one good divided by the percentage change in the price of another good or:

$$\text{Cross–price elasticity of demand} = \frac{\text{Percentage change in quantity demanded of good 1}}{\text{Percentage change in the price of good 2}}$$

The cross-price elasticity of demand is positive for *substitutes* and negative for *complements*.

The Elasticity of Supply

Price elasticity of supply measures how much the quantity supplied responds to a change in the price of that good, computed as the percentage change in quantity supplied divided by the percentage change in price.

If the quantity supplied changes substantially from a change in price, supply is *elastic*. If the quantity supplied changes little from a change in price, supply is *inelastic*. Supply is more elastic when the sellers have greater flexibility to change the amount of a good they produce in response to a change in price. Generally, the shorter the time period considered, the less flexibility the seller has in choosing how much to produce and the more inelastic the supply curve.

The formula for computing the price elasticity of supply is:

$$\text{Price elasticity of supply} = \frac{\text{Percentage change in quantity supplied}}{\text{Percentage change in price}}$$

If price elasticity of supply is greater than one, supply is elastic. If elasticity is less than one, supply is inelastic. If elasticity is equal to one, supply is said to have unit elasticity. If elasticity is zero, supply is perfectly inelastic (vertical). If elasticity is infinite, supply is perfectly elastic (horizontal). In general, the flatter the supply curve, the more elastic. The steeper the supply curve, the more inelastic.

Price elasticity of supply may not be constant along a given supply curve. At low quantities, a small increase in price may stimulate a large increase in quantity supplied because there is excess capacity in the production facility. Therefore, price elasticity is large. At high quantities, a large increase in price may cause only a small increase in quantity supplied because the production facility is at full capacity. Therefore, price elasticity is small.

Three Applications of Supply, Demand, and Elasticity

- *The market for agricultural products:* Advances in technology have shifted the supply curve for agricultural products to the right. The demand for food, however, is generally inelastic (steep) because food is inexpensive and a necessity. As a result, the rightward shift in supply has caused a great reduction in the equilibrium price and a small increase in the equilibrium quantity. Thus, ironically, technological advances in agriculture reduce total revenue paid to farmers as a group.

- *The market for oil:* In the 1970s and early 1980s, the Organization of Petroleum Exporting Countries (OPEC) reduced the supply of oil in order to raise its price. In the short run, the demand for oil tends to be inelastic (steep) because consumers cannot easily find substitutes. Thus, the decrease in supply raised the price substantially and increased total revenue to the producers. In the long run, however, consumers found substitutes and drove more fuel-efficient cars causing the demand for oil to become more elastic, and producers searched for more oil causing supply to become more elastic. As a result, while the price of oil rose a great deal in the short run, it did not rise much in the long run.

- *The market for illegal drugs:* In the short run, the demand for illegal addictive drugs is relatively inelastic. As a result, drug interdiction policies that reduce the supply of drugs tend to greatly increase the price of drugs while reducing the quantity consumed very little, and thus, total revenue paid by drug users increases. This need for additional funds by drug users may cause drug-related crime to rise. This increase in total revenue and in crime is likely to be smaller in the long run because the demand for illegal drugs becomes more elastic as time passes. Alternatively, policies aimed at reducing the demand for drugs reduce total revenue in the drug market and reduce drug-related crime.

Conclusion

The tools of supply and demand allow you to analyze the most important events and policies that shape the economy.

Helpful Hints

1. An easy way to remember the difference between the terms elastic and inelastic is to substitute the word *sensitivity* for elasticity. For example, price elasticity of demand becomes price *sensitivity* of demand. If the quantity demanded is sensitive to a change in price (demand is relatively flat), demand is elastic. If the quantity demanded is insensitive to a change in price (demand is relatively steep), demand is inelastic. The same is true for the price elasticity of supply. If the quantity supplied is sensitive to a change in price, supply is elastic. If the quantity supplied is insensitive to a change in price, supply is inelastic.

2. Although elasticity and slope are similar, they are not the same. Along a straight line, slope is constant. Slope (rise over run) is the same anywhere on the line and is measured as the change in the dependent variable divided by the change in the independent variable. Elasticity, however, is measured as the *percent* change in the dependent variable divided by the *percent* change in the independent variable. This value changes as we move along a line because a one-unit change in a variable is a larger percentage change when the initial values are small as opposed to when they are large. In practice, however, it is still reasonable to suggest that flatter curves tend to be more elastic and steeper curves tend to be more inelastic.

3. The term "elasticity" is used to describe how much the quantity stretches (or changes) in response to some economic event such as a change in price or income.

If the quantity stretches a great deal in response to a change in price or income, it is considered elastic. This mental picture should also help you remember how to calculate an elasticity—in the numerator, you will always find the percentage change in quantity, and in the denominator, you will always find the percentage change in the variable that is the source of the change in quantity.

Terms and Definitions

Choose a definition for each key term.

Key Terms

_____ Elasticity

_____ Price elasticity of demand

_____ Elastic

_____ Inelastic

_____ Total revenue

_____ Income elasticity of demand

_____ Cross-price elasticity of demand

_____ Price elasticity of supply

_____ Normal good

_____ Inferior good

Definitions

1. A measure of how much the quantity demanded of a good responds to a change in consumers' income

2. When the quantity demanded or supplied responds substantially to a change in one of its determinants

3. A good characterized by a negative income elasticity

4. A measure of the responsiveness of the quantity demanded or quantity supplied to a change in one of its determinants

5. A good characterized by a positive income elasticity

6. A measure of how much the quantity supplied of a good responds to a change in the price of that good

7. When the quantity demanded or supplied responds only slightly to a change in one of its determinants

8. The amount paid by buyers and received by sellers of a good computed as $P \times Q$

9. A measure of how much the quantity demanded of a good responds to a change in the price of that good

10. A measure of how much the quantity demanded of one good responds to a change in the price of another good

Problems and Short-Answer Questions

Practice Problems

1. For each pair of goods listed below, which good would you expect to have the more elastic demand? Why?
   a. cigarettes; a trip to Florida over spring break

   _____

   _____

   b.   an AIDS vaccine over the next month; an AIDS vaccine over the next five years

_____

_____

_____

   c.   beer; Budweiser

_____

_____

   d.   insulin; aspirin

_____

_____

_____

2. Suppose the *Daily Newspaper* estimates that if it raises the price of its newspaper from $1.00 to $1.50 then the number of subscribers will fall from 50,000 to 40,000.

   a.   What is the price elasticity of demand for the *Daily Newspaper* when elasticity is calculated using the midpoint method?

_____

   b.   What is the advantage of using the midpoint method?

_____

_____

   c.   If the *Daily Newspaper*'s only concern is to maximize total revenue, should it raise the price of a newspaper from $1.00 to $1.50? Why or why not?

_____

_____

3. The table below provides the demand schedule for motel rooms at Small Town Motel. Use the information provided to complete the table. Answer the following questions based on your responses in the table. Use the midpoint method to calculate the percentage changes used to generate the elasticities.

Price	Quantity Demanded	Total Revenue	% Change in Price	% Change in Quantity	Elasticity
$ 20	24	_____			
			_____	_____	_____
40	20	_____			
			_____	_____	_____
60	16	_____			
			_____	_____	_____
80	12	_____			
			_____	_____	_____
100	8	_____			
			_____	_____	_____
120	4	_____			
			_____	_____	_____

a. Over what range of prices is the demand for motel rooms elastic? To maximize total revenue, should Small Town Motel raise or lower the price within this range?

_____

b. Over what range of prices is the demand for motel rooms inelastic? To maximize total revenue, should Small Town Motel raise or lower the price within this range?

_____

c. Over what range of prices is the demand for motel rooms unit elastic? To maximize total revenue, should Small Town Motel raise or lower the price within this range?

_____

_____

4. The demand schedule from question 3 above is reproduced below along with another demand schedule when consumer incomes have risen to $60,000 from $50,000. Use this information to answer the following questions. Use the midpoint method to calculate the percentage changes used to generate the elasticities.

Price	Quantity Demanded When Income Is $50,000	Quantity Demanded When Income Is $60,000
$ 20	24	34
40	20	30
60	16	26
80	12	22
100	8	18
120	4	14

a. What is the income elasticity of demand when motel rooms rent for $40?

_____

b. What is the income elasticity of demand when motel rooms rent for $100?

_____

c. Are motel rooms normal or inferior goods? Why?

_____

_____

d. Are motel rooms likely to be necessities or luxuries? Why?

_____

_____

5. For each pair of goods listed below, which good would you expect to have the more elastic supply? Why?
   a. televisions; beachfront property

   _____

   _____

   _____

   b. crude oil over the next week; crude oil over the next year

   _____

   _____

   _____

   c. a painting by van Gogh; a print of the same painting by van Gogh

   _____

   _____

   _____

Short-Answer Questions

1. What are the four major determinants of the price elasticity of demand?

   _____

   _____

   _____

   _____

2. If demand is inelastic, will an increase in price raise or lower total revenue? Why?

   _____

   _____

   _____

   _____

3. If the price of soda doubles from $1.00 per can to $2.00 per can and you buy the same amount, what is your price elasticity of demand for soda, and is it considered elastic or inelastic?

   _____

4. If the price of Pepsi increases by one cent and this induces you to stop buying Pepsi altogether and switch to Coca-Cola, what is your price elasticity of demand for Pepsi, and is it considered elastic or inelastic?

   _____

5. Suppose your income rises by 20 percent and your quantity demanded of eggs falls by 10 percent. What is the value of your income elasticity of demand for eggs? Are eggs normal or inferior goods to you?

   _____

6. Suppose a firm is operating at half capacity. Is its supply curve for output likely to be relatively elastic or inelastic? Why?

   _____

   _____

   _____

   _____

7. Is the price elasticity of supply for fresh fish likely to be elastic or inelastic when measured over the time period of one day? Why?

   _____

   _____

   _____

   _____

8. If a demand curve is linear, is the elasticity constant along the demand curve? Which part tends to be elastic and which part tends to be inelastic? Why?

   _____

   _____

   _____

   _____

9. Suppose that at a price of $2.00 per bushel, the quantity supplied of corn is 25 million metric tons. At a price of $3.00 per bushel, the quantity supplied is 30 million metric tons. What is the elasticity of supply for corn? Is supply elastic or inelastic?

   _____

10. Suppose that when the price of apples rises by 20 percent, the quantity demanded of oranges rises by 6 percent. What is the cross-price elasticity of demand between apples and oranges? Are these two goods substitutes or complements?

   _____

   _____

   _____

   _____

Self-Test

True/False Questions

_____ 1. If the quantity demanded of a good is sensitive to a change in the price of that good, demand is said to be price inelastic.

_____ 2. Using the midpoint method to calculate elasticity, if an increase in the price of pencils from 10 cents to 20 cents reduces the quantity demanded from 1,000 pencils to 500 pencils, then the demand for pencils is unit price elastic.

_____ 3. The demand for tires should be more inelastic than the demand for Goodyear brand tires.

_____ 4. The demand for aspirin this month should be more elastic than the demand for aspirin this year.

_____ 5. The price elasticity of demand is defined as the percentage change in the price of that good divided by the percentage change in quantity demanded of that good.

_____ 6. If the cross-price elasticity of demand between two goods is positive, the goods are likely to be complements.

_____ 7. If the demand for a good is price inelastic, an increase in its price will increase total revenue in that market.

_____ 8. The demand for a necessity such as insulin tends to be elastic.

_____ 9. If a demand curve is linear, the price elasticity of demand is constant along it.

_____ 10. If the income elasticity of demand for a bus ride is negative, then a bus ride is an inferior good.

_____ 11. The supply of automobiles for this week is likely to be more price inelastic than the supply of automobiles for this year.

_____ 12. If the price elasticity of supply for blue jeans is 1.3, an increase of 10 percent in the price of blue jeans would increase the quantity supplied of blue jeans by 13 percent.

_____ 13. The price elasticity of supply tends to be more inelastic as the firm's production facility reaches maximum capacity.

_____ 14. An advance in technology that shifts the market supply curve to the right always increases total revenue received by producers.

_____ 15. The income elasticity of demand for luxury items, such as diamonds, tends to be large (greater than 1).

Multiple-Choice Questions

1. If a small percentage increase in the price of a good greatly reduces the quantity demanded for that good, the demand for that good is
   a. price inelastic.
   b. price elastic.
   c. unit price elastic.
   d. income inelastic.
   e. income elastic.

2. The price elasticity of demand is defined as
   a. the percentage change in price of a good divided by the percentage change in the quantity demanded of that good.
   b. the percentage change in income divided by the percentage change in the quantity demanded.
   c. the percentage change in the quantity demanded of a good divided by the percentage change in the price of that good.
   d. the percentage change in the quantity demanded divided by the percentage change in income.
   e. none of the above.

3. In general, a flatter demand curve is more likely to be
   a. price elastic.
   b. price inelastic.
   c. unit price elastic.
   d. none of the above.

4. In general, a steeper supply curve is more likely to be
   a. price elastic.
   b. price inelastic.
   c. unit price elastic.
   d. none of the above.

5. Which of the following would cause a demand curve for a good to be price inelastic?
   a. There are a great number of substitutes for the good.
   b. The good is inferior.
   c. The good is a luxury.
   d. The good is a necessity.

6. The demand for which of the following is likely to be the most price inelastic?
   a. airline tickets
   b. bus tickets
   c. taxi rides
   d. transportation

7. If the cross-price elasticity between two goods is negative, the two goods are likely to be
   a. luxuries.
   b. necessities.
   c. complements.
   d. substitutes.

8. If a supply curve for a good is price elastic, then
   a. the quantity supplied is sensitive to changes in the price of that good.
   b. the quantity supplied is insensitive to changes in the price of that good.
   c. the quantity demanded is sensitive to changes in the price of that good.
   d. the quantity demanded is insensitive to changes in the price of that good.
   e. none of the above.

9. If a fisherman must sell all of his daily catch before it spoils for whatever price he is offered, once the fish are caught, the fisherman's price elasticity of supply for fresh fish is
    a. zero.
    b. one.
    c. infinite.
    d. unable to be determined from this information.

10. A decrease in supply (shift to the left) will increase total revenue in that market if
    a. supply is price elastic.
    b. supply is price inelastic.
    c. demand is price elastic.
    d. demand is price inelastic.

11. If an increase in the price of a good has no impact on the total revenue in that market, demand must be
    a. price inelastic.
    b. price elastic.
    c. unit price elastic.
    d. all of the above.

12. If consumers always spend 15 percent of their income on food, then the income elasticity of demand for food is
    a. 0.15.
    b. 1.00.
    c. 1.15.
    d. 1.50.
    e. none of the above.

13. Technological improvements in agriculture that shift the supply of agricultural commodities to the right tend to
    a. reduce total revenue to farmers as a whole because the demand for food is inelastic.
    b. reduce total revenue to farmers as a whole because the demand for food is elastic.
    c. increase total revenue to farmers as a whole because the demand for food is inelastic.
    d. increase total revenue to farmers as a whole because the demand for food is elastic.

14. If supply is price inelastic, the value of the price elasticity of supply must be
    a. zero.
    b. less than 1.
    c. greater than 1.
    d. infinite.
    e. none of the above.

15. If there is excess capacity in a production facility, it is likely that the firm's supply curve is
    a. price inelastic.
    b. price elastic.
    c. unit price elastic.
    d. none of the above.

Use the following information to answer questions 16 and 17. Suppose that at a price of $30 per month, there are 30,000 subscribers to cable television in Small Town. If Small Town Cablevision raises its price to $40 per month, the number of subscribers will fall to 20,000.

16. Using the midpoint method for calculating the elasticity, what is the price elasticity of demand for cable television in Small Town?
    a.   0.66
    b.   0.75
    c.   1.0
    d.   1.4
    e.   2.0

17. At which of the following prices does Small Town Cablevision earn the greatest total revenue?
    a.   either $30 or $40 per month because the price elasticity of demand is 1.0
    b. $30 per month
    c. $40 per month
    d. $0 per month

18. If demand is linear (a straight line), then price elasticity of demand is
    a.   constant along the demand curve.
    b.   inelastic in the upper portion and elastic in the lower portion.
    c.   elastic in the upper portion and inelastic in the lower portion.
    d.   elastic throughout.
    e.   inelastic throughout.

19. If the income elasticity of demand for a good is negative, it must be
    a.   a luxury good.
    b.   a normal good.
    c.   an inferior good.
    d.   an elastic good.

20. If consumers think that there are very few substitutes for a good, then
    a.   supply would tend to be price elastic.
    b.   supply would tend to be price inelastic.
    c.   demand would tend to be price elastic.
    d.   demand would tend to be price inelastic.
    e.   none of the above is true.

Advanced Critical Thinking

In order to reduce teen smoking, the government places a $2 per pack tax on cigarettes. After one month, while the price to the consumer has increased a great deal, the quantity demanded of cigarettes has been reduced only slightly.

1. Is the demand for cigarettes over the period of one month elastic or inelastic?

_____

2. Suppose you are in charge of pricing for a tobacco firm. The president of your firm suggests that the evidence received over the last month demonstrates that the cigarette industry should get together and raise the price of cigarettes further because total revenue to the tobacco industry will certainly rise. Is the president of your firm correct? Why or why not?

_____

_____

_____

_____

3. As an alternative, suppose the president of your tobacco firm suggests that your firm raise the price of your cigarettes independent of the other tobacco firms because the evidence clearly shows that smokers are insensitive to changes in the price of cigarettes. Is the president of your firm correct if it is his desire to maximize total revenue? Why or why not?

_____

_____

_____

_____

Solutions

Terms and Definitions

__4__ Elasticity

__9__ Price elasticity of demand

__2__ Elastic

__7__ Inelastic

__8__ Total revenue

__1__ Income elasticity of demand

__10__ Cross-price elasticity of demand

__6__ Price elasticity of supply

__5__ Normal good

__3__ Inferior good

Practice Problems

1. a. a trip to Florida because it is a luxury whereas cigarettes are a necessity (to smokers)

   b. an AIDS vaccine over the next five years because there are likely to be more substitutes (alternative medications) developed over this time period and consumers' behavior may be modified over longer time periods

   c. Budweiser because it is a more narrowly defined market than beer so there are more substitutes for Budweiser than for beer

   d. aspirin because there are many substitutes for aspirin but few substitutes for insulin

2. a. $(10,000/45,000)/(\$0.50/\$1.25) = 0.56$

   b. With the midpoint method, the value of the elasticity is the same whether you begin at a price of $1.00 and raise it to $1.50 or begin at a price of $1.50 and reduce it to $1.00.

   c. Yes. Because the price elasticity of demand is less than one (inelastic), an increase in price will increase total revenue.

3. See table below.

   a. $80 to $120; lower its prices

Table for problem #3.

Price	Quantity Demanded	Total Revenue	% Change in Price	% Change in Quantity	Elasticity
$20	24	480			
			0.67	0.18	0.27
40	20	800			
			0.40	0.22	0.55
60	16	960			
			0.29	0.29	1.00
80	12	960			
			0.22	0.40	1.82
100	8	800			
			0.18	0.67	3.72
120	4	480			

   b. $20 to $60; raise its prices

   c. $60 to $80; it doesn't matter. For these prices, a change in price proportionately changes the quantity demanded, so total revenue is unchanged.

4. a. $(10/25)/(\$10,000/\$55,000) = 2.2$

   b. $(10/13)/(\$10,000/\$55,000) = 4.2$

   c. Normal goods, because the income elasticity of demand is positive.

   d. Luxuries, because the income elasticity of demand is large (greater than one). In each case, an 18 percent increase in income caused a much larger increase in quantity demanded.

5. a. Televisions, because the production of televisions can be increased in response to an increase in the price of televisions whereas the quantity of beachfront property is fixed.

   b. Crude oil over the next year, because production of oil over the next year can more easily be increased than the production of oil over the next week.

   c. A van Gogh print, because more of them can be created in response to an increase in price whereas the quantity of an original work is fixed.

Short-Answer Questions

1. Whether the good is a necessity or a luxury, the availability of close substitutes, the definition of the market, and the time horizon over which demand is measured.

2. It will increase total revenue because a large increase in price will be accompanied by only a small reduction in the quantity demanded if demand is inelastic.

3. Zero, therefore it is considered perfectly inelastic.

4. Infinite, therefore it is considered perfectly elastic.

5. $-0.10/0.20 = -1/2$. Eggs are inferior goods.

6. Elastic, because a small increase in price will induce the firm to increase production by a large amount.

7. Inelastic (nearly vertical), because once the fish are caught, the quantity offered for sale is fixed and must be sold before it spoils, regardless of the price.

8. No. The upper part tends to be elastic while the lower part tends to be inelastic. This is because on the upper part, for example, a one-unit change in the price is a small percentage change while a one-unit change in quantity is a large percentage change. This effect is reversed on the lower part of the demand curve.

9. $\dfrac{(30-25)/[(25+30)/2]}{(3-2)/[(2+3)/2]} = 0.45,$

   therefore supply is inelastic.

10. $0.06/0.20 = 0.30$, apples and oranges are substitutes because the cross-price elasticity is positive (an increase in the price of apples increases the quantity demanded of oranges).

True/False Questions

1. F; demand would be price elastic.
2. T
3. T
4. F; the longer the time period considered, the more price elastic the demand curve because consumers have an opportunity to substitute or change their behavior.
5. F; the price elasticity of demand is defined as the percentage change in the quantity demanded of a good divided by the percentage change in the price of that good.
6. F; the two goods are likely to be substitutes.
7. T
8. F; the demand for necessities tends to be inelastic.
9. F; demand will be price elastic in its upper portion and price inelastic in its lower portion.
10. T
11. T
12. T
13. T
14. F; it will increase total revenue only if demand is price elastic.
15. T

Multiple-Choice Questions

1. b
2. c
3. a
4. b
5. d
6. d
7. c
8. a
9. a
10. d
11. c
12. b
13. a
14. b
15. b
16. d
17. b
18. c
19. c
20. d

Advanced Critical Thinking

1. Inelastic.
2. Not necessarily. Demand tends to be more elastic over longer periods. In the case of cigarettes, some consumers will substitute toward cigars and pipes. Others may quit or never start to smoke.
3. No. While the demand for cigarettes (the market broadly defined) may be inelastic, the demand for any one brand (market narrowly defined) is likely to be much more elastic because consumers can substitute toward other lower priced brands.

Chapter 6
Supply, Demand, and Government Policies

Goals
In this chapter you will

- Examine the effects of government policies that place a ceiling on prices

- Examine the effects of government policies that put a floor under prices

- Consider how a tax on a good affects the price of the good and the quantity sold

- Learn that taxes levied on sellers and taxes levied on buyers are equivalent

- See how the burden of a tax is split between buyers and sellers

Outcomes
After accomplishing these goals, you should be able to

- Describe the conditions necessary for a price ceiling to be a binding constraint

- Explain why a binding price floor creates a surplus

- Demonstrate why a tax placed on a good generally reduces the quantity of the good sold

- Demonstrate why the results are the same when a tax is placed on the sellers or buyers of a good

- Show whether the buyers or sellers of a good bear the burden of the tax when demand is inelastic and supply is elastic

Chapter Overview

Context and Purpose

Chapter 6 is the third chapter in a three-chapter sequence that deals with supply and demand and how markets work. Chapter 4 developed the model of supply and demand. Chapter 5 added precision to the model of supply and demand by developing the

85

concept of elasticity—the sensitivity of the quantity supplied and quantity demanded to changes in economic conditions. Chapter 6 addresses the impact of government policies on competitive markets using the tools of supply and demand that you learned in Chapters 4 and 5.

The purpose of Chapter 6 is to consider two types of government policies: price controls and taxes. Price controls set the maximum or minimum price at which a good can be sold while a tax creates a wedge between what the buyer pays and the seller receives. These policies can be analyzed within the model of supply and demand. We will find that government policies sometimes produce unintended consequences.

Chapter Review

Introduction   In Chapters 4 and 5, we acted as scientists because we built the model of supply and demand to describe the world as it is. In Chapter 6, we act as policy advisers because we address how government policies are used to try to improve the world. We address two policies: price controls and taxes. Sometimes these policies produce unintended consequences.

Controls on Prices

There are two types of controls on prices: price ceilings and price floors. A price ceiling sets a legal maximum on the price at which a good can be sold. A price floor sets a legal minimum on the price at which a good can be sold.

- **Price Ceilings**   Suppose the government is persuaded by buyers to set a price ceiling. If the price ceiling is set above the equilibrium price, it is not binding. That is, it has no impact on the market because the price can move to equilibrium without restriction. If the price ceiling is set below the equilibrium price, it is a binding constraint because it does not allow the market to reach equilibrium. A binding price ceiling causes the quantity demanded to exceed the quantity supplied, or a shortage. Because there is a shortage, methods develop to ration the small quantity supplied across a large number of buyers. Buyers willing to wait in long lines might get the good, or sellers could sell only to their friends, family, or members of the same race. Lines are inefficient, and discrimination is both inefficient and unfair. Free markets are impersonal and ration goods with prices.

    Price ceilings are commonly found in the markets for gasoline and apartments. When OPEC restricted the quantity of petroleum in 1973, the supply of gasoline was reduced and the equilibrium price rose above the price ceiling and the price ceiling became binding. This caused a shortage of gas and long lines at the pump. In response, the price ceilings were later repealed. Price ceilings on apartments are known as rent controls. Binding rent controls create a shortage of housing. Both the demand and supply of housing are inelastic in the short run, so the initial shortage is small. In the long run, however, the supply and demand for housing become more elastic, and the shortage is more apparent. This causes waiting lists for apartments, bribes to landlords, unclean and unsafe buildings, and lower quality housing. Once established, however, rent controls are politically difficult to remove.

- **Price Floors**   Suppose the government is persuaded by sellers to set a price floor. If the price floor is set below the equilibrium price, it is *not binding*. That is, it has no impact on the market because the price can move to equilibrium without restriction. If the price floor is set above the equilibrium price, it is a *binding constraint* because it does not allow the market to reach equilibrium. A binding price floor causes the quantity supplied to exceed the quantity demanded, or a surplus. In order to eliminate the surplus, sellers may appeal to the biases of the buyers and sell to buyers that are family, friends, or members of the same race. Free markets are impersonal and ration goods with prices.

    An important example of a price floor is the minimum wage. The minimum wage is a binding constraint in the market for young and unskilled workers. When the wage is set above the market equilibrium wage, the quantity supplied of labor exceeds the quantity demanded. The result is unemployment. Studies show that a 10 percent increase in the minimum wage depresses teenage employment by 1 to 3 percent. The minimum wage also causes teenagers to look for work and drop out of school.

Price controls often hurt those they are trying to help—usually the poor. The minimum wage may help those who find work at the minimum wage but harm those who become unemployed because of the minimum wage. Rent controls reduce the quality and availability of housing.

Taxes

Governments use taxes to raise revenue. A tax on a good will affect the quantity sold and both the price paid by buyers and the price received by sellers. If the tax is collected from the sellers, supply shifts upward by the size of the tax per unit. As a result of the decrease in supply, the quantity sold decreases, the price paid by the buyer increases, and the price received by the seller decreases. If the tax is collected from the buyers, demand shifts downward by the size of the tax per unit. Because of the decrease in demand, the quantity sold decreases, the price paid by the buyer increases, and the price received by the seller decreases. Therefore, a tax levied on buyers has the same effect as a tax levied on sellers. After a tax has been placed on a good, the difference between what the buyer pays and the seller receives is the tax per unit and is known as the *tax wedge*. In summary:

- A tax discourages market activity. That is, the quantity sold is reduced.

- Buyers and sellers share the burden of a tax because the price paid by the buyers increases while the price received by the sellers decreases.

- The effect of a tax collected from buyers is equivalent to a tax collected from sellers.

- The government cannot legislate the relative burden of the tax between buyers and sellers. The relative burden of a tax is determined by the elasticity of supply and demand in that market.

Tax incidence is the manner in which the burden of a tax is shared among participants in a market. That is, it is the division of the tax burden. When a tax wedge is placed between buyers and sellers, the tax burden falls more heavily on the side of the market that is less elastic. That is, the tax burden falls more heavily on the side of the market that is less willing to leave the market when price movements are unfavorable to them. For example, in the market for cigarettes, because cigarettes are addictive, demand is likely to be less elastic than supply. Therefore, a tax on cigarettes tends to raise the price paid by buyers more than it reduces the price received by sellers, and as a result, the burden of a cigarette tax falls more heavily on the buyers of cigarettes. With regard to the payroll tax (Social Security and Medicare tax), because labor supply is less elastic than labor demand, most of the tax burden is borne by the workers as opposed to the 50–50 split intended by lawmakers.

Helpful Hints

1. Price ceilings and price floors only matter if they are binding constraints. Price ceilings do not automatically cause a shortage. A price ceiling only causes a shortage if the price ceiling is set below the equilibrium price. In a similar manner, a price floor only causes a surplus if the price floor is set above the equilibrium price.

2. It is useful to think of taxes as causing vertical shifts in demand and supply. Because demand is the maximum buyers are willing to pay for each quantity, a tax imposed on the buyers in a market reduces or shifts downward the demand faced by sellers by precisely the size of the tax per unit. That is, the buyers now offer the sellers an amount that has been reduced by precisely the size of the tax per unit. Alternatively, because supply is the minimum sellers are willing to accept for each quantity, a tax imposed on the sellers in a market reduces or shifts upward the supply faced by buyers by precisely the size of the tax per unit. This is because the sellers now require an additional amount from the buyers that is precisely the size of the tax per unit.

Terms and Definitions

Choose a definition for each key term.

Key Terms	Definitions
_____ Price ceiling	1. The manner in which the burden of a tax is shared among participants in a market
_____ Price floor	2. A legal maximum on the price at which a good can be sold
_____ Tax incidence	3. The difference between what the buyer pays and the seller receives after a tax has been imposed
_____ Tax wedge	4. A legal minimum on the price at which a good can be sold

Problems and Short-Answer Questions

Practice Problems

1. Use the following supply and demand schedules for bicycles to answer the questions below.

Price	Quantity Demanded	Quantity Supplied
$300	60	30
400	55	40
500	50	50
600	45	60
700	40	70
800	35	80

a. In response to lobbying by the Bicycle Riders Association, Congress places a price ceiling of $700 on bicycles. What effect will this have on the market for bicycles? Why?

_____

_____

b. In response to lobbying by the Bicycle Riders Association, Congress places a price ceiling of $400 on bicycles. Use the information provided above to plot the supply and demand curves for bicycles in Exhibit 1. Impose the price ceiling. What is the result of a price ceiling of $400 on bicycles?

_____

_____

c. Does a price ceiling of $400 on bicycles make all bicycle buyers better off? Why or why not?

_____

_____

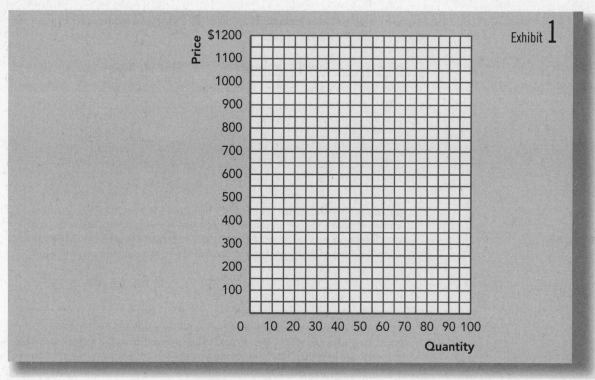

d. Suppose instead, in response to lobbying by the Bicycle Manufacturers As-
    sociation, Congress imposes a price floor on bicycles of $700. Use the information
    provided above to plot the supply and demand curves for bicycles in Exhibit 2.
    Impose the $700 price floor. What is the result of the $700 price floor?

    _____

    _____

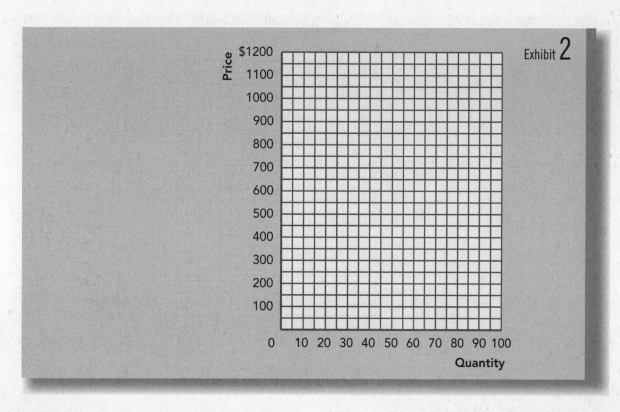

2. Use the following supply and demand schedules for bicycles to answer the questions below.

Price	Quantity Demanded	Quantity Supplied
$300	60	30
400	55	40
500	50	50
600	45	60
700	40	70
800	35	80

a. Plot the supply and demand curves for bicycles in Exhibit 3. On the graph, impose a tax of $300 per bicycle to be collected from the sellers. After the tax, what has happened to the price paid by the buyers, the price received by the sellers, and the quantity sold when compared to the free market equilibrium?

_____

_____

b. Again, plot the supply and demand curves for bicycles in Exhibit 4. On the graph, impose a tax of $300 per bicycle to be collected from the buyers. After the tax, what has happened to the price paid by the buyers, the price received by the sellers, and the quantity sold when compared to the free market equilibrium?

_____

_____

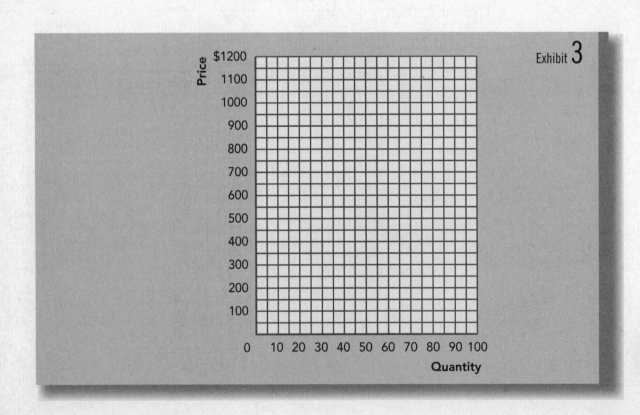

Exhibit 3

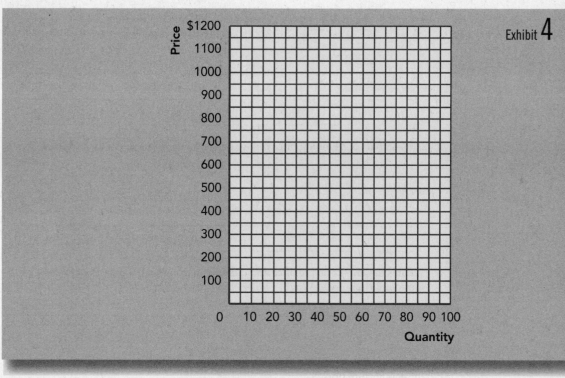

Exhibit 4

c. Compare your answers to questions *a* and *b* above. What conclusion do you draw from this comparison?

_____

_____

d. Who bears the greater burden of this tax, the buyers or the sellers? Why?

_____

_____

_____

_____

Short-Answer Questions

1. What is the impact on the price and quantity in a market if a price ceiling is set above the equilibrium price? Why?

_____

_____

_____

2. What is the impact on the price and quantity in a market if a price ceiling is set below the equilibrium price?

_____

_____

3. What are some of the problems created by a binding price ceiling?

_____

_____

_____

_____

4. Is the impact of a binding price ceiling greater in the short run or the long run? Why?

_____

_____

_____

_____

5. What is the impact on the price and quantity in a market if a price floor is set below the equilibrium price? Why?

_____

_____

6. What is the impact on the price and quantity in a market if a price floor is set above the equilibrium price?

_____

_____

7. When we use the model of supply and demand to analyze a tax that is collected from the sellers, which way do we shift the supply curve? Why?

_____

_____

_____

_____

8. When we use the model of supply and demand to analyze a tax that is collected from the buyers, which way do we shift the demand curve? Why?

_____

_____

_____

_____

9. Why is a tax collected from the buyers equivalent to a tax collected from the sellers?

_____

_____

_____

_____

10. Suppose a gas-guzzler tax is placed on luxury automobiles. Who will likely bear the greater burden of the tax, the buyers of luxury autos or the sellers? Why?

_____

_____

_____

_____

_____

Self-Test

True/False Questions

_____ 1. If the equilibrium price of gasoline is $3.00 per gallon and the government places a price ceiling on gasoline of $4.00 per gallon, the result will be a shortage of gasoline.

_____ 2. A price ceiling set below the equilibrium price causes a surplus.

_____ 3. A price floor set above the equilibrium price is a binding constraint.

_____ 4. The shortage of housing caused by a binding rent control is likely to be more severe in the long run when compared to the short run.

_____ 5. The minimum wage helps all teenagers because they receive higher wages than they would otherwise.

_____ 6. A 10 percent increase in the minimum wage causes a 10 percent reduction in teenage employment.

_____ 7. A price ceiling that is not a binding constraint today could cause a shortage in the future if demand were to increase and raise the equilibrium price above the fixed price ceiling.

_____ 8. A price floor in a market always creates a surplus in that market.

_____ 9. A $10 tax on baseball gloves will always raise the price that the buyers pay for baseball gloves by $10.

_____ 10. The ultimate burden of a tax lands most heavily on the side of the market that is less elastic.

_____ 11. If medicine is a necessity, the burden of a tax on medicine will likely land more heavily on the buyers of medicine.

_____ 12. When we use the model of supply and demand to analyze a tax collected from the buyers, we shift the demand curve upward by the size of the tax.

_____ 13. A tax collected from buyers has an equivalent impact to a same size tax collected from sellers.

_____ 14. A tax creates a tax wedge between a buyer and a seller. This causes the price paid by the buyer to rise, the price received by the seller to fall, and the quantity sold to fall.

_____ 15. The government can choose to place the burden of a tax on the buyers in a market by collecting the tax from the buyers rather than the sellers.

Multiple-Choice Questions

1. For a price ceiling to be a binding constraint on the market, the government must set it
    a. above the equilibrium price.
    b. below the equilibrium price.
    c. precisely at the equilibrium price.
    d. at any price because all price ceilings are binding constraints.

2. A binding price ceiling creates
    a. a shortage.
    b. a surplus.
    c. an equilibrium.
    d. a shortage or a surplus depending on whether the price ceiling is set above or below the equilibrium price.

3. Suppose the equilibrium price for apartments is $800 per month and the government imposes rent controls of $500. Which of the following is *unlikely* to occur as a result of the rent controls?
    a. There will be a shortage of housing.
    b. Landlords may discriminate among apartment renters.
    c. Landlords may be offered bribes to rent apartments.
    d. The quality of apartments will improve.
    e. There may be long lines of buyers waiting for apartments.

4. A price floor
    a. sets a legal maximum on the price at which a good can be sold.
    b. sets a legal minimum on the price at which a good can be sold.
    c. always determines the price at which a good must be sold.
    d. is not a binding constraint if it is set above the equilibrium price.

5. Which of the following statements about a binding price ceiling is true?
    a. The surplus created by the price ceiling is greater in the short run than in the long run.
    b. The surplus created by the price ceiling is greater in the long run than in the short run.
    c. The shortage created by the price ceiling is greater in the short run than in the long run.
    d. The shortage created by the price ceiling is greater in the long run than in the short run.

6. Which side of the market is more likely to lobby government for a price floor?
    a. Neither buyers nor sellers desire a price floor.
    b. Both buyers and sellers desire a price floor.
    c. the sellers
    d. the buyers

7. The surplus caused by a binding price floor will be greatest if
    a. both supply and demand are elastic.
    b. both supply and demand are inelastic.
    c. supply is inelastic and demand is elastic.
    d. demand is inelastic and supply is elastic.

8. Which of the following is an example of a price floor?
    a. rent controls
    b. restricting gasoline prices to $2.00 per gallon when the equilibrium price is $3.00 per gallon
    c. the minimum wage
    d. All of the above are price floors.

9. Which of the following statements is true if the government places a price ceiling on gasoline at $4.00 per gallon and the equilibrium price is $3.00 per gallon?
    a. There will be a shortage of gasoline.
    b. There will be a surplus of gasoline.
    c. A significant increase in the supply of gasoline could cause the price ceiling to become a binding constraint.
    d. A significant increase in the demand for gasoline could cause the price ceiling to become a binding constraint.

10. Studies show that a 10 percent increase in the minimum wage
    a. decreases teenage employment by about 10 to 15 percent.
    b. increases teenage employment by about 10 to 15 percent.
    c. decreases teenage employment by about 1 to 3 percent.
    d. increases teenage employment by about 1 to 3 percent.

11. Within the supply-and-demand model, a tax collected from the buyers of a good shifts the
    a. demand curve upward by the size of the tax per unit.
    b. demand curve downward by the size of the tax per unit.
    c. supply curve upward by the size of the tax per unit.
    d. supply curve downward by the size of the tax per unit.

12. Within the supply-and-demand model, a tax collected from the sellers of a good shifts the
    a. demand curve upward by the size of the tax per unit.
    b. demand curve downward by the size of the tax per unit.
    c. supply curve upward by the size of the tax per unit.
    d. supply curve downward by the size of the tax per unit.

13. Which of the following takes place when a tax is placed on a good?
    a. an increase in the price buyers pay, a decrease in the price sellers receive, and a decrease in the quantity sold
    b. an increase in the price buyers pay, a decrease in the price sellers receive, and an increase in the quantity sold
    c. a decrease in the price buyers pay, an increase in the price sellers receive, and a decrease in the quantity sold
    d. a decrease in the price buyers pay, an increase in the price sellers receive, and an increase in the quantity sold

14. When a tax is collected from the buyers in a market,
    a. the buyers bear the burden of the tax.
    b. the sellers bear the burden of the tax.
    c. the tax burden on the buyers and sellers is the same as an equivalent tax collected from the sellers.
    d. the tax burden falls most heavily on the buyers.

15. A tax of $1.00 per gallon on gasoline
    a. increases the price the buyers pay by $1.00 per gallon.
    b. decreases the price the sellers receive by $1.00 per gallon.
    c. increases the price the buyers pay by precisely $0.50 and reduces the price received by sellers by precisely $0.50.
    d. places a tax wedge of $1.00 between the price the buyers pay and the price the sellers receive.

16. The burden of a tax falls more heavily on the sellers in a market when
    a. demand is inelastic and supply is elastic.
    b. demand is elastic and supply is inelastic.
    c. both supply and demand are elastic.
    d. both supply and demand are inelastic.

17. A tax placed on a good that is a necessity for consumers will likely generate a tax burden that
     a. falls more heavily on buyers.
     b. falls more heavily on sellers.
     c. is evenly distributed between buyers and sellers.
     d. falls entirely on sellers.

18. The burden of a tax falls more heavily on the buyers in a market when
     a. demand is inelastic and supply is elastic.
     b. demand is elastic and supply is inelastic.
     c. both supply and demand are elastic.
     d. both supply and demand are inelastic.

19. Which of the following statements about the burden of a tax is correct?
     a. The tax burden generated from a tax placed on a good consumers perceive to be a necessity will fall most heavily on the sellers of the good.
     b. The tax burden falls most heavily on the side of the market (buyers or sellers) that is most willing to leave the market when price movements are unfavorable to them.
     c. The burden of a tax lands on the side of the market (buyers or sellers) from which it is collected.
     d. The distribution of the burden of a tax is determined by the relative elasticities of supply and demand and is not determined by legislation.

20. For which of the following products would the burden of a tax likely fall more heavily on the sellers?
     a. food
     b. entertainment
     c. clothing
     d. housing

Advanced Critical Thinking

Suppose that the government needs to raise tax revenue. A politician suggests that the government place a tax on food because everyone must eat and, thus, a food tax would surely raise a great deal of tax revenue. However, because the poor spend a large proportion of their income on food, the tax should be collected only from the sellers of food (grocery stores) and not from the buyers of food. The politician argues that this type of tax would place the burden of the tax on corporate grocery store chains and not on poor consumers.

1. Can the government legislate that the burden of a food tax will fall only on the sellers of food? Why or why not?

   _____

   _____

   _____

   _____

   _____

   _____

2. Do you think the burden of a food tax will tend to fall on the sellers of food or the buyers of food? Why?

   _____

   _____

   _____

   _____

   _____

   _____

Solutions

Terms and Definitions

 _2_ Price ceiling

 _4_ Price floor

 _1_ Tax incidence

 _3_ Tax wedge

Practice Problems

1. a. It will have no effect. The price ceiling is not binding because the equilibrium price is $500 and the price ceiling is set at $700.

   b. See Exhibit 5. The quantity demanded rises to 55 units, the quantity supplied falls to 40 units, and there is a shortage of 15 units.

Exhibit 5

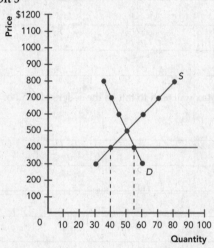

   c. No. It may make those bicycle buyers better off that actually get a bicycle. However, some buyers are unable to get a bike, must wait in line, pay a bribe, or accept a lower quality bicycle.

   d. See Exhibit 6. The quantity supplied rises to 70 units, the quantity demanded falls to 40 units, and there is a surplus of 30 units.

Exhibit 6

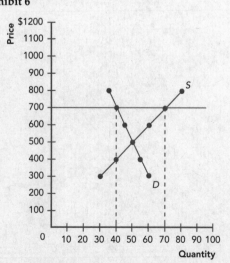

2. a. See Exhibit 7. The price paid by the buyers rises to $700, the price received by the sellers falls to $400, and the quantity sold falls to 40 units.

Exhibit 7

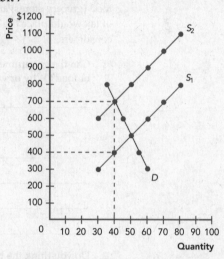

   b. See Exhibit 8. The price paid by the buyers rises to $700, the price received by the sellers falls to $400, and the quantity sold falls to 40 units.

Exhibit 8

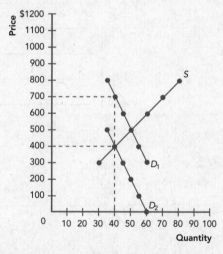

   c. The impact of a tax collected from sellers is equivalent to the impact of a tax collected from buyers.

   d. The greater burden of the tax has fallen on the buyers. The free market equilibrium price was $500. After the tax, the price the buyers pay has risen $200 while the price the sellers receive has fallen $100. This is because demand is less elastic than supply.

Short-Answer Questions

1. There is no impact because the price can move to equilibrium without restriction. That is, the price ceiling is not a binding constraint.

2. The quantity supplied decreases and the quantity demanded increases, causing a shortage.

3. There will be a shortage, buyers may wait in lines, sellers may be able to discriminate among buyers, the quality of the product may be reduced, and bribes may be paid to sellers.

4. The impact is greater in the long run because both supply and demand tend to be more elastic in the long run. As a result, the shortage becomes more severe in the long run.

5. There is no impact because the price can move to equilibrium without restriction. That is, the price floor is not a binding constraint.

6. The quantity supplied increases, and the quantity demanded decreases, causing a surplus.

7. The supply curve is shifted upward by the size of the tax because the amount the seller requires from the buyer has been increased by precisely the size of the tax.

8. The demand curve is shifted downward by the size of the tax because the amount the buyer is willing to offer the seller has been reduced precisely by the size of the tax.

9. A tax places a wedge between what the buyer pays and the seller receives. Whether the buyer or the seller actually hands the tax to the government makes no difference whatsoever.

10. The sellers will bear the greater burden because the demand for luxuries tends to be highly elastic. That is, when the price buyers pay rises due to the tax, wealthy buyers can easily shift their purchases toward alternative items while producers cannot quickly reduce production when the price they receive falls. The burden falls on the side of the market that is less elastic.

True/False Questions

1. F; a price ceiling set above the equilibrium price is not binding.

2. F; it causes a shortage.

3. T

4. T

5. F; some may be helped but others become unemployed and still others quit school to earn what appears to a teenager to be a good wage.

6. F; it causes a 1 to 3 percent reduction in employment.

7. T

8. F; it creates a surplus only if the floor is set above the equilibrium price.

9. F; the difference between what the sellers receive and the buyers pay will be $10, but the price received by the sellers usually will fall some so the price paid by the buyers will rise by less than $10.

10. T

11. T

12. F; we shift the demand curve downward by the size of the tax.

13. T

14. T

15. F; the burden of a tax is determined by the relative elasticities of supply and demand.

Multiple-Choice Questions

1. b
2. a
3. d
4. b
5. d
6. c
7. a
8. c
9. d
10. c
11. b
12. c
13. a
14. c
15. d
16. b
17. a
18. a
19. d
20. b

Advanced Critical Thinking

1. No. The tax burden is determined by the elasticity of supply and demand. The burden of a tax falls most heavily on the side of the market that is less elastic. That is, the burden is on the side of the market least willing to leave the market when the price moves unfavorably.

2. The burden will fall most heavily on the buyers of food regardless of whether the tax is collected from the buyers or the sellers. Food is a necessity, and therefore, the demand for food is relatively inelastic. When the price rises due to the tax, people still must eat. Grocery chains can sell another product lines when the price they receive for food falls due to the tax.

Chapter 7

Consumers, Producers, and the Efficiency of Markets

- Examine the link between buyers' willingness to pay for a good and the demand curve

- Learn how to define and measure consumer surplus

- Examine the link between sellers' costs of producing a good and the supply curve

- Learn how to define and measure producer surplus

- See that the equilibrium of supply and demand maximizes total surplus in a market

Outcomes
After accomplishing these goals, you should be able to

- Derive a demand curve from a group of individual buyers' willingness to pay schedules

- Locate consumer surplus on a supply and demand graph

- Derive a supply curve from a group of individual sellers' cost of production schedules

- Locate producer surplus on a supply-and-demand graph

- Demonstrate why all quantities other than the equilibrium quantity fail to maximize total surplus in a market

Chapter Overview

Context and Purpose

Chapter 7 is the first chapter in a three-chapter sequence on welfare economics and market efficiency. Chapter 7 employs the supply-and-demand model to develop consumer surplus and producer surplus as a measure of welfare and market efficiency. These concepts are then utilized in Chapters 8 and 9 to determine the winners and losers from taxation and restrictions on international trade.

The purpose of Chapter 7 is to develop *welfare economics*—the study of how the allocation of resources affects economic well-being. Chapters 4 through 6 employed supply and demand in a positive framework when we asked the question, "What is the equilibrium price and quantity in a market?" We now address the normative question, "Is the equilibrium price and quantity in a market the best possible solution to the resource allocation problem or is it simply the price and quantity that balances supply and demand?" We will discover that under most circumstances the equilibrium price and quantity is also the one that maximizes welfare.

Chapter Review

Introduction   In this chapter, we address welfare economics—the study of how the allocation of resources affects economic well-being. We measure the benefits that buyers and sellers receive from taking part in a market, and we discover that the equilibrium price and quantity in a market maximizes the total benefits received by buyers and sellers.

Consumer Surplus

Consumer surplus measures the benefits received by buyers from participating in a market. Each potential buyer in a market has some willingness to pay for a good. This willingness to pay is the maximum amount that a buyer will pay for the good. If we plot the value of the greatest willingness to pay for the first unit followed by the next greatest willingness to pay for the second unit and so on (on a price and quantity graph), we have plotted the market demand curve for the good. That is, the height of the demand curve is the marginal buyers' willingness to pay. Because some buyers value a good more than other buyers, the demand curve is downward sloping.

Consumer surplus is the amount a buyer is willing to pay for a good minus the amount the buyer actually pays for it. For example, if you are willing to pay $20 for a new CD by your favorite music artist and you are able to purchase it for $15, you receive consumer surplus on that CD of $5. In general, because the height of the demand curve measures the value buyers place on a good measured by the buyers' willingness to pay, *consumer surplus in a market is the area below the demand curve and above the price.*

When the price of a good falls, consumer surplus increases for two reasons. First, existing buyers receive greater surplus because they are allowed to pay less for the quantities they were already going to purchase, and second, new buyers are brought into the market because the price is now lower than their willingness to pay.

Note that because the height of the demand curve is the value buyers place on a good measured by their willingness to pay, consumer surplus measures the benefits received by buyers *as the buyers themselves perceive it.* Therefore, consumer surplus is an appropriate measure of buyers' benefits if policymakers respect the preferences of buyers. Economists generally believe that buyers are rational and that buyer preferences should be respected except possibly in cases of drug addiction and so on.

Producer Surplus

Producer surplus measures the benefits received by sellers from participating in a market. Each potential seller in a market has some *cost* of production. This cost is the value of everything a seller must give up to produce a good, and it should be interpreted as the producers' opportunity cost of production—actual out-of-pocket expenses plus the value of the producers' time. The cost of production is the minimum amount a seller is willing to accept in order to produce the good. If we plot the cost of the least cost producer of the first unit, then the next least cost producer of the second unit, and so on (on a price and quantity graph), we have plotted the market supply curve for the good. That is, the height of the supply curve is the marginal sellers' cost of production. Because some sellers have a lower cost than other sellers, the supply curve is upward sloping.

Producer surplus is the amount a seller is paid for a good minus the seller's cost of providing it. For example, if a musician can produce a CD for a cost of $10 and sell it for $15, the musician receives a producer surplus of $5 on that CD. In general, because the height of the supply curve measures the sellers' costs, *producer surplus in a market is the area below the price and above the supply curve.*

When the price of a good rises, producer surplus increases for two reasons. First, existing sellers receive greater surplus because they receive more for the quantities they were already going to sell, and second, new sellers are brought into the market because the price is now higher than their cost.

Market Efficiency

We measure economic well-being with *total surplus*—the sum of consumer and producer surplus.

$$\text{Total surplus} = \left(\begin{array}{c} \text{value to} \\ \text{buyers} \end{array} - \begin{array}{c} \text{amount paid} \\ \text{by buyers} \end{array} \right) + \left(\begin{array}{c} \text{amount received} \\ \text{by sellers} \end{array} - \begin{array}{c} \text{cost to} \\ \text{sellers} \end{array} \right)$$

$$\text{Total surplus} = \text{value to buyers} - \text{cost to sellers}$$

Graphically, total surplus is the area below the demand curve and above the supply curve. Resource allocation is said to exhibit efficiency if it maximizes the total surplus received by all members of society. Free market equilibrium is efficient because it maximizes total surplus. This efficiency is demonstrated by the following observations:

- Free markets allocate output to the buyers who value it the most—those with a willingness to pay greater than or equal to the equilibrium price. Therefore, consumer surplus cannot be increased by moving consumption from a current buyer to any other nonbuyer.

- Free markets allocate buyers for goods to the sellers who can produce at the lowest cost—those with a cost of production less than or equal to the equilibrium price. Therefore, producer surplus cannot be increased by moving production from a current seller to any other nonseller.

- Free markets produce the quantity of goods that maximizes the sum of consumer and producer surplus or total surplus. If we produce less than the equilibrium quantity, we fail to produce units where the value to the marginal buyer exceeds the cost to the marginal seller. If we produce more than the equilibrium quantity, we produce units where the cost to the marginal seller exceeds the value to the marginal buyer.

Economists generally advocate free markets because they are efficient. Because markets are efficient, many believe that government policy should be *laissez-faire*, which means "leave to do" or "let people do as they will." Adam Smith's "invisible hand" of the marketplace guides buyers and sellers to an allocation of resources that maximizes total surplus. The efficient outcome cannot be improved upon by a benevolent social planner. In addition to efficiency, however, policymakers may also be concerned with equality—the uniformity of the distribution of well-being among the members of society.

Conclusion: Market Efficiency and Market Failure

There are two main reasons a free market may not be efficient:

- A market may not be perfectly competitive. If individual buyers or sellers (or small groups of them) can influence the price, they have *market power* and they may be able to keep the price and quantity away from equilibrium.

- A market may generate side effects, or *externalities*, which affect people who are not participants in the market at all. These side effects, such as pollution, are not taken into account by buyers and sellers in a market, so the market equilibrium may not be efficient for society as a whole.

Market power and externalities are two types of *market failure*—the inability of some unregulated markets to allocate resources efficiently.

Helpful Hints

1. To better understand "willingness to pay" for the buyer and "cost" to seller, read both demand and supply "backward." That is, read both demand and supply from the quantity axis to the price or dollar axis. When we read demand from quantity to price, we find that the potential buyer for the first unit has a very high willingness to pay because that buyer places a great value on the good. As we move farther out along the quantity axis, the buyers for those quantities have a somewhat lower willingness to pay, and thus, the demand curve slopes negatively. When we read supply from quantity to price, we find that the potential seller for the first unit is extremely efficient and, accordingly, has a very low cost of production. As we move farther out along the quantity axis, the sellers for those quantities have somewhat higher costs, and thus, the supply curve slopes upward. At equilibrium between supply and demand, only those units are produced that generate a value to buyers which exceeds the cost to the sellers.

2. Consumer surplus exists, in part, because in a competitive market, there is one price and all participants are price takers. With a single market price determined by the interactions of many buyers and sellers, individual buyers may have a willingness to pay that exceeds the price, and as a result, some buyers receive consumer surplus. If, however, sellers are aware of the buyers' willingness to pay and the sellers engage in price discrimination, that is, charge each buyer their willingness to pay, there would be no consumer surplus. Each buyer would be forced to pay his individual willingness to pay. This issue will be addressed in later chapters.

Terms and Definitions

Choose a definition for each key term.

Key Terms

_____ Welfare economics

_____ Willingness to pay

_____ Consumer surplus

_____ Cost

_____ Producer surplus

_____ Efficiency

_____ Equality

_____ Market failure

Definitions

1. The amount a buyer is willing to pay for a good minus the amount the buyer actually pays for it

2. The property of a resource allocation of maximizing the total surplus received by all members of society

3. The study of how the allocation of resources affects economic well-being

4. The inability of some unregulated markets to allocate resources efficiently

5. The property of distributing prosperity uniformly among the members of society

6. The amount a seller is paid for a good minus the seller's cost of providing it

7. The maximum amount that a buyer will pay for a good

8. The value of everything a seller must give up to produce a good

Problems and Short-Answer Questions

Practice Problems

1. The following information describes the value Lori Landlord places on having her five apartment houses repainted. She values the repainting of each apartment house at a different amount depending on how badly it needs repainting.

Value of new paint on first apartment house	$5,000
Value of new paint on second apartment house	4,000
Value of new paint on third apartment house	3,000
Value of new paint on fourth apartment house	2,000
Value of new paint on fifth apartment house	1,000

   a. Plot Lori Landlord's willingness to pay in Exhibit 1.

   b. If the price to repaint her apartments is $5,000 each, how many will she repaint? What is the value of her consumer surplus?

   _____

   c. Suppose the price to repaint her apartments falls to $2,000 each. How many apartments will Lori choose to have repainted? What is the value of her consumer surplus?

   _____

   d. What happened to Ms. Landlord's consumer surplus when the price of having her apartments repainted fell? Why?

   _____

   _____

   _____

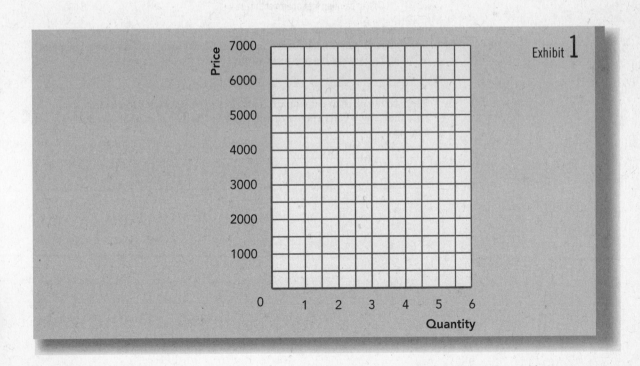

Exhibit 1

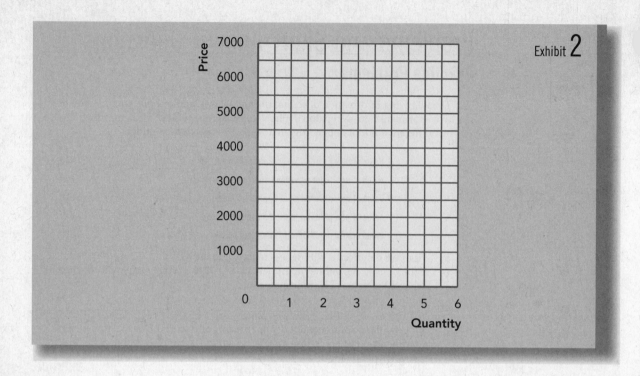

2. The following information shows the costs incurred by Peter Painter when he paints apartments. Because painting is backbreaking work, the more he paints, the higher the costs he incurs in both pain and chiropractic bills.

Cost of painting first apartment house	$1,000
Cost of painting second apartment house	2,000
Cost of painting third apartment house	3,000
Cost of painting fourth apartment house	4,000
Cost of painting fifth apartment house	5,000

a. Plot Peter Painter's cost in Exhibit 2.

b. If the price of painting apartment houses is $2,000 each, how many will he paint? What is the value of his producer surplus?

_____

c. Suppose the price to paint apartments rises to $4,000 each. How many apartments will Peter choose to repaint? What is the value of his producer surplus?

_____

_____

d. What happened to Mr. Painter's producer surplus when the price to paint apartments rose? Why?

_____

_____

_____

3. Use the information about willingness to pay and cost from questions 1 and 2 above to answer the following questions.

a. If a benevolent social planner sets the price for painting apartment houses at $5,000, what is the value of consumer surplus? producer surplus? total surplus?

_____

_____

_____

b. If a benevolent social planner sets the price for painting apartment houses at $1,000, what is the value of consumer surplus? producer surplus? total surplus?

_____

_____

_____

c. If the price for painting apartment houses is allowed to move to its free market equilibrium price of $3,000, what is the value of consumer surplus, producer surplus, and total surplus in the market? How does total surplus in the free market compare to the total surplus generated by the social planner?

_____

_____

_____

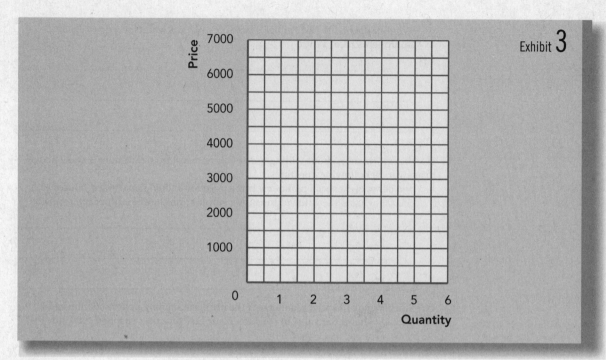

Exhibit 3

4. In Exhibit 3, plot the linear supply and demand curves for painting apartments implied by the information in questions 1 and 2 above (draw them so that they contact the vertical axis). Show consumer and producer surplus for the free market equilibrium price and quantity. Is this allocation of resources efficient? Why or why not?

_____

_____

_____

_____

_____

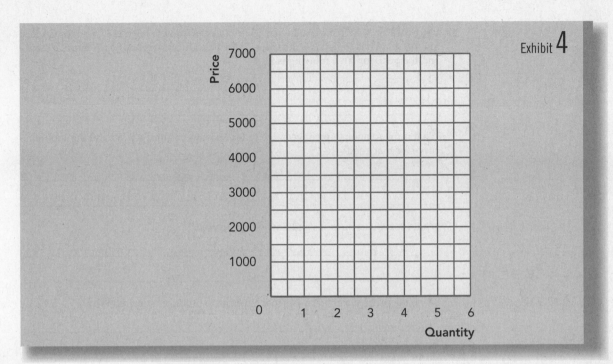

Exhibit 4

5. Suppose Lori Landlord has difficulty renting her dilapidated apartments so she increases her willingness to pay for painting by $2,000 per apartment. Plot Lori's new willingness to pay along with Peter's cost in Exhibit 4. If the equilibrium price rises to $4,000, what is the value of consumer surplus, producer surplus, and total surplus? Show consumer and producer surplus on the graph. Compare your answer to the answer you found in 3c above.

_____

_____

_____

_____

Short-Answer Questions

1. What is the relationship between the buyers' willingness to pay for a good and the demand curve for that good?

_____

_____

2. What is consumer surplus, and how is it measured?

_____

_____

3. What is the value of consumer surplus for the marginal buyer? Why?

_____

_____

4. If the cost for Moe to mow a lawn is $5, for Larry to mow a lawn is $7, and for Curly to mow a lawn is $9, what is the value of their producer surplus if each mows a lawn and the price for lawn mowing is $10?

_____

_____

5. What is the relationship between the sellers' cost to produce a good and the supply curve for that good?

_____

_____

6. What is producer surplus, and how is it measured?

_____

_____

7. When the price of a good rises, what happens to producer surplus? Why?

_____

_____

8. Can a benevolent social planner choose a quantity that provides greater economic welfare than the equilibrium quantity generated in a competitive market? Why?

_____

_____

9. What does an economist mean by "efficiency"?

_____

_____

10. Is a competitive market efficient? Why or why not?

_____

_____

11. How does a competitive market choose which producers will produce and sell a product?

_____

_____

Self-Test

True/False Questions

_____ 1. Consumer surplus is the amount a buyer is willing to pay for a good minus the seller's cost.

_____ 2. If the demand curve in a market is stationary, consumer surplus decreases when the price in that market increases.

_____   3.   If your willingness to pay for a hamburger is $3.00 and the price is $2.00, your consumer surplus is $5.00.

_____   4.   Producer surplus is a measure of the unsold inventories of suppliers in a market.

_____   5.   Consumer surplus is a good measure of buyers' benefits if buyers are rational.

_____   6.   Cost to the seller includes the opportunity cost of the seller's time.

_____   7.   The height of the supply curve is the marginal seller's cost.

_____   8.   Total surplus is the cost to sellers minus the value to buyers.

_____   9.   Free markets are efficient because they allocate output to buyers who have a willingness to pay that is below the price.

_____   10.   Producer surplus is the area above the supply curve and below the price.

_____   11.   The major advantage of allowing free markets to allocate resources is that the outcome of the allocation is efficient.

_____   12.   Equilibrium in a competitive market maximizes total surplus.

_____   13.   The two main types of market failure are market power and externalities.

_____   14.   Externalities are side effects, such as pollution, that are not taken into account by the buyers and sellers in a market.

_____   15.   Producing more of a product always adds to total surplus.

Multiple-Choice Questions

1. Consumer surplus is the area
    a.   above the supply curve and below the price.
    b.   below the supply curve and above the price.
    c.   above the demand curve and below the price.
    d.   below the demand curve and above the price.
    e.   below the demand curve and above the supply curve.

2. A buyer's willingness to pay is
    a.   that buyer's consumer surplus.
    b.   that buyer's producer surplus.
    c.   that buyer's maximum amount he is willing to pay for a good.
    d.   that buyer's minimum amount he is willing to pay for a good.
    e.   none of the above.

3. If a buyer's willingness to pay for a new Honda is $20,000 and she is able to actually buy it for $18,000, her consumer surplus is
    a. $0.
    b. $2,000.
    c. $18,000.
    d. $20,000.
    e. $38,000.

4. An increase in the price of a good along a stationary demand curve
    a.   increases consumer surplus.
    b.   decreases consumer surplus.
    c.   improves the material welfare of the buyers.
    d.   improves market efficiency.

5. Suppose there are three identical vases available to be purchased. Buyer 1 is willing to pay $30 for one, buyer 2 is willing to pay $25 for one, and buyer 3 is willing to pay $20 for one. If the price is $25, how many vases will be sold and what is the value of consumer surplus in this market?
   a. One vase will be sold, and consumer surplus is $30.
   b. One vase will be sold, and consumer surplus is $5.
   c. Two vases will be sold, and consumer surplus is $5.
   d. Three vases will be sold, and consumer surplus is $0.
   e. Three vases will be sold, and consumer surplus is $80.

6. Producer surplus is the area
   a. above the supply curve and below the price.
   b. below the supply curve and above the price.
   c. above the demand curve and below the price.
   d. below the demand curve and above the price.
   e. below the demand curve and above the supply curve.

7. If a benevolent social planner chooses to produce less than the equilibrium quantity of a good, then
   a. producer surplus is maximized.
   b. consumer surplus is maximized.
   c. total surplus is maximized.
   d. the value placed on the last unit of production by buyers exceeds the cost of production.
   e. the cost of production on the last unit produced exceeds the value placed on it by buyers.

8. If a benevolent social planner chooses to produce more than the equilibrium quantity of a good, then
   a. producer surplus is maximized.
   b. consumer surplus is maximized.
   c. total surplus is maximized.
   d. the value placed on the last unit of production by buyers exceeds the cost of production.
   e. the cost of production on the last unit produced exceeds the value placed on it by buyers.

9. The seller's cost of production is
   a. the seller's consumer surplus.
   b. the seller's producer surplus.
   c. the maximum amount the seller is willing to accept for a good.
   d. the minimum amount the seller is willing to accept for a good.
   e. none of the above.

10. Total surplus is the area
    a. above the supply curve and below the price.
    b. below the supply curve and above the price.
    c. above the demand curve and below the price.
    d. below the demand curve and above the price.
    e. below the demand curve and above the supply curve.

11. An increase in the price of a good along a stationary supply curve
    a. increases producer surplus.
    b. decreases producer surplus.
    c. improves market equity.
    d. does all of the above.

12. Adam Smith's "invisible hand" concept suggests that a competitive market outcome
    a. minimizes total surplus.
    b. maximizes total surplus.
    c. generates equality among the members of society.
    d. does both *b* and *c*.

13. In general, if a benevolent social planner wanted to maximize the total benefits received by buyers and sellers in a market, the planner should
    a. choose a price above the market equilibrium price.
    b. choose a price below the market equilibrium price.
    c. allow the market to seek equilibrium on its own.
    d. choose any price the planner wants because the losses to the sellers (buyers) from any change in price are exactly offset by the gains to the buyers (sellers).

14. If buyers are rational and there is no market failure,
    a. free market solutions are efficient.
    b. free market solutions generate equality.
    c. free market solutions maximize total surplus.
    d. all of the above are true.
    e. *a* and *c* are correct.

15. If a producer has market power (can influence the price of the product in the market) then free market solutions
    a. generate equality.
    b. are efficient.
    c. are inefficient.
    d. maximize consumer surplus.

16. If a market is efficient, then
    a. the market allocates output to the buyers who value it the most.
    b. the market allocates buyers to the sellers who can produce the good at least cost.
    c. the quantity produced in the market maximizes the sum of consumer and producer surplus.
    d. all of the above are true.
    e. none of the above is true.

17. If a market generates a side effect or externality, then free market solutions
    a. generate equality.
    b. are efficient.
    c. are inefficient.
    d. maximize producer surplus.

18. Medical care clearly enhances people's lives. Therefore, we should consume medical care until
    a. everyone has as much as they would like.
    b. the benefit buyers place on medical care is equal to the cost of producing it.
    c. buyers receive no benefit from another unit of medical care.
    d. we must cut back on the consumption of other goods.

19. Joe has ten baseball gloves, and Sue has none. A baseball glove costs $50 to produce. If Joe values an additional baseball glove at $100 and Sue values a baseball glove at $40, then to maximize
    a. efficiency, Joe should receive the glove.
    b. efficiency, Sue should receive the glove.
    c. consumer surplus, both should receive a glove.
    d. equity, Joe should receive the glove.

20. Suppose that the price of a new bicycle is $300. Sue values a new bicycle at $400. It costs $200 for the seller to produce the new bicycle. What is the value of total surplus if Sue buys a new bike?
    a. $100
    b. $200
    c. $300
    d. $400
    e. $500

Advanced Critical Thinking

Suppose you are having an argument with your roommate about whether the federal government should subsidize the production of food. Your roommate argues that because food is something that is unambiguously good (unlike liquor, guns, and drugs, which may be considered inherently evil by some members of society), we simply cannot have too much of it. That is, because food is clearly good, having more of it must always improve our economic well-being.

1. Is it true that you cannot have too much of a good thing? Conversely, is it possible to overproduce unambiguously good things such as food, clothing, and shelter? Why or why not?

   _____

   _____

   _____

   _____

2. In Exhibit 5, demonstrate your answer to question 1 above with a supply-and-demand graph for food by showing the impact on economic well-being of producing quantities in excess of the equilibrium quantity.

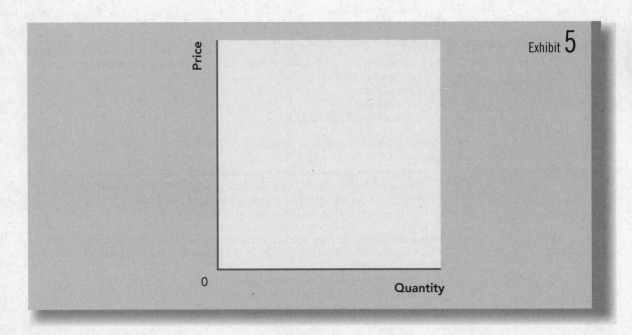

Solutions

Terms and Definitions

__3__ Welfare economics

__7__ Willingness to pay

__1__ Consumer surplus

__8__ Cost

__6__ Producer surplus

__2__ Efficiency

__5__ Equality

__4__ Market failure

Practice Problems

1. a. See Exhibit 6.

Exhibit 6

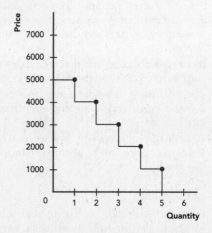

b. One apartment painted. $5,000 – $5,000 = $0, therefore she has no consumer surplus.

c. Four apartments painted. ($5,000 – $2,000) + ($4,000 – $2,000) + ($3,000 – $2,000) + ($2,000 – $2,000) = $6,000 of consumer surplus.

d. Her consumer surplus rose because she gains surplus on the unit she would have already purchased at the old price plus she gains surplus on the new units she now purchases due to the lower price.

2. a. See Exhibit 7.

Exhibit 7

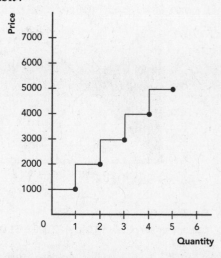

b. Two. ($2,000 – $1,000) + ($2,000 – $2,000) = $1,000 of producer surplus.

c. Four apartments. ($4,000 – $1,000) + ($4,000 – $2,000) + ($4,000 – $3,000) + ($4,000 – $4,000) = $6,000 of producer surplus.

d. He received greater producer surplus on the unit he would have produced anyway plus additional surplus on the units he now chooses to produce due to the increase in price.

3. a. Only one unit will be purchased, so consumer surplus = ($5,000 – $5,000) = $0, producer surplus = ($5,000 – $1,000) = $4,000, and total surplus = $0 + $4,000 = $4,000.

b. Only one unit will be produced, so consumer surplus = ($5,000 – $1,000) = $4,000, producer surplus = ($1,000 – $1,000) = $0, and total surplus = $4,000 + $0 = $4,000.

c. Consumer surplus = ($5,000 – $3,000) + ($4,000 – $3,000) + ($3,000 – $3,000) = $3,000. Producer surplus = ($3,000 – $1,000) + ($3,000 – $2,000) + ($3,000 – $3,000) = $3,000. Total surplus = $3,000 + $3,000 = $6,000. Free market total surplus is greater than social planner total surplus.

4. See Exhibit 8. Yes, it is efficient because at a quantity that is less than the equilibrium quantity, we fail to produce units that buyers value more than their cost. At a quantity above the equilibrium quantity, we produce units that cost more than the buyers value them. At equilibrium, we produce all possible units that are valued in excess of what they cost, which maximizes total surplus.

Exhibit 8

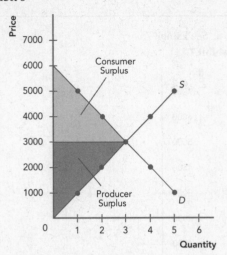

5.   See Exhibit 9.

Consumer surplus = $3,000 + $2,000 + $1,000 + $0 = $6,000.

Producer surplus = $3,000 + $2,000 + $1,000 + $0 = $6,000.

Total surplus = $6,000 + $6,000 = $12,000.

Consumer surplus, producer surplus, and total surplus have all increased.

Exhibit 9

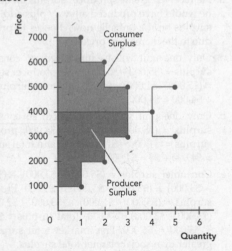

Short-Answer Questions

1.   The height of the demand curve at any quantity is the marginal buyer's willingness to pay. Therefore, a plot of buyers' willingness to pay for each quantity is a plot of the demand curve.

2.   Consumer surplus is the amount a buyer is willing to pay for a good minus the amount the buyer actually pays. It is measured as the area below the demand curve and above the price.

3.   Zero, because the marginal buyer is the buyer who would leave the market if the price were any higher. Therefore, they are paying their willingness to pay and are receiving no surplus.

4.   ($10 − $5) + ($10 − $7) + ($10 − $9) = $9

5.   The height of the supply curve at any quantity is the marginal seller's cost. Therefore, a plot of the sellers' cost for each quantity is a plot of the supply curve.

6.   Producer surplus is the amount a seller is paid for a good minus the seller's cost of providing it. It is measured as the area below the price and above the supply curve.

7.   Producer surplus increases because existing sellers receive a greater surplus on the units they were already going to sell and new sellers enter the market because the price is now above their cost.

8.   Generally, no. At any quantity below the equilibrium quantity, the market fails to produce units where the value to the marginal buyer exceeds the cost. At any quantity above the equilibrium quantity, the market produces units where the cost to the marginal producer exceeds the value to the buyers.

9.   It is a resource allocation that maximizes the total surplus received by all members of society.

10.   Yes, because it maximizes the area below the demand curve and above the supply curve, or total surplus.

11.   Only those producers who have costs at or below the market price will be able to produce and sell that good.

True/False Questions

1.   F; consumer surplus is the amount a buyer is willing to pay for a good minus the amount the buyer actually pays.

2.   T

3.   F; $3.00 − $2.00 = $1.00.

4.   F; it is a measure of the benefits of market participation to the sellers in a market.

5.   T

6.   T

7.   T

8.   F; total surplus is the value to buyers minus the cost to sellers.

9.   F; free markets allocate output to buyers who have a willingness to pay that is above the price.

10.   T

11.   T

12.   T

13.   T

14.   T

15.   F; producing above the equilibrium quantity reduces total surplus because units are produced for which cost exceeds the value to buyers.

Multiple-Choice Questions

1.   d

2.   c

3. b
4. b
5. c
6. a
7. d
8. e
9. d
10. e
11. a
12. b
13. c
14. e
15. c
16. d
17. c
18. b
19. a
20. b

Advanced Critical Thinking

1. You can have too much of a good thing. Yes, any good with a positive cost and a declining willingness to pay from the consumer can be overproduced. This is because at some point of production, the cost per unit will exceed the value to the buyer and there will be a loss to total surplus associated with additional production.

2. See Exhibit 10.

Exhibit 10

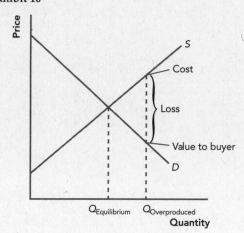

Chapter 8

Application: The Costs of Taxation

- Examine how taxes reduce consumer and producer surplus
- Learn the meaning and causes of the deadweight loss of a tax
- Consider why some taxes have larger deadweight losses than others
- Examine how tax revenue and deadweight loss vary with the size of a tax

- Place a tax wedge in a supply-and-demand graph and determine the tax revenue and the levels of consumer and producer surplus
- Place a tax wedge in a supply-and-demand graph and determine the value of the deadweight loss
- Show why a given tax will generate a greater deadweight loss if supply and demand are elastic than if they are inelastic
- Demonstrate why some very large taxes generate little tax revenue but a great deal of deadweight loss

Chapter Overview

Context and Purpose

Chapter 8 is the second chapter in a three-chapter sequence dealing with welfare economics. In the previous section on supply and demand, Chapter 6 introduced taxes and demonstrated how a tax affects the price and quantity sold in a market. Chapter 6 also described the factors that determine how the burden of the tax

119

is divided between the buyers and sellers in a market. Chapter 7 developed welfare economics—the study of how the allocation of resources affects economic well-being. Chapter 8 combines the lessons learned in Chapters 6 and 7 and addresses the effects of taxation on welfare. Chapter 9 will address the effects of trade restrictions on welfare.

The purpose of Chapter 8 is to apply the lessons learned about welfare economics in Chapter 7 to the issue of taxation, which we addressed in Chapter 6. We will learn that the cost of a tax to buyers and sellers in a market usually exceeds the revenue collected by the government. We will also learn about the factors that determine the degree by which the cost of a tax exceeds the revenue collected by the government.

Chapter Review

Introduction   Taxes raise the price buyers pay, reduce the price sellers receive, and reduce the quantity exchanged. Clearly, the welfare of the buyers and sellers is reduced, and the welfare of the government is increased. However, overall welfare is reduced because the cost of a tax to buyers and sellers exceeds the revenue raised by the government.

The Deadweight Loss of Taxation

Recall from Chapter 6 that a tax places a wedge between what a buyer pays and a seller receives and reduces the quantity sold regardless of whether the tax is collected from the buyer or the seller. With regard to welfare, recall from Chapter 7 that consumer surplus is the amount buyers are willing to pay minus the price they actually pay, whereas producer surplus is the price sellers actually receive minus their costs. The welfare or benefit to the government from a tax is the revenue it collects from the tax, which is the quantity of the good sold *after the tax is placed on the good* multiplied by the tax per unit. This benefit actually accrues to those on whom the tax revenue is spent.

Referring to Exhibit 1, without a tax the price is P_0 and the quantity is Q_0. Thus, consumer surplus is the area A + B + C and producer surplus is D + E + F. Tax revenue is zero. Total surplus is A + B + C + D + E + F.

With a tax, the price to buyers rises to P_B, the price to sellers falls to P_s, and the quantity falls to Q_1. Consumer surplus is now A, producer surplus is now F, and tax revenue is B + D. Total surplus is now A + B + D + F. Consumer surplus and producer surplus have both been reduced and tax revenue has been increased. However, consumer surplus and producer surplus have been reduced by B + C + D + E, and government revenue has been increased by only B + D. Therefore, losses to buyers and sellers from a tax exceed the revenue raised by the government. The reduction in total surplus that results from a tax is known as deadweight loss and is equal to C + E.

Taxes cause deadweight losses because taxes prevent buyers and sellers from realizing some of the gains from trade. That is, taxes distort incentives because taxes raise the price paid by buyers, which reduces the quantity demanded and lowers the price received by sellers, which reduces the quantity supplied. The size of the market is reduced below its optimum, and sellers fail to produce and sell goods for which the benefits to buyers exceed the costs of the producers. Deadweight loss is a loss of potential gains from trade.

The Determinants of the Deadweight Loss

The size of the deadweight loss from a tax depends on the elasticities of supply and demand. Deadweight loss from a tax is caused by the distortion in the price faced by buyers and sellers. The more buyers are sensitive to an increase in the price of the good (more elastic demand), the more they reduce their quantity demanded when a tax is placed on a good. The more sellers are sensitive to a decrease in the price of a good (more elastic supply), the more they reduce their quantity supplied when a tax is placed on a good. A greater reduction in the quantity exchanged in the market causes a greater deadweight loss. As a result, *the greater the elasticities of supply and demand, the greater the deadweight loss of a tax.*

The most important tax in the U.S. economy is the tax on labor—federal and state income taxes and Social Security taxes. Taxes on labor encourage workers to work fewer hours, second earners to stay home, the elderly to retire early, and the unscrupulous to

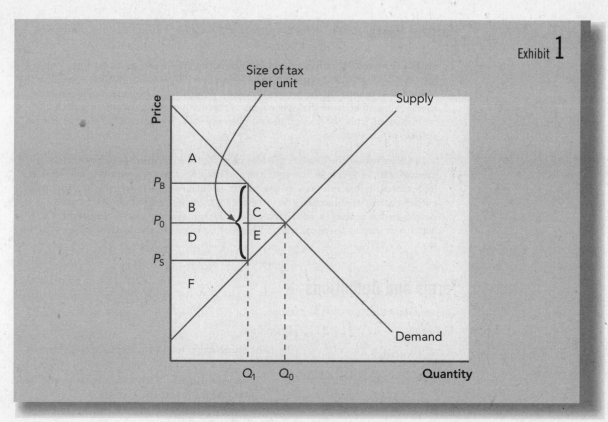

Exhibit 1

enter the underground economy. The more elastic the supply of labor, the greater the deadweight loss of taxation and, thus, the greater the cost of any government program that relies on income tax revenue for funding. Economists and politicians argue about how elastic the supply of labor is and, thus, how large these effects are.

Deadweight Loss and Tax Revenue as Taxes Vary

Deadweight loss increases as a tax increases. Indeed, deadweight loss increases at an increasing rate as a tax increases. It increases as the square of the factor of increase in the tax. For example, if a tax is doubled, the deadweight loss rises by a factor of four. If a tax is tripled, the deadweight loss rises by a factor of nine, and so on.

Tax revenue first increases and then decreases as a tax increases. This is because, at first, an increase in a tax increases the taxes collected per unit more than it reduces the units sold. At some point, however, an ever-increasing tax reduces the size of the market (the quantity sold and taxed) to such a degree that the government begins to collect a large tax on such a small quantity that tax revenue begins to fall.

The idea that a high tax rate could so shrink the market that it reduces tax revenue was expressed by Arthur Laffer in 1974. The *Laffer curve* is a diagram that shows as the size of a tax on a good is increased, revenue first rises and then falls. The implication is that if tax rates are already extremely high, a reduction in tax rates could increase tax revenue. This is a part of what has come to be called supply-side economics. Evidence has shown that this may be true for individuals who are taxed at extremely high rates, but it is less likely to be true for an entire economy. A possible exception is Sweden in the 1980s because its marginal tax rates were about 80 percent for the typical worker.

Conclusion

Taxes place a cost on market participants in two ways:

- Resources are diverted from buyers and sellers to the government.

- Taxes distort incentives so fewer goods are produced and sold than otherwise. That is, taxes cause society to lose some of the benefits of efficient markets.

Helpful Hints

1. As a tax increases, it reduces the size of the market more and more. At some point, the tax is so high that it is greater than or equal to the potential surplus even from the first unit. At that point, the tax has become a *prohibitive tax* because it eliminates the market altogether. Note that when a tax is prohibitive, the government collects no revenue at all from the tax because no units are sold. The market has reached the far side of the Laffer curve.

2. As a tax increases, the deadweight loss increases *at an increasing rate* because there are two sources to the deadweight loss and both sources are generating an increase in deadweight loss as a tax increases. First, an increase in a tax reduces the quantity exchanged and that increases deadweight loss. Second, as quantity exchanged decreases due to the tax, each successive unit that is not produced and sold *has a higher total surplus associated with it*. This further increases the deadweight loss from a tax.

Terms and Definitions

Choose a definition for each key term.

Key Terms	Definitions
_____ Tax wedge	1. The reduction in total surplus that results from a tax
_____ Deadweight loss	2. A graph showing the relationship between the size of a tax and the tax revenue collected
_____ Laffer curve	3. The difference between what the buyer pays and the seller receives when a tax is placed in a market

Problems and Short-Answer Questions

Practice Problems

1. Exhibit 2 shows the market for tires. Suppose that a $12 road-use tax is placed on each tire sold.
   a. In Exhibit 2, locate consumer surplus, producer surplus, tax revenue, and the deadweight loss.
   b. Why is there a deadweight loss in the market for tires after the tax is imposed?

   _____

   _____

   _____

   c. What is the value of the tax revenue collected by the government? Why wasn't the government able to collect $12 per tire on 60 tires sold (the original equilibrium quantity)?

   _____

   _____

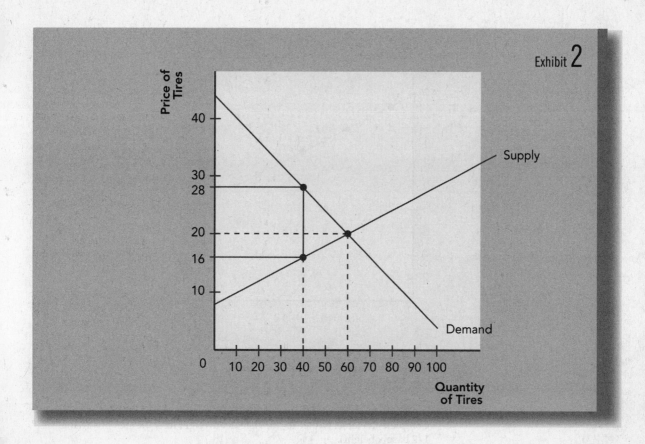

Exhibit 2

d. What is the value of the tax revenue collected from the buyers? What is the value
    of the tax revenue collected from the sellers? Did the burden of the tax fall more
    heavily on the buyers or the sellers? Why?

    _____

    _____

e. Suppose over time, buyers of tires are able to substitute away from auto tires
    (they walk or ride bicycles). Because of this, their demand for tires becomes more
    elastic. What will happen to the size of the deadweight loss in the market for
    tires? Why?

    _____

    _____

    _____

    _____

    _____

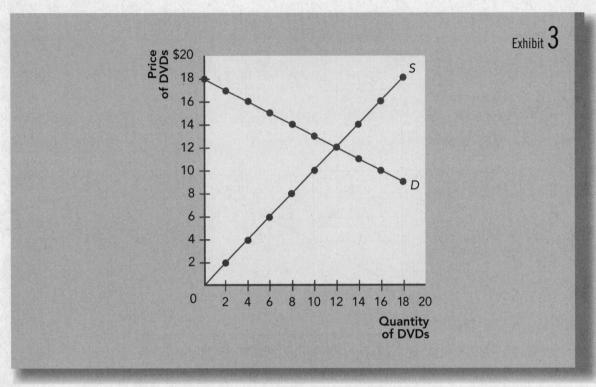

Exhibit 3

2. Use Exhibit 3, which shows the market for DVDs, to answer the following questions.
   a. Complete the table. (Note: To calculate deadweight loss, the area of a triangle is 1/2 base × height).

Tax per unit	Tax revenue collected	Deadweight loss
$ 0	_____	_____
3	_____	_____
6	_____	_____
9	_____	_____
12	_____	_____
15	_____	_____
18	_____	_____

   b. As the tax is increased, what happens to the amount of tax revenue collected? Why?

   _____

   _____

   _____

   c. At a tax of $18 per DVD, how much tax revenue is collected? Why?

   _____

   _____

   _____

    d.   If the government wanted to maximize tax revenue, what tax per unit should it impose?

_____

    e.   If the government wanted to maximize efficiency (total surplus), what tax per unit should it impose?

_____

    f.   What happens to the deadweight loss due to the tax as the tax is increased? Why?

_____

_____

Short-Answer Questions

1. Why does a tax reduce consumer surplus?

_____

_____

_____

2. Why does a tax reduce producer surplus?

_____

_____

_____

3. Why does a tax generally produce a deadweight loss?

_____

_____

_____

_____

4. Under what conditions would a tax fail to produce a deadweight loss?

_____

_____

_____

5. When a tax is placed on a good, does the government collect revenue equal to the loss in total surplus due to the tax? Why or why not?

_____

_____

_____

_____

_____

6. Suppose Rachel values having her house painted at $1,000. The cost for Paul to paint her house is $700. What is the value of the total surplus or the gains from trade on this transaction? What is the size of the tax that would eliminate this trade? What is the deadweight loss from this tax? What generalization can you make from this exercise?

_____

_____

_____

_____

7. Would you expect a tax on gasoline to have a greater deadweight loss in the short run or the long run? Why?

_____

_____

_____

_____

8. Suppose the supply of oil is relatively inelastic. Would a tax on oil generate a large deadweight loss? Why or why not? Who would bear the burden of the tax, the buyer or the seller of oil? Why?

_____

_____

_____

_____

9. As a tax on a good increases, what happens to tax revenue? Why?

_____

_____

_____

_____

10. As a tax on a good increases, what happens to the deadweight loss from the tax? Why?

_____

_____

_____

_____

Self-Test

True/False Questions

_____ 1. In general, a tax raises the price the buyers pay, lowers the price the sellers receive, and reduces the quantity sold.

_____ 2. If a tax is placed on a good and it reduces the quantity sold, there must be a deadweight loss from the tax.

_____ 3. Deadweight loss is the reduction in consumer surplus that results from a tax.

_____ 4. When a tax is placed on a good, the revenue the government collects is exactly equal to the loss of consumer and producer surplus from the tax.

_____ 5. If John values having his hair cut at $20 and Mary's cost of providing the haircut is $10, any tax on haircuts larger than $10 will eliminate the gains from trade and cause a $20 loss of total surplus.

_____ 6. If a tax is placed on a good in a market where supply is perfectly inelastic, there is no deadweight loss and the sellers bear the entire burden of the tax.

_____ 7. A tax on cigarettes would likely generate a larger deadweight loss than a tax on luxury boats.

_____ 8. A tax will generate a greater deadweight loss if supply and demand are inelastic.

_____ 9. A tax causes a deadweight loss because it eliminates some of the potential gains from trade.

_____ 10. A larger tax always generates more tax revenue.

_____ 11. A larger tax always generates a larger deadweight loss.

_____ 12. If an income tax rate is high enough, a reduction in the tax rate could increase tax revenue.

_____ 13. A tax collected from buyers generates a smaller deadweight loss than a tax collected from sellers.

_____ 14. If a tax is doubled, the deadweight loss from the tax more than doubles.

_____ 15. A deadweight loss results when a tax causes market participants to fail to produce and consume units on which the benefits to the buyers exceed the costs to the sellers.

Multiple-Choice Questions

Use Exhibit 4 to answer questions 1 through 10.

1. If there is no tax placed on the product in this market, consumer surplus is the area
    a. A + B + C.
    b. D + C + B.
    c. A + B + E.
    d. C + D + F.
    e. A.

2. If there is no tax placed on the product in this market, producer surplus is the area
    a. A + B + C + D.
    b. C + D + F.
    c. D.
    d. C + F.
    e. A + B + E.

3. If a tax is placed on the product in this market, consumer surplus is the area
    a. A.
    b. A + B.
    c. A + B + E.
    d. A + B + C + D.
    e. D.

4. If a tax is placed on the product in this market, producer surplus is the area
    a. A.
    b. A + B + E.
    c. C + D + F.
    d. D.
    e. A + B + C + D.

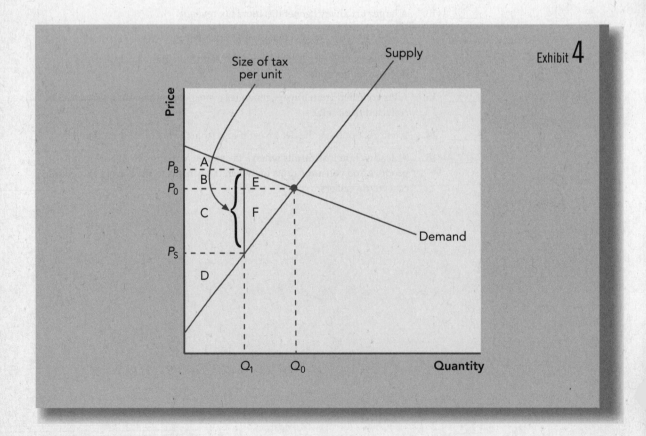

5. If a tax is placed on the product in this market, tax revenue paid by the buyers is the area
   a. A.
   b. B.
   c. C.
   d. B + C.
   e. B + C + E + F.

6. If a tax is placed on the product in this market, tax revenue paid by the sellers is the area
   a. A.
   b. B.
   c. C.
   d. C + F.
   e. B + C + E + F.

7. If there is no tax placed on the product in this market, total surplus is the area
   a. A + B + C + D.
   b. A + B + C + D + E + F.
   c. B + C + E + F.
   d. E + F.
   e. A + D + E + F.

8. If a tax is placed on the product in this market, total surplus is the area
   a. A + B + C + D.
   b. A + B + C + D + E + F.
   c. B + C + E + F.
   d. E + F.
   e. A + D.

9. If a tax is placed on the product in this market, deadweight loss is the area
   a. B + C.
   b. B + C + E + F.
   c. A + B + C + D.
   d. E + F.
   e. A + D.

10. Which of the following is true with regard to the burden of the tax in Exhibit 4?
    a. The buyers pay a larger portion of the tax because demand is more inelastic than supply.
    b. The buyers pay a larger portion of the tax because demand is more elastic than supply.
    c. The sellers pay a larger portion of the tax because supply is more elastic than demand.
    d. The sellers pay a larger portion of the tax because supply is more inelastic than demand.

11. Which of the following would likely cause the greatest deadweight loss?
    a. a tax on cigarettes
    b. a tax on salt
    c. a tax on cruise line tickets
    d. a tax on gasoline

12. A tax on gasoline is likely to
    a. cause a greater deadweight loss in the long run when compared to the short run.
    b. cause a greater deadweight loss in the short run when compared to the long run.
    c. generate a deadweight loss that is unaffected by the time period over which it is measured.
    d. None of the above is correct.

13. Deadweight loss is greatest when
    a. both supply and demand are relatively inelastic.
    b. both supply and demand are relatively elastic.
    c. supply is elastic and demand is perfectly inelastic.
    d. demand is elastic and supply is perfectly inelastic.

14. Suppose the supply of diamonds is relatively inelastic. A tax on diamonds would generate a
    a. large deadweight loss and the burden of the tax would fall on the buyer of diamonds.
    b. small deadweight loss and the burden of the tax would fall on the buyer of diamonds.
    c. large deadweight loss and the burden of the tax would fall on the seller of diamonds.
    d. small deadweight loss and the burden of the tax would fall on the seller of diamonds.

15. Taxes on labor income tend to encourage
    a. workers to work fewer hours.
    b. second earners to stay home.
    c. the elderly to retire early.
    d. the unscrupulous to enter the underground economy.
    e. all of the above.

16. When a tax on a good starts small and is gradually increased, tax revenue will
    a. rise.
    b. fall.
    c. first rise and then fall.
    d. first fall and then rise.
    e. do none of the above.

17. The graph that shows the relationship between the size of a tax and the tax revenue collected by the government is known as a
    a. deadweight curve.
    b. tax revenue curve.
    c. Laffer curve.
    d. Reagan curve.
    e. None of the above is correct.

18. If a tax on a good is doubled, the deadweight loss from the tax
    a. stays the same.
    b. doubles.
    c. increases by a factor of four.
    d. could rise or fall.

19. The reduction of a tax
    a. could increase tax revenue if the tax had been extremely high.
    b. will always reduce tax revenue regardless of the prior size of the tax.
    c. will have no impact on tax revenue.
    d. causes a market to become less efficient.

20. When a tax distorts incentives to buyers and sellers so that fewer goods are produced and sold, the tax has
    a. increased efficiency.
    b. reduced the price buyers pay.
    c. generated no tax revenue.
    d. caused a deadweight loss.

Advanced Critical Thinking

You are watching the local news report on television with your roommate. The news anchor reports that the state budget has a deficit of $100 million. Because the state currently collects exactly $100 million from its 5 percent sales tax, your roommate says, "I can tell them how to fix their deficit. They should simply double the sales tax to 10 percent. That will double their tax revenue from $100 million to $200 million and provide the needed $100 million."

1. Is it true that doubling a tax will always double tax revenue? Why or why not?

   _____

   _____

   _____

   _____

   _____

   _____

2. Will doubling the sales tax affect the tax revenue and the deadweight loss in all markets to the same degree? Explain.

   _____

   _____

   _____

   _____

   _____

   _____

Solutions

Terms and Definitions

_3_   Tax wedge

_1_   Deadweight loss

_2_   Laffer curve

Practice Problems

1. a. See Exhibit 5.

Exhibit 5

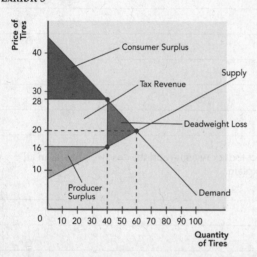

b. The tax raises the price paid by buyers and lowers the price received by sellers causing them to reduce their quantities demanded and supplied. Therefore, they fail to produce and exchange units where the value to buyers exceeds the cost to sellers.

c. $12 × 40 = $480. The tax distorted prices to the buyers and sellers so that the quantity supplied and demanded with the tax is reduced to 40 units from 60 units.

d. $8 × 40 = $320 from buyers. $4 × 40 = $160 from sellers. The burden fell more heavily on the buyers because the demand for tires was less elastic than the supply of tires.

e. Deadweight loss will increase because when buyers are more sensitive to an increase in price (due to the tax), they will reduce their quantity demanded even more and shrink the market more. Thus, even fewer units that are valued by buyers in excess of their cost will be sold.

2. a.

Tax per unit	Tax revenue collected	Deadweight loss
$ 0	$ 0	$0
3	30	($3 × 2)/2 = $3
6	48	($6 × 4)/2 = $12
9	54	($9 × 6)/2 = $27
12	48	($12 × 8)/2 = $48
15	30	($15 × 10)/2 = $75
18	0	($18 × 12)/2 = $108

b. It first rises, then falls. At first, as the tax is increased tax revenue rises. At some point, the tax reduces the size of the market to such a degree that the government is collecting a large tax on such a small quantity that tax revenue begins to fall.

c. No tax revenue is collected because the tax is as large as the total surplus on the first unit. Therefore, there is no incentive to produce and consume even one unit and the entire market is eliminated.

d. $9 per unit.

e. $0 per unit, which causes the market to return to its free market equilibrium.

f. It increases. Indeed, it increases at an increasing rate. This is because as the tax increases, it causes the quantity exchanged to be reduced on units that have an ever larger potential surplus attached to them.

Short-Answer Questions

1. Consumer surplus is what the buyer is willing to pay for a good minus what the buyer actually pays, and a tax raises the price the buyer actually pays.

2. Producer surplus is the amount the seller receives for a good minus the seller's cost, and a tax reduces what the seller receives for a good.

3. A tax raises the price buyers pay and lowers the price sellers receive. This price distortion reduces the quantity demanded and supplied so we fail to produce and consume units where the benefits to the buyers exceed the costs to the sellers.

4. If either supply or demand were perfectly inelastic (insensitive to a change in price), then a tax would fail to reduce the quantity exchanged and the market would not shrink.

5. No. The tax distorts prices to buyers and sellers and causes them to reduce their quantities demanded and supplied. Taxes are collected only on the units sold after the tax is imposed. Those units that are no longer produced and sold generate no tax revenue, but those units would have added to total surplus because they were valued by buyers

in excess of their cost to sellers. The reduction in total surplus is the deadweight loss.

6. Total surplus = $300. Any tax larger than $300. Deadweight loss would be $300. A tax that is greater than the potential gains from trade will eliminate trade and create a deadweight loss equal to the lost gains from trade.

7. There would be a greater deadweight loss in the long run. This is because both demand and supply tend to be more elastic in the long run as consumers and producers are able to substitute away from this market when prices move in an adverse direction. The more a market shrinks from a tax, the greater the deadweight loss.

8. No. Because the supply of oil is highly inelastic, the quantity supplied is not responsive to a decrease in the price received by the seller. The seller would bear the burden of the tax for the same reason—supply of oil is highly inelastic.

9. First tax revenue increases. At some point tax revenue decreases as the distortion in prices to buyers and sellers causes the market to shrink and large taxes are collected on a small number of units exchanged.

10. Deadweight loss increases continuously because as a tax increases, the distortion in prices caused by the tax causes the market to shrink continuously. Thus, we fail to produce more and more units where the benefits to buyers exceed the costs to sellers.

True/False Questions

1. T
2. T
3. F; deadweight loss is the reduction in *total surplus* that results from a tax.
4. F; the loss of producer and consumer surplus exceeds the revenue from the tax. The difference is deadweight loss.
5. F; the loss in total surplus is the buyer's value minus the seller's cost or $20 − $10 = $10.
6. T
7. F; the more elastic the demand curve, the greater the deadweight loss, and the demand for cigarettes (a necessity) should be more inelastic than the demand for luxury boats (a luxury).
8. F; a tax generates a greater deadweight loss when supply and demand are more elastic.
9. T
10. F; as a tax increases, revenue first rises and then falls as the tax shrinks the market to a point where all trades are eliminated and tax revenue is zero.
11. T
12. T
13. F; taxes collected from either the buyers or the sellers are equivalent. That is why economists simply use a tax wedge when analyzing a tax and avoid the issue altogether.

14. T
15. T

Multiple-Choice Questions

1. c
2. b
3. a
4. d
5. b
6. c
7. b
8. a
9. d
10. d
11. c
12. a
13. b
14. d
15. e
16. c
17. c
18. c
19. a
20. d

Advanced Critical Thinking

1. No. Usually an increase in a tax will reduce the size of the market because the tax will increase the price to buyers, causing them to reduce their quantity demanded and will decrease the price to sellers, causing them to reduce their quantity supplied. Therefore, when taxes double, the government collects twice as much per unit on many fewer units, so tax revenue will increase by less than double and could, in some extreme cases, even go down.

2. No. Some markets may have extremely elastic supply-and-demand curves. In these markets, an increase in a tax causes market participants to leave the market, and little revenue is generated from the tax increase, but deadweight loss increases a great deal. Other markets may have inelastic supply-and-demand curves. In these markets, an increase in a tax fails to cause market participants to leave the market and a great deal of additional tax revenue is generated with little increase in deadweight loss.

Chapter 9

Application: International Trade

Goals
In this chapter you will

- Consider what determines whether a country imports or exports a good

- Examine who wins and who loses from international trade

- Learn that the gains to winners from international trade exceed the losses to losers

- Analyze the welfare effects of tariffs

- Examine the arguments people use to advocate trade restrictions

Outcomes
After accomplishing these goals, you should be able to

- Determine whether a country imports or exports a good if the world price is greater than the before-trade domestic price

- Show that the consumer wins and the producer loses when a country imports a good

- Use consumer and producer surplus to show that the gains of the consumer exceed the losses of the producer when a country imports a good

- Show the deadweight loss associated with a tariff

- Defeat the arguments made in support of trade restrictions

Chapter Overview

Context and Purpose

Chapter 9 is the third chapter in a three-chapter sequence dealing with welfare economics. Chapter 7 introduced welfare economics—the study of how the allocation of resources affects economic well-being. Chapter 8 applied the lessons of welfare economics to taxation. Chapter 9 applies the tools of welfare economics from Chapter 7 to the study of international trade, a topic that was first introduced in Chapter 3.

135

The purpose of Chapter 9 is to use our knowledge of welfare economics to address the gains from trade more precisely than we did in Chapter 3 when we studied comparative advantage and the gains from trade. We will develop the conditions that determine whether a country imports or exports a good and discover who wins and who loses when a country imports or exports a good. We will find that when free trade is allowed, the gains of the winners exceed the losses of the losers. Because there are gains from trade, we will see that restrictions on free trade reduce the gains from trade and cause deadweight losses similar to those generated by a tax.

Chapter Review

Introduction   This chapter employs welfare economics to address the following questions:

- How does international trade affect economic well-being?
- Who gains and who loses from free international trade?
- How do the gains from trade compare to the losses from trade?

The Determinants of Trade

In the absence of international trade, a market generates a domestic price that equates the domestic quantity supplied and domestic quantity demanded in that market. The world price is the price of the good that prevails in the world market for that good. Prices represent opportunity costs. Therefore, comparing the world price and the domestic price of a good before trade indicates whether a country has the lower opportunity cost of production and, thus, a comparative advantage in the production of a good or if other countries have a comparative advantage in the production of the good.

- If the world price is above the domestic price for a good, the country has a comparative advantage in the production of that good and that good should be exported if trade is allowed.
- If the world price is below the domestic price for a good, foreign countries have a comparative advantage in the production of that good and that good should be imported if trade is allowed.

The Winners and Losers from Trade

Assume that the country being analyzed is a small country and is, therefore, a *price taker* on world markets. This means that the country takes the world price as given and cannot influence the world price.

Exhibit 1 depicts a situation where the world price is higher than the before-trade domestic price. This country has a comparative advantage in the production of this good. If free trade is allowed, the domestic price will rise to the world price and it will export the difference between the domestic quantity supplied and the domestic quantity demanded.

With regard to gains and losses to an exporting country from trade, before-trade consumer surplus was A + B, and producer surplus was C, so total surplus was A + B + C. After trade, consumer surplus is A and producer surplus is B + C + D (the area below the price and above the supply curve). Total surplus is now A + B + C + D for a gain of area D. This analysis generates two conclusions:

- When a country allows trade and becomes an exporter of a good, domestic producers are better off, and domestic consumers are worse off.
- Trade increases the economic well-being of a nation because the gains of the winners exceed the losses of the losers.

Exhibit 2 depicts a situation where the world price is lower than the before-trade domestic price. Other countries have a comparative advantage in the production of this good. If free trade is allowed, the domestic price will fall to the world price, and it will import the difference between the domestic quantity supplied and the domestic quantity demanded.

With regard to gains and losses to an importing country from trade, before-trade consumer surplus was A and producer surplus was B + C, so total surplus was A + B + C.

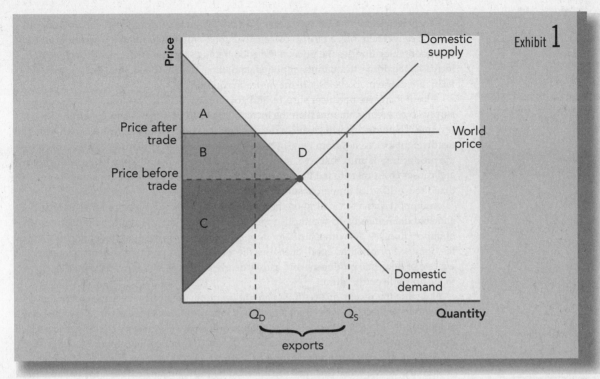

After trade, consumer surplus is A + B + D (the area below the demand curve and above the price), and producer surplus is C. Total surplus is now A + B + C + D for a gain of area D. This analysis generates two conclusions:

- When a country allows trade and becomes an importer of a good, domestic consumers are better off, and domestic producers are worse off.

- Trade increases the economic well-being of a nation because the gains of the winners exceed the losses of the losers.
  Trade can make everyone better off if the winners compensate the losers.
Compensation is rarely paid, so the losers lobby for trade restrictions, such as tariffs.

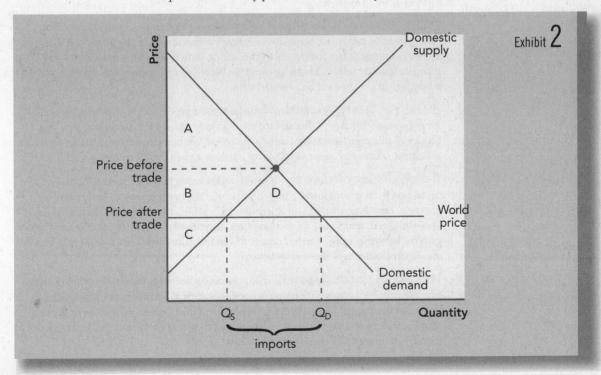

Tariffs restrict international trade. A tariff is a tax on goods produced abroad and sold domestically. Therefore, a tariff is placed on a good only if the country is an importer of that good. A tariff raises the price of the good, reduces the domestic quantity demanded, increases the domestic quantity supplied, and, thus, reduces the quantity of imports. A tariff moves the market closer to the no-trade equilibrium.

A tariff increases producer surplus and government revenue but reduces consumer surplus by a greater amount than the increase in producer surplus and government revenue. Therefore, a tariff creates a deadweight loss because total surplus is reduced. The deadweight loss comes from two sources. The increase in the price due to the tariff causes the production of units that cost more to produce than the world price (overproduction) and causes consumers to fail to consume units where the value to the consumer is greater than the world price (underconsumption).

An import quota sets a limit on the quantity of a good that can be produced abroad and sold domestically. To accomplish this, a government can distribute a limited number of import licenses. As with a tariff, an import quota reduces the quantity of imports, raises the domestic price of the good, decreases the welfare of domestic consumers, increases the welfare of domestic producers, and causes deadweight losses. It moves the market closer to the no-trade equilibrium.

Note that the results of a tariff and an import quota are nearly the same except that the government collects revenue from a tariff. If the import licenses are given away, the license holders earn the surplus generated from the world price being below the domestic price. If the government sells the import licenses for the maximum possible amount, it will collect revenue equal to the tariff revenue and a tariff and a quota become identical. If quotas are "voluntary" in the sense that they are imposed by the exporting country, the revenue from the quota accrues to the foreign firms or governments.

Tariffs cause deadweight losses. Therefore, if economic efficiency is a policy goal, countries should allow free trade and avoid using tariffs.

Free trade offers benefits beyond efficiency. Free trade increases variety for consumers, allows firms to take advantage of economies of scale, makes markets more competitive, and facilitates the spread of technology.

The Arguments for Restricting Trade

Opponents of free trade (often producers hurt by free trade) offer the following arguments in support of trade restrictions:

- **The Jobs Argument**   Opponents of free trade argue that trade destroys domestic jobs. However, while free trade does destroy inefficient jobs in the importing sector, it creates more efficient jobs in the export sector, industries where the country has a comparative advantage. This is always true because each country has a comparative advantage in the production of something.

- **The National-Security Argument**   Some industries argue that their product is vital for national security, so it should be protected from international competition. The danger of this argument is that it runs the risk of being overused, particularly when the argument is made by representatives of industry rather than the defense establishment.

- **The Infant-Industry Argument**   New industries argue that they need temporary protection from international competition until they become mature enough to compete. However, there is a problem choosing which new industries to protect, and once protected, temporary protection often becomes permanent. In addition, industries government truly expects to be competitive in the future don't need protection because the owners will accept short-term losses.

- **The Unfair-Competition Argument**   Opponents of free trade argue that other countries provide their industries with unfair advantages such as subsidies, tax breaks, and lower environmental restrictions. However, the gains of consumers in the importing country will exceed the losses of the producers in that country, and the country will gain when importing subsidized production.

- **The Protection-as-a-Bargaining-Chip Argument** Opponents of free trade argue that the threat of trade restrictions may result in other countries lowering their trade restrictions. However, if this does not work, the threatening country must back down or reduce trade—neither of which is desirable.

When countries choose to reduce trade restrictions, they can take a *unilateral* approach and remove trade restrictions on their own. Alternatively, they can take a *multilateral* approach and reduce trade restrictions along with other countries. Examples of the multilateral approach are NAFTA and GATT. The rules of GATT are enforced by the WTO. The multilateral approach has advantages in that it provides freer overall trade because many countries do it together, and thus, it is sometimes more easily accomplished politically. However, it may fail if negotiations between countries break down. Many economists suggest a unilateral approach because there will be gains to the domestic economy and this will cause other countries to emulate it.

Conclusion

Economists overwhelmingly support free trade. Free trade between states in the United States improves welfare by allowing each area of the country to specialize in the production of goods for which they have a comparative advantage. In the same manner, free trade between countries allows each country to enjoy the benefits of comparative advantage and the gains from trade.

Helpful Hints

1. Countries that restrict trade usually restrict imports rather than exports. This is because producers lose from imports and gain from exports, and producers are better organized to lobby the government to protect their interests. For example, when a country imports a product, consumers win, and producers lose. Consumers are less likely to organize and lobby the government than the affected producers, so imports may be restricted. When a country exports a product, producers win, and consumers lose. Yet again, consumers are less likely to organize and lobby the government to restrict exports so exports, are rarely restricted.

2. The overwhelming majority of economists find no sound *economic* argument in opposition to free trade. The only argument against free trade that may not be defeated on economic grounds is the "national-security argument." This is because it is the only argument against free trade that is not based on economics but rather is based on other strategic objectives.

3. A *prohibitive* tariff or import quota is one that is so restrictive that it returns the domestic market to its original no-trade equilibrium. This occurs if the tariff is greater than or equal to the difference between the world price and the no-trade domestic price or if the import quota is set at zero.

Terms and Definitions

Choose a definition for each key term.

Key Terms

_____ World price

_____ Price takers

_____ Tariff

Definitions

1. Market participants that cannot influence the price so they view the price as given

2. The price of a good that prevails in the world market for that good

3. A tax on goods produced abroad and sold domestically

Problems and Short-Answer Questions

Practice Problems

1. Use Exhibit 3 to answer the following questions.
   a.   If trade is not allowed, what is the equilibrium price and quantity in this market?

   _____

   b.   If trade is allowed, will this country import or export this commodity? Why?

   _____

   _____

   c.   If trade is allowed, what is the price at which the good is sold, the domestic quantity supplied and demanded, and the quantity imported or exported?

   _____

   _____

   d.   What area corresponds to consumer surplus if no trade is allowed?

   _____

   e.   What area corresponds to consumer surplus if trade is allowed?

   _____

   f.   What area corresponds to producer surplus if no trade is allowed?

   _____

   g.   What area corresponds to producer surplus if trade is allowed?

   _____

   h.   If free trade is allowed, who gains and who loses, the consumers or the producers, and what area corresponds to their gain or loss?

   _____

   i.   What area corresponds to the gains from trade?

   _____

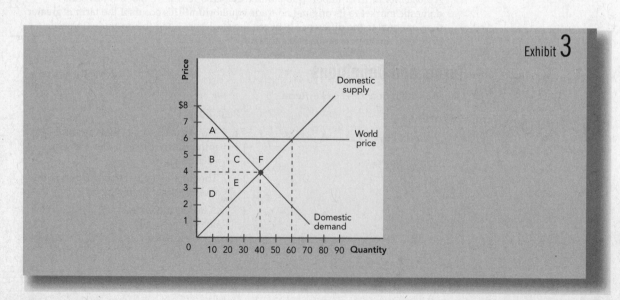

Exhibit 3

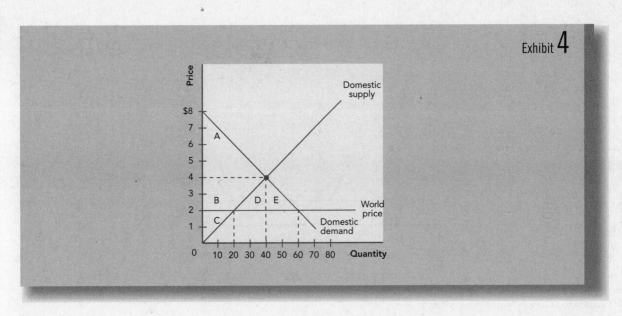

Exhibit 4

2. Use Exhibit 4 to answer the following questions.
   a. If trade is not allowed, what is the equilibrium price and quantity in this market?

   _____

   b. If trade is allowed, will this country import or export this commodity? Why?

   _____

   _____

   c. If trade is allowed, what is the price at which the good is sold, the domestic quantity supplied and demanded, and the quantity imported or exported?

   _____

   _____

   d. What area corresponds to consumer surplus if no trade is allowed?

   _____

   e. What area corresponds to consumer surplus if trade is allowed?

   _____

   f. What area corresponds to producer surplus if no trade is allowed?

   _____

   g. What area corresponds to producer surplus if trade is allowed?

   _____

   h. If free trade is allowed, who gains and who loses, the consumers or the producers, and what area corresponds to their gain or loss?

   _____

   i. What area corresponds to the gains from trade?

   _____

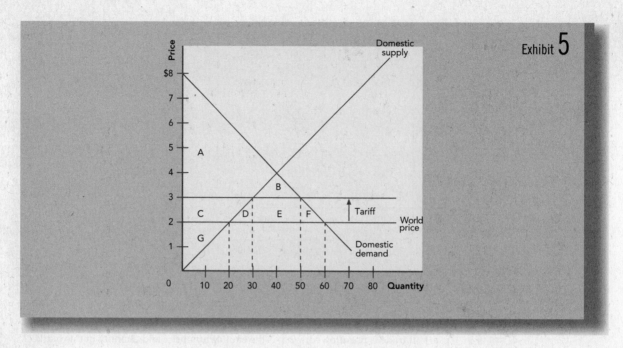

3. Use Exhibit 5 to answer the following questions.

   a. If free trade is allowed, what are the domestic quantity supplied, domestic quantity demanded, and the quantity imported?

      _____

      _____

   b. If a $1 tariff is placed on this good, what are the domestic quantity supplied, domestic quantity demanded, and the quantity imported?

      _____

      _____

   c. What area corresponds to consumer and producer surplus before the tariff is applied?

      _____

      _____

   d. What area corresponds to consumer surplus, producer surplus, and government revenue after the tariff is applied?

      _____

      _____

   e. What area corresponds to the deadweight loss associated with the tariff?

      _____

   f. Describe in words the sources of the deadweight loss from a tariff.

      _____

      _____

      _____

g. What is the size of the tariff that would eliminate trade altogether (i.e., that would return the market to its no-trade domestic solution)?

_____

Short-Answer Questions

The following table shows the amount of output a worker can produce per hour in Partyland and Laborland.

	Beer	Pizza
Partyland	2	4
Laborland	4	12

1. If free trade is allowed, which good will each country export to the other? Why? (Explain in terms of each country's opportunity cost of production.)

_____

_____

_____

2. If the world price for a good is above a country's before-trade domestic price, will this country import or export this good? Why?

_____

_____

3. If residents of a country are allowed to import a good, who gains and who loses when compared to the before-trade equilibrium, the producers or the consumers? Why?

_____

_____

4. Describe in words the source of the gains from trade (the additional total surplus) received by an exporting country.

_____

_____

5. Describe in words the source of the gains from trade (the additional total surplus) received by an importing country.

_____

_____

6. Describe in words the source of the deadweight loss from restricting trade.

_____

_____

7. For every tariff there is an import quota that will generate a similar result. What are the shortcomings of using an import quota to restrict trade versus using a tariff?

_____

_____

8. What arguments are made to support trade restrictions?

_____

_____

9. Present the free-trade response to the argument that imports should be restricted on goods that a country needs for national security.

_____

_____

10. If tariffs reduce total surplus and, therefore, total economic well-being, why do governments employ them?

_____

_____

11. List other benefits of free trade beyond those suggested by our standard analysis.

_____

_____

Self-Test

True/False Questions

_____ 1. If the world price for a good exceeds a country's before-trade domestic price for that good, the country should import that good.

_____ 2. Countries should import products for which they have a comparative advantage in production.

_____ 3. If a worker in Brazil can produce 6 oranges or 2 apples in an hour while a worker in Mexico can produce 2 oranges or 1 apple in an hour, then Brazil should export oranges and Mexico should export apples.

_____ 4. If free trade is allowed and a country imports wheat, domestic buyers of bread are better off and domestic farmers are worse off when compared to the before-trade domestic equilibrium.

_____ 5. If free trade is allowed and a country exports a good, domestic producers of the good are worse off and domestic consumers of the good are better off when compared to the before-trade domestic equilibrium.

_____ 6. If free trade is allowed and a country exports a good, the gains of domestic producers exceed the losses of domestic consumers and total surplus rises.

_____ 7. Trade makes everyone better off.

_____ 8. Trade can make everyone better off if the winners from trade compensate the losers from trade.

_____ 9. Trade increases the economic well-being of a nation because the gains of the winners exceed the losses of the losers.

_____ 10. Tariffs tend to benefit consumers.

_____ 11. A tariff raises the price of a good, reduces the domestic quantity demanded, increases the domestic quantity supplied, and increases the quantity imported.

_____ 12. An import quota that restricts imports to the same degree as an equivalent tariff raises the same amount of government revenue as the equivalent tariff, even if the government gives away the import licenses.

_____ 13. Opponents of free trade often argue that free trade destroys domestic jobs.

_____ 14. If a foreign country subsidizes its export industries, its taxpayers are paying to improve the welfare of consumers in the importing countries.

_____ 15. Tariffs cause deadweight losses because they raise the price of the imported good and cause overproduction and underconsumption of the good in the importing country.

Multiple-Choice Questions

1. If free trade is allowed, a country will export a good if the world price is
   a. below the before-trade domestic price of the good.
   b. above the before-trade domestic price of the good.
   c. equal to the before-trade domestic price of the good.
   d. none of the above.

2. Suppose the world price is below the before-trade domestic price for a good. If a country allows free trade in this good,
   a. consumers will gain and producers will lose.
   b. producers will gain and consumers will lose.
   c. both producers and consumers will gain.
   d. both producers and consumers will lose.

The following table shows the amount of output a worker can produce per hour in the United States and Canada.

	Pens	Pencils
United States	8	4
Canada	8	2

3. Which of the following statements about free trade between the United States and Canada is true?
   a. The United States will export pencils, but there will be no trade in pens because neither country has a comparative advantage in the production of pens.
   b. The United States will export pens, and Canada will export pencils.
   c. The United States will export pencils, and Canada will export pens.
   d. The United States will export both pens and pencils.

4. If the world price for a good exceeds the before-trade domestic price for a good, then that country must have
   a. an absolute advantage in the production of the good.
   b. an absolute disadvantage in the production of the good.
   c. a comparative advantage in the production of the good.
   d. a comparative disadvantage in the production of the good.

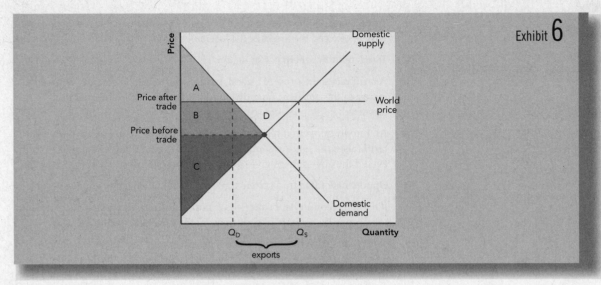

Use Exhibit 6 to answer questions 5 through 9.

5. If trade is not allowed, consumer surplus is the area
   a.   A.
   b.   A + B.
   c.   A + B + C.
   d.   A + B + D.
   e.   A + B + C + D.

6. If free trade is allowed, consumer surplus is the area
   a.   A.
   b.   A + B.
   c.   A + B + C.
   d.   A + B + D.
   e.   A + B + C + D.

7. If trade is not allowed, producer surplus is the area
   a.   C.
   b.   B + C.
   c.   B + C + D.
   d.   A + B + C.
   e.   A + B + C + D.

8. If free trade is allowed, producer surplus is the area
   a.   C.
   b.   B + C.
   c.   B + C + D.
   d.   A + B + C.
   e.   A + B + C + D.

9. The gains from trade correspond to the area
   a.   A.
   b.   B.
   c.   C.
   d.   D.
   e.   B + D.

10. When a country allows trade and exports a good,
    a.   domestic consumers are better off, domestic producers are worse off, and the
         nation is worse off because the losses of the losers exceed the gains of the winners.
    b.   domestic consumers are better off, domestic producers are worse off, and the
         nation is better off because the gains of the winners exceed the losses of the losers.
    c.   domestic producers are better off, domestic consumers are worse off, and the
         nation is worse off because the losses of the losers exceed the gains of the winners.
    d.   domestic producers are better off, domestic consumers are worse off, and the
         nation is better off because the gains of the winners exceed the losses of the losers.

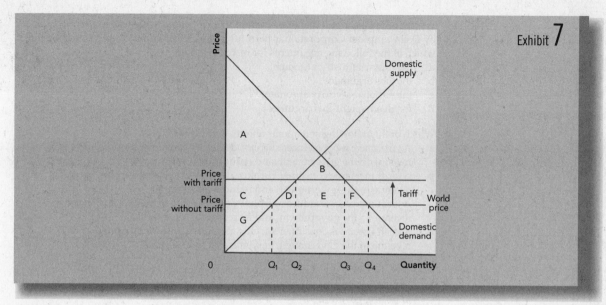

Use Exhibit 7 to answer questions 11 through 15.

11. If free trade is allowed, consumer surplus is the area
    a. A.
    b. A + B.
    c. A + B + C.
    d. A + B + C + D + E + F.
    e. A + B + C + D + E + F + G.

12. If a tariff is placed on this good, consumer surplus is the area
    a. A.
    b. A + B.
    c. A + B + C.
    d. A + B + C + D + E + F.
    e. A + B + C + D + E + F + G.

13. Government revenue from the tariff is the area
    a. C + D + E + F.
    b. D + E + F.
    c. D + F.
    d. G.
    e. E.

14. If a tariff is placed on this good, producer surplus is the area
    a. G.
    b. G + C.
    c. G + C + D + E + F.
    d. G + C + D + E + F + B.
    e. G + C + E.

15. The deadweight loss from the tariff is the area
    a. B + D + E + F.
    b. B.
    c. D + E + F.
    d. D + F.
    e. E.

16. When politicians argue that outsourcing or offshoring of technical support to India by Dell Computer Corporation is harmful to the U.S. economy, they are employing which of the following arguments for restricting trade?
    a. the infant-industry argument
    b. the jobs argument
    c. the national-security argument
    d. the deadweight-loss argument

17. Which of the following statements about a tariff is true?
    a. A tariff increases producer surplus, decreases consumer surplus, increases revenue to the government, and reduces total surplus.
    b. A tariff increases consumer surplus, decreases producer surplus, increases revenue to the government, and reduces total surplus.
    c. A tariff increases producer surplus, decreases consumer surplus, increases revenue to the government, and increases total surplus.
    d. A tariff increases consumer surplus, decreases producer surplus, increases revenue to the government, and increases total surplus.

18. Which of the following statements about import quotas is true?
    a. Import quotas are preferred to tariffs because they raise more revenue for the imposing government.
    b. Voluntary quotas established by the exporting country generate no deadweight loss for the importing country.
    c. For every tariff, there is an import quota that could have generated a similar result.
    d. An import quota reduces the price to the domestic consumers.

19. Which of the following is *not* employed as an argument in support of trade restrictions?
    a. Free trade destroys domestic jobs.
    b. Free trade harms the national security if vital products are imported.
    c. Free trade is harmful to importing countries if foreign countries subsidize their exporting industries.
    d. Free trade harms both domestic producers and domestic consumers and therefore reduces total surplus.
    e. Free trade harms infant industries in an importing country.

20. Because producers are better able to organize than consumers are, we would expect there to be political pressure to create
    a. free trade.
    b. import restrictions.
    c. export restrictions.
    d. none of the above.

Advanced Critical Thinking

You are watching the nightly news. A political candidate being interviewed says, "I'm for free trade, but it must be fair trade. If our foreign competitors will not raise their environmental regulations, reduce subsidies to their export industries, and lower tariffs on their imports of our goods, we should retaliate with tariffs and import quotas on their goods to show them that we won't be played for fools!"

1. If a foreign country artificially lowers the cost of production for its producers with lax environmental regulations and direct subsidies and then exports the products to us, who gains and who loses in our country, producers or consumers?

    _____

    _____

    _____

2. Continuing from question 1 above, does our country gain or lose? Why?

    _____

    _____

    _____

3. If a foreign country subsidizes the production of a good exported to the United States, who bears the burden of their mistaken policy?

    _____

    _____

    _____

4. What happens to our overall economic well-being if we restrict trade with a country that subsidizes its export industries? Explain.

    _____

    _____

    _____

5. Is there any difference in the analysis of our importation of a good sold at the cost of production or sold at a subsidized price? Why?

    _____

    _____

    _____

6. Is it a good policy to threaten trade restrictions in the hope that foreign governments will reduce their trade restrictions? Explain.

    _____

    _____

    _____

Solutions

Terms and Definitions

_2_ World price

_1_ Price takers

_3_ Tariff

Practice Problems

1. a. Price = $4, quantity = 40 units.
   b. Export because the world price is above the domestic price, which implies that this country has a comparative advantage in the production of this good.
   c. Price = $6, quantity supplied = 60 units, quantity demanded = 20 units, quantity exported = 40 units.
   d. A + B + C
   e. A
   f. D + E
   g. B + C + D + E + F
   h. Consumers lose B + C, producers gain B + C + F.
   i. F

2. a. Price = $4, quantity = 40 units.
   b. Import because the world price is below the domestic price, which implies that other countries have a comparative advantage in the production of this good.
   c. Price = $2, quantity supplied = 20 units, quantity demanded = 60 units, quantity imported = 40 units.
   d. A
   e. A + B + D + E
   f. B + C
   g. C
   h. Consumers gain B + D + E, producers lose B.
   i. D + E

3. a. Quantity supplied = 20 units, quantity demanded = 60 units, quantity imported = 40 units.
   b. Quantity supplied = 30 units, quantity demanded = 50 units, quantity imported = 20 units.
   c. Consumer surplus = A + B + C + D + E + F, producer surplus = G.
   d. Consumer surplus = A + B, producer surplus = C + G, government revenue = E.
   e. D + F
   f. First, the rise in the price due to the tariff causes *overproduction* because units are produced that cost more than the world price. Second, the rise in price causes *underconsumption* because consumers fail to consume units where the value to consumers is greater than the world price.
   g. A $2 tariff would raise the price to $4 (the no-trade domestic price) and eliminate trade.

Short-Answer Questions

1. In Partyland, the opportunity cost of 1 beer is 2 pizzas. In Laborland, the opportunity cost of 1 beer is 3 pizzas. Partyland has the lower opportunity cost of beer and, thus, a comparative advantage in beer production, and it will export beer. In Laborland, the opportunity cost of 1 pizza is 1/3 of a beer. In Partyland, the opportunity cost of 1 pizza is 1/2 of a beer. Laborland has the lower opportunity cost of pizza and, thus, a comparative advantage in pizza production, and it will export pizza. The fact that Laborland is more efficient at both is irrelevant.

2. Export, because the domestic opportunity cost of production is lower than the opportunity cost of production in other countries.

3. Consumers gain and producers lose because, if trade is allowed, the domestic price falls to the world price.

4. The gains are the additional value placed on the exported units by buyers in the rest of the world in excess of the domestic cost of production.

5. The gains are the additional value placed by domestic buyers on the imported units in excess of their cost of production in the rest of the world.

6. The rise in price from restricting trade causes overproduction of the good (production of units that cost more than the world price) and underconsumption of the good (failure to consume units valued more than the world price).

7. The revenue from an import quota will accrue to the license holders or foreign firms and governments unless the domestic government sells the import licenses for the maximum possible amount.

8. Free trade will destroy domestic jobs, reduce national security, harm infant industries, force domestic producers to compete with foreign companies that have unfair advantages, and allow other countries to have trade restrictions while our country does not.

9. The danger is that nearly any good (far beyond standard military items) can be argued by representatives of industry to be necessary for national security.

10. Tariffs harm domestic consumers while helping domestic producers. Producers are better able to organize than are consumers, and thus, they are better able to lobby the government on their behalf.

11. Free trade increases the variety of goods for consumers, allows firms to take advantage of economies of scale, makes markets more competitive, and facilitates the spread of technology.

True/False Questions

1. F; the country should *export* that good.
2. F; countries should export goods for which they have a comparative advantage in production.
3. T
4. T
5. F; producers gain, consumers lose.
6. T
7. F; some gain and some lose but the gains of the winners outweigh the losses of the losers.
8. T
9. T
10. F; tariffs benefit producers.
11. F; tariffs decrease imports.
12. F; at most, a quota can raise the same revenue if the government sells the import licenses for the maximum amount possible (the difference between the world price and the domestic price).
13. T
14. T
15. T

Multiple-Choice Questions

1. b
2. a
3. c
4. c
5. b
6. a
7. a
8. c
9. d
10. d
11. d
12. b
13. e
14. b
15. d
16. b
17. a
18. c
19. d
20. b

Advanced Critical Thinking

1. Consumers gain, producers lose.
2. Our country gains because the gains of the consumers exceed the losses of the producers.
3. The taxpayers of the foreign country.
4. Producers gain, consumers lose, but consumers lose more than producers gain so total surplus is reduced and there is a deadweight loss. The result is no different than restricting trade when the foreign producer has no unfair advantage.

5. No. In either case, the world price is lower than the before-trade domestic price, causing consumers to gain and producers to lose from trade. Also, restrictions on trade cause consumers to lose more than producers gain whether the production of the good was subsidized or not.
6. Usually not. If the other country fails to give in to the threat, the threatening country has to choose between backing down and reducing trade—neither of which is desirable.

Chapter 10
Externalities

Goals
In this chapter you will

- Learn what an externality is
- See why externalities can make market outcomes inefficient
- Examine the various government policies aimed at solving the problem of externalities
- Examine how people can sometimes solve the problem of externalities on their own
- Consider why private solutions to externalities sometimes do not work

Outcomes
After accomplishing these goals, you should be able to

- Distinguish between a positive and a negative externality
- Demonstrate why the optimal quantity and the market quantity differ in the presence of an externality
- Demonstrate the potential equality of a corrective tax and pollution permits
- Define the Coase theorem
- Explain how transaction costs may impede a private solution to an externality

Chapter Overview

Context and Purpose

Chapter 10 is the first chapter in the microeconomic section of the text. It is the first chapter in a two-chapter sequence on the economics of the public sector. Chapter 10 addresses externalities—the uncompensated impact of one person's actions on the well-being of a bystander. Chapter 11 will address public goods and common resources (goods that will be defined in Chapter 11).

In Chapter 10, we address different sources of externalities and a variety of potential cures for externalities. Markets maximize total surplus to buyers and sellers in a market. However, if a market generates an externality (a cost or benefit to someone external to the market), the market equilibrium may not maximize the total benefit to society. Thus, in Chapter 10 we will see that while markets are usually a good way to organize economic activity, governments can sometimes improve market outcomes.

Chapter Review

Introduction   An externality is the uncompensated impact of one person's actions on the well-being of a bystander. If the effect is beneficial, it is called a *positive externality*. If the effect is adverse, it is called a *negative externality*. Markets maximize total surplus to buyers and sellers in a market, and this is usually efficient. However, if a market generates an externality, the market equilibrium may not maximize the total benefit to society as a whole, and thus, the market is inefficient. Government policy may potentially improve efficiency. Examples of negative externalities are pollution from exhaust and noise. Examples of positive externalities are historic building restorations and research into new technologies.

Externalities and Market Inefficiency

The height of the demand curve measures the value of the good to the marginal consumer. The height of the supply curve measures the cost to the marginal producer. If there is no government intervention, the price adjusts to balance supply and demand. The quantity produced maximizes consumer and producer surplus. If there is no externality, the market solution is efficient because it maximizes the well-being of buyers and sellers in the market and their well-being is all that matters. However, if there is an externality and bystanders are affected by this market, the market does not maximize the total benefit to society as a whole because others beyond just the buyers and sellers in the market are affected.

There are two types of externalities:

- Negative externality: When the production of a good generates pollution, costs accrue to society beyond those that accrue to the producing firm. Thus, the social cost exceeds the private cost of production, and graphically, the social cost curve is above the supply curve (private cost curve). Total surplus is the value to the consumers minus the true social cost of production. Therefore, the optimal quantity that maximizes total surplus is less than the equilibrium quantity generated by the market.

- Positive externality: A good such as education generates benefits to people beyond just the buyers of education. As a result, the social value of education exceeds the private value. Graphically, the social value curve is above the demand curve (private value curve). Total surplus is the true social value minus the cost to producers. Therefore, the optimal quantity that maximizes total surplus is greater than the equilibrium quantity generated by the market.

Internalizing an externality is the altering of incentives so that people take into account the external effects of their actions. To internalize externalities, the government can create taxes and subsidies to shift the supply and demand curves until they are the same as the true social cost and social value curves. This will make the equilibrium quantity and the optimal quantity the same, and the market becomes efficient. Negative externalities can be internalized with taxes while positive externalities can be internalized with subsidies.

High technology production (robotics, etc.) generates a positive externality for other producers known as a *technology spillover*. Some economists consider this spillover effect to be so pervasive that they believe the government should have an industrial policy—government intervention to promote technology-enhancing industries. Other economists are skeptical. At present, the U.S. government provides a property right for new ideas in the form of patent protection and offers special tax breaks for expenditures on research and development.

Public Policies Toward Externalities

The government can sometimes improve the outcome by responding in one of two ways: command-and-control policies or market-based policies.

- Command-and-control policies are regulations that require or prohibit (or limit) certain behaviors. The problem here is that the regulator must know all of the details of an industry and alternative technologies in order to create the efficient rules. Prohibiting a behavior altogether can be best if the cost of a particular type of pollution is enormous.

- Market-based policies align private incentives with social efficiency. There are two types of market-based policies: corrective taxes and subsidies, and tradable pollution permits.

A tax enacted to correct the effects of a negative externality is known as a corrective tax or Pigovian tax. An ideal corrective tax or subsidy would equal the external cost or benefit from the activity generating the externality. Corrective taxes can reduce negative externalities at a lower cost than regulations because the tax essentially places a price on a negative externality, say pollution. Those firms that can reduce their pollution with the least cost reduce their pollution a great deal while other firms that have higher costs of reducing their pollution reduce their pollution very little. The same amount of total reduction in pollution can be achieved with the tax as with regulation but at lower cost. In addition, with the tax firms have incentive to develop cleaner technologies and reduce pollution even further than the regulation would have required. Unlike other taxes, corrective taxes enhance efficiency rather than reduce efficiency. For example, the tax on gasoline is a corrective tax, because, rather than causing a deadweight loss, it causes there to be less traffic congestion, safer roads, and a cleaner environment. Gasoline taxes are politically unpopular.

Tradable pollution permits allow the holder of the permit to pollute a certain amount. Those firms that have a high cost of reducing their pollution will be willing to pay a high price for the permits, and those firms that can reduce pollution at a low cost will sell their permits and will instead reduce their pollution. The initial allocation of the permits among industries does not affect the efficient outcome. This method is similar to a corrective tax. While a corrective tax sets the price of pollution (the tax), tradable pollution permits set the quantity of pollution permitted. In the market for pollution, either method can reach the efficient solution. Tradable pollution permits may be superior because the regulator does not need to know the demand to pollute in order to restrict pollution to a particular quantity. The EPA is increasingly and successfully using pollution permits to reduce pollution. At present, to reduce carbon emissions and global warming, the United States is moving toward a cap-and-trade system for carbon, which is very similar to a tax on carbon.

Some people object to an economic analysis of pollution. They feel that any pollution is too much and that putting a price on pollution is immoral. Because all economic activity creates pollution to some degree and all activities involve trade-offs, economists have little sympathy for this argument. Rich productive countries demand a cleaner environment, and market-based policies reduce pollution at a lower cost than alternatives, further increasing the demand for a clean environment.

Private Solutions to Externalities

Government action is not always needed to solve the externality problem. Some private solutions to the externality problem are as follows:

- Moral codes and social sanctions: People "do the right thing" and do not litter.
- Charities: People give tax-deductible gifts to environmental groups and private colleges and universities.
- Private markets that harness self-interest and cause efficient mergers: The beekeeper merges with the apple orchard, and the resulting firm produces more apples and more honey.
- Private markets that harness self-interest and create contracts among affected parties: The apple orchard and the beekeeper can agree to produce the optimal combined quantity of apples and honey.

The Coase theorem is the proposition that if private parties can bargain without cost over the allocation of resources, they can solve the problem of externalities on their own. In other words, regardless of the initial distribution of rights, the interested parties can always reach a bargain in which everyone is better off and the outcome is efficient. For example, if the value of peace and quiet exceeds the value of owning a barking dog, the party desiring quiet will buy the right to quiet from the dog owner and remove the dog, or the dog owner will fail to buy the right to own a barking dog from the owner of quiet space. Regardless of whether one has the property right to peace and quiet or the other has the right to make noise, there is no barking dog, which, in this case, is efficient. The result is the opposite and is also efficient if the value of owning a dog exceeds the value of peace and quiet.

Private parties often fail to reach efficient agreements, however, due to transaction costs. Transaction costs are the costs that parties incur in the process of agreeing and following through on a bargain. If transaction costs exceed the potential gains from the agreement, no private solution will occur. Some sources of high transaction costs are:

- lawyers' fees to write the agreement
- costs of enforcing the agreement
- a breakdown in bargaining when there is a range of prices that would create efficiency
- a large number of interested parties.

Conclusion

Markets maximize total surplus to buyers and sellers in a market and this is usually efficient. However, if a market generates an externality, the market equilibrium may not maximize the total benefit to society as a whole, and thus, the market is inefficient. The Coase theorem says that people can bargain among themselves and reach an efficient solution. If transaction costs are high, however, government policy may be needed to improve efficiency. Corrective taxes and pollution permits are preferred to command-and-control policies because they reduce pollution at a lower cost and, therefore, increase the quantity demanded of a clean environment.

Helpful Hints

1. Why do we use the word "externality" to refer to the uncompensated impact of one person's actions on the well-being of a bystander? An easy way to remember is to know that the word externality refers to the "external effects" of a market transaction or to costs and benefits that land on a bystander who is "external to the market."

2. Negative externalities cause the socially optimal quantity of a good to be less than the quantity produced by the market. Positive externalities cause the socially optimal quantity of a good to be greater than the quantity produced by the market. To remedy the problem, the government can tax goods that produce negative externalities by the size of the external cost, and subsidize goods that produce positive externalities by the size of the external benefit.

Terms and Definitions

Choose a definition for each key term.

Key Terms

_____ Externality

_____ Positive externality

_____ Negative externality

_____ Social cost

_____ Internalizing an externality

_____ Corrective tax

_____ Coase theorem

_____ Transaction costs

Definitions

1. The proposition that if private parties can bargain without cost over the allocation of resources, they can solve the problem of externalities on their own

2. The costs that parties incur in the process of agreeing and following through on a bargain

3. A situation when a person's actions have an adverse impact on a bystander

4. A tax designed to induce private decision makers to take into account the social costs that arise from a negative externality

5. The uncompensated impact of one person's actions on the well-being of a bystander

6. Altering incentives so that people take into account the external effects of their actions

7. The sum of private costs and external costs

8. A situation when a person's actions have a beneficial impact on a bystander

Problems and Short-Answer Questions

Practice Problems

1. The information below provides the prices and quantities in a hypothetical market for automobile antifreeze.

Price per gallon	Quantity demanded	Quantity supplied
$1	700	300
2	600	400
3	500	500
4	400	600
5	300	700
6	200	800
7	100	900
8	0	1,000

a. Plot the supply and demand curves for antifreeze in Exhibit 1.
b. What is the equilibrium price and quantity generated by buyers and sellers in the market?

_____

_____

c. Suppose that the production of antifreeze generates pollution in the form of chemical runoff and that the pollution imposes a $2 cost on society for each gallon of antifreeze produced. Plot the social cost curve in Exhibit 1.
d. What is the optimal quantity of antifreeze production? Does the market overproduce or underproduce antifreeze?

_____

_____

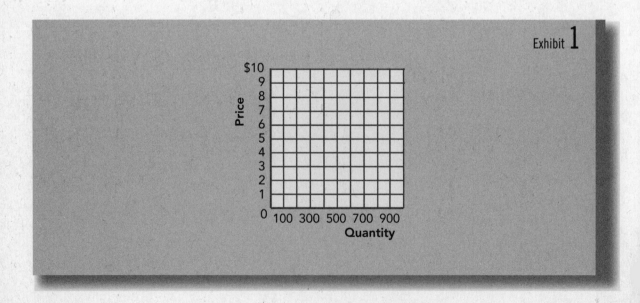

Exhibit 1

e.   If the government were to intervene to make this market efficient, should it impose a corrective tax or a subsidy? What is the value of the appropriate tax or subsidy?

_____

_____

2. Suppose citizens living around Metropolitan Airport value peace and quiet at a value of $3 billion.

a.   If it costs the airlines $4 billion to make their planes quieter (the airlines value noise at $4 billion), is it efficient for the government to require that the planes be muffled? Why or why not?

_____

_____

_____

b.   If it costs the airlines $2 billion to make their planes quieter, is it efficient for the government to require that the planes be muffled? Why or why not?

_____

_____

c.   Suppose there are no transaction costs and suppose that people have the right to peace and quiet. If it costs the airlines $2 billion to make their planes quieter, what is the private solution to the problem?

_____

_____

d.   Suppose there are no transaction costs and suppose that airlines have the right to make as much noise as they please. If it costs the airlines $2 billion to make their planes quieter, what is the private solution to the problem?

_____

_____

e.   Compare your answers to *c* and *d* above. What are the similarities, and what are the differences? What general rule can you make from the comparison?

_____

_____

_____

f.   Suppose it costs the airlines $2 billion to make their planes quieter. If a private solution to the noise problem requires an additional $2 billion of transaction costs (due to legal fees, the large number of affected parties, and enforcement costs), can there be a private solution to the problem? Why or why not?

_____

_____

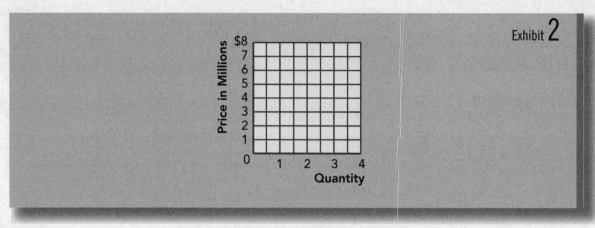

3. Suppose there are four firms that each wish to dump one barrel of waste chemicals into the river. Firm 1 produces a product that is so valued by society and sells for such a high price that it is willing to pay $8 million to dump a barrel. Firm 2 produces a somewhat less valuable product and is only willing to pay $6 million to dump a barrel. In similar fashion, suppose firm 3 is willing to pay $4 million to dump a barrel and firm 4 will pay $2 million.

   a. Draw the demand for the right to pollute in Exhibit 2.

   b. Suppose the EPA estimates that the safe level of pollutants in the river is 3 barrels. At what value should they set a corrective tax?

   _____

   _____

   c. Suppose the EPA estimates that the safe level of pollutants in the river is 3 barrels. How many tradable pollution permits should they allocate? At what price will the permits trade?

   _____

   _____

   d. Compare parts *b* and *c* above. How many barrels are dumped in each case? What is the price paid to pollute in each case? Is there an advantage to one method of internalizing the externality compared to the other?

   _____

   _____

   _____

Short-Answer Questions

Use the following information for questions 1 through 3:
   Suppose that a commercial apple orchard uses pesticides in the production of apples. In the process, dangerous fumes drift across a nearby neighborhood.

   1. Is this an example of a positive or a negative externality? Explain.

   _____

   _____

2. If this externality is not internalized, does the market overproduce or underproduce apples? What does it mean to overproduce or underproduce a product?

_____

_____

_____

3. To internalize this externality, should the government tax or subsidize apples? Why or why not?

_____

_____

_____

4. What are the two types of public policies toward externalities? Describe them. Which one do economists prefer? Why?

_____

_____

_____

5. Does a corrective tax reduce or increase efficiency? Why?

_____

_____

_____

6. Why are tradable pollution permits considered superior to corrective taxes at reducing pollution?

_____

_____

_____

7. Suppose an individual enjoys lawn care and gardening a great deal. He uses pesticides to control insects and the harmful residue drifts across the neighborhood. He values the use of the pesticides at $10,000, and the neighborhood values clean air at $15,000. What does the Coase theorem suggest will take place?

_____

_____

_____

8. In question 7 above, how large would the transaction costs need to be in order to ensure that no private solution to the problem can be found?

_____

_____

_____

9. What are the sources of transaction costs when affected parties try to eliminate an externality?

_____

_____

_____

10. What are some types of private solutions to externalities?

_____

_____

_____

Self-Test

True/False Questions

_____ 1.   A positive externality is an external benefit that accrues to the buyers in a market while a negative externality is an external cost that accrues to the sellers in a market.

_____ 2.   If a market generates a negative externality, the social cost curve is above the supply curve (private cost curve).

_____ 3.   If a market generates a positive externality, the social value curve is above the demand curve (private value curve).

_____ 4.   A market that generates a negative externality that has not been internalized generates an equilibrium quantity that is less than the optimal quantity.

_____ 5.   If a market generates a negative externality, a corrective tax will move the market toward a more efficient outcome.

_____ 6.   According to the Coase theorem, an externality always requires government intervention in order to internalize the externality.

_____ 7.   To reduce pollution by some targeted amount, it is most efficient if each firm that pollutes reduces its pollution by an equal amount.

_____ 8.   When Smokey the Bear says, "Only you can prevent forest fires," society is attempting to use moral codes and social sanctions to internalize the externality associated with using fire while camping.

_____ 9.   A tax always makes a market less efficient.

_____ 10. If Bob values smoking in a restaurant at $10 and Sue values clean air while she eats at $15, according to the Coase theorem, Bob will not smoke in the restaurant only if Sue owns the right to clean air.

_____ 11. If transaction costs exceed the potential gains from an agreement between affected parties to an externality, there will be no private solution to the externality.

_____ 12. A corrective tax sets the price of pollution while tradable pollution permits set the quantity of pollution.

_____ 13. An advantage of using tradable pollution permits to reduce pollution is that the regulator need not know anything about the demand for pollution rights.

_____ 14. The majority of economists do not like the idea of putting a price on polluting the environment.

_____ 15. For any given demand curve for pollution, a regulator can achieve the same level of pollution with either a corrective tax or by allocating tradable pollution permits.

Multiple-Choice Questions

1. An externality is
   a. the benefit that accrues to the buyer in a market.
   b. the cost that accrues to the seller in a market.
   c. the uncompensated impact of one person's actions on the well-being of a bystander.
   d. the compensation paid to a firm's external consultants.
   e. none of the above.

2. A negative externality generates
   a. a social cost curve that is above the supply curve (private cost curve) for a good.
   b. a social cost curve that is below the supply curve (private cost curve) for a good.
   c. a social value curve that is above the demand curve (private value curve) for a good.
   d. none of the above.

3. A positive externality generates
   a. a social cost curve that is above the supply curve (private cost curve) for a good.
   b. a social value curve that is above the demand curve (private value curve) for a good.
   c. a social value curve that is below the demand curve (private value curve) for a good.
   d. none of the above.

4. A negative externality (that has not been internalized) causes the
   a. optimal quantity to exceed the equilibrium quantity.
   b. equilibrium quantity to exceed the optimal quantity.
   c. equilibrium quantity to equal the optimal quantity.
   d. equilibrium quantity to be either above or below the optimal quantity.

5. A positive externality (that has not been internalized) causes the
   a. optimal quantity to exceed the equilibrium quantity.
   b. equilibrium quantity to exceed the optimal quantity.
   c. equilibrium quantity to equal the optimal quantity.
   d. equilibrium quantity to be either above or below the optimal quantity.

6. To internalize a negative externality, an appropriate public policy response would be to
   a. ban the production of all goods creating negative externalities.
   b. have the government take over the production of the good causing the externality.
   c. subsidize the good.
   d. tax the good.

7. The government engages in an industrial policy
   a. to internalize the negative externality associated with industrial pollution.
   b. to internalize the positive externality associated with technology-enhancing industries.
   c. to help stimulate private solutions to the technology externality.
   d. by allocating tradable technology permits to high technology industry.

8. When an individual buys a car in a congested urban area, it generates
   a. an efficient market outcome.
   b. a technology spillover.
   c. a positive externality.
   d. a negative externality.

9. The most efficient pollution control system would ensure that
   a. each polluter reduce its pollution an equal amount.
   b. the polluters with the lowest cost of reducing pollution reduce their pollution the greatest amount.
   c. no pollution of the environment is tolerated.
   d. the regulators decide how much each polluter should reduce its pollution.

10. According to the Coase theorem, private parties can solve the problem of externalities if
    a. each affected party has equal power in the negotiations.
    b. the party affected by the externality has the initial property right to be left alone.
    c. there are no transaction costs.
    d. the government requires them to negotiate with each other.
    e. there are a large number of affected parties.

11. To internalize a positive externality, an appropriate public policy response would be to
    a. ban the good creating the externality.
    b. have the government produce the good until the value of an additional unit is zero.
    c. subsidize the good.
    d. tax the good.

12. Which of the following is not considered a transaction cost incurred by parties in the process of contracting to eliminate a pollution externality?
    a. costs incurred to reduce the pollution
    b. costs incurred due to lawyers' fees
    c. costs incurred to enforce the agreement
    d. costs incurred due to a large number of parties affected by the externality
    e. All of the above are considered transaction costs.

13. Bob and Tom live in a university dorm. Bob values playing loud music at a value of $100. Tom values peace and quiet at a value of $150. Which of the following statements is *true*?
    a. It is efficient for Bob to continue to play loud music.
    b. It is efficient for Bob to stop playing loud music only if Tom has the property right to peace and quiet.
    c. It is efficient for Bob to stop playing loud music only if Bob has the property right to play loud music.
    d. It is efficient for Bob to stop playing loud music regardless of who has the property right to the level of sound.

14. Bob and Tom live in a university dorm. Bob values playing loud music at a value of $100. Tom values peace and quiet at a value of $150. Which of the following statements is *true* about an efficient solution to this externality problem if Bob has the right to play loud music and if there are no transaction costs?
    a. Bob will pay Tom $100, and Bob will stop playing loud music.
    b. Tom will pay Bob between $100 and $150, and Bob will stop playing loud music.
    c. Bob will pay Tom $150, and Bob will continue to play loud music.
    d. Tom will pay Bob between $100 and $150, and Bob will continue to play loud music.

15. Which of the following is *true* regarding tradable pollution permits and corrective taxes?
    a. Corrective taxes are more likely to reduce pollution to a targeted amount than tradable pollution permits.
    b. Tradable pollution permits efficiently reduce pollution only if they are initially distributed to the firms that can reduce pollution at the lowest cost.
    c. To set the quantity of pollution with tradable pollution permits, the regulator must know everything about the demand for pollution rights.
    d. Corrective taxes and tradable pollution permits create an efficient market for pollution.
    e. All of the above are true.

16. The gas-guzzler tax that is placed on new vehicles that get very poor mileage is an example of
    a. a tradable pollution permit.
    b. an application of the Coase theorem.
    c. an attempt to internalize a positive externality.
    d. an attempt to internalize a negative externality.

17. A corrective tax on pollution
    a. sets the price of pollution.
    b. sets the quantity of pollution.
    c. determines the demand for pollution rights.
    d. reduces the incentive for technological innovations to further reduce pollution.

18. Tradable pollution permits
    a. set the price of pollution.
    b. set the quantity of pollution.
    c. determine the demand for pollution rights.
    d. reduce the incentive for technological innovations to further reduce pollution.

19. When wealthy alumni provide charitable contributions to their alma mater to reduce the tuition payments of current students, it is an example of
    a. an attempt to internalize a positive externality.
    b. an attempt to internalize a negative externality.
    c. a corrective tax.
    d. a command-and-control policy.

20. Suppose an industry emits a negative externality such as pollution, and the possible methods to internalize the externality are command-and-control policies, corrective taxes, and tradable pollution permits. If economists were to rank these methods for internalizing a negative externality based on efficiency, ease of implementation, and the incentive for the industry to further reduce pollution in the future, they would likely rank them in the following order (from most favored to least favored):
    a. corrective taxes, command-and-control policies, tradable pollution permits.
    b. command-and-control policies, tradable pollution permits, corrective taxes.
    c. tradable pollution permits, corrective taxes, command-and-control policies.
    d. tradable pollution permits, command-and-control policies, corrective taxes.
    e. They would all rank equally high because the same result can be obtained from any one of the policies.

Advanced Critical Thinking

You are home for semester break. Your father opens the mail. One of the letters is your parents' property tax bill. On the property tax bill, there is a deduction if the property owner has done anything to beautify his property. The property owner can deduct 50 percent of any expenditure on things such as landscaping from his property taxes. For example, if your parents spent $2,000 on landscaping, they can reduce their tax bill by $0.50 \times \$2,000 = \$1,000$ so that the true cost of the landscaping was only $1,000. Your father announces, "This is an outrage. If someone wants to improve his house, it is no one's business but his own. I remember some of my college economics, and I know that taxes and subsidies are always inefficient."

1. What is the city government trying to subsidize with this tax break?

    _____

    _____

2. What is the externality that this subsidy is trying to internalize?

    _____

    _____

    _____

3. Although taxes and subsidies usually create inefficiencies, are taxes and subsidies always inefficient? Why or why not?

    _____

    _____

    _____

    _____

Solutions

Terms and Definitions

_5_ Externality

_8_ Positive externality

_3_ Negative externality

_7_ Social cost

_6_ Internalizing an externality

_4_ Corrective tax

_1_ Coase theorem

_2_ Transaction costs

Practice Problems

1. a. See Exhibit 3.

Exhibit 3

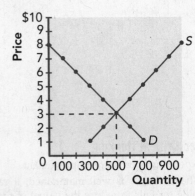

b. Price = $3, quantity = 500 units.

c. See Exhibit 4.

Exhibit 4

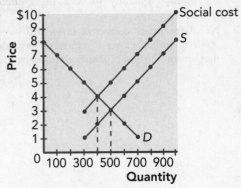

d. 400 units. The market overproduces because the market quantity is 500 while the optimal quantity is 400 units.

e. The government should impose a corrective tax of $2 per unit.

2. a. No, because the cost of correcting the externality exceeds the value placed on it by the affected parties.

b. Yes, because the value placed on peace and quiet exceeds the cost of muffling the planes.

c. The airlines could spend $2 billion and make their planes quieter or buy the right to make noise for $3 billion, so they will choose to make the planes quieter for $2 billion.

d. The affected citizens must pay at least $2 billion and are willing to pay up to $3 billion to the airlines to have the planes made quieter.

e. Similarities: The planes will be made quieter regardless of the original property rights because it is efficient. Differences: If the citizens have the right to quiet, citizens gain and airlines lose. If the airlines have the right to make noise, airlines gain and citizens lose.

f. No, because the transaction costs exceed the potential gains from trade. (The potential gains are the $3 billion value of quiet minus the $2 billion cost to quiet the planes, or $1 billion.)

3. a. See Exhibit 5.

Exhibit 5

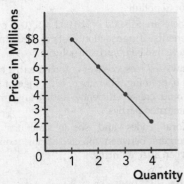

b. $4 million per barrel

c. Three permits should be sold. They will trade at a price of $4 million per permit.

d. Three barrels. $4 million per barrel. Yes, with the tradable pollution permits, the regulator does not need to know anything about the demand for pollution in this market in order to target pollution at 3 barrels and the initial allocation of pollution permits will not have an impact on the efficient solution.

Short-Answer Questions

1. Negative externality, because the social cost of producing apples exceeds the private cost of producing apples.

2. Overproduce. To overproduce is to produce units where the true cost exceeds the true value. To underproduce is to fail to produce units where the true value exceeds the true cost.

3. Tax apples because to internalize this externality, it requires that the supply curve for apples be shifted upward until it equals the true social cost curve.

4. Command-and-control policies are regulations that prohibit certain behaviors. Market-based policies align private incentives with social efficiency. Economists prefer market-based policies because they are more efficient and they provide incentives for even further reduction in, say, pollution through advances in technology.

5. It increases efficiency by shifting the supply or demand curve toward the true social cost or value curve, thereby making the market solution equal to the optimal or efficient solution.

6. The regulator doesn't need to know anything about the demand to pollute in order to arrive at the targeted amount of pollution.

7. No pesticides will be used, and the air will be clean, regardless of whether the individual owns the right to use pesticides or the neighborhood residents own the right to clean air. Either the individual will fail to buy the right to pollute or the neighborhood residents will pay the individual not to pollute.

8. There are $15,000 − $10,000 = $5,000 of potential benefits. If transaction costs exceed this amount, there will be no private solution.

9. Lawyers' fees, costs of enforcement, a breakdown in bargaining when there is a range of prices that would create efficiency, and a large number of interested parties.

10. Moral codes and social sanctions, charities, mergers between affected firms, contracts between affected firms.

True/False Questions

1. F; a positive externality is a benefit that accrues to a bystander, and a negative externality is a cost that accrues to a bystander.
2. T
3. T
4. F; the equilibrium quantity is greater than the optimal quantity.
5. T
6. F; the Coase theorem suggests that private parties can solve the problem of an externality on their own if there are no transaction costs.
7. F; firms that can reduce pollution at a lower cost should reduce their pollution more than firms that can reduce pollution at a greater cost.
8. T
9. F; corrective taxes can make a market more efficient.
10. F; the original distribution of property rights to the air will not affect the efficient solution.
11. T
12. T
13. T
14. F; economists generally think that a market for pollution will reduce pollution most efficiently.

15. T

Multiple-Choice Questions

1. c
2. a
3. b
4. b
5. a
6. d
7. b
8. d
9. b
10. c
11. c
12. a
13. d
14. b
15. d
16. d
17. a
18. b
19. a
20. c

Advanced Critical Thinking

1. Expenditures on home improvement.
2. When a house is well maintained, it raises the value (or fails to reduce the value) of the nearby property. Individual buyers and sellers in the market for home repair do not consider this when choosing the quantity of home repair, and thus, the optimal quantity exceeds the equilibrium quantity.
3. No. Appropriate corrective taxes and subsidies move a market closer to efficiency because the market equilibrium is inefficient to begin with.

Chapter 11

Public Goods and Common Resources

Goals
In this chapter you will

- Learn the defining characteristics of public goods and common resources

- Examine why private markets fail to provide public goods

- Consider some of the important public goods in our economy

- See why the cost–benefit analysis of public goods is both necessary and difficult

- Examine why people tend to use common resources too much

- Consider some of the important common resources in our economy

Outcomes
After accomplishing these goals, you should be able to

- Classify goods into the categories of public goods, private goods, common resources, or club goods

- Explain why production of public goods is unprofitable to private industry

- Explain the public good nature of national defense

- Explain why surveys to determine the benefits of public goods are a less precise valuation of benefits than prices of private goods

- Tell the story of the Tragedy of the Commons

- Explain why fish and wildlife are common resources

Chapter Overview

Context and Purpose

Chapter 11 is the second chapter in a two-chapter sequence on the economics of the public sector. Chapter 10 addressed externalities.

169

Chapter 11 addresses public goods and common resources—goods for which it is difficult to charge prices to users.

The purpose of Chapter 11 is to address a group of goods that are free to the consumer. When goods are free, market forces that normally allocate resources are absent. Therefore, free goods, such as playgrounds and public parks, may not be produced and consumed in the proper amounts. Government can potentially remedy this market failure and improve economic well-being.

Chapter Review

Introduction   Some goods are free to the consumer—beaches, lakes, playgrounds. When goods are available without prices, market forces that normally allocate resources are absent. Therefore, free goods, such as playgrounds and public parks, may not be produced and consumed in the proper amounts. Government can potentially remedy this market failure and improve economic well-being.

The Different Kinds of Goods

There are two characteristics of goods that are useful when defining types of goods:

- Excludability: the property of a good whereby a person can be prevented from using it. A good is excludable if a seller can exclude nonpayers from using it (food in the grocery store) and not excludable if a seller cannot exclude nonpayers from using it (broadcast television or radio signal).

- Rivalry in consumption: the property of a good whereby one person's use of a good diminishes other people's use. A good is rival in consumption if only one person can consume the good (food) and not rival if the good can be consumed by more than one at the same time (streetlight).

With these characteristics, goods can be divided into four categories:

1. Private goods: Goods that are both excludable and rival in consumption. Most goods like bread and blue jeans are private goods and are allocated efficiently by supply and demand in markets.

2. Public goods: Goods that are neither excludable nor rival in consumption, such as national defense and streetlights.

3. Common resources: Goods that are rival in consumption but not excludable, such as fish in the ocean.

4. Club goods: Goods that are excludable but not rival in consumption, such as fire protection and cable television. Club goods are one type of natural monopoly.

This chapter examines the two types of goods that are not excludable and, thus, are free: public goods and common resources.

Public Goods

Public goods are difficult for a private market to provide because of the *free-rider problem*. A free rider is a person who receives the benefit of a good but avoids paying for it. Because public goods are not excludable, firms cannot prevent nonpayers from consuming the good, and thus, there is little incentive for a firm to produce a public good. The outcome of a public good is similar to that of a positive externality because consumers of a good fail to consume the efficient quantity of the good because they do not take into account the benefit to others.

For example, a streetlight may be valued at $1,000 by each of ten homeowners in a neighborhood. If the cost is $5,000, no individual will buy a streetlight because no one can sell the right to use the light to their neighbors for $1,000 each. This is because after the streetlight is in place, their neighbors can consume the light whether they pay or not. Even though the neighborhood values the streetlight at a total value of $10,000 and the cost of a streetlight is only $5,000, the private market will not be able to provide it. Public goods are related to positive externalities in that each neighbor ignores the external benefit provided to others when deciding whether to buy a streetlight. Often government steps in, provides goods, such as streetlights, where benefits exceed the costs, and pays for them with tax revenue. In this case, the government could provide the streetlight and tax each resident $500, and everyone would be better off.

Some important public goods are national defense, basic research that produces general knowledge, and programs to fight poverty.

Some goods can switch between being public goods and private goods depending on the circumstances. A lighthouse is a public good if the owner cannot charge each ship as it passes the light. A lighthouse becomes a private good if the owner can charge the port to which the ships are traveling.

When a private market cannot produce a public good, governments must decide whether to produce the good. Their decision tool is often cost–benefit analysis: a study that compares the costs and benefits to society of providing a public good. There are two problems with cost–benefit analysis:

- Quantifying benefits is difficult using the results of a questionnaire.

- Respondents have little incentive to tell the truth.

When governments decide whether to spend money on additional safety measures such as stoplights and stop signs, they must consider the value of a human life because the benefit of such an expenditure is the probability of saving a life times the value of a life. Studies suggest that the value of a human life is about $10 million.

Common Resources

Common resources are not excludable but are rival in consumption (say fish in the ocean). Therefore, common resources are free, but when one person uses it, it diminishes other people's enjoyment of it. The outcome of a common resource is similar to that of a negative externality because consumers of a good do not take into account the negative impact on others from their consumption. The result is that common resources are used excessively.

The Tragedy of the Commons is a parable that illustrates why common resources get used more than is desirable from the standpoint of society as a whole. The town common (open land to be grazed) will be overgrazed to the point where it becomes barren because, since it is free, private incentives suggest that each individual should graze as many sheep as possible, yet this is overgrazing from a social perspective. Possible solutions are to regulate the number of sheep grazed, tax sheep, auction off sheep-grazing permits, or divide the land and sell it to individual sheep herders, making grazing land a private good.

Some important common resources are clean air and water, congested nontoll roads, and fish, whales, and other wildlife. Private decision makers use a common resource too much, so governments regulate behavior or impose fees to reduce the problem of overuse. For example, imposing tolls on congested roads reduces congestion and shortens travel times.

Conclusion: The Importance of Property Rights

In the case of public goods and common resources, markets fail to allocate resources efficiently because property rights are not clearly established. In a private market, no one owns the clean air so no one can charge people when they pollute. The result is that people pollute too much (externality example) or use too much clean air (common resource example). Furthermore, no one can charge those who are protected by national defense for the benefit they receive so people produce too little national defense (public good example).

The government can potentially solve these problems by selling pollution permits, regulating private behavior, or providing the public good.

Helpful Hints

1. In general, public goods are underproduced and common resources are overconsumed. This is because they are both free. Because public goods are free, it is not profitable to produce them (streetlights and national defense). Because common resources are free, people overconsume them (clean air and fish in the ocean).

2. Public goods are defined by their characteristics, not by who provides them. A streetlight is a public good because it is not excludable and not rival in consumption. This is true even if, as an individual, I choose to buy one and put it in my front yard. Once in my front yard, I cannot charge you for standing near it, and when you do, it does not reduce my benefits from using it. Therefore, a streetlight is a public good whether I buy it or the city government buys it. Further, if the city government sets up a food stand and sells hot dogs, the hot dogs are private goods even though they are provided by the government because the hot dogs are both excludable and rival in consumption.

3. When governments use cost–benefit analysis as a tool to help them decide whether to produce a public good, we noted that it is difficult to collect data on the true benefits that people would receive from a public good. This is because they have an incentive to exaggerate their benefit if they would use the public good and underreport their benefit if they don't plan to use the public good very much. This is sometimes called the *liars problem*.

Terms and Definitions

Choose a definition for each key term.

Key Terms

_____ Excludability

_____ Rivalry in consumption

_____ Private goods

_____ Public goods

_____ Common resources

_____ Club goods

_____ Free rider

_____ Cost–benefit analysis

_____ Tragedy of the Commons

Definitions

1. Goods that are both excludable and rival in consumption

2. The property of a good whereby one person's use diminishes other people's use

3. A person who receives the benefit of a good but avoids paying for it

4. A study that compares the costs and benefits to society of providing a public good

5. Goods that are rival in consumption but not excludable

6. The property of a good whereby a person can be prevented from using it

7. A parable that illustrates why common resources get used more than is desirable from the standpoint of society as a whole

8. Goods that are neither excludable nor rival in consumption

9. Goods that are excludable but not rival in consumption

Problems and Short-Answer Questions

Practice Problems

1. Consider the rivalry in consumption and excludability of each of the following goods. Use this information to determine whether the goods are public goods, private goods, common resources, or club goods. Explain.

   a. Fish in a private pond

   _____

   _____

   b. Fish in the ocean

   _____

   _____

   c. Broadcast television signals

   _____

   _____

   d. Cable television signals

   _____

   _____

   e. Basic research on lifestyle and cholesterol levels

   _____

   _____

   f. Specific research on a cholesterol-lowering drug for which a patent can be obtained

   _____

   _____

   g. An uncongested highway (no tolls)

   _____

   _____

   h. A congested highway (no tolls)

   _____

   _____

   i. An uncongested toll road

   _____

   _____

j.   A hot dog served at a private party

_____

_____

k.   A hot dog sold at a stand owned by the city government

_____

_____

2.   Suppose the city of Roadville is debating whether to build a new highway from its airport to the downtown area. The city surveys its citizens and finds that, on average, each of the one million residents values the new highway at a value of $50 and the highway costs $40 million to construct.

a.   Assuming the survey was accurate, is building a new highway efficient? Why or why not?

_____

_____

b.   Under what conditions would private industry build the road?

_____

_____

c.   Is it likely that private industry will build the road? Why or why not?

_____

_____

_____

d.   Should the city build the road? On average, how much should it increase each resident's tax bill to pay for the road?

_____

_____

e.   Is it certain that building the highway is efficient? That is, what are the problems associated with using cost–benefit analysis as a tool for deciding whether to provide a public good?

_____

_____

_____

Short-Answer Questions

1.   What does it mean to say that a good is excludable?

_____

_____

2. Why is it difficult for private industry to provide public goods?

_____

_____

3. How is a streetlight (a public good) related to a positive externality?

_____

_____

4. Suppose the value of a human life is $10 million. Suppose the use of airbags in cars reduces the probability of dying in a car accident over one's lifetime from 0.2 percent to 0.1 percent. Further, suppose that a lifetime supply of airbags will cost the average consumer $12,000. If these numbers were accurate, would it be efficient for the government to require airbags in cars? Why or why not?

_____

_____

5. What type of problem are hunting and fishing licenses intended to relieve? Explain.

_____

_____

6. How are fish in the ocean (a common resource) related to a negative externality?

_____

_____

_____

7. How can the establishment of individual property rights eliminate the problems associated with a common resource?

_____

_____

8. Food is more important than roads to the public, yet the government provides roads for the public and rarely provides food. Why?

_____

_____

_____

9. Why did buffalo almost become extinct while cows (a similar animal) are unlikely to ever become extinct?

_____

_____

10. Were the buffalo hunters who almost made the buffalo extinct behaving irrationally? Explain.

_____

_____

_____

Self-Test

True/False Questions

_____ 1. A public good is both rival in consumption and excludable.

_____ 2. A common resource is neither rival in consumption nor excludable.

_____ 3. An apple sold in a grocery store is a private good.

_____ 4. Club goods are free to the consumer of the good.

_____ 5. Private markets have difficulty providing public goods due to the free-rider problem.

_____ 6. If the city government sells apples at a roadside stand, the apples are public goods because they are provided by the government.

_____ 7. Public goods are related to positive externalities because the potential buyers of public goods ignore the external benefits those goods provide to other consumers when they make their decision about whether to purchase public goods.

_____ 8. Common resources are overused because common resources are free to the consumer.

_____ 9. The socially optimal price for a fishing license is zero.

_____ 10. The government should continue to spend to improve the safety of our highways until there are no deaths from auto accidents.

_____ 11. Common resources are related to negative externalities because consumers of common resources ignore the negative impact of their consumption on other consumers of the common resource.

_____ 12. If someone owned the property rights to clean air, that person could charge for the use of the clean air in a market for clean air, and thus, air pollution could be reduced to the optimal level.

_____ 13. A fireworks display at a private amusement park is a good provided by a natural monopoly.

_____ 14. When the government uses cost–benefit analysis to decide whether to provide a public good, the potential benefit of the public good can easily be established by surveying the potential consumers of the public good.

_____ 15. National defense is a classic example of a common resource.

Multiple-Choice Questions

1. If one person's consumption of a good diminishes other people's use of the good, the good is said to be
   a. a common resource.
   b. a club good.
   c. rival in consumption.
   d. excludable.

2. A public good is
   a. both rival in consumption and excludable.
   b. neither rival in consumption nor excludable.
   c. rival in consumption but not excludable.
   d. not rival in consumption but excludable.

3. A private good is
   a. both rival in consumption and excludable.
   b. neither rival in consumption nor excludable.
   c. rival in consumption but not excludable.
   d. not rival in consumption but excludable.

4. A club good is
   a. both rival in consumption and excludable.
   b. neither rival in consumption nor excludable.
   c. rival in consumption but not excludable.
   d. not rival in consumption but excludable.

5. A common resource is
   a. both rival in consumption and excludable.
   b. neither rival in consumption nor excludable.
   c. rival in consumption but not excludable.
   d. not rival in consumption but excludable.

6. Public goods are difficult for a private market to provide due to
   a. the public goods problem.
   b. the rivalness problem.
   c. the Tragedy of the Commons.
   d. the free-rider problem.

7. Suppose each of 20 neighbors on a street values street repairs at $3,000. The cost of the street repair is $40,000. Which of the following statements is *true*?
   a. It is not efficient to have the street repaired.
   b. It is efficient for each neighbor to pay $3,000 to repair the section of street in front of his home.
   c. It is efficient for the government to tax the residents $2,000 each and repair the road.
   d. None of the above is true.

8. A free rider is a person who
   a. receives the benefit of a good but avoids paying for it.
   b. produces a good but fails to receive payment for the good.
   c. pays for a good but fails to receive any benefit from the good.
   d. fails to produce goods but is allowed to consume goods.

9. Which of the following is an example of a public good?
   a. whales in the ocean
   b. apples on a tree in a public park
   c. hot dogs at a picnic
   d. national defense

10. A positive externality affects market efficiency in a manner similar to a
    a. private good.
    b. public good.
    c. common resource.
    d. rival good.

11. Suppose that requiring motorcycle riders to wear helmets reduces the probability of a motorcycle fatality from 0.3 percent to 0.2 percent over the lifetime of a motorcycle rider and that the cost of a lifetime supply of helmets is $500. It is efficient for the government to require riders to wear helmets if human life is valued at
    a. $100 or more.
    b. $150 or more.
    c. $500 or more.
    d. $50,000 or more.
    e. $500,000 or more.

12. A negative externality affects market efficiency in a manner similar to
    a. a private good.
    b. a public good.
    c. a common resource.
    d. an excludable good.

13. When governments employ cost–benefit analysis to help them decide whether to provide a public good, measuring benefits is difficult because
    a. one can never place a value on human life or the environment.
    b. respondents to questionnaires have little incentive to tell the truth.
    c. there are no benefits to the public because a public good is not excludable.
    d. the benefits are infinite because a public good is not rival in consumption and an infinite amount of people can consume it at the same time.

14. Which of the following is an example of a common resource?
    a. a national park
    b. a fireworks display
    c. national defense
    d. iron ore

15. The Tragedy of the Commons is a parable that illustrates why
    a. public goods are underproduced.
    b. private goods are underconsumed.
    c. common resources are overconsumed.
    d. club goods are overconsumed.

16. Which of the following are potential solutions to the problem of air pollution?
    a. auction off pollution permits
    b. grant rights of the clean air to citizens so that firms must purchase the right to pollute
    c. regulate the amount of pollutants that firms can put in the air
    d. all of the above

17. When markets fail to allocate resources efficiently, the ultimate source of the problem is usually
    a. that prices are not high enough so people overconsume.
    b. that prices are not low enough so firms overproduce.
    c. that property rights have not been well established.
    d. government regulation.

18. If a person can be prevented from using a good, the good is said to be
    a. a common resource.
    b. a public good.
    c. rival in consumption.
    d. excludable.

19. A congested toll road is
    a. a private good.
    b. a public good.
    c. a common resource.
    d. a club good.

20. A person who regularly watches public television but fails to contribute to public television's fundraising drives is known as
    a. a common rider.
    b. a costly rider.
    c. a free rider.
    d. an unwelcome rider.
    e. excess baggage.

Advanced Critical Thinking

Broadcast television and broadcast radio send out signals that can be received by an infinite number of receivers without reducing the quality of the reception of other consumers of the signal and it is not possible to charge any of the consumers of the signal.

1. What type of good (private, public, common resource, club good) is a broadcast television or broadcast radio signal? Explain.

   _____

   _____

   _____

2. Is this type of good normally provided by private industry? Why or why not?

   _____

   _____

   _____

3. Private companies have been providing broadcast television and radio since the invention of the medium. How do they make it profitable if they cannot charge the recipient of the signal?

   _____

   _____

   _____

4. What are the "recent" alternatives to traditional commercial television and commercial radio?

   _____

   _____

5. What type of good (private, public, common resource, club good) is this newer type of television and music provision?

   _____

   _____

Solutions

Terms and Definitions

<u>6</u> Excludability
<u>2</u> Rivalry in consumption
<u>1</u> Private goods
<u>8</u> Public goods
<u>5</u> Common resources
<u>9</u> Club good
<u>3</u> Free rider
<u>4</u> Cost–benefit analysis
<u>7</u> Tragedy of the Commons

Practice Problems

1. a. Rival in consumption and excludable, private good. Only one can eat a fish. Because it is private, nonpayers can be excluded from fishing.

   b. Rival in consumption but not excludable, common resource. Only one can eat a fish but the ocean is not privately owned, so nonpayers cannot be excluded.

   c. Not rival in consumption and not excludable, public good. Additional viewers can turn on their televisions without reducing the benefits to other consumers and nonpayers cannot be excluded.

   d. Not rival in consumption but excludable, club good. More houses can be wired without reducing the benefit to other consumers, and the cable company can exclude nonpayers.

   e. Not rival in consumption and not excludable, public good. Once discovered, additional people can benefit from the knowledge without reducing the benefit to other consumers of the knowledge, and once in the public domain, nonpayers cannot be excluded.

   f. Not rival in consumption but excludable, club good. Additional users of the knowledge could use it without reducing the benefit to other consumers; therefore, it is not rival. If a patent can be obtained, no one else can produce the anti-cholesterol pill, so it is excludable.

   g. Not rival in consumption and not excludable, public good. Additional cars can travel the road without reducing the benefit to other consumers, and the additional cars cannot be forced to pay for the road.

   h. Rival in consumption but not excludable, common resource. Additional cars reduce the benefits of current users, but they cannot be forced to pay for the use of the highway.

   i. Not rival in consumption but excludable, club good. Additional cars do not reduce the benefits to current users, but they can be excluded if they don't pay the toll.

   j. Rival in consumption but not excludable, common resource. If one eats the hot dog, another cannot.

However, once provided, partygoers cannot be charged for eating the hot dogs.

   k. Rival in consumption and excludable, private good. If one eats the hot dog, another cannot. Even though it is supplied by the government, it is being sold, so nonpayers can be excluded.

2. a. Yes, because the total benefit is $50 × 1,000,000 = $50 million while the cost is $40 million.

   b. If the road could be built as a toll road, then private industry could make the road excludable, and the project could be profitable.

   c. No. Toll roads are usually in rural areas where they can be made as limited-access roads and, therefore, excludable. It would be very difficult to make a downtown urban road limited access or excludable.

   d. Yes. $40.

   e. No. Quantifying benefits is difficult using the results from a questionnaire and respondents have little incentive to tell the truth. Therefore, those who would use the road exaggerate their benefit, and those that would rarely use it understate their benefit.

Short-Answer Questions

1. It means that those who do not pay for the good can be excluded from consuming it.

2. Because public goods are not excludable, the free-rider problem makes it unprofitable for private industry to produce public goods.

3. When people consider buying a streetlight, they fail to consider the external benefit it would provide to others and only consider their personal benefit. Thus, there is an underproduction and consumption of both public goods and goods that generate positive externalities.

4. No, because the expected benefit from airbags is $(0.2 - 0.1) × $10,000,000 = $10,000$ while the cost is $12,000.

5. The overconsumption of common resources. Because common resources are free, people use them excessively. Selling a limited number of hunting or fishing licenses restricts the number of users.

6. A common resource is free so it is overconsumed. Each consumer of fish fails to take into account the negative impact on others of their consumption causing overuse of the resource from a social perspective.

7. People overuse common resources because their benefit is positive and their cost is zero. If ownership over the resource exists, the cost of using the resource is realized and a socially optimal price is generated.

8. Food is both rival in consumption and excludable, so it can be efficiently provided by the private market. Roads are often neither rival in

consumption nor excludable, so they will not be provided by private markets and may be most efficiently provided by government.

9. Buffalo were a common resource and over-consumed. Cows are private goods and are produced and sold at the socially efficient price and quantity.

10. No. Because the buffalo were a common property resource, the buffalo were free. Each hunter pursued his own best interest but failed to take into account the impact of his actions on other people.

True/False Questions

1. F; it is neither rival in consumption nor excludable.
2. F; it is rival in consumption but not excludable.
3. T
4. F; they are excludable so a price must be paid to receive them, but they are not rival in consumption, so they can be enjoyed by many at the same time.
5. T
6. F; goods are categorized as public or private based on their characteristics, not who provided them, so an apple sold to a consumer is private regardless of who provided the apple.
7. T
8. T
9. F; a positive price is optimal so that the price reduces the quantity demanded of fish to the socially optimal level.
10. F; at some point, the cost of increasing safety (reducing highway deaths) exceeds the value of a life.
11. T
12. T
13. T
14. F; quantifying benefits is difficult and respondents have little incentive to tell the truth.
15. F; national defense is an example of a public good.

Multiple-Choice Questions

1. c
2. b
3. a
4. d
5. c
6. d
7. c
8. a
9. d
10. b
11. e
12. c
13. b
14. a
15. c
16. d
17. c
18. d
19. a
20. c

Advanced Critical Thinking

1. Public good. A broadcast signal is not rival in consumption and not excludable.
2. No, because it is not profitable to produce a good for which nonpayers cannot be excluded from consuming it.
3. Broadcasters charge advertisers for the commercials they show during the broadcasters' programming. That is why it is called commercial television or commercial radio.
4. Cable television, pay-per-view television, TV shows on DVD, cable music included with cable television, and satellite radio.
5. Club good because it is not rival in consumption but is excludable.

Chapter 12

The Costs of Production

Chapter Overview

Context and Purpose

Chapter 12 is the first chapter in a three-chapter sequence dealing with firm behavior and the organization of industry. It is important that you become comfortable with the material in Chapter 12 because Chapter 13 is based on the concepts developed in Chapter 12. To be more specific, Chapter 12 develops the cost curves on which firm behavior is based. The remaining chapter in this section (Chapter 13) utilizes these cost curves to develop the behavior of firms in different market structures—competitive and monopolistic.

The purpose of Chapter 12 is to address the costs of production and develop the firm's cost curves. These cost curves underlie the firm's supply curve. In previous chapters, we summarized the firm's production decisions by starting with the supply curve. Although this is suitable for answering many questions, it is now necessary to address the costs that underlie the supply curve in order to address the part of economics known as *industrial organization*—the study of how firms' decisions about prices and quantities depend on the market conditions they face.

Chapter Review

Introduction   In previous chapters, we summarized the firm's production decisions by starting with the supply curve. Although this is suitable for answering many questions, it is now necessary to address the costs that underlie the supply curve in order to address the part of economics known as *industrial organization*—the study of how firms' decisions about prices and quantities depend on the market conditions they face.

What Are Costs?

Economists generally assume that the goal of a firm is to maximize profits.

Profit = total revenue − total cost.

Total revenue is the quantity of output the firm produces times the price at which it sells the output. Total cost is more complex. An economist considers the firm's cost of production to include all of the opportunity costs of producing its output. The total opportunity cost of production is the sum of the explicit and implicit costs of production. Explicit costs are input costs that require an outlay of money by the firm, such as when money flows out of a firm to pay for raw materials, workers' wages, rent, and so on. Implicit costs are input costs that do not require an outlay of money by the firm. Implicit costs include the value of the income forgone by the owner of the firm had the owner worked for someone else plus the forgone interest on the financial capital that the owner invested in the firm.

Accountants are usually only concerned with the firm's flow of money, so they record only explicit costs. Economists are concerned with the firm's decision making, so they are concerned with total opportunity costs, which are the sum of explicit costs and implicit costs. Because accountants and economists view costs differently, they view profits differently:

- Economic profit = total revenue − (explicit costs + implicit costs)
- Accounting profit = total revenue − explicit costs

Because an accountant ignores implicit costs, accounting profit is greater than economic profit. A firm's decision about supplying goods and services is motivated by *economic* profits.

Production and Costs

For the following discussion, we assume that the size of the production facility (factory) is fixed in the short run. Therefore, this analysis describes production decisions in the short run.

A firm's costs reflect its production process. A production function shows the relationship between the quantity of inputs used to make a good (horizontal axis) and the quantity of output of that good (vertical axis). The marginal product of any input is the increase in output that arises from an additional unit of that input. The marginal product of an input can be measured as the slope of the production function or "rise over run." Production functions exhibit diminishing marginal product—the property whereby the marginal product of an input declines as the quantity of the input increases. Hence, the slope of a production function gets flatter as more and more inputs are added to the production process.

The *total-cost curve* shows the relationship between the quantity of output produced and the total cost of production. Because the production process exhibits diminishing marginal product, the quantity of inputs necessary to produce equal increments of output rises as we produce more output, and thus, the total-cost curve rises at an increasing rate or gets steeper as the amount produced increases.

The Various Measures of Cost

Several measures of cost can be derived from data on the firm's total cost. Costs can be divided into fixed costs and variable costs. Fixed costs are costs that do not vary with the quantity of output produced—for example, rent. Variable costs are costs that do vary with the quantity of output produced—for example, expenditures on raw materials and temporary workers. The sum of fixed and variable costs equals total costs.

In order to choose the optimal amount of output to produce, the producer needs to know the cost of the typical unit of output and the cost of producing one additional unit. The cost of the typical unit of output is measured by average total cost, which is total cost divided by the quantity of output. Average total cost is the sum of average fixed cost (fixed costs divided by the quantity of output) and average variable cost (variable costs divided by the quantity of output). Marginal cost is the cost of producing one additional unit. It is measured as the increase in total costs that arises from an extra unit of production. In symbols, if Q = quantity, TC = total cost, ATC = average total cost, FC = fixed costs, AFC = average fixed costs, VC = variable costs, AVC = average variable costs, and MC = marginal cost, then:

$$ATC = TC/Q,$$

$$AVC = VC/Q,$$

$$AFC = FC/Q,$$

$$MC = \Delta TC/\Delta Q.$$

When these cost curves are plotted on a graph with cost on the vertical axis and quantity produced on the horizontal axis, these cost curves will have predictable shapes. At low levels of production, the marginal product of an extra worker is large, so the marginal cost of another unit of output is small. At high levels of production, the marginal product of a worker is small, so the marginal cost of another unit is large. Therefore, because of diminishing marginal product, the marginal-cost curve is increasing or upward sloping. The average-total-cost curve is U-shaped because at low levels of output, average total costs are high due to high average fixed costs. As output increases, average total costs fall because fixed costs are spread across additional units of output. However, at some point, diminishing returns cause an increase in average variable costs, which in turn begins to increase average costs. The efficient scale of the firm is the quantity of output that minimizes average total cost. Whenever marginal cost is less than average total cost, average total cost is falling. Whenever marginal cost is greater than average total cost, average total cost is rising. Therefore, the marginal-cost curve crosses the average-total-cost curve at the efficient scale.

To this point, we have assumed that the production function exhibits diminishing marginal product at all levels of output, and therefore, there are rising marginal costs at all levels of output. Often, however, production first exhibits increasing marginal product and decreasing marginal costs at very low levels of output as the addition of workers allows for specialization of skills. At higher levels of output, diminishing returns eventually set in and marginal costs begin to rise, causing all cost-curve relationships previously described to continue to hold. In particular:

- Marginal cost eventually rises with the quantity of output.

- The average-total-cost curve is U-shaped.

- The marginal-cost curve crosses the average-total-cost curve at the minimum of average total cost.

Costs in the Short Run and in the Long Run

The division of costs between fixed and variable depends on the time horizon. In the short run, the size of the factory is fixed, and for many firms, the only way to vary output is hiring or firing workers. In the long run, the firm can change the size of the factory, and all costs are variable. The long-run average-total-cost curve, although flatter than the short-run average-total-cost curves, is still U-shaped. For each particular factory size, there is a short-run average-total-cost curve that lies on or above the long-run average-total-cost curve. In the long run, the firm gets to choose on which short-run curve it wants to operate. In the short run, it must operate on the short-run curve it chose in the past. Some firms reach the long run faster than do others because some firms can change the size of their factory relatively easily.

At low levels of output, firms tend to have economies of scale—the property whereby long-run average total cost falls as the quantity of output increases. At high levels of output, firms tend to have diseconomies of scale—the property whereby long-run average total cost rises as the quantity of output increases. At intermediate levels of output, firms tend to have constant returns to scale—the property whereby long-run average total cost stays the same as the quantity of output changes. Economies of scale may be caused by increased *specialization* among workers as the factory gets larger while diseconomies of scale may be caused by *coordination problems* inherent in extremely large organizations. Adam Smith, 200 years ago, recognized the efficiencies captured by large factories that allowed workers to specialize in particular jobs.

Conclusion

This chapter developed a typical firm's cost curves. These cost curves will be used in the following chapters to see how firms make production and pricing decisions.

Helpful Hints

1. Because accountants and economists view costs and, thus, profits differently, it is possible for a firm that appears profitable according to an accountant to be unprofitable according to an economist. For example, suppose a firm incurs $20,000 in explicit costs to produce output that is sold for total revenue of $30,000. According to the accountant, the firm's profit is $10,000. However, suppose that the owner/ manager of the firm could have worked for another firm and earned $15,000 during this period. Although the accountant would still record the firm's profits at $30,000 − $20,000 = $10,000, the economist would argue that the firm is not profitable because the total explicit and implicit costs are $20,000 + $15,000 = $35,000, which exceeds the $30,000 of total revenue.

2. In the case of discrete numerical examples, marginal values are determined over a range of a variable rather than at a point. Therefore, when we plot a marginal value, we plot it halfway between the two end points of the range of the variable of concern. For example, if we are plotting the marginal cost of production as we move from the fifth unit to the sixth unit of production, we calculate the change in cost as we move from producing five units to producing six units, and then we plot this marginal cost as if it is for the fifth and a half unit. Notice the marginal-cost curves in your text. Each marginal-cost curve is plotted in this manner. Similarly, if we were plotting the marginal cost of production as we move from producing 50 units to producing 60 units, we would plot the marginal cost of that change in production as if it were for the 55th unit.

3. The long run is usually defined as the period of time necessary for all inputs to become variable. That is, the long run is the period of time necessary for the firm to be able to change the size of the production facility or factory. Note that this

period of time differs across industries. For example, it may take many years for all of the inputs of a railroad to become variable because the railroad tracks are quite permanent and the right-of-way for new track is difficult to obtain. However, an ice cream shop could add on to its production facility in just a matter of months. Thus, it takes longer for a railroad to reach the long run than it does for an ice cream shop.

Terms and Definitions

Choose a definition for each key term.

Key Terms		Definitions
_____ Total revenue		1. Costs that do not vary with the quantity of output produced
_____ Total cost		2. Total revenue minus total cost
_____ Profit		3. The increase in total cost that arises from an extra unit of production
_____ Explicit costs		4. The property whereby long-run average total cost falls as the quantity of output increases
_____ Implicit costs		5. The property whereby long-run average total cost stays the same as the quantity of output changes
_____ Economic profit		
_____ Accounting profit		6. Input costs that do not require an outlay of money by the firm
_____ Production function		7. The increase in output that arises from an additional unit of input
_____ Marginal product		8. The market value of the inputs a firm uses in production
_____ Diminishing marginal product		9. The property whereby long-run average total cost rises as the quantity of output increases
_____ Fixed costs		10. Fixed costs divided by the quantity of output
_____ Variable costs		11. Costs that vary with the quantity of output produced
_____ Average total cost		12. The quantity of output that minimizes average total cost
_____ Average fixed cost		13. The amount a firm receives for the sale of its output
_____ Average variable cost		14. The relationship between quantity of inputs used to make a good and the quantity of output of that good
_____ Marginal cost		
_____ Efficient scale		15. Variable costs divided by the quantity of output
_____ Economies of scale		16. Total cost divided by the quantity of output
_____ Diseconomies of scale		17. The property whereby the marginal product of an input declines as the quantity of the input increases
_____ Constant returns to scale		18. Total revenue minus total cost, including both explicit and implicit costs
		19. Total revenue minus total explicit cost
		20. Input costs that require an outlay of money by the firm

Problems and Short-Answer Questions

Practice Problems

1. Joe runs a small boat factory. He can make ten boats per year and sell them for $35,000 each. It costs Joe $250,000 for the raw materials (fiberglass, wood, paint, and so on) to build the ten boats. Joe has invested $500,000 in the factory and equipment needed to produce the boats: $200,000 from his own savings and $300,000 borrowed at 10 percent interest (assume that Joe could have loaned his money out at 10 percent, too). Joe can work at a competing boat factory for $60,000 per year.

    a.   What is the total revenue Joe can earn in a year?

    _____

    _____

    b.   What are the explicit costs Joe incurs while producing ten boats?

    _____

    _____

    c.   What are the total opportunity costs of producing ten boats (explicit and implicit)?

    _____

    _____

    d.   What is the value of Joe's accounting profit?

    _____

    _____

    e.   What is the value of Joe's economic profit?

    _____

    _____

    f.   Is it truly profitable for Joe to operate his boat factory? Explain.

    _____

    _____

    _____

    _____

    _____

    _____

2. a. Complete the following table. It describes the production and cost of hamburgers at a roadside stand. All figures are measured per hour.

Number of Workers	Output	Marginal Product of Labor	Cost of Factory	Cost of Workers	Total Cost
0	0		$25	$0	_____
		_____			
1	6		25	5	_____
		_____			
2	11		25	10	_____
		_____			
3	15		25	15	_____
		_____			
4	18		25	20	_____
		_____			
5	20		25	25	_____

b. Plot the production function in Exhibit 1.

c. What happens to the marginal product of labor as more workers are added to the production facility? Why? Use this information about the marginal product of labor to explain the slope of the production function you plotted above.

_____

_____

_____

d. Plot the total-cost curve in Exhibit 2.

e. Explain the shape of the total-cost curve.

_____

_____

_____

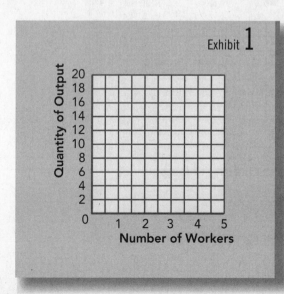

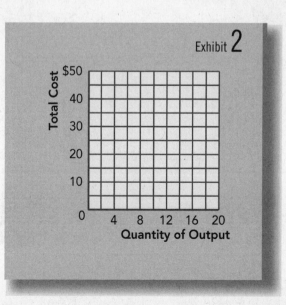

3. a. The information below is for Barbara's blue jeans manufacturing plant. All data are per hour. Complete the table. Note the following abbreviations: *FC* (fixed cost), *VC* (variable cost), *TC* (total cost), *AFC* (average fixed cost), *AVC* (average variable cost), *ATC* (average total cost), *MC* (marginal cost).

Quantity	FC	VC	TC	AFC	AVC	ATC	MC
0	$16	$0	___	___	___	___	
							___
1	16	18	___	___	___	___	
							___
2	16	31	___	___	___	___	
							___
3	16	41	___	___	___	___	
							___
4	16	49	___	___	___	___	
							___
5	16	59	___	___	___	___	
							___
6	16	72	___	___	___	___	
							___
7	16	90	___	___	___	___	
							___
8	16	114	___	___	___	___	
							___
9	16	145	___	___	___	___	
							___
10	16	184	___	___	___	___	

b. Plot AFC, AVC, ATC, and MC in Exhibit 3. (Note: Read Helpful Hint 2 above before plotting MC).

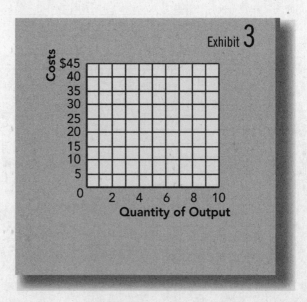

Exhibit 3

c.   Explain the shape of each of the curves you plotted in part *b* above.

_____

_____

_____

_____

_____

d.   Explain the relationship between *ATC* and *MC*.

_____

_____

_____

e.   Explain the relationship among *ATC, AFC,* and *AVC*.

_____

f.   What is Barbara's efficient scale? How do you find the efficient scale? Explain.

_____

_____

_____

Short-Answer Questions

1.   What is profit?

_____

_____

2.   How does economic profit differ from accounting profit?

_____

_____

_____

3. Suppose you own and operate your own business. Furthermore, suppose that interest rates rise and another firm offers you a job paying twice what you thought you were worth in the labor market. What has happened to your accounting profit? What has happened to your economic profit? Are you more or less likely to continue to operate your own firm?

_____

_____

_____

_____

4. Explain the relationship between the production function and the total-cost curve.

_____

_____

_____

_____

5. Is the salary of management in a firm a fixed cost or a variable cost? Why?

_____

_____

_____

_____

6. What is the efficient scale of a firm?

_____

_____

_____

7. Explain the relationship between marginal cost and average total cost.

_____

_____

_____

_____

8. What is the shape of the marginal-cost curve in the typical firm? Why is it shaped this way?

_____

_____

_____

_____

9. If a firm is operating in the area of constant returns to scale, what will happen to average total costs in the short run if the firm expands production? Why? What will happen to average total costs in the long run? Why?

_____

_____

_____

_____

10. When a small firm expands the scale of its operation, why does it usually first experience increasing returns to scale? When the same firm grows to be extremely large, why might a further expansion of the scale of operation generate decreasing returns to scale?

_____

_____

_____

_____

Self-Test

True/False Questions

_____ 1. Total revenue equals the quantity of output the firm produces times the price at which it sells its output.

_____ 2. Wages and salaries paid to workers are an example of implicit costs of production.

_____ 3. If total revenue is $100, explicit costs are $50, and implicit costs are $30, then accounting profit equals $50.

_____ 4. If there are implicit costs of production, accounting profits will exceed economic profits.

_____ 5. When a production function gets flatter, the marginal product is increasing.

_____ 6. If a firm continues to employ more workers within the same size factory, it will eventually experience diminishing marginal product.

_____ 7. If the production function for a firm exhibits diminishing marginal product, the corresponding total-cost curve for the firm will become flatter as the quantity of output expands.

_____ 8. Fixed costs plus variable costs equal total costs.

_____ 9. Average total costs are total costs divided by marginal costs.

_____ 10. When marginal costs are below average total costs, average total costs must be falling.

_____ 11. If, as the quantity produced increases, a production function first exhibits increasing marginal product and later diminishing marginal product, the corresponding marginal-cost curve will be U-shaped.

_____ 12. The average-total-cost curve crosses the marginal-cost curve at the minimum of the marginal-cost curve.

_____ 13. The average-total-cost curve in the long run is flatter than the average-total-cost curve in the short run.

_____ 14. The efficient scale for a firm is the quantity of output that minimizes marginal cost.

_____ 15. In the long run, as a firm expands its production facilities, it generally first experiences diseconomies of scale, then constant returns to scale, and finally economies of scale.

Multiple-Choice Questions

1. Accounting profit is equal to total revenue minus
   a. implicit costs.
   b. explicit costs.
   c. the sum of implicit and explicit costs.
   d. marginal costs.
   e. variable costs.

2. Economic profit is equal to total revenue minus
   a. implicit costs.
   b. explicit costs.
   c. the sum of implicit and explicit costs.
   d. marginal costs.
   e. variable costs.

Use the following information to answer questions 3 and 4. Madelyn owns a small pottery factory. She can make 1,000 pieces of pottery per year and sell them for $1.00 each. It costs Madelyn $20,000 for the raw materials to produce the 1,000 pieces of pottery. She has invested $100,000 in her factory and equipment: $50,000 from her savings and $50,000 borrowed at 10 percent (assume that she could have loaned her money out at 10 percent, too). Madelyn can work at a competing pottery factory for $40,000 per year.

3. The accounting profit at Madelyn's pottery factory is
   a. $30,000.
   b. $35,000.
   c. $70,000.
   d. $75,000.
   e. $80,000.

4. The economic profit at Madelyn's pottery factory is
   a. $30,000.
   b. $35,000.
   c. $70,000.
   d. $75,000.
   e. $80,000.

5. If there are implicit costs of production,
   a. economic profit will exceed accounting profit.
   b. accounting profit will exceed economic profit.
   c. economic profit and accounting profit will be equal.
   d. economic profit will always be zero.
   e. accounting profit will always be zero.

6. If a production function exhibits diminishing marginal product, its slope
   a. becomes flatter as the quantity of the input increases.
   b. becomes steeper as the quantity of the input increases.
   c. is linear (a straight line).
   d. could be any of the above.

7. If a production function exhibits diminishing marginal product, the slope of the corresponding total-cost curve
   a. becomes flatter as the quantity of output increases.
   b. becomes steeper as the quantity of output increases.
   c. is linear (a straight line).
   d. could be any of the above.

Use the following information to answer questions 8 and 9.

Number of Workers	Output
0	0
1	23
2	40
3	50

8. The marginal product of labor as production moves from employing one worker to employing two workers is
   a. 0.
   b. 10.
   c. 17.
   d. 23.
   e. 40.

9. The production process described above exhibits
   a. constant marginal product of labor.
   b. increasing marginal product of labor.
   c. diminishing marginal product of labor.
   d. increasing returns to scale.
   e. decreasing returns to scale.

10. Which of the following is a variable cost in the short run?
   a. wages paid to factory labor
   b. payment on the lease for factory equipment
   c. rent on the factory
   d. interest payments on borrowed financial capital
   e. salaries paid to upper management

Use the following information to answer questions 11 through 14.

Quantity of Output	Fixed Costs	Variable Costs	Total Costs	Marginal Costs
0	$10	$0	_____	
				_____
1	10	5	_____	
				_____
2	10	11	_____	
				_____
3	10	18	_____	
				_____
4	10	26	_____	
				_____
5	10	36	_____	

11. The average fixed cost of producing four units is
    a. $26.
    b. $10.
    c. $5.
    d. $2.50.
    e. none of the above.

12. The average total cost of producing three units is
    a. $3.33.
    b. $6.
    c. $9.33.
    d. $18.
    e. $28.

13. The marginal cost of changing production from three units to four units is
    a. $5.
    b. $6.
    c. $7.
    d. $8.
    e. $9.

14. The efficient scale of production is
    a. one unit.
    b. two units.
    c. three units.
    d. four units.
    e. five units.

15. When marginal costs are below average total costs,
    a. average fixed costs are rising.
    b. average total costs are falling.
    c. average total costs are rising.
    d. average total costs are minimized.

16. If marginal costs equal average total costs,
    a. average total costs are rising.
    b. average total costs are falling.
    c. average total costs are minimized.
    d. average total costs are maximized.

17. If, as the quantity produced increases, a production function first exhibits increasing marginal product and later diminishing marginal product, the corresponding marginal-cost curve will
    a. slope upward.
    b. be U-shaped.
    c. slope downward.
    d. be flat (horizontal).

18. In the long run, if a very small factory were to expand its scale of operations, it is likely that it would initially experience
    a. economies of scale.
    b. constant returns to scale.
    c. diseconomies of scale.
    d. an increase in average total costs.

19. The efficient scale of production is the quantity of output that minimizes
    a. average total cost.
    b. marginal cost.
    c. average fixed cost.
    d. average variable cost.

20. Which of the following statements is *true?*
    a. All costs are fixed in the long run.
    b. All costs are variable in the long run.
    c. All costs are fixed in the short run.
    d. All costs are variable in the short run.

Advanced Critical Thinking

Your friend has a large garden and grows fresh fruit and vegetables to be sold at a local "farmer's market." Your friend comments, "I hired a college student who was on summer vacation to help me this summer, and my production more than doubled. Next summer, I think I'll hire two or maybe three helpers, and my output should go up more than three- or fourfold."

1. If all production processes eventually exhibit diminishing marginal product of the variable inputs, could it be true that your friend hired a helper (doubled the labor) and more than doubled his production? Why or why not?

   _____

   _____

   _____

   _____

2. Is it likely that he could hire more workers and continue to reap greater than proportional increases in production? Why or why not?

   _____

   _____

   _____

   _____

   _____

3. In the long run, what must your friend do to the scale of his operation if he wants to continue to hire workers and have those workers generate proportional increases in production? Explain. Even in the long run, could your friend expand his scale of operation forever and continue to keep average total costs at a minimum? Explain.

_____

_____

_____

_____

_____

_____

_____

_____

Solutions

Terms and Definitions

<u>13</u>   Total revenue
<u>8</u>   Total cost
<u>2</u>   Profit
<u>20</u>   Explicit costs
<u>6</u>   Implicit costs
<u>18</u>   Economic profit
<u>19</u>   Accounting profit
<u>14</u>   Production function
<u>7</u>   Marginal product
<u>17</u>   Diminishing marginal product
<u>1</u>   Fixed costs
<u>11</u>   Variable costs
<u>16</u>   Average total cost
<u>10</u>   Average fixed cost
<u>15</u>   Average variable cost
<u>3</u>   Marginal cost
<u>12</u>   Efficient scale
<u>4</u>   Economies of scale
<u>9</u>   Diseconomies of scale
<u>5</u>   Constant returns to scale

Practice Problems

1. a. 10 × $35,000 = $350,000
   b. $250,000 + ($300,000 × 0.10) = $280,000
   c. $250,000 + ($500,000 × 0.10) + $60,000 = $360,000
   d. $350,000 − $280,000 = $70,000
   e. $350,000 − $360,000 = −$10,000
   f. No. Joe could make $60,000 plus 10 percent interest on his $200,000 financial capital for a total of $80,000 if he worked for the competition instead of running his own factory. His factory makes an accounting profit of only $70,000 per year, so it costs him $10,000 to run his own factory (the size of the economic loss).

2. a.

Number of Workers	Output	Marginal Product of Labor	Cost of Factory	Cost of Workers	Total Cost
0	0		$25	$0	$25
		6			
1	6		25	5	30
		5			
2	11		25	10	35
		4			
3	15		25	15	40
		3			
4	18		25	20	45
		2			
5	20		25	25	50

b. See Exhibit 4.

Exhibit 4

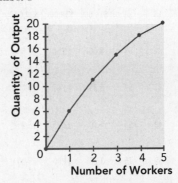

c. It diminishes because additional workers have to share the production equipment and the work area becomes more crowded. The slope of the production function is the change in output from a change in a unit of input, which is the marginal product of labor. Because it is diminishing, the slope of the production function gets flatter as a greater number of inputs are used.

d. See Exhibit 5.

Exhibit 5

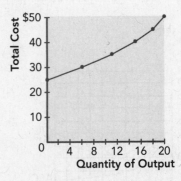

e. The total-cost curve gets steeper as the quantity produced rises due to the diminishing marginal product of labor. That is, in order to produce additional equal increments of output, the firm must employ ever greater amounts of inputs, and costs rise at an increasing rate.

3. a.

Quantity	FC	VC	TC	AFC	AVC	ATC	MC
0	$16	$0	$16	—	—	—	
							$18
1	16	18	34	$16.00	$18.00	$34.00	
							13
2	16	31	47	8.00	15.50	23.50	
							10
3	16	41	57	5.33	13.67	19.00	
							8
4	16	49	65	4.00	12.25	16.25	
							10
5	16	59	75	3.20	11.80	15.00	
							13
6	16	72	88	2.67	12.00	14.67	
							18
7	16	90	106	2.29	12.86	15.14	
							24
8	16	114	130	2.00	14.25	16.25	
							31
9	16	145	161	1.78	16.11	17.88	
							39
10	16	184	200	1.60	18.40	20.00	

b. See Exhibit 6.

Exhibit 6

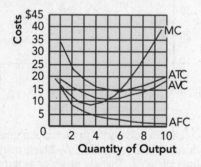

c. *AFC* declines as the quantity goes up because a fixed cost is spread across a greater number of units. *MC* declines for the first four units due to an increasing marginal product of the variable input. *MC* rises thereafter due to decreasing marginal product. *AVC* is U-shaped for the same reason as *MC*. *ATC* declines due to falling *AFC* and increasing marginal product. *ATC* rises at higher levels of production due to decreasing marginal product.

d. When *MC* is below *ATC*, *ATC* must be declining. When *MC* is above *ATC*, *ATC* must be rising. Therefore, *MC* crosses *ATC* at the minimum of *ATC*.

e. *AFC* plus *AVC* equals *ATC*.

f. Six pairs of blue jeans. Efficient scale is the output that minimizes *ATC*. It is also the place where *MC* crosses the average-total-cost curve.

Short-Answer Questions

1. Profit = total revenue – total cost.

2. Economic profit is total revenue minus explicit costs and implicit costs. Accounting profit is total revenue minus explicit costs.

3. Accounting profit is unchanged. Economic profit is reduced because implicit costs have risen—the opportunity cost of your invested money and of your time both went up. You are less likely to continue to operate your own firm because it is less profitable.

4. The total-cost curve reflects the production function. When an input exhibits diminishing marginal product, the production function gets flatter because additional increments of inputs increase output by ever smaller amounts. Correspondingly, the total-cost curve gets steeper as the amount produced rises.

5. It is a fixed cost because the salary paid to management doesn't vary with the quantity produced.

6. It is the quantity of production that minimizes average total cost.

7. When marginal cost is below average total cost, the average-total-cost curve must be falling. When marginal cost is above average total cost, the average-total-cost curve must be rising. Thus, the marginal-cost curve crosses the average-total-cost curve at the minimum of average total cost.

8. Typically, the marginal-cost curve is U-shaped. The firm often experiences increasing marginal product at very small levels of output as workers are allowed to specialize in their activities. Thus, marginal cost falls. At some point, the firm will experience diminishing marginal product, and the marginal-cost curve will begin to rise.

9. In the short run, the size of the production facility is fixed, so the firm will experience diminishing returns and increasing average total costs when adding additional workers. In the long run, the firm will expand the size of the factory and the number of workers together, and if the firm experiences constant returns to scale, average total costs will remain fixed at the minimum.

10. As a small firm expands the scale of operation, the higher production level allows for greater specialization of the workers and long-run average total costs fall. As an enormous firm continues to expand, it will likely develop coordination problems and long-run average total costs begin to increase.

True/False Questions

1. T

2. F; wages and salaries are explicit costs of production because dollars flow out of the firm.
3. T
4. T
5. F; marginal product is the slope of the production function, so marginal product is decreasing when the production function gets flatter.
6. T
7. F; diminishing marginal product means that it requires ever greater amounts of an input to produce equal increments of output so total costs rise at an increasing rate.
8. T
9. F; average total costs are total costs divided by the quantity of output.
10. T
11. T
12. F; the marginal-cost curve crosses the average-total-cost curve at the minimum of the average-total-cost curve.
13. T
14. F; efficient scale minimizes average total costs.
15. F; a firm generally experiences economies of scale, constant returns to scale, and diseconomies of scale as the scale of production expands.

Multiple-Choice Questions

1. b
2. c
3. d
4. a
5. b
6. a
7. b
8. c
9. c
10. a
11. d
12. c
13. d
14. d
15. b
16. c
17. b
18. a
19. a
20. b

Advanced Critical Thinking

1. Yes. Many production processes first exhibit increasing marginal product of the variable inputs (in this case, workers). This result may occur due to specialization of labor. After the second worker is hired, one worker specializes in weeding while the other specializes in watering.

2. No. At some point, if any input is fixed (say, the size of the garden), the firm will experience diminishing marginal product of the variable inputs. That is, at some point, the garden will become crowded, and additional workers will add smaller and smaller amounts to output.

3. It is likely that the garden is small enough that the firm would experience economies of scale if it increased its scale of operation by expanding the size of the garden and hiring more workers. No, your friend cannot expand his scale of operation forever because, at some point, the firm becomes so large that it develops coordination problems and the firm experiences diseconomies of scale.

Chapter 13

Firms in Competitive Markets

Goals
In this chapter you will

- Learn what characteristics make a market competitive

- Examine how competitive firms decide how much output to produce

- Examine how competitive firms decide when to shut down production temporarily

- Examine how competitive firms decide whether to exit or enter a market

- See how firm behavior determines a market's short-run and long-run supply curves

Outcomes
After accomplishing these goals, you should be able to

- List up to three conditions that characterize a competitive market

- Locate the supply curve for a competitive firm on a graph of its cost curves

- Demonstrate why firms temporarily shut down if the price they receive for their output is less than average variable cost

- Demonstrate why firms exit a market permanently if the price they receive for their output is less than average total cost

- Show why the long-run supply curve in a competitive market is more elastic than the short-run supply curve

Chapter Overview

Context and Purpose

Chapter 13 is the second chapter in a three-chapter sequence dealing with firm behavior and the organization of industry. Chapter 12 developed the cost curves on which firm behavior is based.

203

These cost curves are employed in Chapter 13 to show how a competitive firm responds to changes in market conditions. Chapter 14 will employ these cost curves to see how firms with market power (monopolistic) respond to changes in market conditions.

The purpose of Chapter 13 is to examine the behavior of competitive firms—firms that do not have market power. The cost curves developed in the previous chapter shed light on the decisions that lie behind the supply curve in a competitive market.

Chapter Review

Introduction In this chapter, we examine the behavior of competitive firms—firms that do not have *market power*. Firms that have market power can influence the market price of the goods they sell. The cost curves developed in the previous chapter shed light on the decisions that lie behind the supply curve in a competitive market.

What Is a Competitive Market?

A competitive market has two main characteristics:

- There are many buyers and sellers in the market.

- The goods offered for sale are largely the same.

The result of these two conditions is that each buyer and seller is a *price taker*. A third condition sometimes thought to characterize perfectly competitive markets is:

- Firms can freely enter or exit the market.

Firms in competitive markets try to maximize profit, which equals total revenue minus total cost. Total revenue (TR) is $P \times Q$. Because a competitive firm is small compared to the market, it takes the price as given. Thus, total revenue is proportional to the amount of output sold—doubling output sold doubles total revenue.

Average revenue (AR) equals total revenue (TR) divided by the quantity of output (Q) or $AR = TR/Q$. Because $TR = P \times Q$, then $AR = (P \times Q) / Q = P$. That is, for all firms, *average revenue equals the price of the good.*

Marginal revenue (MR) equals the change in total revenue from the sale of an additional unit of output or $MR = \Delta TR/\Delta Q$. When Q rises by one unit, total revenue rises by P dollars. Therefore, for competitive firms, *marginal revenue equals the price of the good.*

Profit Maximization and the Competitive Firm's Supply Curve

Firms maximize profit by comparing marginal revenue and marginal cost. For the competitive firm, marginal revenue is fixed at the price of the good and marginal cost is increasing as output rises. There are three general rules for profit maximization:

- If marginal revenue exceeds marginal cost, the firm should increase output to increase profit.

- If marginal cost exceeds marginal revenue, the firm should decrease output to increase profit.

- At the profit-maximizing level of output, marginal revenue and marginal cost are exactly equal.

Assume that we have a firm with typical cost curves. Graphically, marginal cost (MC) is upward sloping, average total cost (ATC) is U-shaped, and MC crosses ATC at the minimum of ATC. If we draw $P = AR = MR$ on this graph, we can see that the firm will choose to produce a quantity that will maximize profit based on the intersection of MR and MC. That is, the firm will choose to produce the quantity where $MR = MC$. At any quantity lower than the optimal quantity, $MR > MC$ and profit is increased if output is increased. At any quantity above the optimal quantity, $MC > MR$ and profit is increased if output is reduced.

If the price were to increase, the firm would respond by increasing production to the point where the new higher $P = AR = MR$ is equal to MC. That is, the firm moves up its MC curve until $MR = MC$ again. Therefore, *because the firm's marginal-cost curve determines how much the firm is willing to supply at any price, it is the competitive firm's supply curve.*

A firm will temporarily *shut down* (produce nothing) *if the revenue that it would get from producing is less than the variable costs (VC) of production.* Examples of temporary shutdowns are farmers leaving land idle for a season and restaurants closing for lunch. For the temporary shutdown decision, the firm ignores fixed costs because these are considered to be sunk costs, or costs that are not recoverable because the firm must pay them whether they produce output or not. Mathematically, the firm should temporarily shut down if $TR < VC$. Divide by Q and get $TR/Q < VC/Q$, which is $AR = MR = P < AVC$. That is, the firm should shut down if $P < AVC$. Therefore, *the competitive firm's short-run supply curve is the portion of its marginal-cost curve that lies above the average-variable-cost curve.*

In general, beyond the example of a competitive firm, all rational decision makers think at the margin and ignore sunk costs when making economic decisions. Rational decision makers undertake activities where the marginal benefit exceeds the marginal cost.

In the long run, a firm will *exit the market* (permanently cease operations) *if the revenue it would get from producing is less than its total costs.* If the firm exits the industry, it avoids both its fixed and variable costs, or total costs. Mathematically, the firm should exit if $TR < TC$. Divide by Q and get $TR/Q = TC/Q$, which is $AR = MR = P < ATC$. That is, the firm should exit if $P < ATC$. Therefore, *the competitive firm's long-run supply curve is the portion of its marginal-cost curve that lies above the average-total-cost curve.*

A competitive firm's profit = $TR - TC$. Divide and multiply by Q and get profit = $(TR/Q - TC/Q) \times Q$ or profit = $(P - ATC) \times Q$. If price is above ATC, the firm is profitable. If price is below ATC, the firm generates losses and would choose in the long run to exit the market.

The Supply Curve in a Competitive Market

In the short run, the number of firms in the market is fixed because firms cannot quickly enter or exit the market. Therefore, in the short run, the market supply curve is the horizontal sum of the portion of the individual firm's marginal-cost curves that lie above their average-variable-cost curves. That is, the market supply curve is simply the sum of the quantities supplied by each firm in the market at each price. Because the individual marginal-cost curves are upward sloping, *the short-run market supply curve is also upward sloping.*

In the long run, firms are able to enter and exit the market. Suppose all firms have the same cost curves. If firms in the market are making profits, new firms will enter the market, increasing the quantity supplied and causing the price to fall until economic profits are zero. If firms in the market are making losses, some existing firms will exit the market, decreasing the quantity supplied and causing the price to rise until economic profits are zero. In the long run, *firms that remain in the market must be making zero economic profit.* Because profit = $(P - ATC) \times Q$, *profit equals zero only when $P = ATC$.* For the competitive firm, $P = MC$ and MC intersects ATC at the minimum of ATC. Thus, *in the long-run equilibrium of a competitive market with free entry and exit, firms must be operating at their efficient scale.* Also, because firms enter or exit the market if the price is above or below minimum ATC, the price always returns to the minimum of ATC for each firm, but the total quantity supplied in the market rises and falls with the number of firms. Thus, there is only one price consistent with zero profits, and *the long-run market supply curve must be horizontal* (perfectly elastic) at that price.

Competitive firms stay in business even though they are making zero economic profits in the long run. Recall that economists define total costs to include all the opportunity costs of the firm, so the zero-profit equilibrium is compensating the owners of the firm for their time and their money invested.

In the short run, an increase in demand increases the price of a good and existing firms make economic profits. In the long run, this attracts new firms to enter the market causing a corresponding increase in the market supply. This increase in supply reduces the price to its original level consistent with zero profits but the quantity sold in the market is now higher. Thus, if at present firms are earning high profits in a competitive industry, they can expect new firms to enter the market and prices and profits to fall in the future.

Although the standard case is one where the long-run market supply curve is perfectly elastic, the long-run market supply curve might be upward sloping for two reasons:

- If an input necessary for production is in limited supply, an expansion of firms in that industry will raise the costs for all existing firms and increase the price as output supplied increases.

- If firms have different costs (some are more efficient than others) in order to induce new less efficient firms to enter the market, the price must increase to cover the less efficient firm's costs. In this case, only the marginal firm earns zero economic profits while more efficient firms earn profits in the long run.

Regardless, because firms can enter and exit more easily in the long run than in the short run, *the long-run market supply curve is more elastic than the short-run market supply curve.*

Conclusion: Behind the Supply Curve

The supply decision is based on marginal analysis. Profit-maximizing firms that supply goods in competitive markets produce where marginal cost equals price equals minimum average total cost.

Helpful Hints

1. We have determined that, in the short run, the firm will produce the quantity of output where $P = MC$ as long as the price equals or exceeds average variable cost. An additional way to see the logic of this behavior is to recognize that because fixed costs must be paid regardless of the level of production, any time the firm can at least cover its variable costs, any additional revenue beyond its variable costs can be applied to its fixed costs. Therefore, in the short run, the firm loses less money than it would if it shut down if the price exceeds its average variable costs. As a result, the short-run supply curve for the firm is the portion of the marginal-cost curve that is above the average-variable-cost curve.

2. Recall that rational decision makers think at the margin. The decision rule for any action is that we should do things for which the marginal benefit exceeds the marginal cost and continue to do that thing until the marginal benefit equals the marginal cost. This decision rule translates directly to the firm's production decision in that the firm should continue to produce additional output until marginal revenue (the marginal benefit to the firm) equals marginal cost.

3. In this chapter, we derived the equation for profit as profit = $(P - ATC) \times Q$. It helps to remember that, in words, this formula says that profit simply equals the average profit per unit times the number of units sold. This holds true even in the case of losses. If the price is less than average total cost, then we have the average loss per unit times the number of units sold.

Terms and Definitions

Choose a definition for each key term.

Key Terms

_____ Price takers

_____ Competitive market

_____ Average revenue

_____ Marginal revenue

_____ Shut down

_____ Exit

_____ Sunk cost

Definitions

1. A short-run decision to temporarily cease production during a specific period of time due to current market conditions

2. A market with many buyers and sellers trading identical products so that each buyer and seller is a price taker

3. Total revenue divided by the quantity sold

4. A cost to which one is already committed and is not recoverable

5. The change in total revenue from an additional unit sold

6. Buyers and sellers in a competitive market that must accept the price that the market determines

7. A long-run decision to permanently cease production and leave the market

Problems and Short-Answer Questions

Practice Problems

1. Are the following markets likely to be perfectly competitive? Explain.
   a. The market for gasoline

   _____

   _____

   b. The market for blue jeans

   _____

   _____

   c. The market for agricultural products such as corn and beans

   _____

   _____

   d. The market for the common stock of IBM

   _____

   _____

   e. The market for electricity

   _____

   _____

   f. The market for cable television

   _____

   _____

2. a. The following table contains information about the revenues and costs for Barry's Baseball Manufacturing. All data are per hour. Complete the first group of columns that correspond to Barry's production if $P = \$3$. ($TR$ = total revenue, TC = total cost, MR = marginal revenue, MC = marginal cost.)

Q	TR, P = $3	TC	Profit	MR	MC	TR, P = $2	Profit	MR
0	_____	$1	_____			_____	_____	
				_____				_____
1	_____	$2	_____			_____	_____	
				_____	_____			_____
2	_____	$4	_____			_____	_____	
				_____	_____			_____
3	_____	$7	_____			_____	_____	
				_____	_____			_____
4	_____	$11	_____			_____	_____	
				_____	_____			_____
5	_____	$16	_____			_____	_____	

b. If the price is $3 per baseball, what is Barry's optimal level of production? What criteria did you use to determine the optimal level of production?

_____

_____

_____

c. Is $3 per baseball a long-run equilibrium price in the market for baseballs? Explain. What adjustment will take place in the market for baseballs, and what will happen to the price in the long run?

_____

_____

_____

d. Suppose the price of baseballs falls to $2. Fill out the remaining three columns of the table above. What is the profit-maximizing level of output when the price is $2 per baseball? How much profit does Barry's Baseball Manufacturing earn when the price of baseballs is $2?

_____

_____

_____

e. Is $2 per baseball a long-run equilibrium price in the market for baseballs? Explain. Why would Barry continue to produce at this level of profit?

_____

_____

_____

f. Describe the slope of the short-run supply curve for the market for baseballs. Describe the slope of the long-run supply curve in the market for baseballs.

_____

_____

_____

3. a. In Exhibit 1, show the cost curves of a representative firm in long-run equilibrium alongside the corresponding market equilibrium for an industry that has a perfectly elastic long-run market supply curve.

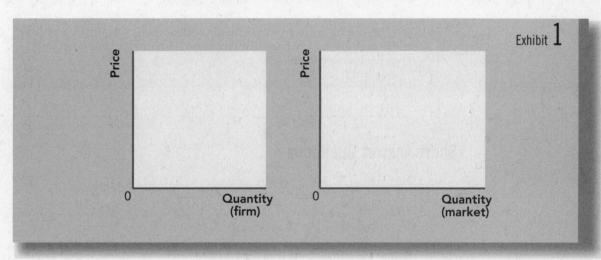

Exhibit 1

b. Suppose there is a decrease in the demand for this product. In Exhibit 2, show the shift in demand in the market for this product and the corresponding profit or loss on the cost curves of the representative firm.

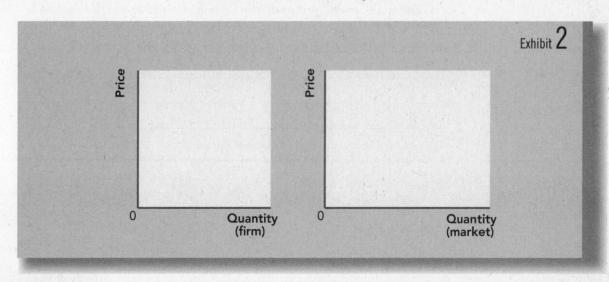

Exhibit 2

c. In Exhibit 3, show the adjustment that takes place in order to return the market and firm to long-run equilibrium.

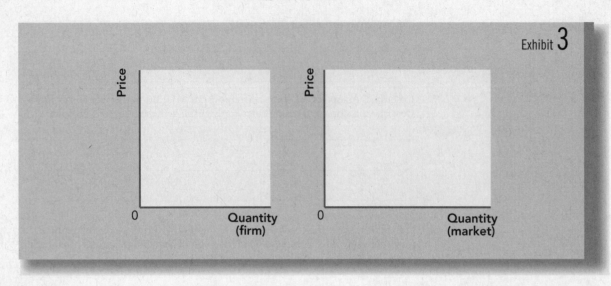

Exhibit 3

d. After the market has returned to long-run equilibrium, is the price higher, lower, or the same as the initial price? Are there more, fewer, or the same number of firms producing in the market?

_____

_____

Short-Answer Questions

1. What are the three conditions that characterize a competitive market?

_____

_____

_____

_____

2. If a firm is in a competitive market, what happens to its total revenue if it doubles its output? Why?

_____

_____

_____

_____

3. If a firm is producing a level of output where marginal revenue exceeds marginal cost, would it improve profits by increasing output, decreasing output, or keeping output unchanged? Why?

_____

_____

_____

_____

4. What constitutes a competitive firm's short-run supply curve? Explain.

_____

_____

_____

_____

5. What constitutes a competitive firm's long-run supply curve? Explain.

_____

_____

_____

_____

6. You go to your campus bookstore and see a coffee mug emblazoned with your university's shield. It costs $5, and you value it at $8, so you buy it. On the way to your car, you drop it, and it breaks into pieces. Should you buy another one or should you go home because the total expenditure of $10 now exceeds the $8 value that you place on it? Why?

_____

_____

_____

_____

7. Suppose the price for a firm's output is above the average variable cost of production but below the average total cost of production. Will the firm shut down in the short run? Explain. Will the firm exit the market in the long run? Explain.

_____

_____

_____

_____

8. Why must the long-run equilibrium in a competitive market (with free entry and exit) have all firms operating at their efficient scale?

_____

_____

_____

_____

9. Why is the short-run market supply curve upward sloping while the standard long-run market supply curve is perfectly elastic?

_____

_____

_____

_____

10. Under what conditions would the long-run market supply curve be upward sloping?

_____

_____

_____

_____

Self-Test

True/False Questions

_____ 1. The only requirement for a market to be perfectly competitive is for the market to have many buyers and sellers.

_____ 2. For a competitive firm, marginal revenue equals the price of the good it sells.

_____ 3. If a competitive firm sells three times the amount of output, its total revenue also increases by a factor of three.

_____ 4. A firm maximizes profit when it produces output up to the point where marginal cost equals marginal revenue.

_____ 5. If marginal cost exceeds marginal revenue at a firm's current level of output, the firm can increase profit if it increases its level of output.

_____ 6. A competitive firm's short-run supply curve is the portion of its marginal-cost curve that lies above its average-total-cost curve.

_____ 7. A competitive firm's long-run supply curve is the portion of its marginal-cost curve that lies above its average-variable-cost curve.

_____ 8. In the short run, if the price a firm receives for a good is above its average variable costs but below its average total costs of production, the firm will temporarily shut down.

_____ 9. In a competitive market, both buyers and sellers are price takers.

_____ 10. In the long run, if the price firms receive for their output is below their average total costs of production, some firms will exit the market.

_____ 11. In the short run, the market supply curve for a good is the sum of the quantities supplied by each firm at each price.

_____ 12. The short-run market supply curve is more elastic than the long-run market supply curve.

_____ 13. In the long run, perfectly competitive firms earn small but positive economic profits.

_____ 14. In the long run, if firms are identical and there is free entry and exit in the market, all firms in the market operate at their efficient scale.

_____ 15. If the price of a good rises above the minimum average total cost of production, positive economic profits will cause new firms to enter the market, which drives the price back down to the minimum average total cost of production.

Multiple-Choice Questions

1. Which of the following is *not* a characteristic of a competitive market?
    a. There are many buyers and sellers in the market.
    b. The goods offered for sale are largely the same.
    c. Firms can freely enter or exit the market.
    d. Firms generate small but positive economic profits in the long run.
    e. All of the above are characteristics of a competitive market.

2. Which of the following markets would most closely satisfy the requirements for a competitive market?
    a. gold bullion
    b. electricity
    c. cable television
    d. soda
    e. All of the above represent competitive markets.

3. If a competitive firm doubles its output, its total revenue
    a. more than doubles.
    b. doubles.
    c. less than doubles.
    d. cannot be determined because the price of the good may rise or fall.

4. For a competitive firm, marginal revenue is
    a. equal to the price of the good sold.
    b. average revenue divided by the quantity sold.
    c. total revenue divided by the price.
    d. equal to the quantity of the good sold.

5. The competitive firm maximizes profit when it produces output up to the point where
    a. marginal cost equals total revenue.
    b. marginal revenue equals average revenue.
    c. marginal cost equals marginal revenue.
    d. price equals average variable cost.

6. If a competitive firm is producing a level of output where marginal revenue exceeds marginal cost, the firm could increase profits if it
    a. increased production.
    b. decreased production.
    c. maintained production at the current level.
    d. temporarily shut down.

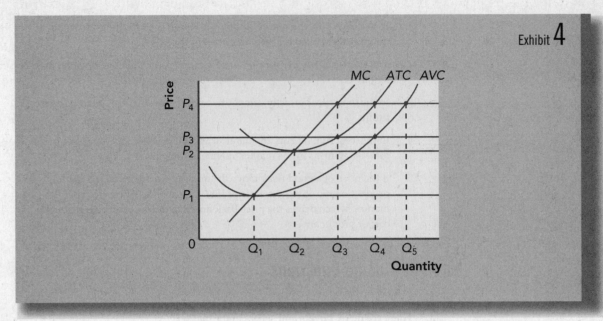

Use Exhibit 4 to answer questions 7 through 11.

7. If the price is P_4, a competitive firm will maximize profits if it produces
   a. Q_1.
   b. Q_2.
   c. Q_3.
   d. Q_4.
   e. Q_5.

8. If the price is P_4, the firm will earn profits equal to the area
   a. $(P_2 - P_1) \times Q_2$.
   b. $(P_3 - P_2) \times Q_3$.
   c. $(P_4 - P_2) \times Q_4$.
   d. $(P_4 - P_3) \times Q_3$.
   e. None of the above is correct.

9. In the short run, competitive firms will temporarily shut down production if the price falls below
   a. P_1.
   b. P_2.
   c. P_3.
   d. P_4.

10. In the long run, some competitive firms will exit the market if the price is below
    a. P_1.
    b. P_2.
    c. P_3.
    d. P_4.

11. In the long run, the competitive equilibrium is
    a. P_1, Q_1.
    b. P_2, Q_2.
    c. P_4, Q_3.
    d. P_4, Q_4.
    e. P_4, Q_5.

12. In the short run, the competitive firm's supply curve is the
    a. entire marginal-cost curve.
    b. portion of the marginal-cost curve that lies above the average-total-cost curve.
    c. portion of the marginal-cost curve that lies above the average-variable-cost curve.
    d. upward-sloping portion of the average-total-cost curve.
    e. upward-sloping portion of the average-variable-cost curve.

13. In the long run, the competitive firm's supply curve is the
    a. entire marginal-cost curve.
    b. portion of the marginal-cost curve that lies above the average-total-cost curve.
    c. portion of the marginal-cost curve that lies above the average-variable-cost curve.
    d. upward-sloping portion of the average-total-cost curve.
    e. upward-sloping portion of the average-variable-cost curve.

14. A grocery store should close at night if the
    a. total costs of staying open are greater than the total revenue due to staying open.
    b. total costs of staying open are less than the total revenue due to staying open.
    c. variable costs of staying open are greater than the total revenue due to staying open.
    d. variable costs of staying open are less than the total revenue due to staying open.

15. The long-run market supply curve
    a. is always more elastic than the short-run market supply curve.
    b. is always less elastic than the short-run market supply curve.
    c. has the same elasticity as the short-run market supply curve.
    d. is always perfectly elastic.

16. In the long run, some firms will exit the market if the price of the good offered for sale is less than
    a. marginal revenue.
    b. marginal cost.
    c. average revenue.
    d. average total cost.

17. If all firms in a market have identical cost structures and if inputs used in the production of the good in that market are readily available, then the long-run market supply curve for that good should be
    a. perfectly elastic.
    b. downward sloping.
    c. upward sloping.
    d. perfectly inelastic.

18. If an input necessary for production is in limited supply so that an expansion of the industry raises costs for all existing firms in the market, then the long-run market supply curve for a good could be
    a. perfectly elastic.
    b. downward sloping.
    c. upward sloping.
    d. perfectly inelastic.

19. If the long-run market supply curve for a good is perfectly elastic, an increase in the demand for that good will, in the long run, cause
    a. an increase in the price of the good and an increase in the number of firms in the market.
    b. an increase in the price of the good but no increase in the number of firms in the market.
    c. an increase in the number of firms in the market but no increase in the price of the good.
    d. no impact on either the price of the good or the number of firms in the market.

20. In long-run equilibrium in a competitive market, firms are operating at
    a. the minimum of their average-total-cost curves.
    b. the intersection of marginal cost and marginal revenue.
    c. their efficient scale.
    d. zero economic profit.
    e. all of the above.

Advanced Critical Thinking

In some regions of the country, it is common for Walmart stores and large supermarkets to stay open 24 hours a day, 365 days a year.

1. You walk into a Walmart store at 2:00 a.m. with a friend to buy some blank CDs. Your friend says, "I can't believe that these stores stay open all night. Only one out of fifteen checkout lines is open. There can't be more than ten shoppers in this store. It just doesn't make any sense for this store to be open all night." Explain to your friend what conditions must be true for it to be to the advantage of Walmart to stay open all night.

_____

_____

_____

_____

2. Are the costs of rent, equipment, fixtures, salaries of management, and so on relevant when Walmart makes the decision whether to stay open all night? Why or why not?

_____

_____

_____

_____

3. If Walmart had the same number of customers during its daytime hours as you observed during its nighttime hours, do you think it would continue to operate? Explain.

_____

_____

_____

_____

Solutions

Terms and Definitions

__6__ Price takers

__2__ Competitive market

__3__ Average revenue

__5__ Marginal revenue

__1__ Shut down

__7__ Exit

__4__ Sunk cost

Practice Problems

1. a. Yes, many buyers and sellers and the product of different sellers is nearly identical.

   b. Probably not, many buyers and sellers but the product is not identical (Levi's vs. Lee), so each seller is not a price taker.

   c. Yes, many buyers and sellers and the product of different sellers is identical.

   d. Yes, many buyers and sellers and the product of different sellers is identical.

   e. No, few sellers (often only one). If there were multiple sellers, the product would be identical.

   f. No, few sellers (often only one). If there were multiple sellers, the product would be nearly identical.

2. a.

Q	TR, P = $3	TC	Profit	MR	MC	TR, P = $2	Profit	MR
0	$0	$1	−$1			$0	−$1	
				$3	$1			$2
1	3	2	1			2	0	
				3	2			2
2	6	4	2			4	0	
				3	3			2
3	9	7	2			6	−1	
				3	4			2
4	12	11	1			8	−3	
				3	5			2
5	15	16	−1			10	−6	

   b. Optimal production is either two or three baseballs per hour. This level of production maximizes profit (at $2) and it is the level of output where $MC = MR$ (at $3).

   c. No, because Barry is earning positive economic profits of $2. These profits will attract new firms to enter the market for baseballs, the market supply will increase, and the price will fall until economic profits are zero.

   d. See answers for the table in part a above. Optimal production is either one or two baseballs per hour. Zero economic profit is earned by Barry.

   e. Yes. Economic profits are zero and firms neither enter nor exit the industry. Zero economic profits means that Barry doesn't earn anything beyond his opportunity costs of production but his revenues do cover the cost of his inputs and the value of his time and money.

   f. The slope of the short-run supply curve is positive because when $P = \$2$, quantity supplied is one or two units per firm and when $P = \$3$, quantity supplied is two or three units per firm. In the long run, supply is horizontal (perfectly elastic) at $P = \$2$ because any price above $2 causes firms to enter and drives the price back to $2.

3. a. See Exhibit 5.

Exhibit 5

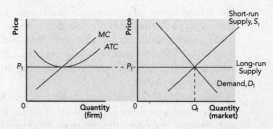

   b. See Exhibit 6.

Exhibit 6

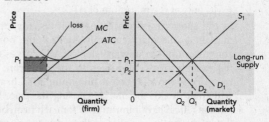

   c. See Exhibit 7.

Exhibit 7

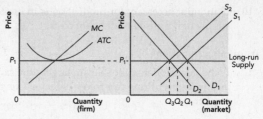

   d. The price has returned to its initial level. There are fewer firms producing in this market.

Short-Answer Questions

1. There are many buyers and sellers, the goods offered for sale are largely the same, and firms can freely enter or exit the market.

2. Total revenue doubles. This is because, in a competitive market, the price is unaffected by the amount sold by any individual firm.

3. If $MR > MC$, increasing output will increase profits because an additional unit of production increases revenue more than it increases costs.

4. It is the portion of the firm's marginal-cost curve that lies above its average-variable-cost curve because the firm maximizes profit where $P = MC$, and in the short run, fixed or sunk costs are irrelevant and the firm must only cover its variable costs.

5. It is the portion of the firm's marginal-cost curve that lies above its average-total-cost curve because the firm maximizes profit where $P = MC$, and in the long run, the firm must cover its total costs or it should exit the market.

6. You should buy another mug because the marginal benefit ($8) still exceeds the marginal cost ($5). The broken mug is a sunk cost and is not recoverable. Therefore, it is irrelevant.

7. No. In the short run, the firm's fixed costs are sunk costs so the firm will not shut down because it only needs to cover its variable costs. Yes. In the long run, the firm must cover total costs, and if $P < ATC$, the firm generates losses in the long run and it will exit the market.

8. In the long-run equilibrium, firms must be making zero economic profits so that firms are not entering or exiting the industry. Zero profits occur when $P = ATC$, and for the competitive firm $P = MC$ determines the production level. $P = ATC = MC$ only at the minimum of ATC.

9. In the short run, firms cannot exit or enter the market, so the market supply curve is the horizontal sum of the upward-sloping MC curves of the existing firms. However, in the long run, if the price is above or below minimum ATC, firms will enter or exit the market causing the price to always return to minimum ATC for each firm, but the total quantity supplied in the market rises and falls with the number of firms. Thus, the market supply curve is horizontal.

10. If an input necessary for production is in limited supply or if firms have different costs.

True/False Questions

1. F; the goods offered for sale are largely the same and (possibly) firms can freely enter or exit the market.

2. T

3. T

4. T

5. F; the firm increases profits if it reduces output.

6. F; it is the portion of the MC curve that lies above its average-variable-cost curve.

7. F; it is the portion of the MC curve that lies above its average-total-cost curve.

8. F; the firm will continue to operate in the short run as long as price exceeds average variable costs.

9. T

10. T

11. T

12. F; the long-run market supply curve is more elastic than the short-run market supply curve.

13. F; they earn zero economic profits in the long run.

14. T

15. T

Multiple-Choice Questions

1.	d	11.	b
2.	a	12.	c
3.	b	13.	b
4.	a	14.	c
5.	c	15.	a
6.	a	16.	d
7.	c	17.	a
8.	d	18.	c
9.	a	19.	c
10.	b	20.	e

Advanced Critical Thinking

1. For Walmart to stay open all night (and not undertake a temporary shutdown), it must be true that its total revenue at night must equal or exceed its variable costs incurred from staying open the additional hours (electricity, wages of night shift workers, etc.).

2. No. These costs are fixed costs or sunk costs—costs that cannot be recovered even if Walmart chooses not to operate at night.

3. It is unlikely. This is because the temporary shutdown decision (staying open additional hours at night) depends on whether total revenue equals or exceeds variable costs, but the decision to remain in the market in the long-run depends on whether total revenue equals or exceeds total costs. It is unlikely that the revenue earned at night covers total costs (both fixed and variable costs).

Chapter 14
Monopoly

- Learn why some markets have only one seller
- Analyze how a monopoly determines the quantity to produce and the price to charge
- See how the monopoly's decisions affect economic well-being
- See why monopolies try to charge different prices to different customers
- Consider the various public policies aimed at solving the problem of monopoly

- List three reasons why a monopoly can remain the sole seller of a product in a market
- Use a monopolist's cost curves and the demand curve it faces to show the profit earned by a monopolist
- Show the deadweight loss from a monopolist's production decision
- Demonstrate the surprising result that price discrimination by a monopolist can raise economic welfare above that generated by standard monopoly pricing
- Show why forcing a natural monopoly to charge its marginal cost of production creates losses for the monopolist

Chapter Overview

Context and Purpose

Chapter 14 is the third chapter in a three-chapter sequence dealing with firm behavior and the organization of industry. Chapter 12 developed the cost curves on which firm behavior is based. These cost curves were employed in Chapter 13 to show how

219

a competitive firm responds to changes in market conditions. In Chapter 14, these cost curves are again employed, this time to show how a monopolistic firm chooses the quantity to produce and the price to charge.

A monopolist is the sole seller of a product without close substitutes. As such, it has market power because it can influence the price of its output. That is, a monopolist is a price maker as opposed to a price taker. The purpose of Chapter 14 is to examine the production and pricing decisions of monopolists, the social implications of their market power, and the ways in which governments might respond to the problems caused by monopolists.

Chapter Review

Introduction   Monopolists have market power because they can influence the price of their output. That is, monopolists are *price makers* as opposed to *price takers*. While competitive firms choose to produce a quantity of output such that the given market price equals the marginal cost of production, monopolists charge prices that exceed marginal costs. In this chapter, we examine the production and pricing decisions of monopolists, the social implications of their market power, and the ways in which governments might respond to the problems caused by monopolists.

Why Monopolies Arise

A monopoly is a firm that is the sole seller of a product without close substitutes. A monopoly is able to remain the only seller in a market only if there are *barriers to entry*. That is, other firms are unable to enter the market and compete with it. There are three sources of barriers to entry:

- *Monopoly resources:* A key resource required for production is owned by a single firm. For example, if a firm owns the only well in town, it has a monopoly for the sale of water. DeBeers essentially has a monopoly in the market for diamonds because it controls 80 percent of the world's production of diamonds. This source of monopoly is somewhat rare.

- *Government created monopolies:* The government gives a single firm the exclusive right to produce some good. When the government grants patents (which last for twenty years) to inventors and copyrights to authors, it is giving someone the right to be the sole producer of that good. The benefit is that it increases incentives for creative activity. The costs will be discussed later in this chapter.

- *Natural monopolies:* The costs of production make a single producer more efficient than a large number of producers. A natural monopoly arises when a single firm can supply a good to an entire market at a smaller cost than could two or more firms. This happens when there are economies of scale over the relevant range of output. That is, the average-total-cost curve for an individual firm continually declines at least to the quantity that could supply the entire market. This cost advantage is a natural barrier to entry because firms with higher costs find it undesirable to enter the market. Common examples are utilities such as water and electricity distribution. Club goods are generally produced by natural monopolies.

How Monopolies Make Production and Pricing Decisions

A competitive firm is small relative to the market, so it takes the price of the good it produces as given. Because it can sell as much as it chooses at the given market price, the competitive firm faces a demand curve that is perfectly elastic at the market price. A monopoly is the sole producer in its market, so it faces the entire downward-sloping market demand curve. The monopolist can choose any price/quantity combination on the demand curve by choosing the quantity and seeing what price buyers will pay. As with competitive firms, monopolies choose a quantity of output that maximizes profit (total revenue minus total cost).

Because the monopolist faces a downward-sloping demand curve, it must lower the price of the good if it wishes to sell a greater quantity. Therefore, when it sells an additional unit, the sale of the additional unit has two effects on total revenue ($P \times Q$):

- The output effect: Q is higher.
- The price effect: P is lower (on the marginal unit and on the units it was already selling).

Because the monopolist must reduce the price on every unit it sells when it expands output by one unit, marginal revenue ($\Delta TR / \Delta Q$) for the monopolist declines as Q increases and marginal revenue is always less than the price of the good.

As with a competitive firm, the monopolist maximizes profit at the level of output where marginal revenue (MR) equals marginal cost (MC). As Q increases, MR decreases, and MC increases. Therefore, at low levels of output, $MR > MC$, and an increase in Q increases profit. At high levels of output, $MC > MR$, and a decrease in output increases profit. The monopolist, therefore, should produce up to the point where $MR = MC$. That is, the profit-maximizing level of output is determined by the intersection of the marginal-revenue and marginal-cost curves. Because the MR curve lies below the demand curve, the price the monopolist charges is found by reading up to the demand curve from the $MR = MC$ intersection. That is, it charges the highest price consistent with that quantity.

Recall that for the competitive firm, because the demand curve facing the firm is perfectly elastic so that $P = MR$, the profit-maximizing equilibrium requires that $P = MR = MC$. However, for the monopoly firm, $MR < P$, so the profit-maximizing equilibrium requires that $P > MR = MC$. As a result, *in competitive markets, price equals marginal cost while in monopolized markets, price exceeds marginal cost.*

Evidence from the pharmaceutical drug market is consistent with our theory. While the patent is enforced, the price of a drug is high. When the patent expires and generic drugs become available, the price falls substantially.

As with the competitive firm, profit = $(P - ATC) \times Q$, or profit equals the average profit per unit times the number of units sold.

The Welfare Cost of Monopolies

Does a monopoly market maximize economic well-being as measured by total surplus? Recall that total surplus is the sum of consumer surplus and producer surplus. Equilibrium of supply and demand in a competitive market naturally maximizes total surplus because all units are produced where the value to buyers is greater than or equal to the cost of production to the sellers.

For a monopolist to produce the socially efficient quantity (maximize total surplus by producing all units where the value to buyers exceeds or equals the cost of production), it would have to produce the level of output where the marginal-cost curve intersects the demand curve. However, the monopolist chooses to produce the level of output where the marginal-revenue curve intersects the marginal-cost curve. Because for the monopolist the marginal-revenue curve is always below the demand curve, *the monopolist produces less than the socially efficient quantity of output.*

The small quantity produced by the monopolist allows the monopolist to charge a price that exceeds the marginal cost of production. Therefore, the monopolist generates a *deadweight loss* because, at the high monopoly price, consumers fail to buy units of output where the value to them exceeds the cost to the monopolist.

The deadweight loss from a monopoly is similar to the deadweight loss from a tax, and the monopolist's profit is similar to tax revenue except that the revenue is received by a private firm. Because the profit earned by a monopolist is simply a transfer of consumer surplus to producer surplus, a monopoly's profit is not a social cost. The social cost of a monopoly is the deadweight loss generated when the monopolist produces a quantity of output below that which is efficient.

Price Discrimination

Price discrimination is the business practice of selling the same good at different prices to different customers. Price discrimination can only be practiced by a firm with market power such as a monopolist. There are three lessons to note about price discrimination:

- Price discrimination is a rational strategy for a profit-maximizing monopolist because a monopolist's profits are increased when it charges each customer a price closer to his individual willingness to pay.

- Price discrimination is only possible if the monopolist is able to separate customers according to their willingness to pay—by age, income, location, etc. If there is *arbitrage*—the process of buying a good in one market at a low price and selling it in another market at a higher price—price discrimination is not possible.

- Price discrimination can raise economic welfare because output increases beyond that which would result under monopoly pricing. However, the additional surplus (reduced deadweight loss) is received by the producer, not the consumer.

Perfect price discrimination occurs when a monopolist charges each customer her exact willingness to pay. In this case, the efficient quantity is produced and consumed and there is no deadweight loss. However, total surplus goes to the monopolist in the form of profit. In reality, perfect price discrimination cannot be accomplished. Imperfect price discrimination may raise, lower, or leave unchanged total surplus in a market.

Examples of price discrimination include movie tickets, airline tickets, discount coupons, financial aid for college tuition, quantity discounts, and tickets for Broadway shows.

Public Policy Toward Monopolies

Monopolies fail to allocate resources efficiently because they produce less than the socially optimal quantity of output and charge prices that exceed marginal cost. Policymakers can respond to the problem of monopoly in one of four ways:

- *By trying to make monopolized industries more competitive.* The Justice Department can employ antitrust laws (statutes aimed at reducing monopoly power) to prevent mergers that reduce competition, break up extremely large companies to increase competition, and prevent companies from colluding. However, some mergers result in synergies that reduce costs and raise efficiency. Therefore, it is difficult for government to know which mergers to block and which ones to allow.

- *By regulating the behavior of the monopolies.* The prices charged by natural monopolies such as utilities are often regulated by government. If a natural monopoly is required to set its price equal to its marginal cost, the efficient quantity will be consumed, but the monopoly will lose money because marginal cost must be below average variable cost if average variable cost is declining. Thus, the monopolist will exit the industry. In response, regulators can subsidize a natural monopoly with tax revenue (which creates its own deadweight loss) or allow average-total-cost pricing, which is an improvement over monopoly pricing, but it is not as efficient as marginal-cost pricing. Another problem with regulating prices is that monopolists have no incentive to reduce costs because their prices are reduced when their costs are reduced.

- *By turning some private monopolies into public enterprises.* Instead of regulating the prices charged by a natural monopoly, the government can run the monopoly itself. The Postal Service is an example. Economists generally prefer private ownership to government ownership because private owners have a greater incentive to minimize costs.

- *By doing nothing at all.* Because each of the previously listed solutions has its own shortcomings, some economists urge that monopolies be left alone. They believe that the "political failure" in the real world is more costly than the "market failure" caused by monopoly pricing.

Conclusion: The Prevalence of Monopolies

In one sense, monopolies are common because most firms have some control over the prices they charge. On the other hand, firms with substantial monopoly power are rare. Monopoly power is a matter of degree.

Helpful Hints

1. A monopolist can choose the quantity and see what price buyers will pay or can choose the price and see what quantity buyers will purchase. That is, a monopolist is still subject to the demand curve for its product. The monopolist cannot choose both a high price and a large quantity if that combination does not lie on the demand curve facing the monopolist.

2. A monopolist is not guaranteed to earn profits. Any one of us can be the monopolist in the production of gold-plated textbook covers (because there is currently no producer of such a product), but the demand for such a product is likely to be too low to cover the costs of production. In like manner, gaining a patent on a product does not guarantee the holder of the patent future profits.

Terms and Definitions

Choose a definition for each key term.

Key Terms	Definitions
_____ Monopoly	1. A monopoly that arises because a single firm can supply a good or service to an entire market at a smaller cost than could two or more firms
_____ Natural monopoly	2. A firm that is the sole seller of a product without close substitutes
_____ Price discrimination	3. A situation in which the monopolist is able to charge each customer precisely his willingness to pay
_____ Arbitrage	4. The business practice of selling the same good at different prices to different customers
_____ Perfect price discrimination	5. The process of buying a good in one market at a low price and selling it in another market at a higher price

Problems and Short-Answer Questions

Practice Problems

1. a. What are the three sources of the barriers to entry that allow a monopoly to remain the sole seller of a product?

   _____

   _____

   _____

   b. What is the entry barrier that is the source of the monopoly power for the following products or producers? List some competitors that keep these products or producers from having absolute monopoly power.
   (1) United States Postal Service

   _____

   _____

(2) Perrier Spring Water

_____

_____

(3) Prozac (a brand-name drug)

_____

_____

(4) DeBeers Diamonds

_____

_____

(5) *Principles of Economics* by N. Gregory Mankiw (your textbook)

_____

_____

(6) Edison Power Company

_____

_____

2. Suppose a firm has a patent on a special process to make a unique smoked salmon. The following table provides information about the demand facing this firm for this unique product.

Pounds of Salmon	Price	$(P \times Q)$ Total Revenue	$(\Delta TR/\Delta Q)$ Marginal Revenue
0	$20	_____	
			_____
1	18	_____	
			_____
2	16	_____	
			_____
3	14	_____	
			_____
4	12	_____	
			_____
5	10	_____	
			_____
6	8	_____	
			_____
7	6	_____	

a. Complete the table above.
b. Plot the demand curve and the marginal-revenue curve in Exhibit 1. (Read Helpful Hint 2 in Chapter 12 of this study guide for a reminder on how to plot marginal values.)

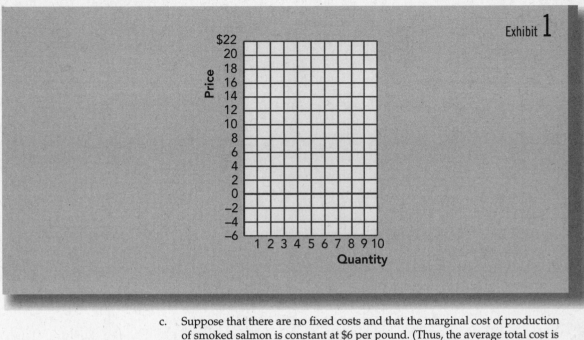

Exhibit 1

c. Suppose that there are no fixed costs and that the marginal cost of production of smoked salmon is constant at $6 per pound. (Thus, the average total cost is also constant at $6 per pound.) What is the quantity and price chosen by the monopolist? What is the profit earned by the monopolist? Show your solution on the graph you created in part *b* above.

_____

_____

_____

d. What is the price and quantity that maximizes total surplus?

_____

_____

e. Compare the monopoly solution and the efficient solution. That is, is the monopolist's price too high or too low? Is the monopolist's quantity too high or too low? Why?

_____

_____

_____

f. Is there a deadweight loss in this market if the monopolist charges the monopoly price? Explain.

_____

_____

_____

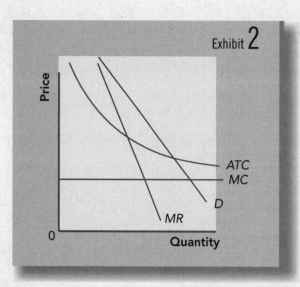

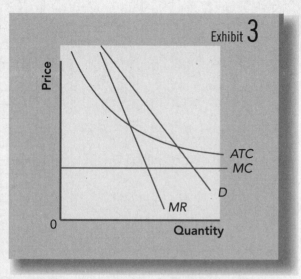

g.   If the monopolist is able to costlessly and perfectly price discriminate, is the outcome efficient? Explain. What is the value of consumer surplus, producer surplus, and total surplus? Explain.

_____

_____

_____

3.   a.   What type of market is represented in Exhibit 2: perfect competition, monopoly, or natural monopoly? Explain.

_____

_____

_____

b.   Show the profit or loss generated by this firm in Exhibit 2 assuming that the firm maximizes profit.

c.   Suppose government regulators force this firm to set the price equal to its marginal cost in order to improve efficiency in this market. In Exhibit 3, show the profit or loss generated by this firm.

d.   In the long run, will forcing this firm to charge a price equal to its marginal cost improve efficiency? Explain.

_____

_____

_____

Short-Answer Questions

1. What is a *barrier to entry?* What are the three sources of barriers to entry that allow a monopoly to remain the sole seller in a market?

_____

_____

_____

_____

_____

_____

2. If a natural monopoly is forced through regulation to charge a price equal to its marginal cost, will the outcome be efficient? Why or why not?

_____

_____

3. Does a monopolist charge the highest possible price for its output? Why or why not? How does a monopolist choose the price it will charge for its product?

_____

_____

_____

_____

4. Why does a monopolist produce less than the socially efficient quantity of output?

_____

_____

_____

5. Are the monopolist's profits part of the social cost of monopoly? Explain.

_____

_____

_____

_____

6. Is perfect price discrimination efficient? Explain. Who receives the surplus?

_____

_____

_____

_____

7. What is the necessary condition for a monopolist to be able to price discriminate?

_____

_____

_____

_____

8. What are the four ways that policymakers can respond to the problem of monopoly?

_____

_____

_____

_____

9. Should antitrust laws be utilized to stop all mergers? Why or why not?

_____

_____

_____

_____

10. What are some of the problems associated with regulating the price charged by a natural monopoly?

_____

_____

_____

Self-Test

True/False Questions

_____ 1. Monopolists are price takers.

_____ 2. The most common source of a barrier to entry into a monopolist's market is that the monopolist owns a key resource necessary for production of that good.

_____ 3. A monopoly is the sole seller of a product with no close substitutes.

_____ 4. A natural monopoly is a monopoly that uses its ownership of natural resources as a barrier to entry into its market.

_____ 5. The demand curve facing a monopolist is the market demand curve for its product.

_____ 6. For the monopolist, marginal revenue is always less than the price of the good.

_____ 7. The monopolist chooses the quantity of output at which marginal revenue equals marginal cost and then uses the demand curve to find the price that will induce consumers to buy that quantity.

_____ 8. The supply curve for a monopolist is always positively sloped.

_____ 9. A monopolist produces an efficient quantity of output, but it is still inefficient because it charges a price that exceeds marginal cost and the resulting profit is a social cost.

_____ 10. Price discrimination is only possible if there is no arbitrage.

_____ 11. Price discrimination can raise economic welfare because output increases beyond that which would result under monopoly pricing.

_____ 12. Perfect price discrimination is efficient, but all of the surplus is received by the consumer.

_____ 13. Universities are engaging in price discrimination when they charge different levels of tuition to poor and wealthy students.

_____ 14. Using regulations to force a natural monopoly to charge a price equal to its marginal cost of production will cause the monopoly to lose money and exit the industry.

_____ 15. Most economists argue that the most efficient solution to the problem of monopoly is that the monopoly should be publicly owned.

Multiple-Choice Questions

1. Which of the following is _not_ a barrier to entry in a monopolized market?
    a. The government gives a single firm the exclusive right to produce some good.
    b. The costs of production make a single producer more efficient than a large number of producers.
    c. A key resource is owned by a single firm.
    d. A single firm is very large.

2. A firm whose average total cost continually declines at least to the quantity that could supply the entire market is known as a
    a. perfect competitor.
    b. natural monopoly.
    c. government monopoly.
    d. regulated monopoly.

3. When a monopolist produces an additional unit, the marginal revenue generated by that unit must be
    a. above the price because the output effect outweighs the price effect.
    b. above the price because the price effect outweighs the output effect.
    c. below the price because the output effect outweighs the price effect.
    d. below the price because the price effect outweighs the output effect.

4. A monopolist maximizes profit by producing the quantity at which
    a. marginal revenue equals marginal cost.
    b. marginal revenue equals price.
    c. marginal cost equals price.
    d. marginal cost equals demand.
    e. none of the above occurs.

5. Which of the following statements about price and marginal cost in competitive and monopolized markets is _true?_
    a. In competitive markets, price equals marginal cost; in monopolized markets, price equals marginal cost.
    b. In competitive markets, price exceeds marginal cost; in monopolized markets, price exceeds marginal cost.
    c. In competitive markets, price equals marginal cost; in monopolized markets, price exceeds marginal cost.
    d. In competitive markets, price exceeds marginal cost; in monopolized markets, price equals marginal cost.

6. Cengage Learning is a monopolist in the production of your textbook because
   a. Cengage Learning owns a key resource in the production of textbooks.
   b. Cengage Learning is a natural monopoly.
   c. the government has granted Cengage Learning exclusive rights to produce this textbook.
   d. Cengage Learning is a very large company.

Use Exhibit 4 to answer questions 7 through 10.

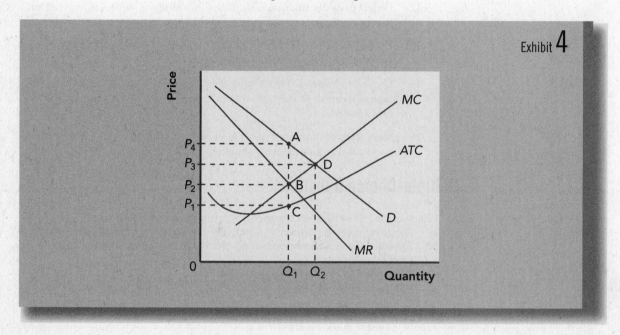

Exhibit 4

7. The profit-maximizing monopolist will choose the price and quantity represented by point
   a. A.
   b. B.
   c. C.
   d. D.
   e. None of the above is correct.

8. The profit earned by the profit-maximizing monopolist is represented by the area
   a. P_4ABP_2.
   b. P_4ACP_1.
   c. P_4AQ_10.
   d. P_3DQ_20.
   e. None of the above is correct.

9. The deadweight loss associated with monopoly pricing is represented by the area
   a. P_4ABP_2.
   b. P_4ACP_1.
   c. ABD.
   d. P_2BCP_1.
   e. None of the above is correct.

10. The efficient price and quantity are represented by point
    a. A.
    b. B.
    c. C.
    d. D.
    e. None of the above is correct.

11. The inefficiency associated with monopoly is due to
    a. the monopoly's profits.
    b. the monopoly's losses.
    c. overproduction of the good.
    d. underproduction of the good.

12. Compared to a perfectly competitive market, a monopoly market will usually generate
    a. higher prices and higher output.
    b. higher prices and lower output.
    c. lower prices and lower output.
    d. lower prices and higher output.

13. The monopolist's supply curve
    a. is the marginal-cost curve above average variable cost.
    b. is the marginal-cost curve above average total cost.
    c. is the upward-sloping portion of the average-total-cost curve.
    d. is the upward-sloping portion of the average variable cost.
    e. does not exist.

14. Using government regulations to force a natural monopoly to charge a price equal to its marginal cost will
    a. improve efficiency.
    b. raise the price of the good.
    c. attract additional firms to enter the market.
    d. cause the monopolist to exit the market.

15. The purpose of antitrust laws is to
    a. regulate the prices charged by a monopoly.
    b. increase competition in an industry by preventing mergers and breaking up large firms.
    c. increase merger activity to help generate synergies that reduce costs and raise efficiency.
    d. create public ownership of natural monopolies.
    e. do all of the above.

16. Public ownership of natural monopolies
    a. tends to be inefficient.
    b. usually lowers the cost of production dramatically.
    c. creates synergies between the newly acquired firm and other government-owned companies.
    d. does none of the above.

17. Which of the following statements about price discrimination is *not* true?
    a. Price discrimination can raise economic welfare.
    b. Price discrimination requires that the seller be able to separate buyers according to their willingness to pay.
    c. Perfect price discrimination generates a deadweight loss.
    d. Price discrimination increases a monopolist's profits.
    e. For a monopolist to engage in price discrimination, buyers must be unable to engage in arbitrage.

18. If regulators break up a natural monopoly into many smaller firms, the cost of production
    a. will fall.
    b. will rise.
    c. will remain the same.
    d. could either rise or fall depending on the elasticity of the monopolist's supply curve.

19. A monopoly is able to continue to generate economic profits in the long run because
    a. potential competitors sometimes don't notice the profits.
    b. there is some barrier to entry to that market.
    c. the monopolist is financially powerful.
    d. antitrust laws eliminate competitors for a specified number of years.
    e. of all of the above.

20. If marginal revenue exceeds marginal cost, a monopolist should
    a. increase output.
    b. decrease output.
    c. keep output the same because profits are maximized when marginal revenue exceeds marginal cost.
    d. raise the price.

Advanced Critical Thinking

You are watching a television news show. A consumer advocate is discussing the airline industry. He says, "There are so many rates offered by airlines that it is technically possible for a 747 to be carrying a full load of passengers where no two of them paid the same price for their tickets. This is clearly unfair and inefficient." He continues, "In addition, the profits of the airlines have doubled in the last few years since they began this practice, and these additional profits are clearly a social burden. We need legislation that requires airlines to charge all passengers on an airplane the same price for their travel."

1. List some of the ways airlines divide their customers according to their willingness to pay.

   _____
   _____
   _____
   _____

2. Is it necessarily inefficient for airlines to charge different prices to different customers? Why or why not?

   _____
   _____
   _____
   _____

3. Is the increase in profits generated by this type of price discrimination a social cost? Explain.

   _____
   _____
   _____
   _____

Solutions

Terms and Definitions

<u> 2 </u> Monopoly

<u> 1 </u> Natural monopoly

<u> 4 </u> Price discrimination

<u> 5 </u> Arbitrage

<u> 3 </u> Perfect price discrimination

Practice Problems

1. a. A key resource is owned by a single firm (monopoly resource), the government gives a single firm the exclusive right to produce a good (government-created monopoly), the costs of production make a single producer more efficient (natural monopoly).

   b. (1) Natural monopoly. E-mail, fax machines, telephone, private delivery such as FedEx.

   (2) Monopoly resource. Other bottled water, soft drinks.

   (3) Government-created monopoly due to a patent. Other drugs for depression, generic drugs when the patent expires.

   (4) Monopoly resource. Other gems such as emeralds, rubies, sapphires.

   (5) Government-created monopoly due to copyright. Other principles of economics texts.

   (6) Natural monopoly. Wood-burning stoves, gas lanterns, home generators.

2. a.

Pounds of Salmon	Price	($P \times Q$) Total Revenue	($\Delta TR/\Delta Q$) Marginal Revenue
0	$20	0	
			18
1	18	18	
			14
2	16	32	
			10
3	14	42	
			6
4	12	48	
			2
5	10	50	
			−2
6	8	48	
			−6
7	6	42	

b. See Exhibit 5.

Exhibit 5

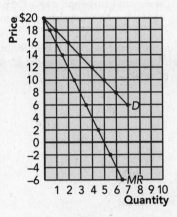

c. Q = between 3 and 4 units (say 3.5), P = between $12 and $14 (say $13). Profit = $TR - TC$ or profit = $(3.5 \times \$13) - (3.5 \times \$6) = \$45.50 - \$21.00 = \$24.50$. (Or profit = $(P - ATC) \times Q = (\$13 - \$6) \times 3.5 = \$24.50$.) See Exhibit 6.

Exhibit 6

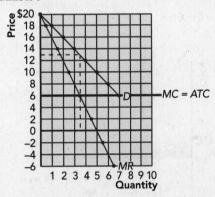

d. Seven units at $6 each. (The efficient solution is where the market produces all units where benefits exceed or equal costs of production, which is where demand intersects MC.)

e. The monopolist's price is too high and quantity produced too low because the monopolist faces a downward-sloping demand curve that makes $MR < P$. Therefore, when the profit-maximizing monopolist sets $MR = MC$ and the MR curve is below the demand curve, the quantity is less than optimal and the price charged exceeds the MC of production.

f. Yes. Units from 3.5 to 7, or an additional 3.5 pounds of salmon are valued by the consumer at values in excess of the $6 per pound MC of production and these units are not produced and consumed when the price is $13. (Deadweight loss = the deadweight loss triangle = $1/2 (7 - 3.5) \times (\$13 - \$6) = \$12.25$.)

g. Yes, all units are produced where the value to buyers is greater than or is equal to the cost of production (7 units). Total surplus is now producer surplus, and there is no consumer surplus. Total surplus and producer surplus is the area under the demand curve and above the price or 1/2($20 − $6) × 7 = $49. Consumer surplus = $0.

3. a. Natural monopoly because ATC is still declining at the quantity that could satisfy the entire market.

b. See Exhibit 7.

Exhibit 7

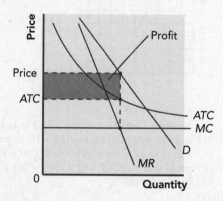

c. See Exhibit 8.

Exhibit 8

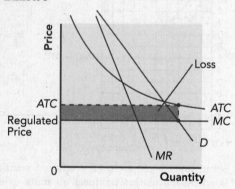

d. No. Because marginal cost must be below average total cost if average total cost is declining, this firm will generate losses if forced to charge a price equal to marginal cost. It will simply exit the market, which eliminates all surplus associated with this market.

Short-Answer Questions

1. Anything that restricts new firms from entering a market. A key resource is owned by a single firm, the government gives a single firm the exclusive right to produce a good, or the costs of production make a single producer more efficient than a large number of producers.

2. No. The monopolist will generate losses and will exit the market.

3. No. Even a monopolist is subject to the demand for its product, so a high price would cause buyers to buy very little of the good. The monopolist chooses its price by first choosing the optimal quantity based on the intersection of MR and MC and then charging the price consistent with that quantity.

4. For a monopolist, P > MR because for a monopolist to sell another unit, it must reduce the price on the marginal unit and all of its previous units. Therefore, while a monopolist equates MR and MC, it charges a price that is greater than MC, which causes consumers to buy less than the efficient amount of the good.

5. No. The monopolist's profits are a redistribution of consumer surplus to producer surplus. The social cost of monopoly is the deadweight loss associated with the reduced production of output.

6. Yes, because every unit is produced where the value to buyers is greater than or equal to the cost to the producer. However, the entire total surplus is received by the producer (the monopolist).

7. The monopolist must be able to separate buyers according to their willingness to pay.

8. Try to make monopolized industries more competitive, regulate the behavior of the monopolies, turn private monopolies into public enterprises, or do nothing at all.

9. No, many mergers capture synergies between the merging firms that reduce costs and increase efficiency.

10. The monopolist may lose money and exit the market. Subsidies to prevent this require taxes that also generate deadweight losses. Regulated monopolists have little incentive to reduce costs.

True/False Questions

1. F; monopolists are price makers.

2. F; owning a key resource is the rarest source of barriers to entry.

3. T

4. F; a natural monopoly is a firm with an average total cost curve that continually declines at least to the quantity that satisfies the entire market.

5. T

6. T

7. T

8. F; monopolists have no supply curve.

9. F; the inefficiency generated by a monopoly results from the failure of the monopolist to produce units of output where the value to consumers equals or exceeds the cost of production. The monopolist's profits are not a cost to society but are just a redistribution from consumer surplus to producer surplus.

10. T

11. T

12. F; all of the surplus is received by the producer.
13. T
14. T
15. F; economists usually prefer private ownership to public ownership because private owners have a greater incentive to reduce costs.

Multiple-Choice Questions

1. d
2. b
3. d
4. a
5. c
6. c
7. a
8. b
9. c
10. d
11. d
12. b
13. e
14. d
15. b
16. a
17. c
18. b
19. b
20. a

Advanced Critical Thinking

1. Airlines segment people by age (young and old fly cheaper), by location (more competitive routes are cheaper), by length of time between leaving and returning (tourists fly cheaper than business travelers), by length of time of advance booking (later bookings can be more expensive until the very last minute when it may become cheaper again), and so on.

2. No. Price discrimination can improve efficiency. By charging buyers their willingness to pay, the monopolist increases production to the point where all units are produced where the value to buyers is greater than or equal to the cost of production.

3. No. Some of the additional profits are from the creation of additional surplus that accrues entirely to the producer, and some of the profits are a redistribution of surplus from consumer surplus to producer surplus.

Chapter 15
Measuring a Nation's Income

Chapter Overview

Context and Purpose

Chapter 15 is the first chapter in the macroeconomic section of the text. It is the first of a two-chapter sequence that introduces you to two vital statistics that economists use to monitor the macroeconomy—Gross Domestic Product (GDP) and the consumer price index. Chapter 15 develops how economists measure production and income in the macroeconomy. Chapter 16 develops how economists measure the level of prices in the macroeconomy. Taken together, Chapter 15 concentrates on the *quantity* of output in the macroeconomy while Chapter 16 concentrates on the *price* of output in the macroeconomy.

The purpose of this chapter is to provide you with an understanding of the measurement and the use of gross domestic product. GDP is the single most important measure of the health of the macroeconomy. Indeed, it is the most widely reported statistic in every developed economy.

Chapter Review

Introduction   Microeconomics is the study of individual markets and the decision making of individual firms and households that meet in those markets. Macroeconomics is the study of the entire economy as a whole. This chapter and the remainder of this text deals with macroeconomics.

The Economy's Income and Expenditure

In a nation's macroeconomy, income must equal expenditure. This is true because, in every transaction, the income of the seller must be equal to the expenditure of the buyer. Gross domestic product (GDP) is a measure of the *total income* or total output in the economy. Since income equals expenditure, GDP can be measured by adding up the income earned in the economy (wages, rent, and profit) or the expenditure on goods and services produced in the economy. That is, income equals expenditure equals GDP.

The Measurement of GDP

GDP is defined as the market value of all final goods and services produced within a country in a given period of time.

- "Market value" means that production is valued at the price paid for the output. Hence, items sold at higher prices are more heavily weighted in GDP.

- "Of all" means that GDP attempts to measure all production in the economy that is legally sold in markets. For example, GDP excludes the production and sale of illegal drugs and household production such as when homeowners clean their own houses. However, in an attempt to be comprehensive, GDP does include the estimated rental value of owner-occupied housing as an expenditure on housing services.

- "Final" means that GDP includes only goods and services that are sold to the end user. Thus, GDP counts the sale of a Ford Taurus when it is sold at retail, but it excludes Ford's purchases of intermediate goods such as glass, steel, and tires used up during the production of the car. *Intermediate goods* are goods that are produced by one firm to be further processed by another firm. Counting only final goods and services avoids double counting *intermediate production*.

- "Goods and services" means that while GDP clearly includes tangible manufactured items such as cars and trucks, it also includes intangible items such as lawyers' and doctors' services.

- "Produced" means that we exclude the sale of used items that were produced (and counted) in a previous period. Again, this avoids double counting.

- "Within a country" means that GDP measures the value of production within the geographic borders of a country.

- "In a given period of time" means that we measure GDP per year or per quarter.

GDP data are statistically "seasonally adjusted" to eliminate the systematic variations in the data that are caused by seasonal events such as Christmas and crop harvest. Our definition of GDP focuses on expenditures. The government also adds up income to measure GDP. The difference between the two calculations is statistical discrepancy.

Other measures of income besides GDP are listed below, from largest to smallest.

- *Gross national product (GNP):* GNP measures the income or production of a nation's permanent residents or "nationals" (both people and their factories) no matter where they are located.

- *Net national product (NNP):* NNP is the total income of a nation's residents (GNP) minus depreciation. *Depreciation* is the value of the wear and tear on the economy's capital stock.

- *National income:* National income is the total income earned by a nation's residents. It differs from NNP because of the statistical discrepancy from data collection.

- *Personal income:* Personal income is the income of households and noncorporate businesses. It excludes retained earnings (corporate income not paid out as dividends) and subtracts indirect business taxes, corporate taxes, and contributions for social insurance. It includes interest income households receive from government debt and government *transfer payments* (welfare and Social Security).

- *Disposable personal income:* This is income of households and nonincorporated businesses after they pay their obligations to the government (taxes, traffic tickets).

The Components of GDP

GDP can be measured by adding up the value of the expenditures on final goods and services. Economists divide expenditures into four components: consumption (*C*), investment (*I*), government purchases (*G*), and net exports (*NX*).

- Consumption (71 percent) is spending by households on goods and services, with the exception of new housing.

- Investment (13 percent) is spending on capital equipment, inventories, and structures such as new housing. Investment does not include spending on stocks, bonds, and mutual funds.

- Government purchases (20 percent) is spending on goods and services by all levels of government (federal, state, and local). Government purchases do not include *transfer payments* such as government payments for Social Security, welfare, and *unemployment* benefits because the government does not receive any product or service in return.

- Net exports (–4 percent) is the value of foreign purchases of U.S. domestic production (exports) minus U.S. domestic purchases of foreign production (imports). Imports must be subtracted because consumption, investment, and government purchases include expenditures on all goods, foreign and domestic, and the foreign component must be removed so that only spending on domestic production remains.

Denoting GDP as *Y*, we can say that $Y = C + I + G + NX$. The variables are defined in such a way that this equation is an identity.

Real versus Nominal GDP

Nominal GDP is the value of output measured in the prices that existed during the year in which the output was produced (current prices). Real GDP is the value of output measured in the prices that prevailed in some arbitrary (but fixed) *base year* (constant prices). If we observe that nominal GDP has risen from one year to the next, we are unable to determine whether the quantity of goods and services has risen or whether the prices of goods and services have risen. However, if we observe that real GDP has risen, we are certain that the quantity of goods and services has risen because the output from each year is valued in terms of the same base-year prices. Thus, real GDP is the better measure of production in the economy.

The GDP deflator = (nominal GDP/real GDP) × 100. The GDP deflator is a price index that measures the level of prices in the current year relative to the level of prices in the base year. The percentage change in the GDP deflator is a measure of the rate of inflation.

In the United States, real GDP has grown on average at about 3 percent per year since 1965. Occasional periods of decline in real GDP are known as *recessions*.

Is GDP a Good Measure of Economic Well-Being?

Real GDP is a strong indicator of the economic well-being of a society because countries with a large real GDP per person tend to have better educational systems, better health care systems, more literate citizens, better housing, a better diet, a longer life expectancy, and so on. However, GDP is not a perfect measure of material well-being because it excludes leisure, the quality of the environment, and goods and services produced at home and not sold in markets such as child rearing, housework, and volunteer work. In addition, GDP says nothing about the *distribution* of income. GDP also fails to capture the underground or shadow economy—the portion of the economy that does not report its economic activity. For example, GDP does not measure illegal drug sales or income that is unreported to avoid taxation. The underground economy is relatively small in the United States. Regardless, international data clearly shows a close relationship between a nation's GDP per person and the standard of living of its citizens.

Helpful Hints

1. GDP measures production. When we set out to measure GDP, we must first remember that we are measuring production (and the income earned from producing it) over a period of time. If we can remember that, we will generally account for unusual types of production correctly. Examples:

   - How should we handle the measurement of the production of a cruise ship that takes three years to build and is sold at the end of the third year? Logically, we should count the portion of the ship that was completed during each year and apply it to that year's GDP. In fact, that is what economists do. If we had accounted for the entire ship in the year in which it was sold, we would have overestimated GDP in the third year and underestimated GDP in the previous two years.

   - Similarly, if a new house were built during one year but sold for the first time during the next year, we should account for it during the first year because that is when it was produced. That is, the builder "purchased" the finished home during the first year and added it to his or her inventory of homes.

   While in general we only wish to count final goods and services, we do count the production of intermediate goods that were not used during the period but were added to a firm's inventory because this production will not be captured by counting all of the final goods.

2. GDP does not include all expenditures. We have learned that we can measure GDP by adding the expenditures on final goods and services ($Y = C + I + G + NX$). Once we have learned the expenditure approach, however, we must not forget the words "on final goods and services" and mistakenly count all expenditures. When we include expenditures on used items, intermediate goods, stocks and bonds, or government transfer payments, we get a very large dollar value, but it has nothing to do with GDP. The dollar value of total transactions in the economy is enormous and many times that of GDP.

3. Intermediate goods and final goods are distinct. It should be helpful to clarify the distinction between intermediate goods and final goods with an example. Recall:

    ♦ Intermediate goods are goods that are produced by one firm to be further processed by another firm.

    ♦ Final goods are sold to the end user.

    GDP only includes the value of the final goods and services because the value of the intermediate goods used in the production of a final good or service is fully captured in the price of the final good or service. If we include the value of intermediate production in GDP, we would double count the intermediate goods.

    If we understand this distinction, can we list the items in the economy that are intermediate or final? For example, is a tire an intermediate good or a final good? The answer is: It depends on who bought it. When General Motors buys a tire from Goodyear, the tire is an intermediate good because General Motors will attach it to a car and sell it. When you buy a tire from your Goodyear dealer, it is a final good and should be counted in GDP. Thus, it is difficult to list items in the economy that are intermediate or final without knowledge of the buyer.

4. Comparisons of GDP across countries and time can be biased. We should be cautious when we compare GDP across nations of different levels of market development and when we compare GDP across long periods of time within a single nation. This is because GDP excludes most nonmarket activities. Clearly, a greater proportion of the output of lesser-developed nations is likely to be household production such as when someone does their own farming, cleaning, sewing, and maybe even home construction. Since these activities are not captured by a market transaction, they are not recorded in lesser-developed nations or in earlier periods of industrialized nations when market development was less extensive. The result is an even lower estimate of their GDP.

Terms and Definitions

Choose a definition for each key term.

Key Terms	Definitions

Key Terms

_____Inflation

_____Unemployment

_____Macroeconomics

_____Microeconomics

_____Total income

_____Total expenditure

_____Gross domestic product

_____Intermediate production

_____Final production

_____Gross national product

_____Depreciation

_____Consumption

_____Investment

_____Government purchases

_____Net exports

_____Transfer payment

_____Real GDP

_____Nominal GDP

_____Base year

_____GDP deflator

_____Recession

Definitions

1. The production of goods and services valued at current prices

2. Spending by households on goods and services, excluding new housing

3. Spending on domestically produced goods by foreigners (exports) minus spending on foreign goods by domestic residents (imports)

4. Period of decline in GDP

5. Market value of all final goods and services produced within a country in a given period of time

6. Wages, rent, and profit

7. The rate at which prices are rising

8. Market value of all final goods and services produced by a nation's residents in a given period of time

9. Spending on capital equipment, inventories, and structures, including household purchases of new housing

10. Spending on goods and services by all levels of government

11. A measure of the price level calculated as the ratio of nominal GDP to real GDP then multiplied by 100

12. Expenditures by government for which they receive no goods or services

13. Percent of the labor force that is out of work

14. The study of how households and firms make decisions and how they interact in markets

15. Goods that are produced by one firm to be further processed by another firm

16. The study of economy-wide phenomena

17. The production of goods and services valued at base-year prices

18. Finished products sold to the end user

19. Consumption, investment, government purchases, and net exports

20. The year from which prices are used to measure real GDP

21. Value of worn-out equipment and structures

Problems and Short-Answer Questions

Practice Problems

1. a. Complete the following table.

	Year 1	Year 2	Year 3
Gross Domestic Product	4,532	4,804	_____
Consumption	_____	3,320	3,544
Investment	589	629	673
Government Purchases	861	_____	977
Net Exports	−45	−58	−54

b. What is the largest expenditure component of GDP?

c. Does investment include the purchase of stocks and bonds? Why?

d. Do government purchases include government spending on unemployment checks? Why?

e. What does it mean to say that net exports are negative?

2. Suppose the base year in the following table is 2011.

Year	Production of X	Price per Unit of X
2011	20 units	$ 5
2012	20 units	10
2013	20 units	20

a. What is nominal GDP for 2011, 2012, and 2013?

b. What is real GDP for 2011, 2012, and 2013?

3. Suppose the following table records the total output and prices for an entire economy. Furthermore, suppose the base year in the following table is 2012.

Year	Price of Soda	Quantity of Soda	Price of Jeans	Quantity of Jeans
2012	$1.00	200	$10.00	50
2013	1.00	220	11.00	50

a.   What is the value of nominal GDP in 2012?

_____

b.   What is the value of real GDP in 2012?

_____

c.   What is the value of nominal GDP in 2013?

_____

d.   What is the value of real GDP in 2013?

_____

e.   What is the value of the GDP deflator in 2012?

_____

f.   What is the value of the GDP deflator in 2013?

_____

g.   From 2012 to 2013, prices rose approximately what percentage?

_____

h.   Was the increase in nominal GDP from 2012 to 2013 mostly due to an increase in real output or due to an increase in prices?

_____

4. Complete the following table.

Year	Nominal GDP	Real GDP	GDP Deflator
1	_____	$100	100
2	$120	_____	120
3	150	125	_____

a.   What year is the base year? How can you tell?

_____

_____

b.   From year 1 to year 2, did real output rise or did prices rise? Explain.

_____

_____

c.   From year 2 to year 3, did real output rise or did prices rise? Explain.

_____

_____

Short-Answer Questions

1. Why does income = expenditure = GDP?

_____

_____

_____

2. Define GDP and explain the important terms in the definition.

_____

_____

_____

3. What are the components of expenditure? Provide an example of each.

_____

_____

_____

4. Provide an example of a transfer payment. Do we include it in GDP? Why or why not?

_____

_____

_____

5. If nominal GDP in 2013 exceeds nominal GDP in 2012, did real output rise? Did prices rise?

_____

_____

_____

6. If real GDP in 2013 exceeds real GDP in 2012, did real output rise? Did prices rise?

_____

_____

_____

7. If you buy a $20,000 Toyota that was produced entirely in Japan, does this affect U.S. GDP? Show how this transaction would affect the appropriate expenditure categories that make up GDP.

_____

_____

_____

8. Explain the difference between GDP and GNP. If the residents of the United States generate as much production in the rest of the world as the rest of the world produces in the United States, what should be true about U.S. GDP and GNP?

_____

_____

_____

9. Which contributes more when measuring GDP, a new diamond necklace purchased by a wealthy person or a soda purchased by a thirsty person? Why?

_____

_____

_____

10. If your neighbor hires you to mow her lawn instead of doing it herself, what will happen to GDP? Why? Did output change?

_____

_____

_____

Self-Test

True/False Questions

_____ 1. For an economy as a whole, income equals expenditure because the income of the seller must be equal to the expenditure of the buyer.

_____ 2. The production of an apple contributes more to GDP than the production of a gold ring because food is necessary for life itself.

_____ 3. If the lumberyard sells $1,000 of lumber to a carpenter and the carpenter uses the lumber to build a garage that he sells for $5,000, the contribution to GDP is $6,000.

_____ 4. A country with a larger GDP per person generally has a greater standard of living or quality of life than a country with a smaller GDP per person.

_____ 5. If nominal GDP in 2013 exceeds nominal GDP in 2012, real output must have risen.

_____ 6. If U.S. GDP exceeds U.S. GNP, then foreigners produce more in the United States than U.S. citizens produce in the rest of the world.

_____ 7. Wages are an example of a transfer payment because there is a transfer of payment from the firm to the worker.

_____ 8. In the United States, investment is the largest component of GDP.

_____ 9. Nominal GDP employs current prices to value output while real GDP employs constant base-year prices to value output.

_____ 10. A new car produced in 2012, but first sold in 2013, should be counted in 2013 GDP because that is when it was first sold as a final good.

_____ 11.   When the city of Chicago purchases a new school building, the investment component of GDP increases.

_____ 12.   A recession occurs when real GDP declines.

_____ 13.   Depreciation is the value of the wear and tear on the economy's equipment and structures.

_____ 14.   Cigarettes should be valued in GDP at $5.50 per pack even though $1.00 of that price is tax because the buyers paid $5.50 per pack.

_____ 15.   Net national product always exceeds a nation's GNP because of depreciation.

Multiple-Choice Questions

1. An example of a transfer payment is
    a.   wages.
    b.   profit.
    c.   rent.
    d.   government purchases.
    e.   unemployment benefits.

2. The value of plant and equipment worn out in the process of manufacturing goods and services is measured by
    a.   consumption.
    b.   depreciation.
    c.   net national product.
    d.   investment.
    e.   intermediate production.

3. Which of the following would be excluded from 2013 GDP? The sale of
    a.   a 2013 Honda made in Tennessee.
    b.   a haircut.
    c.   a realtor's services.
    d.   a home built in 2012 and first sold in 2013.
    e.   All of the above should be counted in 2013 GDP.

4. Gross domestic product can be measured as the sum of
    a.   consumption, investment, government purchases, and net exports.
    b.   consumption, transfer payments, wages, and profits.
    c.   investment, wages, profits, and intermediate production.
    d.   final goods and services, intermediate goods, transfer payments, and rent.
    e.   net national product, gross national product, and disposable personal income.

5. U.S. gross domestic product (in contrast to gross national product) measures the production and income of
    a.   Americans and their factories no matter where they are located in the world.
    b.   people and factories located within the borders of the United States.
    c.   the domestic service sector only.
    d.   the domestic manufacturing sector only.
    e.   none of the above.

6. Gross domestic product is the sum of the market value of the
    a.   intermediate goods.
    b.   manufactured goods.
    c.   normal goods and services.
    d.   inferior goods and services.
    e.   final goods and services.

7. If nominal GDP in 2013 exceeds nominal GDP in 2012, then the production of output must have
    a. risen.
    b. fallen.
    c. stayed the same.
    d. risen or fallen because there is not enough information to determine what happened to real output.

8. If a cobbler buys leather for $100 and thread for $50 and uses them to produce and sell $500 worth of shoes to consumers, the contribution to GDP is
    a. $50.
    b. $100.
    c. $500.
    d. $600.
    e. $650.

9. GDP would include which of the following?
    a. housework
    b. illegal drug sales
    c. intermediate sales
    d. consulting services
    e. the value of taking a day off from work

10. Real GDP is measured in _____ prices while nominal GDP is measured in _____ prices.
    a. current year; base year
    b. base year; current year
    c. intermediate; final
    d. domestic; foreign
    e. foreign; domestic

The following table contains information about an economy that produces only pens and books. The base year is 2011. Use this information to answer questions 11 through 16.

Year	Price of Pens	Quantity of Pens	Price of Books	Quantity of Books
2011	$3	100	$10	50
2012	3	120	12	70
2013	4	120	14	70

11. What is the value of nominal GDP for 2012?
    a. $800
    b. $1,060
    c. $1,200
    d. $1,460
    e. none of the above

12. What is the value of real GDP for 2012?
    a. $800
    b. $1,060
    c. $1,200
    d. $1,460
    e. none of the above

13. What is the value of the GDP deflator in 2012?
    a. 100
    b. 113
    c. 116
    d. 119
    e. 138

14. What is the percentage increase in prices from 2011 to 2012?
    a. 0 percent
    b. 13 percent
    c. 16 percent
    d. 22 percent
    e. 38 percent

15. What is the approximate percentage increase in prices from 2012 to 2013?
    a. 0 percent
    b. 13 percent
    c. 16 percent
    d. 22 percent
    e. 38 percent

16. What is the percentage increase in real GDP from 2012 to 2013?
    a. 0 percent
    b. 7 percent
    c. 22 percent
    d. 27 percent
    e. 32 percent

17. If U.S. GDP exceeds U.S. GNP, then
    a. foreigners are producing more in the United States than Americans are producing in foreign countries.
    b. Americans are producing more in foreign countries than foreigners are producing in the United States.
    c. real GDP exceeds nominal GDP.
    d. real GNP exceeds nominal GNP.
    e. intermediate production exceeds final production.

18. U.S. GDP would exclude which of the following?
    a. lawyer services purchased by a home buyer
    b. lawn care services purchased by a homeowner
    c. a new bridge purchased by the state of Texas
    d. cotton purchased by Lee Jeans
    e. the purchase of a new Mazda produced in Illinois

19. How is your purchase of a $40,000 BMW automobile that was produced entirely in Germany recorded in the U.S. GDP accounts?
    a. Investment increases by $40,000, and net exports increase by $40,000.
    b. Consumption increases by $40,000, and net exports decrease by $40,000.
    c. Net exports decrease by $40,000.
    d. Net exports increase by $40,000.
    e. There is no impact because this transaction does not involve domestic production.

20. If your grandparents buy a new retirement home, this transaction would affect
    a. consumption.
    b. investment.
    c. government purchases.
    d. net exports.
    e. none of the above.

Advanced Critical Thinking

You are watching a news report with your father. The news anchor points out that a certain troubled Caribbean nation generates a GDP per capita of only $430 per year. Since your father knows that U.S. GDP per capita is approximately $43,000, he suggests that we are materially 100 times better off in the United States than in the Caribbean nation.

1. Is your father's statement accurate?

    _____

    _____

2. What general category of production is not captured by GDP in both the United States and the Caribbean nation?

    _____

    _____

3. Provide some examples of this type of activity.

    _____

    _____

    _____

4. Why would the exclusion of this type of production affect the measurement of Caribbean output more than U.S. output?

    _____

    _____

    _____

5. Does this mean that residents of the Caribbean nation are actually as well off materially as residents in the United States?

    _____

    _____

    _____

Solutions

Terms and Definitions

_7_ Inflation

_13_ Unemployment

_16_ Macroeconomics

_14_ Microeconomics

_6_ Total income

_19_ Total expenditure

_5_ Gross domestic product

_15_ Intermediate production

_18_ Final production

_8_ Gross national product

_21_ Depreciation

_2_ Consumption

_9_ Investment

_10_ Government purchases

_3_ Net exports

_12_ Transfer payment

_17_ Real GDP

_1_ Nominal GDP

_20_ Base year

_11_ GDP deflator

_4_ Recession

Practice Problems

1. a.

	Year 1	Year 2	Year 3
Gross Domestic Product	4,532	4,804	5,140
Consumption	3,127	3,320	3,544
Investment	589	629	673
Government Purchases	861	913	977
Net Exports	−45	−58	−54

   b. consumption

   c. No, because that transaction is a purchase of an asset, not a purchase of currently produced capital goods.

   d. No, because unemployment benefits are expenditures for which the government receives no production in return.

   e. It means that imports exceed exports.

2. a. $100, $200, $400

   b. $100, $100, $100

3. a. $700

   b. $700

   c. $770

   d. $720

   e. 100

   f. 107

   g. (107 − 100)/100 = 0.07 = 7%

   h. Percent increase in nominal = ($770 − $700)/700 = 0.10 = 10%. Percent increase in prices = 7%; therefore, most of the increase was due to prices.

4.

Year	Nominal GDP	Real GDP	GDP Deflator
1	$100	$100	100
2	120	100	120
3	150	125	120

   a. Year 1, because the deflator = 100.

   b. Prices rose 20 percent and real output stayed the same.

   c. Prices stayed the same and real output rose 25 percent.

Short-Answer Questions

1. Because the income of the seller equals the expenditure of the buyer and GDP can be measured with either one.

2. Market value of all final goods and services produced within a country in a given period of time. "Market value" = price paid, "of all" = all legal production, "final" = to end users, "goods and services" = includes services, "produced" = no used items, "within a country" = inside borders, "in a given period" = per quarter or year.

3. Consumption (food), investment (factory), government purchases (military equipment), net exports (sale of a Ford to France minus purchase of a Toyota produced in Japan).

4. Social Security payments. No, because the government received no good or service in return.

5. We can't be certain which rose, prices or real output, because an increase in either prices or real output will cause nominal output to rise.

6. Real output rose because the value of output in each year is measured in constant base-year prices. We have no information on prices.

7. No. Consumption would increase by $20,000 and net exports would decrease by $20,000. As a result, U.S. GDP is unaffected.

8. GDP is the production within the borders of the United States. GNP is the production of Americans no matter where the production takes place. They should be equal.

9. A diamond necklace because GDP measures market value.

10. GDP will rise because the mowing of the lawn was a market transaction. However, output didn't really rise.

True/False Questions

1. T

2. F; contribution is based on market value.

3.   F; the garage is the final good, valued at $5,000.
4.   T
5.   F; prices or real output could have risen.
6.   T
7.   F; transfer payments are expenditures for which no good or service is received in return.
8.   F; consumption is the largest component of GDP.
9.   T
10. F; goods are counted in the year produced.
11. F; the purchase is included in government purchases.
12. T
13. T
14. T
15. F; GNP – depreciation = NNP.

Multiple-Choice Questions

1.   e
2.   b
3.   d
4.   a
5.   b
6.   e
7.   d
8.   c
9.   d
10. b
11. c
12. b
13. b
14. b
15. d
16. a
17. a
18. d
19. b
20. b

Advanced Critical Thinking

1.   No.
2.   Nonmarket activities such as household production.
3.   Household production done by an individual without pay such as gardening, cleaning, sewing, home improvement or construction, child supervision, etc.
4.   A greater proportion of the output produced by less-developed nations is nonmarket output. That is, it is not sold and recorded as a market transaction.
5.   No. It just means that quantitative comparisons between nations of greatly different levels of development are very difficult to do and are often inaccurate.

Chapter 16

Measuring the Cost of Living

Chapter Overview

Context and Purpose

Chapter 16 is the second chapter of a two-chapter sequence that deals with how economists measure output and prices in the macro-economy. Chapter 15 addressed how economists measure output. Chapter 16 develops how economists measure the overall price level in the macroeconomy.

The purpose of Chapter 16 is twofold: first, to show you how to generate a price index and, second, to teach you how to employ a price index to compare dollar figures from different points in time and to adjust interest rates for inflation. In addition, you will learn some of the shortcomings of using the consumer price index as a measure of the cost of living.

Chapter Review

Introduction   To compare the income of a worker in, say, 1930 to the income of a worker today, we must first convert the dollar amount of each of their incomes into a comparable measure of purchasing power because there has been inflation over this time period. This chapter explains how economists correct economic variables for the effects of inflation. Inflation is generally measured by the consumer price index (CPI).

The Consumer Price Index

The consumer price index is a measure of the overall cost of the goods and services bought by a typical consumer. It is calculated by the *Bureau of Labor Statistics*.

There are five steps to calculating a CPI:

* *Fix the basket.* Estimate the *quantities* of the products purchased by the typical consumer (i.e., the *basket of goods and services*).

* *Find the prices.* Locate the prices of each item in the basket for each point in time (each year for an annual CPI).

* *Compute the basket's cost.* Use the prices and quantities to calculate the cost of the basket for each year.

* *Choose a base year and compute the index.* Choose a year as the benchmark against which the other years can be compared (i.e., the *base year*). The choice of the base year is arbitrary. Make a ratio of the cost of the basket for each year to the cost in the base year. Multiply each ratio by 100. Each resulting number is the value of the index for that year.

* *Compute inflation.* Inflation is the percentage change in the price index from the preceding year. For example:

$$\text{Inflation rate in 2013} = \left[\frac{\text{CPI in year 2013} - \text{CPI in year 2012}}{\text{CPI in year 2012}} \right] \times 100$$

The actual CPI is calculated both monthly and annually. In addition, the Bureau of Labor Statistics calculates a producer price index (PPI), which measures the cost of a basket of goods and services purchased by firms. Changes in the PPI usually precede changes in the CPI because firms often pass on higher costs in the form of higher consumer prices.

The major categories in the CPI basket are housing (41 percent), transportation (17 percent), food and beverages (15 percent), medical care (7 percent), education and communication (6 percent), recreation (6 percent), apparel (4 percent), and other goods and services (3 percent).

The *cost of living* is the amount by which incomes must rise in order to maintain a constant *standard of living*. There are three problems with using the CPI to measure changes in the cost of living:

* *Substitution bias:* Over time, some prices rise more than others. Consumers will substitute toward goods that have become relatively less expensive. The CPI, however, is based on a fixed basket of purchases. Because the CPI fails to acknowledge the consumer's substitution of less expensive products for more expensive products, the CPI overstates the increase in the cost of living.

* *Introduction of new goods:* When new goods are introduced, a dollar has increased in value because it can buy a greater variety of products. Because the CPI is based on a

fixed consumer basket, it does not reflect this increase in the purchasing power of the dollar (equivalent to a reduction in prices). Thus, again, the CPI overstates the increase in the cost of living.

• *Unmeasured quality change:* If the quality of a good rises from year to year, as with tires and computers, then the value of a dollar is rising even if actual prices are constant. This is equivalent to a reduction in prices. To the degree that an increase in quality is not accounted for by the Bureau of Labor Statistics, the CPI overstates the increase in the cost of living. The opposite is true for a deterioration of quality.

Economists believe that these three factors have caused the CPI to overestimate inflation by about 1 percent each year. This small overestimation of inflation may cause overpayment of Social Security benefits because Social Security benefits are tied to the CPI. Recent technical changes to the CPI may have reduced the upward bias in the CPI by about one-half.

Recall that the *GDP deflator* is the ratio of *nominal GDP* (current output valued at current prices) to *real GDP* (current output valued at base-year prices). Thus, the GDP deflator is a price index, too. It differs from the CPI in two ways:

• First, the basket of goods is different. The GDP deflator utilizes the prices of all goods and services produced domestically. The CPI utilizes the prices of goods and services *bought by consumers* only, regardless of where the goods were produced. Therefore, a change in the price of foreign oil, which raises the price of gasoline, is captured by the CPI but not by the GDP deflator, while a change in the price of a domestically produced nuclear missile is captured by the GDP deflator but not by the CPI.

• Second, the GDP deflator utilizes the quantities of goods and services in *current* output, so the "basket" changes each year. The CPI utilizes the quantities in a *fixed* basket, so the basket changes only when the Bureau of Labor Statistics chooses. Although the CPI and GDP deflator should track each other very closely, the CPI may tend to rise slightly faster due to its inherent substitution bias and the bias associated with the introduction of new goods.

Correcting Economic Variables for the Effects of Inflation

Economists use the CPI to correct *dollar figures*, such as income, and *interest rates* for the effects of inflation.

We correct income for inflation so that we can compare income from different years. The general formula for comparing dollar values from different years is as follows:

Value in year X dollars = Value in year Y dollars × (CPI in year X/CPI in year Y)

In words, to make the above conversion, multiply the dollar value you wish to adjust by the ratio of the ending price level to the starting price level. Your value will now be measured in dollars consistent with the ending price level.

For example, suppose your grandfather earned $17,000 in 1969 and earned $55,000 in 1994. Over those 25 years, did his standard of living increase?

CPI in 1969 = 36.7

CPI in 1994 = 148.2

$17,000 × (148.2/36.7) = $68,649 > $55,000

A $17,000 salary in 1969 would buy as much as a $68,649 salary in 1994. Since your grandfather only earned $55,000 in 1994, his real income fell and his standard of living actually decreased.

When a dollar amount, for example a Social Security payment, is automatically adjusted for inflation, we say that it has been *indexed* for inflation. A contract with this provision is said to contain a *COLA* or *cost-of-living allowance.*

We also correct interest rates for inflation. A correction is necessary because, if prices have risen during the term of a loan, the dollars used for repayment will not buy as much as the dollars originally borrowed.

The nominal interest rate is the interest rate uncorrected for the effects of inflation. The real interest rate is the interest rate corrected for the effects of inflation. The formula for correcting the nominal interest rate for inflation is:

$$\text{real interest rate} = \text{nominal interest rate} - \text{inflation rate}$$

For example, if the bank paid you a nominal interest rate of 4 percent on your account, and if the inflation rate were 3 percent, the real interest rate on your account would be only 1 percent: 4% − 3% = 1%.

Helpful Hints

1. Your particular consumption basket may not be typical. Since the GDP deflator and the CPI are based on different baskets of goods and services, each will provide a slightly different measurement of the cost of living. Continuing in this same line of thinking, your particular consumption basket may differ from the typical consumption basket used by the Bureau of Labor Statistics when they calculate the CPI. For example, when you are a young adult, your basket may be more heavily weighted toward electronics and clothing. If clothing prices are rising faster than average, young people may have a greater increase in the cost of living than is suggested by the CPI. In like manner, when you become old, your consumption basket may be more heavily weighted toward medicine and travel. Exceptional increases in these prices may cause the cost of living for the elderly to rise more quickly than suggested by the CPI.

2. Dollar values can be adjusted backward in time as well as adjusted forward. In the earlier section, there is a numerical example that converts $17,000 of income in 1969 into the amount of income that would be necessary in 1994 to generate the same purchasing power. We discovered that it would take $68,649 for your grandfather to have had the same standard of living in 1994 as he had in 1969. Because he only made $55,000 in 1994, we argued that his standard of living actually fell over the 25-year period.

   Alternatively, we can convert his 1994 salary of $55,000 into its equivalent purchasing power measured in 1969 dollars and compare the resulting figure with his $17,000 income in 1969. We arrive at the same conclusion—he was better off in 1969.

$$\$55,000 \times (36.7/148.2) = \$13,620 < \$17,000$$

   His $55,000 income in 1994 is equivalent to (or generates the same standard of living as) a $13,620 income in 1969. Since he actually made $17,000 in 1969, he had a higher standard of living in 1969.

3. When correcting interest rates for inflation, think like a lender. If you loan someone $100 for one year, and you charge them 7 percent interest, you will receive $107 at the end of the year. Did you receive 7 additional dollars of purchasing power? Suppose inflation was 4 percent. You would need to receive $104 at the end of the year just to break even. That is, you would need $104 just to be able to buy the same set of goods and services that you could have purchased for $100 at the time you granted the loan. In this sense, you received only 3 additional dollars of purchasing power for having made the $100 loan, or a 3 percent real return. Thus, the real interest rate on the loan is 3 percent. Using your formula:

$$7\% - 4\% = 3\%$$

Terms and Definitions

Choose a definition for each key term.

Key Terms

_____ Consumer price index

_____ Inflation rate

_____ GDP deflator

_____ Basket (of goods and services)

_____ Base year

_____ Bureau of Labor Statistics

_____ Producer price index

_____ Cost of living

_____ Standard of living

_____ Substitution bias

_____ Nominal GDP

_____ Real GDP

_____ Indexed contract

_____ Cost-of-living allowance (COLA)

_____ Nominal interest rate

_____ Real interest rate

Definitions

1. The income necessary to maintain a constant standard of living

2. A contract that requires that a dollar amount be automatically corrected for inflation

3. The ratio of the value of the fixed basket purchased by the typical consumer to the basket's value in the base year multiplied by 100

4. The quantities of each item purchased by the typical consumer

5. The ratio of the value of a fixed basket of goods and services purchased by firms to the basket's value in the base year multiplied by 100

6. The percent change in a price index

7. The interest rate corrected for the effects of inflation

8. An automatic increase in income in order to maintain a constant standard of living

9. The inability of the CPI to account for consumers' substitution toward relatively cheaper goods and services

10. Material well-being

11. Output valued at base-year prices

12. Output valued at current prices

13. The ratio of nominal GDP to real GDP multiplied by 100

14. The interest rate uncorrected for the effects of inflation

15. The benchmark year against which other years are compared

16. The government agency responsible for tracking prices

Problems and Short-Answer Questions

Practice Problems

1. The following table shows the prices and the quantities consumed in the country known as the University States. Suppose the base year is 2011. *Also, suppose that 2011 is the year the typical consumption basket was determined, so the quantities consumed during 2011 are the only quantities needed to calculate the CPI in every year.*

Year	Price of Books	Quantity of Books	Price of Pencils	Quantity of Pencils	Price of Pens	Quantity of Pens
2011	$50	10	$1.00	100	$5	100
2012	50	12	1.00	200	10	50
2013	60	12	1.50	250	20	20

a. What is the value of the CPI in 2011?

_____

b. What is the value of the CPI in 2012?

_____

c. What is the value of the CPI in 2013?

_____

d. What is the inflation rate in 2012?

_____

e. What is the inflation rate in 2013?

_____

f. What type of bias do you observe in the CPI and corresponding inflation rates you generated above? Explain.

_____

_____

_____

g. If you had a COLA clause in your wage contract based on the CPI calculated above, would your standard of living likely increase, decrease, or stay the same during the years 2011 through 2013? Why?

_____

_____

_____

h. Again, suppose you had a COLA clause in your wage contract based on the CPI calculated above. If you personally only consume pens (no paper or pencils), would your standard of living likely increase, decrease, or stay the same during the years 2011 through 2013? Why?

_____

_____

2. The following table contains the CPI and the Federal Minimum Hourly Wage Rates for the period 1965 through 2012.

Year	CPI	Minimum Wage	Year	CPI	Minimum Wage	Year	CPI	Minimum Wage
1965	31.5	$1.25	1981	90.9	3.35	1997	160.5	5.15
1966	32.4	1.25	1982	96.5	3.35	1998	163.0	5.15
1967	33.4	1.40	1983	99.6	3.35	1999	166.6	5.15
1968	34.8	1.60	1984	103.9	3.35	2000	172.2	5.15
1969	36.7	1.60	1985	107.6	3.35	2001	177.0	5.15
1970	38.8	1.60	1986	109.6	3.35	2002	179.9	5.15
1971	40.5	1.60	1987	113.6	3.35	2003	184.0	5.15
1972	41.8	1.60	1988	118.3	3.35	2004	188.9	5.15
1973	44.4	1.60	1989	124.0	3.35	2005	195.3	5.15
1974	49.3	2.00	1990	130.7	3.80	2006	201.6	5.15
1975	53.8	2.10	1991	136.2	4.25	2007	207.3	5.85
1976	56.9	2.30	1992	140.3	4.25	2008	215.3	6.55
1977	60.6	2.30	1993	144.5	4.25	2009	214.5	7.25
1978	65.2	2.65	1994	148.2	4.25	2010	218.1	7.25
1979	72.6	2.90	1995	152.4	4.25	2011	224.9	7.25
1980	82.4	3.10	1996	156.9	4.75	2012	229.6	7.25

a. Inflate the 1965 minimum wage to its equivalent value measured in 2012 prices.

b. What happened to the standard of living of minimum-wage workers over this forty-seven-year period?

c. Deflate the 2012 minimum wage to its equivalent value measured in 1965 prices.

d. Do these two methods give you consistent results with regard to the standard of living of minimum-wage workers over time?

e. The minimum wage did not change over the eight-year period from 1981 to 1989. By what percentage did the purchasing power of the minimum wage decline over this period? (Hint: Inflate the value of the minimum wage in 1981 to its equivalent in 1989. Then generate the percent change.)

f. What happened to the standard of living of minimum-wage workers over the period from 1990 to 2000? (Inflate the 1990 minimum wage and compare it to the 2000 minimum wage.)

3. Suppose that you lend your roommate $100 for one year at 9 percent nominal interest.
   a. How many dollars of interest will your roommate pay you at the end of the year?

   _____

   b. Suppose at the time you both agreed to the terms of the loan, you both expected the inflation rate to be 5 percent during the year of the loan. What do you both expect the real interest rate to be on the loan?

   _____

   c. Suppose at the end of the year, you are surprised to discover that the actual inflation rate over the year was 8 percent. What was the actual real interest rate generated by this loan?

   _____

   d. In the case described above, actual inflation turned out to be higher than expected. Which of the two of you had the unexpected gain or loss—your roommate (the borrower) or you (the lender)? Why?

   _____

   _____

   e. What would the real interest rate on the loan have been if the actual inflation rate had turned out to be a whopping 11 percent?

   _____

   f. Explain what it means to have a negative real interest rate.

   _____

   _____

Short-Answer Questions

1. What does the consumer price index attempt to measure?

   _____

   _____

   _____

2. What are the steps that one must go through in order to construct a consumer price index?

   _____

   _____

   _____

3. Which would have a greater impact on the CPI: a 20 percent increase in the price of Rolex watches or a 20 percent increase in the price of new cars? Why?

   _____

   _____

   _____

4. Suppose there is an increase in the price of imported BMW automobiles (which are produced in Germany). Would this have a larger impact on the CPI or the GDP deflator? Why?

_____

_____

_____

5. If the Bureau of Labor Statistics failed to recognize the increase in memory, power, and speed of newer model computers, in which direction would the CPI be biased? What do we call this type of bias?

_____

_____

_____

6. From 1978 to 1979, the minimum wage increased 25 cents. Did minimum-wage workers see an increase in their standard of living? (Use the data from question 2 in the Practice Problems above.)

_____

_____

_____

7. What does the real interest rate measure?

_____

_____

_____

8. Suppose you lend money to your sister at a nominal interest rate of 10 percent because you both expect the inflation rate to be 6 percent. Furthermore, suppose that after the loan has been repaid, you discover that the actual inflation rate over the life of the loan was only 2 percent. Who gained at the other's expense—you or your sister? Why?

_____

_____

_____

9. Paying close attention to question 8, make a general statement with regard to who gains or loses (the borrower or the lender) on a loan contract when inflation turns out to be either higher or lower than expected.

_____

_____

_____

10. If workers and firms negotiate a wage increase based on their expectation of inflation, who gains or loses (the workers or the firms) if actual inflation turns out to be higher than expected? Why?

_____

_____

_____

Self-Test

True/False Questions

_____ 1. An increase in the price of imported cameras is captured by the CPI but not by the GDP deflator.

_____ 2. An increase in the price of helicopters purchased by the U.S. military is captured by the CPI.

_____ 3. Because an increase in gasoline prices causes consumers to ride their bikes more and drive their cars less, the CPI tends to underestimate the cost of living.

_____ 4. An increase in the price of diamonds will have a greater impact on the CPI than an equal percentage increase in the price of food because diamonds are so much more expensive.

_____ 5. The "base year" in a price index is the benchmark year against which other years are compared.

_____ 6. If the CPI rises at 5 percent per year, then every individual in the country needs exactly a 5 percent increase in their income for their standard of living to remain constant.

_____ 7. The producer price index (PPI) is constructed to measure the change in price of total production.

_____ 8. If the Bureau of Labor Statistics fails to recognize that recently produced automobiles can be driven for many more miles than older models, then the CPI tends to overestimate the cost of living.

_____ 9. If your wage rises from $5.00 to $6.25 while the CPI rises from 112 to 121, you should feel an increase in your standard of living.

_____ 10. The largest category of goods and services in the CPI is medical care.

_____ 11. It is impossible for real interest rates to be negative.

_____ 12. If the nominal interest rate is 12 percent and the rate of inflation is 7 percent, then the real rate of interest is 5 percent.

_____ 13. If lenders demand a real rate of return of 4 percent and they expect inflation to be 5 percent, then they should charge 9 percent interest when they extend loans.

_____ 14. If borrowers and lenders agree on a nominal interest rate and inflation turns out to be greater than they had anticipated, lenders will gain at the expense of borrowers.

_____ 15. If workers and firms agree on an increase in wages based on their expectations of inflation and inflation turns out to be less than they expected, workers will gain at the expense of firms.

Multiple-Choice Questions

1. Inflation can be measured by all of the following *except* the
   a. GDP deflator.
   b. consumer price index.
   c. producer price index.
   d. finished goods price index.
   e. All of the above are used to measure inflation.

2. The CPI will be most influenced by a 10 percent increase in the price of which of the following consumption categories?
   a. housing
   b. transportation
   c. medical care
   d. food and beverages
   e. All of the above would produce the same impact.

3. In 1989, the CPI was 124.0. In 1990, it was 130.7. What was the rate of inflation over this period?
   a. 5.1 percent
   b. 5.4 percent
   c. 6.7 percent
   d. 30.7 percent
   e. You can't tell without knowing the base year.

4. Which of the following would likely cause the CPI to rise more than the GDP deflator?
   a. an increase in the price of Fords
   b. an increase in the price of tanks purchased by the military
   c. an increase in the price of domestically produced fighter planes sold exclusively to Israel
   d. an increase in the price of Hondas produced in Japan and sold in the United States
   e. an increase in the price of John Deere tractors

5. The "basket" on which the CPI is based is composed of
   a. raw materials purchased by firms.
   b. total current production.
   c. products purchased by the typical consumer.
   d. consumer production.
   e. none of the above.

6. If there is an increase in the price of apples that causes consumers to purchase fewer pounds of apples and more pounds of oranges, the CPI will suffer from
   a. substitution bias.
   b. bias due to the introduction of new goods.
   c. bias due to unmeasured quality change.
   d. base-year bias.
   e. none of the above.

Use the following table to answer questions 7 through 12. The table shows the prices and the quantities consumed in Carnivore Country. Suppose the base year is 2011. *Also, suppose that 2011 is the year the typical consumption basket was determined, so the quantities consumed in 2011 are the only quantities needed to calculate the CPI in each year.*

Year	Price of Beef	Quantity of Beef	Price of Pork	Quantity of Pork
2011	$2.00	100	$1.00	100
2012	2.50	90	0.90	120
2013	2.75	105	1.00	130

7. What is the value of the basket in the base year?
   a. $300
   b. $333
   c. $418.75
   d. $459.25
   e. none of the above

8. What are the values of the CPI in 2011, 2012, and 2013, respectively?
   a. 100, 111, 139.6
   b. 100, 109.2, 116
   c. 100, 113.3, 125
   d. 83.5, 94.2, 100
   e. none of the above

9. What is the inflation rate for 2012?
   a. 0 percent
   b. 9.2 percent
   c. 11 percent
   d. 13.3 percent
   e. none of the above

10. What is the inflation rate for 2013?
    a. 0 percent
    b. 10.3 percent
    c. 11 percent
    d. 13.3 percent
    e. none of the above

11. The table shows that the 2012 inflation rate is biased upward because of
    a. bias due to the introduction of new goods.
    b. bias due to unmeasured quality change.
    c. substitution bias.
    d. base-year bias.
    e. none of the above.

12. Suppose the base year is changed in the table from 2011 to 2013. Also, suppose that the typical consumption basket was now determined in 2013 (now use the 2013 consumption basket). What is the new value of the CPI in 2012?
    a. 90.6
    b. 100.0
    c. 114.7
    d. 134.3
    e. none of the above

13. Suppose your income rises from $19,000 to $31,000 while the CPI rises from 122 to 169. Your standard of living has likely
    a. fallen.
    b. risen.
    c. stayed the same.
    d. You can't tell without knowing the base year.

14. If the nominal interest rate is 7 percent and the inflation rate is 3 percent, then the real interest rate is
    a.   −4 percent.
    b.   3 percent.
    c.   4 percent.
    d.   10 percent.
    e.   21 percent.

15. Which of the following statements is correct?
    a.   The real interest rate is the sum of the nominal interest rate and the inflation rate.
    b.   The real interest rate is the nominal interest rate minus the inflation rate.
    c.   The nominal interest rate is the inflation rate minus the real interest rate.
    d.   The nominal interest rate is the real interest rate minus the inflation rate.
    e.   None of the above is true.

16. If inflation is 8 percent and the real interest rate is 3 percent, then the nominal interest rate should be
    a.   3/8 percent.
    b.   5 percent.
    c.   11 percent.
    d.   24 percent.
    e.   −5 percent.

17. Under which of the following conditions would you prefer to be the lender?
    a.   The nominal rate of interest is 20 percent, and the inflation rate is 25 percent.
    b.   The nominal rate of interest is 15 percent, and the inflation rate is 14 percent.
    c.   The nominal rate of interest is 12 percent, and the inflation rate is 9 percent.
    d.   The nominal rate of interest is 5 percent, and the inflation rate is 1 percent.

18. Under which of the following conditions would you prefer to be the borrower?
    a.   The nominal rate of interest is 20 percent, and the inflation rate is 25 percent.
    b.   The nominal rate of interest is 15 percent, and the inflation rate is 14 percent.
    c.   The nominal rate of interest is 12 percent, and the inflation rate is 9 percent.
    d.   The nominal rate of interest is 5 percent, and the inflation rate is 1 percent.

19. If borrowers and lenders agree on a nominal interest rate and inflation turns out to be less than they had expected,
    a.   borrowers will gain at the expense of lenders.
    b.   lenders will gain at the expense of borrowers.
    c.   neither borrowers nor lenders will gain because the nominal interest rate has been fixed by contract.
    d.   none of the above is true.

20. If workers and firms agree on an increase in wages based on their expectations of inflation and inflation turns out to be more than they expected,
    a.   firms will gain at the expense of workers.
    b.   workers will gain at the expense of firms.
    c.   neither workers nor firms will gain because the increase in wages is fixed in the labor agreement.
    d.   none of the above is true.

Advanced Critical Thinking

Your grandfather quit smoking cigarettes in 1995. When you ask him why he quit, you get a surprising answer. Instead of reciting the health benefits of quitting smoking, he says, "I quit because it was just getting too expensive. I started smoking in 1965 in Vietnam and cigarettes were only 45 cents a pack. The last pack I bought was $2.00, and I just couldn't justify spending more than four times as much on cigarettes as I used to."

1. In 1965, the CPI was 31.5. In 1995, the CPI was 152.4. While it is commendable that your grandfather quit smoking, what is wrong with his explanation?

   _____

   _____

   _____

   _____

2. What is the equivalent cost of a 1965 pack of cigarettes measured in 1995 prices?

   _____

   _____

3. What is the equivalent cost of a 1995 pack of cigarettes measured in 1965 prices?

   _____

   _____

4. Do both methods give you the same conclusion?

   _____

   _____

   _____

5. The preceding example demonstrates what economists refer to as "money illusion." Why do you think economists might choose the phrase "money illusion" to describe this behavior?

   _____

   _____

   _____

   _____

   _____

Solutions

Terms and Definitions

_3_ Consumer price index

_6_ Inflation rate

_13_ GDP deflator

_4_ Basket (of goods and services)

_15_ Base year

_16_ Bureau of Labor Statistics

_5_ Producer price index

_1_ Cost of living

_10_ Standard of living

_9_ Substitution bias

_12_ Nominal GDP

_11_ Real GDP

_2_ Indexed contract

_8_ Cost-of-living allowance (COLA)

_14_ Nominal interest rate

_7_ Real interest rate

Practice Problems

1. a. ($1,100/$1,100) × 100 = 100

   b. ($1,600/$1,100) × 100 = 145.5

   c. ($2,750/$1,100) × 100 = 250

   d. [(145.5 − 100)/100] × 100 = 45.5 percent

   e. [(250 − 145.5)/145.5] × 100 = 71.8 percent

   f. Substitution bias, because as the price of pens increased, the quantity consumed declined significantly.

   g. Increase, because this CPI overstates the increase in the cost of living.

   h. Decrease, because the price of pens has increased a greater percentage than the CPI.

2. a. $1.25 × (229.6/31.5) = $9.11

   b. It went down because $9.11 > $7.25

   c. $7.25 × (31.5/229.6) = $0.99

   d. Yes, because $0.99 < $1.25. Minimum-wage workers were better off in 1965.

   e. $3.35 × (124.0/90.9) = $4.57

   Further, ($3.35 − $4.57)/$4.57 = −27%

   Alternatively, you can deflate the minimum wage from 1989 to 1981 and get the same result.

   f. $3.80 × (172.2/130.7) = $5.01 < $5.15, so the standard of living of a worker earning the minimum wage improved slightly during the 1990s.

3. a. $9

   b. 9% − 5% = 4%

   c. 9% − 8% = 1%

   d. Your roommate (the borrower) gained; you lost because the borrower repaid the loan with dollars of surprisingly little value.

   e. 9% − 11% = −2%

f. Because of inflation, the interest payment is not large enough to allow the lender to break even (maintain constant purchasing power compared to the day the loan was made).

Short-Answer Questions

1. The overall cost of the goods and services purchased by the typical consumer.

2. Fix the basket, find the prices, compute the basket's cost, choose a base year, and compute the index.

3. New cars, because there are a greater number of new cars in the typical consumption basket.

4. The CPI, because BMWs are in the typical consumption basket, but BMWs are not included in U.S. GDP.

5. Upward, unmeasured quality change.

6. No, $2.65 × (72.6/65.2) = $2.95, which is greater than $2.90.

7. The interest rate adjusted for the effects of inflation.

8. Expected real interest rate = 4 percent. Actual real interest rate = 8 percent. You gained and your sister lost.

9. When inflation is higher than expected, borrowers gain. When inflation is lower than expected, lenders gain.

10. Firms gain, workers lose, because wages didn't rise as much as the cost of living.

True/False Questions

1. T

2. F; military helicopters are not consumer goods.

3. F; the CPI tends to overstate the cost of living because people substitute toward cheaper goods.

4. F; prices in the CPI are weighted according to how much consumers buy of each and food is a larger portion of the consumption basket.

5. T

6. F; the CPI tends to overstate the effects of inflation.

7. F; the PPI measures the price of raw materials.

8. T

9. T

10. F; the largest category is housing.

11. F; if inflation exceeds the nominal interest rate, the real interest rate is negative.

12. T

13. T

14. F; borrowers will gain at the expense of lenders.

15. T

Multiple-Choice Questions

1. d

2. a

3. b
4. d
5. c
6. a
7. a
8. c
9. d
10. b
11. c
12. a
13. b
14. c
15. b
16. c
17. d
18. a
19. b
20. a

Advanced Critical Thinking

1. He is only looking at the cost of cigarettes uncorrected for inflation. It is likely that the real cost has not risen as much as first appears or maybe even gone down.

2. $\$0.45 \times (152.4/31.5) = \$2.18 > \$2.00$

3. $\$2.00 \times (31.5/152.4) = \$0.41 < \$0.45$

4. Yes, each method suggests that, after correcting for inflation, cigarettes were actually more expensive in 1965.

5. When people base decisions on values uncorrected for inflation, there may be an illusion that the cost of living has risen.

Chapter 17
Production and Growth

Goals
In this chapter you will

- See how much economic growth differs around the world
- Consider why productivity is the key determinant of a country's standard of living
- Analyze the factors that determine a country's productivity
- Examine how a country's policies influence its productivity growth

Outcomes
After accomplishing these goals, you should be able to

- List the countries with the highest GDP per person and the countries whose GDP per person is growing the fastest
- Explain why production limits consumption in the long run
- List and explain the factors of production
- Explain seven areas of policy action that may influence a country's productivity and growth

Chapter Overview

Context and Purpose

Chapter 17 is the first chapter in a four-chapter sequence on the production of output in the long run. Chapter 17 addresses the determinants of the level and growth rate of output. We find that capital and labor are among the primary determinants of output. In Chapter 18, we address how saving and investment in capital goods affect the production of output, and in Chapter 19, we learn about some of the tools people and firms use when choosing capital projects in which to invest. In Chapter 20, we address the market for labor.

The purpose of Chapter 17 is to examine the long-run determinants of both the level and the growth rate of real GDP per person. Along the way, we will discover the factors that determine the productivity of workers and address what governments might do to improve the productivity of their citizens.

Chapter Review

Introduction There is great variation in the standard of living across countries at a point in time and within a country across time—for example, between the United States and India today, and between the United States of today and the United States of 100 years ago. Growth rates also vary from country to country with East Asia growing quickly and sub-Saharan Africa growing slowly. This chapter examines the long-run determinants of both the *level* and the *growth rate* of *real GDP per person*.

Economic Growth around the World

There is great variation across countries in both the *level* of real GDP per person and the *growth rate* of real GDP per person.

- At present, the *level* of real GDP per person in the United States is about sixteen times that of India and eight times that of China.

- However, since the *growth rate* of real GDP per person also varies across countries, the ranking of countries by real GDP per person changes over time. For example, over the past 100 years, the ranking of Japan has risen relative to others because it has had an above average growth rate while the ranking of the United Kingdom has fallen due to its below average growth rate.

  Due to economic growth, the average American today enjoys conveniences such as television, air conditioning, cars, telephones, and medicines that the richest American didn't have 150 years ago. Since measures of inflation and output fail to fully capture the introduction of new goods, we overestimate inflation and underestimate economic growth.

Productivity: Its Role and Determinants

A country's standard of living depends directly on the productivity of its citizens because an economy's income is equal to an economy's output. Productivity refers to the quantity of goods and services produced from each unit of labor input. The productivity of a worker is determined by the available physical capital, human capital, natural resources, and technological knowledge. These inputs or *factors of production* are explained below:

- Physical capital per worker (or just capital): Physical capital is the stock of equipment and structures that are used to produce goods and services. Note that these tools and machines are themselves the output from prior human production.

- Human capital per worker: Human capital is the knowledge and skills that workers acquire through education, training, and experience. Note that human capital, like physical capital, is a human-made or produced factor of production.

- Natural resources per worker: Natural resources are inputs provided by nature's bounty, such as land, rivers, and mineral deposits. Natural resources come in two forms: *renewable* and *nonrenewable*.

- Technological knowledge: Technological knowledge is the understanding about the best ways to produce goods and services. Examples of advances in technology are the discovery and application of herbicides and pesticides in agriculture and of the assembly line in manufacturing.

  Technological knowledge differs from human capital. Technological knowledge is society's understanding of the best production methods while human capital is the amount of understanding of these methods that has been transmitted to the labor force.

  A *production function* establishes the relationship between the quantity of inputs used in production and the quantity of output from production. If a production function has *constant returns to scale*, then doubling all of the inputs doubles output.

  In summary, output per worker (labor productivity) depends on physical capital per worker, human capital per worker, natural resources per worker, and the state of technology.

The only factor of production that is not a produced factor is natural resources. Since there is a fixed supply of nonrenewable natural resources, many people have argued that there is a limit to how much the world's economies can grow. So far, however, technological advances have found ways around these limits. Evidence of stable or falling prices of natural resources suggests that we are continuing to succeed at stretching our limited resources.

Economic Growth and Public Policy

Physical capital per worker, human capital per worker, natural resources per worker, and technological knowledge determine productivity. Productivity determines living standards. If a government wishes to raise the productivity and standard of living of its citizens, it should pursue policies that:

- *Encourage saving and investment.* If society consumes less and saves more, it has more resources available to invest in the production of capital. Additional capital increases productivity and living standards. This additional growth has an opportunity cost—society must give up current consumption in order to attain more growth. Investment in capital may be subject to diminishing returns: As the stock of capital rises, the extra output produced by an additional unit of capital declines. Thus, an additional increment of capital in a poor country increases growth more than the same increment in an already rich country. This is known as the catch-up effect because it is easier for a relatively poor country to grow quickly. However, because of diminishing returns to capital, higher saving and investment in a poor country will lead to higher growth only for a period of time, with growth slowing down again as the economy accumulates a higher level of capital stock.

- *Encourage investment from abroad.* Investment from abroad can be encouraged by removing restrictions on the ownership of domestic capital and by providing a stable political environment. In addition to using domestic saving to invest in capital, countries can attract investment by foreigners. There are two categories of foreign investment. *Foreign direct investment* is capital investment that is owned and operated by a foreign entity. *Foreign portfolio investment* is capital investment that is financed with foreign money but is operated by domestic residents. Investment from abroad increases a country's GDP more than its GNP because the investing country earns the profits from the investment. The World Bank and the International Monetary Fund help channel foreign investment toward poor countries.

- *Encourage education.* Education is investment in human capital. Education not only increases the productivity of the recipient, it may provide a positive *externality*. An externality occurs when the actions of one person affect the well-being of a bystander. An educated individual may generate ideas that become useful to others. This is an argument for public education. Poor countries may suffer from *brain drain* when their educated workers emigrate to rich countries.

- *Improve health and nutrition.* Expenditures on the health and nutrition of workers can significantly increase labor productivity. These expenditures are sometimes viewed as an investment in human capital, similar to expenditures on education.

- *Protect property rights and establish political stability. Property rights* refer to the ability of people to exercise control over their resources. For individuals to be willing to work, save and invest, and trade with others by contract, they must be confident that their production and capital will not be stolen and that their agreements will be enforced. Even a remote possibility of political instability creates uncertainty with regard to property rights because a revolutionary government might confiscate property—particularly capital.

- *Encourage free trade.* Free trade is like a technological advance. It allows a country to transform the output from its production into products that another country produces more efficiently. The *infant-industry argument* suggests that developing countries should pursue *inward-oriented policies* by restricting international trade to protect fledgling domestic industry from foreign competition. Most economists disagree with the infant-industry argument and promote *outward-oriented policies* that reduce or eliminate trade barriers. Advantageous natural geography, such as good natural seaports and long coastlines, promotes trade and growth.

- *Encourage research and development.* Most of the increase in the standard of living is due to an increase in technological knowledge that comes from research and development. After a time, knowledge is a *public good* in that we all can use it at the same time without diminishing another's benefits. Research and development might be encouraged with grants, tax breaks, and patents to establish temporary property rights to an invention. Alternatively, it might be encouraged by simply maintaining property rights and political stability.

- *Address population growth.* Population growth may affect productivity in both positive and negative ways. Rapid population growth may *stretch natural resources* across more people. Thomas Malthus (1766–1834) argued that population growth will always rise to the limit imposed by the food supply, causing mankind to live forever in poverty. Any attempt to alleviate poverty will simply cause the poor to have more children, returning them to subsistence living. Malthus' predictions have not come true because he underestimated the ability of technological progress to expand the food supply. Rapid population growth *dilutes the capital stock* (both physical and human capital) by spreading it across more workers. Educated women tend to have fewer children because the opportunity cost of having children increases as opportunities grow. However, a larger population may *promote technological progress.* Throughout history, most technological progress has come from larger population centers where there are more people who are able to discover things and exchange ideas.

Helpful Hints

1. A simple example more clearly defines the factors of production. The simpler the production process, the easier it is to separate and analyze the factors of production. For example, suppose output is "holes dug in the ground." Then the production function is:

$$Y = A \, F(L, K, H, N)$$

where Y is the number of holes dug, A is technological knowledge, L is labor, K is physical capital, H is human capital, and N is natural resources. If we have more workers, there is an increase in L, and Y would increase. If we have more shovels, there is an increase in K, and Y would increase. If workers are educated so that more of them dig with the spaded end of the shovel as opposed to digging with the handle, there is an increase in H, and Y would increase. (Note: The number of workers and the number of shovels is unchanged.) If our country has softer soil so that digging is easier here, N is larger, and therefore, Y is larger. Finally, if we discover that it is more productive to dig after it rains rather than during a drought, there is an increase in A, and Y should increase.

Terms and Definitions

Choose a definition for each key term.

Key Terms	Definitions

Key Terms

_____ Real GDP per person

_____ Growth rate

_____ Productivity

_____ Physical capital

_____ Factors of production

_____ Human capital

_____ Natural resources

_____ Renewable resource

_____ Nonrenewable resource

_____ Technological knowledge

_____ Production function

_____ Constant returns to scale

_____ Diminishing returns

_____ Catch-up effect

_____ Foreign direct investment

_____ Foreign portfolio investment

_____ Externality

_____ Property rights

_____ Infant-industry argument

_____ Inward-oriented policies

_____ Outward-oriented policies

_____ Public good

Definitions

1. The knowledge and skills that workers acquire through education, training, and experience

2. Capital investment owned and operated by foreigners

3. The relationship between inputs and outputs from production

4. A good that we may all use at the same time without diminishing another's benefits

5. The ability of people to exercise control over their resources

6. The quantity of goods and services available for the average individual in the economy

7. The stock of equipment and structures used to produce output

8. When the incremental increase in output declines as equal increments of an input are added to production

9. A production process where doubling all of the inputs doubles the output

10. Natural resource that can be reproduced

11. Restricting international trade to protect fledgling domestic industry from foreign competition

12. Policies that decrease international trade restrictions

13. The property that poorer countries tend to grow more rapidly than richer countries

14. The annual percentage change in output

15. Inputs used in production, such as labor, capital, and natural resources

16. Natural resource that is limited in supply

17. When the actions of one person affect the well-being of a bystander

18. Policies that increase international trade restrictions

19. A society's understanding about the best ways to produce goods and services

20. The quantity of goods and services produced from each unit of labor input

21. Inputs into production provided by nature

22. Capital investment financed with foreign money but operated by domestic residents

Problems and Short-Answer Questions

Practice Problems

1.

Country	Current Real GDP/Person	Current Growth Rate
Northcountry	$15,468	1.98%
Southcountry	13,690	2.03
Eastcountry	6,343	3.12
Westcountry	1,098	0.61

a. Which country is richest? How do you know?

_____

b. Which country is advancing most quickly? How do you know?

_____

c. Which country would likely see the greatest benefit from an increase in capital investment? Why?

_____

_____

_____

d. Referring to question *c* above: Would this country continue to see the same degree of benefits from an increase in capital investment forever? Why or why not?

_____

_____

_____

e. Referring to question *d* above: Why might investment in human capital and research and development fail to exhibit the same degree of diminishing returns as investment in physical capital?

_____

_____

f. Which country has the potential to grow most quickly? List some reasons why it may not be living up to its potential.

_____

_____

_____

_____

g. If real GDP per person in Northcountry next year is $15,918, what is its annual growth rate?

_____

_____

2. Imagine a kitchen. It contains a cook, the cook's diploma, a recipe book, a stove and utensils, and some venison harvested from the open range.
    a. Link each object in the kitchen to a general category within the factors of production.

    _____

    _____

    b. While the different factors of production exhibit different levels of durability, which one is special in that it does not wear out?

    _____

    _____

3. a. List the policies governments might pursue to increase the productivity of their citizens.

    _____

    _____

    b. Which one is, at the very least, fundamentally necessary as a background in which the other policies may operate? Why?

    _____

    _____

    _____

    c. Does a growing population enhance or inhibit growth in productivity? Explain.

    _____

    _____

    _____

Short-Answer Questions

1. Economists measure both the level of real GDP per person and the growth rate of real GDP per person. What different concept does each statistic capture?

    _____

    _____

    _____

2. Must poor countries stay relatively poor forever and must rich countries stay relatively rich forever? Why?

    _____

    _____

    _____

3. What factors determine productivity? Which ones are human produced?

    _____

    _____

    _____

4. How does human capital differ from physical capital?

    _____

    _____

    _____

5. Explain the opportunity cost of investing in capital. Is there any difference in the opportunity cost of investing in human capital versus physical capital?

    _____

    _____

    _____

6. Why does an increase in the rate of saving and investment only increase the rate of growth temporarily?

    _____

    _____

    _____

7. If foreigners buy newly issued stock in Ford, and Ford uses the proceeds to expand capacity by building new plants and equipment, which will rise more in the future: GDP or GNP? Why? What do we call this type of investment?

    _____

    _____

    _____

8. Some economists argue for lengthening patent protection while some economists argue for shortening it. Why might patents increase productivity? Why might they decrease productivity?

    _____

    _____

    _____

Self-Test

True/False Questions

_____ 1. The United States should grow faster than Japan because the United States has a larger economy.

_____ 2. Evidence of rising prices for natural resources demonstrates that nonrenewable resources will become so scarce that economic growth will be limited.

_____ 3. The rate of economic growth is probably underestimated.

_____ 4. Human capital refers to human-made capital such as tools and machinery, as opposed to natural capital such as rivers and timber.

_____ 5. If a production function exhibits constant returns to scale, then doubling all of the inputs doubles output.

_____ 6. In very poor countries, paying parents to send their children to school may increase the education of poor children and decrease the use of child labor.

_____ 7. An increase in capital should cause the growth rate of a relatively poor country to increase more than that of a rich country.

_____ 8. An increase in the rate of saving and investment permanently increases a country's rate of growth.

_____ 9. A country can only increase its level of investment by increasing its saving.

_____ 10. The only factor of production that is not "produced" is natural resources.

_____ 11. Investment in human capital and technology may be particularly productive because of positive spillover effects.

_____ 12. If Germans invest in the U.S. economy by building a new Mercedes factory, in the future U.S. GDP will rise by more than U.S. GNP.

_____ 13. Most economists believe that inward-oriented policies that protect infant industries improve the growth rates of developing nations.

_____ 14. Economic evidence supports the predictions of Thomas Malthus regarding the effects of population growth and the food supply on the standard of living.

_____ 15. The opportunity cost of additional growth is that someone must forgo current consumption.

Multiple-Choice Questions

1. A reasonable measure of the standard of living in a country is
   a. real GDP per person.
   b. real GDP.
   c. nominal GDP per person.
   d. nominal GDP.
   e. the growth rate of nominal GDP per person.

2. Many East Asian countries are growing very quickly because
   a. they have enormous natural resources.
   b. they are imperialists and have collected wealth from previous victories in war.
   c. they save and invest an unusually high percentage of their GDP.
   d. they have always been wealthy and will continue to be wealthy, which is known as the "snowball effect."

3. When a nation has very little GDP per person,
    a. it is doomed to being relatively poor forever.
    b. it must be a small nation.
    c. it has the potential to grow relatively quickly due to the "catch-up effect."
    d. an increase in capital will likely have little impact on output.
    e. none of the above is true.

4. Once a country is wealthy,
    a. it is nearly impossible for it to become relatively poorer.
    b. it may be harder for it to grow quickly because of the diminishing returns to capital.
    c. capital becomes more productive due to the "catch-up effect."
    d. it no longer needs any human capital.
    e. none of the above is true.

5. The opportunity cost of growth is a reduction in
    a. current investment.
    b. current saving.
    c. current consumption.
    d. taxes.

6. *For a given level of technology*, we should expect an increase in labor productivity within a nation when there is an increase in each of the following *except*
    a. human capital per worker.
    b. physical capital per worker.
    c. natural resources per worker.
    d. labor.

7. Which of the following statements is *true*?
    a. Countries may have a different level of GDP per person, but they all grow at the same rate.
    b. Countries may have a different growth rate, but they all have the same level of GDP per person.
    c. Countries all have the same growth rate and level of output because any country can obtain the same factors of production.
    d. Countries have great variance in both the level and growth rate of GDP per person; thus, poor countries can become relatively rich over time.

8. If a production function exhibits constant returns to scale, doubling all of the inputs
    a. has absolutely no impact on output because output is constant.
    b. doubles output.
    c. more than doubles output due to the catch-up effect.
    d. less than doubles output due to diminishing returns.

9. Copper is an example of
    a. human capital.
    b. physical capital.
    c. a renewable natural resource.
    d. a nonrenewable natural resource.
    e. technology.

10. Which of the following statements regarding the impact of population growth on productivity is *true*?
    a. There is no evidence yet that rapid population growth stretches natural resources to the point that it limits growth in productivity.
    b. Rapid population growth may dilute the capital stock, lowering productivity.
    c. Rapid population growth may promote technological progress, increasing productivity.
    d. All of the above are true.

11. Thomas Malthus argued that
    a. technological progress will continuously generate improvements in productivity and living standards.
    b. labor is the only true factor of production.
    c. an ever-increasing population is constrained only by the food supply, resulting in chronic famines.
    d. private charities and government aid will improve the welfare of the poor.
    e. None of the above is true.

12. Madelyn goes to college and reads many books while at school. Her education increases which of the following factors of production?
    a. human capital
    b. physical capital
    c. natural resources
    d. technology
    e. All of the above would be increased.

13. Which of the following describes an increase in technological knowledge?
    a. A farmer discovers that it is better to plant in the spring rather than in the fall.
    b. A farmer buys another tractor.
    c. A farmer hires another day laborer.
    d. A farmer sends his child to agricultural college, and the child returns to work on the farm.

14. Our standard of living is most closely related to
    a. how hard we work.
    b. our supply of capital because everything of value is produced by machinery.
    c. our supply of natural resources because they limit production.
    d. our productivity because our income is equal to what we produce.

15. Which of the following is an example of foreign portfolio investment?
    a. A naturalized U.S. citizen, who was originally born in Germany, buys stock in Ford, and Ford uses the proceeds to buy a new plant.
    b. Toyota builds a new plant in Tennessee.
    c. Toyota buys stock in Ford, and Ford uses the proceeds to build a new plant in Michigan.
    d. Ford builds a new plant in Michigan.
    e. None of the above is an example of foreign portfolio investment.

16. Which of the following government policies is *least* likely to increase growth in Africa?
    a. increase expenditures on public education
    b. increase restrictions on the importing of Japanese automobiles and electronics
    c. eliminate civil war
    d. reduce restrictions on foreign capital investment
    e. All of the above would increase growth.

17. If Mazda builds a new plant in Illinois,
    a. in the future, U.S. GDP will rise more than U.S. GNP.
    b. in the future, U.S. GDP will rise less than U.S. GNP.
    c. in the future, U.S. GDP and GNP will both fall because some income from this investment will accrue to foreigners.
    d. there has been an increase in foreign portfolio investment in the United States.
    e. None of the above is true.

18. If real GDP per person in 2009 is $18,073 and real GDP per person in 2010 is $18,635, what is the growth rate of real output over this period?
    a. 3.0 percent
    b. 3.1 percent
    c. 5.62 percent
    d. 18.0 percent
    e. 18.6 percent

19. Which of the following expenditures to enhance productivity is most likely to emit a positive externality?
    a. Megabank buys a new computer.
    b. Susan pays her college tuition.
    c. Exxon leases a new oil field.
    d. General Motors buys a new drill press.

20. To increase growth, governments should do all of the following *except*
    a. promote free trade.
    b. encourage saving and investment.
    c. encourage foreigners to invest in your country.
    d. encourage research and development.
    e. nationalize major industries.

Advanced Critical Thinking

You are having a discussion with other with people from the Millennial generation. The conversation turns to a supposed lack of growth and opportunity in the United States when compared to some Asian countries such as Japan, South Korea, Taiwan, China, and Singapore. Your roommate says, "These Asian countries must have cheated somehow. That's the only way they could have possibly grown so quickly."

1. Have you learned anything in this chapter that would make you question your roommate's assertion?

   _____

   _____

   _____

   _____

   _____

2. The phenomenal growth rate of Japan since World War II has often been referred to as the "Japanese miracle." Is it a miracle or is it explainable?

   _____

   _____

   _____

   _____

   _____

3. Are the high growth rates found in these Asian countries without cost?

   _____

   _____

   _____

   _____

   _____

Solutions

Terms and Definitions

_6_ Real GDP per person

_14_ Growth rate

_20_ Productivity

_7_ Physical capital

_15_ Factors of production

_1_ Human capital

_21_ Natural resources

_10_ Renewable resource

_16_ Nonrenewable resource

_19_ Technological knowledge

_3_ Production function

_9_ Constant returns to scale

_8_ Diminishing returns

_13_ Catch-up effect

_2_ Foreign direct investment

_22_ Foreign portfolio investment

_17_ Externality

_5_ Property rights

_11_ Infant-industry argument

_18_ Inward-oriented policies

_12_ Outward-oriented policies

_4_ Public good

Practice Problems

1. a. Northcountry because it has the largest real GDP per person.

   b. Eastcountry because it has the largest growth rate.

   c. Westcountry is the poorest and likely has the least capital. Since capital exhibits diminishing returns, it is most productive when it is relatively scarce.

   d. No. Because of diminishing returns to capital, the additional growth from increasing capital declines as a country has more capital.

   e. Human capital emits a positive externality. Research and development is a public good after dissemination.

   f. Westcountry because it is currently the poorest and could easily benefit from additional capital. It may have trade restrictions (inward-oriented policies), a corrupt or unstable government, few courts, and a lack of established property rights, etc.

   g. ($15,918 − $15,468)/$15,468 = 0.029 = 2.9%

2. a. cook = labor, diploma = human capital, recipes = technological knowledge, stove and utensils = capital, venison = natural resource.

   b. Recipes (technological knowledge) never wear out. Labor and human capital die, the stove and utensils wear out slowly, and the venison is used up (although it is probably renewable).

3. a. Encourage saving and investment, investment from abroad, education, health and nutrition, free trade, research and development, protect property rights, and establish political stability.

   b. Property rights and political stability are necessary for there to be any incentive to save, invest, trade, or educate.

   c. The answer is uncertain. A rapidly growing population may reduce productivity by stretching natural resources across more people and by diluting the capital stock across more workers. However, there is evidence that more technological progress takes place in areas with large populations.

Short-Answer Questions

1. Level of real GDP per person measures standard of living. Growth rate measures rate of advance of the standard of living.

2. No. Since growth rates vary widely across countries, rich countries can become relatively poorer and poor countries can become relatively richer.

3. Physical capital per worker, human capital per worker, natural resources per worker, and technological knowledge. All except natural resources.

4. Human capital is the knowledge and skills of the worker. Physical capital is the stock of equipment and structures.

5. Someone must forgo current consumption. No, someone must save instead of consume regardless of whether education or machines are purchased with the saving.

6. Because there are diminishing returns to physical capital.

7. GDP. GNP measures only the income of Americans while GDP measures income generated inside the United States. Therefore, GDP will rise more than GNP because some of the profits from the capital investment will accrue to foreigners in the form of dividends. Foreign portfolio investment.

8. Patents provide a property right to an idea; therefore, people are willing to invest in research and development because it is more profitable. Research and development is a public good once the information is disseminated, and a patent restricts this public use.

True/False Questions

1. F; growth depends on the rate of increase in productivity.

2. F; the prices of natural resources, adjusted for inflation, are stable or falling, so our ability to conserve these resources is growing more rapidly than their supplies are dwindling.

3. T

4. F; human capital is the knowledge and skills of workers.

5. T

6. T

7. T

8. F; due to diminishing returns to capital, growth rises temporarily.

9. F; it can attract foreign investment.

10. T

11. T

12. T

13. F; most economists believe that outward-oriented policies improve growth.

14. F; Malthus underestimated technological improvements in food production. Thus, people are not doomed to live at subsistence.

15. T

Multiple-Choice Questions

1. a
2. c
3. c
4. b
5. c
6. d
7. d
8. b
9. d
10. d
11. c
12. a
13. a
14. d
15. c
16. b
17. a
18. b
19. b
20. e

Advanced Critical Thinking

1. Yes. There are many sources of growth and a country can influence all of them except natural resources.

2. Japan's growth is explainable. Indeed, all of the high-growth Asian countries have extremely high investment as a percentage of GDP.

3. No. The opportunity cost of investment is that someone must forgo current consumption in order to save and invest.

Chapter 18
Saving, Investment, and the Financial System

Goals
In this chapter you will

- Learn about some of the important financial institutions in the U.S. economy
- Consider how the financial system is related to key macroeconomic variables
- Develop a model of the supply and demand for loanable funds in financial markets
- Use the loanable-funds model to analyze various government policies
- Consider how government budget deficits affect the U.S. economy

Outcomes
After accomplishing these goals, you should be able to

- List and describe four important types of financial institutions
- Describe the relationship between national saving, government deficits, and investment
- Explain the slope of the supply and demand for loanable funds
- Shift supply and demand in the loanable-funds market in response to a change in taxes on interest or investment
- Shift supply and demand in the loanable-funds market in response to a change in the government's budget deficit

Chapter Overview

Context and Purpose

Chapter 18 is the second chapter in a four-chapter sequence on the production of output in the long run. In Chapter 17, we found that capital and labor are among the primary determinants of output. For this reason, Chapter 18 addresses the market for saving and investment in capital, and Chapter 19 addresses the tools people

283

and firms use when choosing capital projects in which to invest. Chapter 20 will address the market for labor.

The purpose of Chapter 18 is to show how saving and investment are coordinated by the loanable-funds market. Within the framework of the loanable-funds market, we are able to see the effects of taxes and government deficits on saving, investment, the accumulation of capital, and ultimately, the growth rate of output.

Chapter Review

Introduction   Some people save some of their income and have funds that are available to loan. Some people wish to invest in capital equipment and thus need to borrow. The financial system consists of those institutions that help match, or balance, the lending of savers to the borrowing of investors. This is important because investment in capital contributes to economic growth.

Financial Institutions in the U.S. Economy

The financial system is made up of financial institutions that match borrowers and lenders. Financial institutions can be grouped into two categories: financial markets and financial intermediaries.

Financial markets allow firms to borrow *directly* from those who wish to lend. The two most important financial markets are the bond market and the stock market.

- The *bond market* allows large borrowers to borrow directly from the public. The borrower sells a bond (a certificate of indebtedness or IOU), which specifies the *date of maturity* (the date the loan will be repaid), the amount of interest that will be paid periodically, and the *principal* (the amount borrowed and to be repaid at maturity). The buyer of the bond is the lender.

Bond issues differ in three main ways:

(1)   Bonds are of different *terms* (time to maturity). Longer-term bonds are riskier and, thus, usually pay higher interest because the owner of the bond may need to sell it before maturity at a depressed price.

(2)   Bonds have different *credit risk* (probability of default). Higher risk bonds pay higher interest. *Junk bonds* are exceptionally risky bonds.

(3)   Bonds have different types of *tax treatment*. The interest received from owning a *municipal bond* (bond issued by state or local government) is tax exempt. Thus, municipal bonds pay lower interest.

- The *stock market* allows large firms to raise funds for expansion by taking on additional "partners" or owners of the firm. The sale of stock is called *equity finance*, while the sale of bonds is called *debt finance*. Owners of stock share in the profits or losses of the firm, while owners of bonds receive fixed interest payments as creditors. The stockholder accepts more risk than the bondholder accepts but has a higher potential return. Stocks don't mature or expire and are traded on stock exchanges such as the New York Stock Exchange and NASDAQ. Stock prices are determined by supply and demand and reflect expectations of the firm's future profitability. A *stock index*, such as the Dow Jones Industrial Average, is an average of an important group of stock prices.

Financial intermediaries are financial institutions through which savers (lenders) can indirectly loan funds to borrowers. That is, financial intermediaries are middlepersons between borrowers and lenders. The two most important financial intermediaries are banks and mutual funds.

- *Banks* collect deposits from people and businesses (savers) and lend them to other people and businesses (borrowers). Banks pay interest on deposits and charge a slightly higher rate on their loans. Small businesses usually borrow from banks because they are too small to sell stock or bonds. Banks create a *medium of exchange* when they accept a deposit because individuals can access the deposit for a transaction by writing a check or using a debit card. Other intermediaries only offer savers a *store of value* because their saving is not as accessible.

- Mutual funds are institutions that sell shares to the public and use the proceeds to buy a group of stocks and/or bonds. This allows small savers to *diversify* their asset *portfolios* (own a variety of assets). It also allows small savers access to professional money managers. However, few money managers can beat *index funds*, which buy all of the stocks in a stock index without the aid of active management. There are two reasons why index funds outperform actively managed funds. First, it is hard to pick stocks whose prices will rise because the market price of a stock is already a good reflection of a company's true value. Second, index funds keep costs low by rarely buying and selling and by not having to pay the salaries of professional money managers.

Although there are many differences among these financial institutions, the overriding similarity is that they all direct resources from lenders to borrowers.

Saving and Investment in the National Income Accounts

In order to truly appreciate the role of the financial system in directing saving into investment, we must begin to understand saving and investment from a macroeconomic perspective. The national income accounts record the relationship among income, output, saving, investment, expenditures, taxes, and so on. There are a number of national income *identities* (equations that are true by definition) that expose relationships between these variables.

Recall, GDP is the value of output, the value of income earned from producing it, and *the value of expenditures* on it. Therefore,

$$Y = C + I + G + NX$$

where Y = GDP, C = consumption expenditures, I = investment expenditures, G = government purchases, and NX = net exports. To simplify, we assume there is no international sector, which means that we have a *closed economy*. (An *open economy* includes a foreign sector.) Therefore, for our example

$$Y = C + I + G.$$

National saving, or just saving, is the income left over after paying for consumption and government purchases. To find saving, subtract C and G from both sides.

$$Y - C - G = I$$

or $S = I$

which says, saving = investment.

To appreciate the impact of the government's purchases and taxes on saving, we need to define saving as above:

$$S = Y - C - G,$$

which says again that saving is income left over after consumption and government purchases. Now add and subtract T (taxes) from the right side:

$$S = (Y - T - C) + (T - G).$$

This says that saving is equal to private saving $(Y - T - C)$, which is income left over after paying taxes and consumption, and public saving $(T - G)$, which is the government's budget surplus. Often G is greater than T, and the government runs a negative surplus or a budget deficit.

In summary, $S = I$ for the economy as a whole, and the amount of saving available for investment is the sum of private saving and public saving. Although $S = I$ for the entire economy, it is not true for each individual. That is, some people invest less than they save and have funds to lend, while others invest more than they save and need to borrow funds. These groups meet in the market for loanable funds. Note that saving is the income that remains after paying for consumption and government purchases, while investment is the purchase of new capital.

The Market for Loanable Funds

For simplicity, imagine that there is one loanable funds market where all savers take their funds to be loaned and where all investors go to borrow funds.

- The *supply of loanable funds* comes from national saving. A higher real interest rate increases the incentive to save and increases the quantity supplied of loanable funds.

- The *demand for loanable funds* comes from households and firms that wish to borrow to invest. A higher real interest rate increases the cost of borrowing and reduces the quantity demanded of loanable funds.

The supply and demand for loanable funds combine to generate a market for loanable funds. This market determines the equilibrium real interest rate and the equilibrium quantity of funds loaned and borrowed. Since the funds that are loaned are national saving and the funds that are borrowed are used for investment, the loanable-funds market also determines the equilibrium level of saving and investment.

The following three policies increase saving, investment, and capital accumulation, and hence, these policies increase economic growth.

Reduced taxation on interest and dividends increases the return to saving for any real interest rate and, thus, increases the desire to save and loan at each real interest rate. Graphically, this policy will shift the supply of loanable funds to the right, lower the real interest rate, and raise the quantity demanded of funds for investment. Real interest rates fall while saving and investment rise.

Reduced taxation if one invests, for example an investment tax credit, will increase the return to investment in capital for any real interest rate and, thus, increase the desire to borrow and invest at each real interest rate. Graphically, this policy will shift the demand for loanable funds to the right, raise the real interest rate, and increase the quantity supplied of funds. Real interest rates, saving, and investment rise.

A reduction in government debt and deficits (or an increase in a budget surplus) increases public saving $(T - G)$ so more national saving is available at each real interest rate. Graphically, this policy will shift the supply of loanable funds to the right, decrease the real interest rate, and increase the quantity demanded of funds for investment. Real interest rates fall, and saving and investment rise.

Note that a *budget deficit* is an excess of government spending over tax revenue. The accumulation of past government borrowing is called the *government debt*. A budget surplus is an excess of tax revenue over government spending. When government spending equals tax revenue, there is a *balanced budget*. An increase in the deficit reduces national saving, shifts the supply of loanable funds to the left, raises the real interest rate, and reduces the quantity demanded of funds for investment. When private borrowing and investment are reduced due to government borrowing, we say that government is *crowding out* investment. Government surpluses do just the opposite of budget deficits.

The debt–to-GDP ratio usually rises during wars, and this is considered appropriate. However, it rose during the 1980s. Policymakers from both parties viewed this with alarm, and deficits were reduced during the 1990s, and a surplus arose. During the George W. Bush presidency, the budget returned to a deficit for a number of reasons: tax cuts, a recession, spending on homeland security, and the wars in Iraq and Afghanistan. There was a dramatic increase in the debt-to-GDP ratio associated with the financial crisis and recession that started in 2008.

In 2008 and 2009, the U.S. economy experienced a financial crisis with the following key elements: (1) a decline in real estate prices; (2) insolvencies at financial institutions; (3) declining confidence in financial institutions, which lead to people removing uninsured deposits, and financial institutions selling assets at reduced prices; (4) a credit crunch; (5) an economic downturn and a reduction in overall demand for output; and (6) reduced profitability of companies, which reduced the value of assets and fed back into (1).

Helpful Hints

1. A financial intermediary is a middleperson. An intermediary is someone who gets between two groups and negotiates a solution. For example, we have intermediaries in labor negotiations that sit between a firm and a union. In like manner, a bank is a financial intermediary in that it sits between the ultimate lender (the depositor) and the ultimate borrower (the firm or homebuilder) and "negotiates" the terms of the loan contracts. Banks don't lend their own money. They lend the depositor's money.

2. Investment is not the purchase of stocks and bonds. In casual conversation, people use the word "investment" to mean the purchase of stocks and bonds. For example, "I just invested in ten shares of IBM." (Even an economist might say this.) However, when speaking in economic terms, *investment* is the actual purchase of capital equipment and structures. In this technical framework, when I buy ten shares of newly issued IBM stock, there has been only an exchange of assets—IBM has my money, and I have their stock certificates. If IBM takes my money and buys new equipment with it, their purchase of the equipment is economic *investment*.

3. Don't include consumption loans in the supply of loanable funds. In casual conversation, people use the word "saving" to refer to their new deposit in a bank. For example, "I just saved $100 this week." (An economist might say this, too.) However, if that deposit were loaned out to a consumer who used the funds to purchase airline tickets for a vacation, there has been no increase in *national saving* (or just *saving*) in a macroeconomic sense. This is because saving, in a macroeconomic sense, is income (GDP) that remains after *national* consumption expenditures and government purchases ($S = Y - C - G$). No national saving took place if your personal saving was loaned and used for consumption expenditures by another person. Since national saving is the source of the supply of loanable funds, consumption loans do not affect the supply of loanable funds.

4. Demand for loanable funds is private demand for investment funds. The demand for loanable funds only includes private (households and firms) demand for funds to invest in capital structures and equipment. When the government runs a deficit, it does absorb national saving, but it does not buy capital equipment with the funds. Therefore, when the government runs a deficit, we consider it a reduction in the supply of loanable funds, not an increase in the demand for loanable funds.

Terms and Definitions

Choose a definition for each key term.

Key Terms

_____ Financial system

_____ Financial markets

_____ Financial intermediaries

_____ Bank

_____ Medium of exchange

_____ Bond

_____ Stock

_____ Mutual fund

_____ Closed economy

_____ National saving (saving)

_____ Private saving

_____ Public saving

_____ Budget surplus

_____ Budget deficit

_____ Government debt

_____ Investment

_____ Market for loanable funds

_____ Demand for loanable funds

_____ Supply of loanable funds

_____ Crowding out

Definitions

1. Spendable asset such as a checking deposit

2. A shortfall of tax revenue relative to government spending causing public saving to be negative

3. An economy with no international transactions

4. Financial institutions through which savers can indirectly lend to borrowers

5. The group of institutions in the economy that help match borrowers and lenders

6. The amount of borrowing for investment desired at each real interest rate

7. The income that remains after consumption expenditures and taxes

8. The accumulation of past budget deficits

9. The amount of saving made available for lending at each real interest rate

10. Institution that collects deposits and makes loans

11. Institution that sells shares and uses the proceeds to buy a diversified portfolio

12. Financial institutions through which savers can directly lend to borrowers

13. Certificate of ownership of a small portion of a large firm

14. An excess of tax revenue over government spending causing public saving to be positive

15. The income that remains after consumption expenditures and government purchases

16. A decrease in investment as a result of government borrowing

17. Expenditures on capital equipment and structures

18. Certificate of indebtedness or IOU

19. The market in which those who want to save supply funds and those who want to borrow to invest demand funds

20. The tax revenue that the government has left after paying for its spending

Problems and Short-Answer Questions

Practice Problems

1. Fly-by-Night Corporation is in need of capital funds to expand its production capacity. It is selling short- and long-term bonds and is issuing stock. You are considering the prospect of helping finance their expansion.

    a. If you are to buy both short- and long-term bonds from Fly-by-Night, from which bond would you demand a higher rate of return: short- or long-term? Why?

    _____

    _____

    _____

    b. If Standard & Poor's lowered the creditworthiness of Fly-by-Night, would this affect the rate of return you would demand when buying their bonds? Why or why not?

    _____

    _____

    _____

    c. If Fly-by-Night has exactly the same creditworthiness as Deadbeat City and each is issuing the same term to maturity bonds, which issuer must pay the higher interest rate on its bonds? Why?

    _____

    _____

    _____

    d. If Fly-by-Night is issuing both stocks and bonds, from which would you expect to earn the higher rate of return over the long run? Why?

    _____

    _____

    _____

    e. Which would be safer: putting all of your personal saving into Fly-by-Night stock or putting all of your personal saving into a mutual fund that has some Fly-by-Night stock in its portfolio? Why?

    _____

    _____

    _____

2. Use the saving and investment identities from the national income accounts to answer the following questions. Suppose the following values are from the national income accounts of a country with a closed economy (all values are in billions).

$Y = \$6,000$

$T = \$1,000$

$C = \$4,000$

$G = \$1,200$

a. What is the value of saving and investment in this country?

_____

b. What is the value of private saving?

_____

c. What is the value of public saving?

_____

d. Is the government's budget policy contributing to growth in this country or harming it? Why?

_____

_____

3. The following information describes a loanable-funds market. Values are in billions.

Real Interest Rate	Quantity of Loanable Funds Supplied	Quantity of Loanable Funds Demanded
6%	$1,300	$700
5	1,200	800
4	1,000	1,000
3	800	1,200
2	600	1,500

a. Plot the supply and demand for loanable funds in Exhibit 1. What is the equilibrium real interest rate and the equilibrium level of saving and investment?

_____

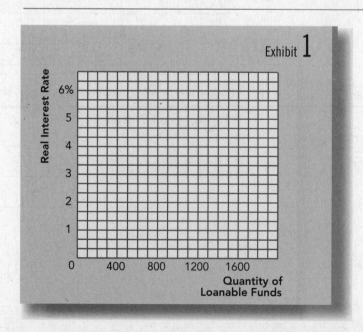

Exhibit 1

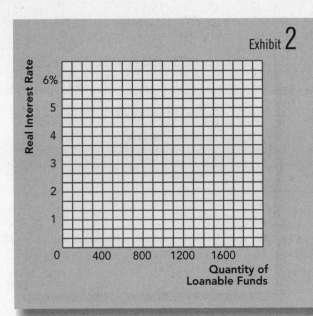

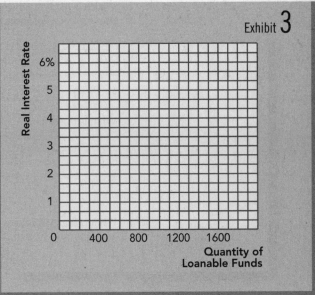

b. What "market forces" will not allow 2 percent to be the real interest rate?

_____

_____

_____

c. Suppose the government suddenly increases its budget deficit by $400 billion. What is the new equilibrium real interest rate and equilibrium level of saving and investment? (Show graphically in Exhibit 2.)

_____

d. Starting at the original equilibrium, suppose the government enacts an investment tax credit that stimulates the demand for loanable funds for capital investment by $400 billion at any real interest rate. What is the new equilibrium real interest rate and equilibrium level of saving and investment? (Show graphically in Exhibit 3.)

_____

e. With regard to questions *c* and *d*, which policy is most likely to increase growth? Why?

_____

_____

_____

Short-Answer Questions

1. Explain why a mutual fund is likely to be less risky than an individual stock.

_____

_____

_____

2. Which is likely to give you a greater rate of return: a checking deposit at a bank or the purchase of a corporate bond? Why?

_____

_____

_____

3. What is the difference between debt finance and equity finance?

_____

_____

_____

4. What is meant by the words "saving" and "investment" in the national income accounts, and how does that use of the words differ from the casual use of the words?

_____

_____

_____

5. In a closed economy, why can't investment ever exceed saving?

_____

_____

_____

6. What is private saving? What is public saving?

_____

_____

_____

_____

7. Utilizing the national income identities, if government purchases were to rise, and if output, taxes, and consumption were to remain unchanged, what would happen to national saving, investment, and growth?

_____

_____

_____

8. Suppose Americans become more frugal. That is, they consume a smaller percent of their income and save a larger percent. Describe the changes in the loanable-funds market. What would likely happen to growth?

_____

_____

_____

9. Suppose the government runs a smaller deficit. Describe the changes in the loanable-funds market. What would likely happen to growth?

_____

_____

_____

10. An increase in the government's budget deficit forces the government to borrow more. Why doesn't an increase in the deficit increase the demand for loanable funds in the loanable-funds market?

_____

_____

_____

11. What is the fundamental difference between financial markets and financial intermediaries?

_____

_____

_____

Self-Test

True/False Questions

_____ 1. When a business firm sells a bond, it has engaged in equity finance.

_____ 2. People who buy stock in a firm have loaned money to the firm.

_____ 3. Mutual funds reduce a shareholder's risk by purchasing a diversified portfolio.

_____ 4. Municipal bonds pay less interest than comparable risk corporate bonds because the interest payments are tax exempt to the bondholder.

_____ 5. In a closed economy, saving is what remains after consumption expenditures and government purchases.

_____ 6. The financial crisis of 2008 and 2009 began with a sharp economic downturn and a reduction in the overall demand for output.

_____ 7. In a closed economy, investment is always equal to saving regardless of where the saving came from—public or private sources.

_____ 8. Investment is the purchase of capital equipment and structures.

_____ 9. If you save money this week and lend it to your roommate to buy food for consumption, your act of personal saving has increased national saving.

_____ 10. The quantity supplied of loanable funds is greater if real interest rates are higher.

_____ 11. If the real interest rate in the loanable-funds market is temporarily held above the equilibrium rate, desired borrowing will exceed desired lending and the real interest rate will fall.

_____ 12. A reduction in the budget deficit should shift the supply of loanable funds to the right, lower the real interest rate, and increase the quantity demanded of loanable funds.

_____ 13. Public saving and the government's budget surplus are the same thing.

_____ 14. If the government wanted to increase the rate of growth, it should raise taxes on interest and dividends to shift the supply of loanable funds to the right.

_____ 15. An increase in the budget deficit that causes the government to increase its borrowing shifts the demand for loanable funds to the right.

Multiple-Choice Questions

1. Which of the following is an example of equity finance?
    a.   corporate bonds
    b.   municipal bonds
    c.   stock
    d.   bank loan
    e.   All of the above are equity finance.

2. Credit risk refers to a bond's
    a.   term to maturity.
    b.   probability of default.
    c.   tax treatment.
    d.   dividend.
    e.   price–earnings ratio.

3. A financial intermediary is a middleperson between
    a.   labor unions and firms.
    b.   husbands and wives.
    c.   buyers and sellers.
    d.   borrowers and lenders.

4. National saving (or just saving) is equal to
    a.   private saving + public saving.
    b.   investment + consumption expenditures.
    c.   GDP – government purchases.
    d.   GDP + consumption expenditures + government purchases.
    e.   none of the above.

5. Which of the following statements is _true_?
    a.   A stock index is a directory used to locate information about selected stocks.
    b.   Longer-term bonds tend to pay less interest than shorter-term bonds.
    c.   Municipal bonds pay less interest than comparable corporate bonds.
    d.   Mutual funds are riskier than single stock purchases because the performance of so many different firms can affect the return of a mutual fund.

6. If government spending exceeds tax collections,
    a.   there is a budget surplus.
    b.   there is a budget deficit.
    c.   private saving is positive.
    d.   public saving is positive.
    e.   none of the above is true.

7. If GDP = $1,000, consumption = $600, taxes = $100, and government purchases = $200, how much is saving and investment?
    a.   saving = $200, investment = $200
    b.   saving = $300, investment = $300
    c.   saving = $100, investment = $200
    d.   saving = $200, investment = $100
    e.   saving = $0, investment = $0

8. If the public consumes $100 billion less and the government purchases $100 billion more (other things unchanging), which of the following statements is *true?*
   a. There is an increase in saving, and the economy should grow more quickly.
   b. There is a decrease in saving, and the economy should grow more slowly.
   c. Saving is unchanged.
   d. There is not enough information to determine what will happen to saving.

9. Which of the following financial market securities would likely pay the highest interest rate?
   a. a municipal bond issued by the state of Texas
   b. a mutual fund with a portfolio of blue chip bonds
   c. a bond issued by a blue chip company
   d. a bond issued by a start-up company

10. Investment is
    a. the purchase of stocks and bonds.
    b. the purchase of capital equipment and structures.
    c. when we place our saving in the bank.
    d. the purchase of goods and services.

11. If Americans become more thrifty, we would expect
    a. the supply of loanable funds to shift to the right and the real interest rate to rise.
    b. the supply of loanable funds to shift to the right and the real interest rate to fall.
    c. the demand for loanable funds to shift to the right and the real interest rate to rise.
    d. the demand for loanable funds to shift to the right and the real interest rate to fall.

12. Which of the following sets of government policies is the most growth oriented?
    a. lower taxes on the returns to saving, provide investment tax credits, and lower the deficit
    b. lower taxes on the returns to saving, provide investment tax credits, and increase the deficit
    c. increase taxes on the returns to saving, provide investment tax credits, and lower the deficit
    d. increase taxes on the returns to saving, provide investment tax credits, and increase the deficit

13. An increase in the budget deficit that causes the government to increase its borrowing
    a. shifts the demand for loanable funds to the right.
    b. shifts the demand for loanable funds to the left.
    c. shifts the supply of loanable funds to the left.
    d. shifts the supply of loanable funds to the right.

14. An increase in the budget deficit will
    a. raise the real interest rate and decrease the quantity of loanable funds demanded for investment.
    b. raise the real interest rate and increase the quantity of loanable funds demanded for investment.
    c. lower the real interest rate and increase the quantity of loanable funds demanded for investment.
    d. lower the real interest rate and decrease the quantity of loanable funds demanded for investment.

15. If the supply of loanable funds is very inelastic (steep), which policy would likely increase saving and investment the most?
    a. an investment tax credit
    b. a reduction in the budget deficit
    c. an increase in the budget deficit
    d. none of the above

16. An increase in the budget deficit is
    a. a decrease in public saving.
    b. an increase in public saving.
    c. a decrease in private saving.
    d. an increase in private saving.
    e. none of the above.

17. If an increase in the budget deficit reduces national saving and investment, we have witnessed a demonstration of
    a. equity finance.
    b. the mutual fund effect.
    c. intermediation.
    d. crowding out.

18. If Americans become less concerned with the future and save less at each real interest rate,
    a. real interest rates fall, and investment falls.
    b. real interest rates fall, and investment rises.
    c. real interest rates rise, and investment falls.
    d. real interest rates rise, and investment rises.

19. If the government increases investment tax credits and reduces taxes on the return to saving at the same time,
    a. the real interest rate should rise.
    b. the real interest rate should fall.
    c. the real interest rate should not change.
    d. the impact on the real interest rate is indeterminate.

20. An increase in the budget surplus
    a. shifts the demand for loanable funds to the right and increases the real interest rate.
    b. shifts the demand for loanable funds to the left and reduces the real interest rate.
    c. shifts the supply of loanable funds to the left and increases the real interest rate.
    d. shifts the supply of loanable funds to the right and reduces the real interest rate.

Advanced Critical Thinking

You are watching a presidential debate. When a candidate is questioned about his position on economic growth, the presidential candidate steps forward and says, "We need to get this country growing again. We need to use tax incentives to stimulate saving and investment, and we need to get that budget deficit down so that the government stops absorbing our nation's saving."

1. If government spending remains unchanged, what inconsistency is implied by the presidential candidate's statement?

    _____

    _____

    _____

    _____

    _____

2. If the presidential candidate truly wishes to decrease taxes and decrease the budget deficit, what has the candidate implied about his plans for government spending?

_____

_____

_____

3. If policymakers want to increase growth, and if policymakers have to choose between tax incentives to stimulate saving and tax incentives to stimulate investment, what might they want to know about supply and demand in the loanable-funds market before making their decision? Explain.

_____

_____

_____

_____

_____

_____

Solutions

Terms and Definitions

<u>5</u>   Financial system
<u>12</u>   Financial markets
<u>4</u>   Financial intermediaries
<u>10</u>   Bank
<u>1</u>   Medium of exchange
<u>18</u>   Bond
<u>13</u>   Stock
<u>11</u>   Mutual fund
<u>3</u>   Closed economy
<u>15</u>   National saving (saving)
<u>7</u>   Private saving
<u>20</u>   Public saving
<u>14</u>   Budget surplus
<u>2</u>   Budget deficit
<u>8</u>   Government debt
<u>17</u>   Investment
<u>19</u>   Market for loanable funds
<u>6</u>   Demand for loanable funds
<u>9</u>   Supply of loanable funds
<u>16</u>   Crowding out

Practice Problems

1. a. Long term because it is more likely that you may need to sell the long-term bond at a depressed price prior to maturity.

   b. Yes, the credit risk has increased, and lenders would demand a higher rate of return.

   c. Fly-by-Night. Unlike municipal bonds, interest receipts are taxable to the owners of corporate bonds.

   d. Owners of stock demand a higher rate of return because it is riskier.

   e. It is safer to put money in a mutual fund because it is diversified (not all of your eggs in one basket).

2. a. ($6,000 − $1,000 − $4,000) + ($1,000 − $1,200) = $800 billion

   b. $6,000 − $1,000 − $4,000 = $1,000 billion

   c. $1,000 − $1,200 = −$200 billion

   d. It is harming growth because public saving is negative so less is available for investment.

3. a. Equilibrium real interest rate = 4%, equilibrium S and I = $1,000 billion. (See Exhibit 4.)

Exhibit 4

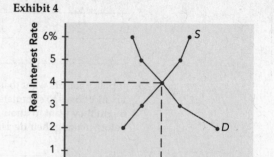

b. At 2 percent interest, the quantity demanded of loanable funds exceeds the quantity supplied by $900 billion. This excess demand for loans (borrowing) will drive interest rates up to 4 percent.

c. Equilibrium real interest rate = 5%, equilibrium S and I = $800 billion. (See Exhibit 5.)

Exhibit 5

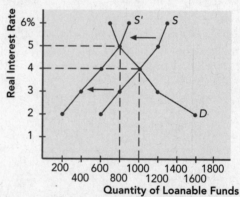

d. Equilibrium real interest rate = 5%, equilibrium S and I = $1,200 billion. (See Exhibit 6.)

Exhibit 6

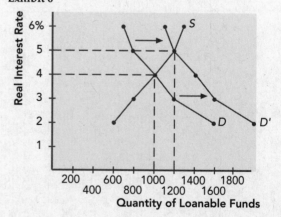

e. An investment tax credit because it shifts the demand for loanable funds to invest in capital to the right, raising the level of investment in capital and stimulating growth.

Short-Answer Questions

1. Because a mutual fund is diversified. When one stock in the fund is performing poorly, it is likely that another stock is performing well.

2. A corporate bond because the bond is riskier and because "direct" lending through a financial market has fewer overhead costs than "indirect" lending through an intermediary.

3. Debt finance is borrowing such as when a firm sells a bond. Equity finance is taking on additional partners such as when a firm sells stock.

4. Saving is what remains after consumption and government purchases. Investment is the purchase of equipment and structures. In casual conversation, saving is what remains out of our income (even if someone else borrows it for consumption) and investment is the purchase of stocks and bonds.

5. Because saving is the GDP left over after consumption expenditures and government purchases, and this is the limit of the output available to be used to purchase equipment and structures.

6. Private saving = $Y - T - C$; public saving = $T - G$.

7. Public saving would decrease and cause national saving and investment to decrease by the same amount, slowing growth.

8. The supply of loanable funds would shift right, the real interest rate would fall, and the quantity demanded of loanable funds to purchase capital would increase. Growth would increase.

9. The supply of loanable funds would shift right, the real interest rate would fall, and the quantity demanded of loanable funds to purchase capital would increase. Growth would increase.

10. The demand for loanable funds is defined as private demand for borrowing to purchase capital equipment and structures. An increase in the deficit absorbs saving and reduces the supply of loanable funds.

11. In a financial market, savers lend directly to borrowers. Through financial intermediaries, savers lend to an intermediary who then lends to the ultimate borrower.

True/False Questions

1. F; to sell a bond is to engage in debt finance.
2. F; stockholders are owners.
3. T
4. T
5. T
6. F; the financial crisis began with a decline in real estate prices.
7. T
8. T
9. F; consumption loans do not increase national saving.
10. T
11. F; desired lending exceeds desired borrowing.
12. T
13. T
14. F; it should lower taxes on interest and dividends.
15. F; it decreases the supply of loanable funds.

Multiple-Choice Questions

1. c
2. b
3. d
4. a
5. c
6. b
7. a
8. c
9. d
10. b
11. b
12. a
13. c
14. a
15. b
16. a
17. d
18. c
19. d
20. d

Advanced Critical Thinking

1. Tax incentives to stimulate saving and investment require a reduction in taxes. This would increase the deficit, which would reduce national saving and investment.

2. The candidate plans to reduce government spending.

3. Policymakers would want to know the elasticity (similar to the steepness) of the supply and demand curves. If loanable funds demand is inelastic, changes in loanable funds supply have little effect on saving and investment, so tax incentives to increase saving at each interest rate do little for growth. If loanable funds supply is inelastic, changes in loanable funds demand have little effect on saving and investment, so tax incentives to increase investment at each interest rate do little for growth.

Chapter 19

The Basic Tools of Finance

- Learn the relationship between present value and future value

- Consider the effects of compound growth

- Learn how risk-averse people reduce the risk they face

- Analyze how asset prices are determined

- Choose between receiving $100 now or $120 two years from now, given an interest rate of 8 percent

- Explain why two people whose incomes grow at slightly different rates may end up with significantly different incomes after a number of years

- Explain the benefits of diversification

- Show why randomly choosing stocks may be as good as more sophisticated stock-picking methods

Chapter Overview

Context and Purpose

Chapter 19 is the third chapter in a four-chapter sequence on the level and growth of output in the long run. In Chapter 17, we learned that capital and labor are among the primary determinants of output and growth. In Chapter 18, we addressed how saving and investment in capital goods affect the production of output. In Chapter 19, we will learn about some of the tools people and firms use when choosing capital projects in which to invest. Since both capital and labor are among the primary determinants of output, Chapter 20 will address the market for labor.

The purpose of Chapter 19 is to introduce you to some tools that people use when they participate in financial markets. We will learn how people compare different sums of money at different points in time, how they manage risk, and how these concepts combine to help determine the value of a financial asset, such as a share of stock.

301

Chapter Review

Introduction   Financial markets coordinate saving and investment. Financial decisions involve two elements—time and risk. For example, people and firms must make decisions today about saving and investment based on expectations of future earnings, but future returns are uncertain. The field of finance studies how people make decisions regarding the allocation of resources over time and the handling of risk. We will learn how people compare different sums of money at different points in time, how they manage risk, and how these concepts combine to help determine the value of a financial asset, such as a share of stock.

Present Value: Measuring the Time Value of Money

The present value of any future value is the amount today that would be needed, at current interest rates, to produce that future sum. The future value is the amount of money in the future that an amount of money today will yield, given prevailing interest rates. Suppose r = the interest rate expressed in decimal form, n = years to maturity, PV = present value, and FV = future value. Furthermore, suppose that interest is paid annually and that the interest is put in the account to earn more interest—a process called compounding. Then:

(1) $PV(1 + r)^n = FV$, and

(2) $FV/(1 + r)^n = PV$.

For example, suppose a person deposited \$100 into a bank account for three years earning 7 percent interest. Using equation (1) where $r = 0.07$, $PV = \$100$, and $n = 3$, we find that in three years the account will hold about \$122.50. That is, the future value is \$122.50.

Alternatively, suppose you were offered a bank deposit that would provide you with \$122.50 three years from now. At an interest rate of 7 percent, what would you pay for that account today? Using equation (2) where $r = 0.07$, $FV = \$122.50$, and $n = 3$, we find that the present value of \$122.50 three years from today is \$100. Finding the present value of a future sum is called *discounting*.

The relationship between present value and future value demonstrates the following:

- Receiving a given sum in the present is preferred to receiving the same sum in the future. The larger the interest rate, the more pronounced is this result.

- In order to choose between two sums—a value today or a larger value at some later date—find the present value of the larger future sum and compare it to the value today.

- Firms undertake investment projects if the present value of the future returns exceeds the cost. The larger the interest rate, the less likely the project will be undertaken because the present value of the project becomes smaller. Thus, investment declines as interest rates rise.

Small differences in growth rates can make enormous differences in a country's level of income after many years. This result is also true for an individual's income or for money deposited in a bank. The concept of *compound growth* shows why. Each year's growth is applied to the previous year's accumulated growth, or in the case of interest, interest is earned on previously earned interest. The effects of compound growth are demonstrated by the *rule of 70*, which states that if some variable grows at a rate of x percent per year, its value will double in approximately $70/x$ years. If your income grows at 1 percent per year, it will about double in 70 years. However, if your income grows at 4 percent, it will double in approximately 17.5 years.

Managing Risk

Most people are risk averse, which means that they dislike bad things more than they like comparable good things. This is because people's utility functions exhibit diminishing marginal utility of wealth. Thus, the utility lost from losing a \$1,000 bet is greater than that gained from winning a \$1,000 bet. People can reduce risk by buying insurance, diversifying their risk, and accepting a lower return on their assets.

- *People can reduce the risk they face by buying insurance.* Insurance allows the economy to spread the risk more efficiently because it is easier for 100 people to bear 1/100 of the group's risk of a house fire than for each to bear the entire risk of one house fire alone. There are two problems with insurance markets. *Adverse selection* occurs because a high-risk person is more likely to buy insurance than a low-risk person. *Moral hazard* occurs because after people buy insurance, they have less incentive to be careful. Some low-risk people don't buy insurance because these problems may cause the price of insurance to be too high for low-risk people.

- *People can reduce the risk they face through diversification.* Diversification is the reduction of risk achieved by replacing a single risk with a large number of smaller unrelated risks. This is summarized by the phrase, "Don't put all of your eggs in one basket." Risk is diversified through insurance because it is easier for 100 people to bear 1/100 of the group's risk of a house fire than for each to bear the entire risk of one house fire alone. The risk on a portfolio of stocks, as measured by the *standard deviation* (volatility) of the returns, is reduced by diversifying the portfolio— buying a small amount of a large number of stocks instead of a large amount of one stock. Diversification can eliminate firm-specific risk—the uncertainty associated with specific companies. It cannot eliminate market risk—the uncertainty associated with the entire economy, which affects all companies traded on the stock market.

- *People can reduce the risk they face by accepting a lower rate of return on their investments.* People face a trade-off between risk and return in their portfolio. In order to earn greater returns, people must accept more risk. In order to have less risk, people must accept lower returns. The optimal combination of risk and return for a person depends on the person's degree of risk aversion, which depends on the person's preferences.

Asset Valuation

The price of a share of stock is determined by supply and demand. People often try to buy stock that is *undervalued*—shares of a business whose value exceeds its price. If the price exceeds the value, the stock is considered *overvalued* and if the price and value are equal, the stock is *fairly valued*. The price of the stock is known. The value of a stock is uncertain because it is the present value of the future stream of dividends and the final sales price. The dividends and final sales price depend on the firm's future profitability. Fundamental analysis is a detailed analysis of a company's accounting statements and future prospects to determine its value. You can perform fundamental analysis yourself, rely on Wall Street analysts, or buy shares in a mutual fund whose manager does fundamental analysis.

According to the efficient markets hypothesis, asset prices reflect all publicly available information about the value of an asset. This theory argues that professional money managers monitor news to determine a stock's value. The stock's price is set by supply and demand, so at any point in time, shares sold equal shares bought, implying that an equal number believe that the stock is overvalued as think it is undervalued. Thus, the average analyst thinks it is fairly valued all the time. According to this theory, the stock market is informationally efficient, which means that prices in the stock market reflect all available information in a rational way. If this is true, stock prices should follow a random walk, the path of which is impossible to predict from available information because all available information has already been incorporated into the price. As a result, no stock is a better buy than any other is, and the best you can do is to buy a diversified portfolio.

Index funds provide evidence in support of the efficient markets hypothesis. Index funds are mutual funds that buy all of the stocks in a particular stock index. Actively managed funds use research to try to buy only the best stocks. Actively managed funds fail to outperform index funds because they trade more frequently, incurring trading costs, plus they charge fees for their alleged expertise.

Some people suggest that markets are irrational. That is, stock prices often move in ways that are hard to explain on the basis of rational analysis of news and so appear to be driven by psychological trends. However, if this were true, traders should be able to take advantage of this fact and buy better than average stocks, but beating the market is nearly impossible. Since the value of a stock depends on its dividends and final sales price, it may not be irrational to purchase a stock at a price that appears to exceed its fundamental value (speculative bubble) if others are willing to pay even more for it at a later date.

Conclusion

The concept of present value shows us that a dollar today is worth more than a dollar at a later date, and it allows us to compare sums at different points in time. Risk management shows us ways that risk-averse people can reduce their risk exposure. Asset valuation reflects a firm's future profitability. There is controversy regarding whether stock prices are a rational estimate of a company's true value.

Helpful Hints

1. Compound growth is the same as compound interest. Compound interest is when you earn interest on your previously earned interest. Assuming annual compounding, when you deposit $100 in a bank at 10 percent, you receive $110 at the end of the year. If you leave it in for two years, you receive compound interest in that you receive $121 at the end of two years—the $100 principal, $10 interest from the first year, $10 interest from the second year, *plus $1 interest on the first year's $10 interest payment.* Next year, interest would be earned not on $100, or $110, but on $121, and so on.

   In like manner, after a number of years, a faster growing economy is applying its percentage growth rate to a much larger base (size of economy), and total output accelerates away from economies that are growing more slowly. For example, applying the rule of 70, an economy that is growing at 1 percent should double in size after about 70 years (70/1). An economy growing at 4 percent should double in size every 17 1/2 years (70/4). After 70 years, the 4 percent growth economy is 16 times its original size (24) while the 1 percent growth economy is only twice its original size. If both economies started at the same size, the 4 percent growth economy is now eight times the size of the 1 percent growth economy thanks to compound growth.

2. Risk-averse people benefit from insurance because, due to their diminishing marginal utility of wealth, the reduction in utility from a single big expense exceeds the reduction in utility from a number of small payments into the insurance fund. For example, suppose there are 50 people in town. One house burns down each year so each person has a 1 in 50 chance of losing his entire home in any given year. People can pay 1/50 of the value of their home into the insurance fund each year, and thus, they will have paid premiums equal to the value of their home after 50 years. Alternatively, they can fail to buy insurance, but they will replace their home once every 50 years due to fire. Although the expected values of these two expenses are the same, risk-averse people choose to buy insurance because the reduction in utility from paying once for one entire home exceeds the reduction in utility from paying 50 times for 1/50 of a home.

3. The volatility of the return of a stock portfolio decreases as the number of stocks in the portfolio increases. When a portfolio is comprised of just one stock, the volatility of the portfolio is the same as the volatility of the single stock. When a portfolio is comprised of two stocks, it could be that when one stock is paying a return that is less than its average, the other may be paying more than its average, and the two tend to cancel out. As a result, the portfolio has less volatility than each of the stocks in the portfolio. This effect continues as the number of stocks in the portfolio increases. However, the majority of the risk reduction occurs by the time there are 20 or 30 stocks in the portfolio. Note that in order to achieve the projected risk reduction from diversification, the risks on the stocks must be unrelated. Therefore, randomly choosing stocks should generate more risk reduction than choosing stocks of firms that are, for example, all in the same industry or all located in the same geographic area.

4. The price of a stock depends on supply and demand. The demand for a stock depends on the present value of the stream of dividend payments and the final sales price. Therefore, an increase in either the expected dividends or the final sales price, or a decrease in the prevailing interest rate, will increase the demand for a stock and

increase its price. The demand for a stock also depends on risk factors associated with the stock. Because people are risk averse, an increase in aggregate risk will reduce the demand for all stocks and all stock prices should decrease. Oddly, an increase in firm-specific risk (the portion of the standard deviation in the returns on a particular stock that are associated with the specific company) should not affect the demand for the stock because this type of risk can be eliminated through diversification.

Terms and Definitions

Choose a definition for each key term.

Key Terms	Definitions
_____ Finance	1. Reflecting all available information in a rational way
_____ Present value	2. The amount of money today that would be needed to produce, using prevailing interest rates, a given future amount of money
_____ Future value	
_____ Compounding	3. The study of a company's accounting statements and future prospects to determine its value
_____ Risk averse	
_____ Diversification	4. The field that studies how people make decisions regarding the allocation of resources over time and the handling of risk
_____ Firm-specific risk	
_____ Market risk	5. The path of a variable whose changes are impossible to predict
_____ Fundamental analysis	6. Risk that affects only a single company
_____ Efficient markets hypothesis	7. The accumulation of a sum of money in an account where interest is earned on previously paid interest
_____ Informational efficiency	8. The theory according to which asset prices reflect all publicly available information about the value of an asset
_____ Random walk	9. The amount of money in the future that an amount of money today will yield, given prevailing interest rates
	10. The reduction of risk achieved by replacing a single risk with a large number of smaller unrelated risks
	11. Risk that affects all companies in the stock market
	12. Exhibiting a dislike of uncertainty

Problems and Short-Answer Questions

Practice Problems

1. Whitewater Raft Tour Company can purchase rafts today for $100,000. They will earn a $40,000 return on the rafts at the end of each of the next three years.
   a.   If the interest rate were 12 percent, what is the present value of each of the future returns that Whitewater Raft expects to receive?

   _____

   _____

b. If the interest rate were 12 percent, should Whitewater Raft invest in the rafts? Explain.

_____

_____

c. If the interest rate were 7 percent, should Whitewater Raft invest in the rafts? Explain.

_____

_____

d. Compare your answers to parts *b* and *c* above. What general principle about the relationship between investment and the interest rate is demonstrated?

_____

_____

2. Use the *rule of 70* to answer the following questions. Suppose that real GDP/person in Fastcountry grows at an annual rate of 2 percent and that real GDP/person in Slowcountry grows at an annual rate of 1 percent.

a. How many years does it take for real GDP/person to double in Fastcountry?

_____

b. If real GDP per person in Fastcountry is $2,000 in 1940, how much will it be in the year 2010?

_____

c. How many years does it take for real GDP/person to double in Slowcountry?

_____

d. If real GDP per person in Slowcountry is $2,000 in 1940, how much will it be in the year 2010?

_____

e. Use the numbers you calculated above to help explain the concept of compound growth.

_____

_____

_____

f. If Fastcountry stopped growing in the year 2010, how many years would it take for the standard of living in Slowcountry to catch that of Fastcountry?

_____

3. For each of the following, determine the type of problem from which the insurance market suffers (adverse selection or moral hazard) and explain.

a. Susan buys health insurance at the nonsmoker rate. After she obtains the insurance, she begins smoking again.

_____

_____

_____

b.   Bryce discovers that he has a liver condition that will shorten his life. He seeks life insurance to help pay for his children's college expenses.

_____

_____

_____

c.   Fred gets a new job and will have to commute to Chicago. Fearing that he will get into an auto accident in the heavy traffic, he increases his auto coverage.

_____

_____

_____

d.   After Lisa gets fire insurance on her house, she burns fires in the fireplace without closing the fireplace doors.

_____

_____

_____

4.   Rachel is an extremely picky eater. When choosing a restaurant, she always chooses to eat at a buffet. At a buffet, she doesn't have to order off a menu, so she doesn't have to risk ordering something she may not like. Rachel knows that buffet food is very ordinary, and because she avoids nice restaurants, she misses the chance to eat some exceptional foods that she would enjoy very much. On the other hand, she never has a meal that she is unwilling to eat.

a.   Does Rachel gain as much utility from a truly great meal as she loses from eating a meal she dislikes? Explain.

_____

_____

_____

b.   What can you say about Rachel's utility function with regard to her preferences toward risk? Explain.

_____

_____

_____

c.   How does the availability of a buffet help Rachel reduce her risk? Explain.

_____

_____

_____

Short-Answer Questions

1. Suppose that the interest rate is 6 percent. Which would you prefer to receive: $100 today or $110 one year from today? Why?

   _____

   _____

   _____

2. Suppose you put $100 in your savings account at your bank. If your account earns 8 percent interest and it is compounded annually, how much will be in your account after one year? after two years? How much more interest did you earn in the second year? Why?

   _____

   _____

   _____

3. You just won a lottery that pays you $100,000 at the end of each of the next three years. Alternatively, the lottery is willing to pay you a lesser amount in one lump sum today. What is the least you should accept in a lump sum payment today if the interest rate is 9 percent? Explain.

   _____

   _____

   _____

4. According to the *rule of 70*, how long will it take for your income to double if you get a 5 percent raise every year? If you start work at the age of 23 earning $40,000 per year and get a 5 percent raise every year, how much will you be earning if you retire at age 65?

   _____

   _____

   _____

5. What property of an individual's utility function is necessary for that individual to be risk averse? Explain.

   _____

   _____

   _____

6. Suppose that people wreck their autos once every ten years and the autos are a total loss. People can buy insurance with annual premiums of 1/10 of the value of a car. Would a risk-averse person buy collision insurance for his auto? Why or why not?

   _____

   _____

   _____

7. What are the two types of problems from which insurance markets suffer? Explain. What problem does this cause for low-risk people?

_____

_____

_____

8. What are the two types of risk someone faces when they buy stock? Which type of risk can be reduced with diversification and which type cannot? Explain.

_____

_____

_____

9. Which are riskier, stocks or government bonds? Why? How can people use this information to adjust the amount of risk they face? If people reduce risk in this way, what happens to their return? Explain.

_____

_____

_____

10. What are three ways that people can reduce the risk they face in their investment portfolios?

_____

_____

_____

_____

_____

11. What is fundamental analysis, and what are three ways to perform fundamental analysis?

_____

_____

_____

Self-Test

True/False Questions

_____ 1. If the prevailing interest rate is 10 percent, a rational person should be indifferent between receiving $1,000 today and $1,000 one year from today.

_____ 2. You are going to receive a $100,000 inheritance in ten years. If the prevailing interest rate is 6 percent, the present value of your inheritance is $55,839.48.

_____ 3. The rule of 70 suggests that, on average, people's incomes double every 70 years.

_____ 4. If interest is compounded annually, $100 placed in a bank account earning 10 percent interest should generate $30 interest after three years.

_____ 5. According to the rule of 70, if your income grows at 7 percent per year, it will double in ten years.

_____ 6. The present value of a future sum is the amount of money today that would be needed, at prevailing interest rates, to produce that future sum.

_____ 7. If people are risk averse, the utility gained from winning $1,000 is equal to the utility lost from losing a $1,000 bet.

_____ 8. If someone's utility function exhibits diminishing marginal utility of wealth, this person is risk averse.

_____ 9. The insurance market demonstrates the problem of adverse selection when those who are sicker than average seek health insurance.

_____ 10. People can reduce what is known as market risk by diversifying their portfolios.

_____ 11. Increasing the diversification of a portfolio from one stock to ten stocks reduces the portfolio's risk by the same amount as increasing the diversification from ten to twenty stocks.

_____ 12. As a person allocates more of his savings to stocks and less to government bonds, he will earn a higher rate of return but he must accept additional risk.

_____ 13. The efficient markets hypothesis suggests that since markets are efficient, it is easy to engage in fundamental analysis to purchase undervalued stock and then earn greater than average market returns.

_____ 14. If the efficient markets hypothesis is true, stock prices follow a random walk. Therefore, buying a diversified portfolio, by purchasing an index fund or by throwing darts at the stock page, is probably the best that you can do.

_____ 15. The value of a stock is based on the present value of the future stream of dividend payments and the final sales price.

Multiple-Choice Questions

1. The amount today that would be needed, at prevailing interest rates, to produce a particular sum in the future is known as
   a. compound value.
   b. future value.
   c. present value.
   d. fair value.
   e. beginning value.

2. If a depositor puts $100 in a bank account that earns 4 percent interest compounded annually, how much will be in the account after five years?
   a. $104.00
   b. $120.00
   c. $121.67
   d. $123.98
   e. $400.00

3. General Electric has the opportunity to purchase a new factory today that will provide them with a $50 million return four years from now. If prevailing interest rates are 6 percent, what is the maximum that the project can cost for General Electric to be willing to undertake the project?
   a. $34,583,902
   b. $39,604,682
   c. $43,456,838
   d. $50,000,000
   e. $53,406,002

4. An increase in the prevailing interest rate
   a. decreases the present value of future returns from investment and decreases investment.
   b. decreases the present value of future returns from investment and increases investment.
   c. increases the present value of future returns from investment and decreases investment.
   d. increases the present value of future returns from investment and increases investment.

5. If two countries start with the same real GDP per person, and one country grows at 2 percent while the other grows at 4 percent,
   a. one country will always have 2 percent more real GDP per person than the other.
   b. the standard of living in the country growing at 4 percent will start to accelerate away from the slower growing country due to compound growth.
   c. the standard of living in the two countries will converge.
   d. next year the country growing at 4 percent will have twice the GDP per person as the country growing at 2 percent.

6. Using the *rule of 70*, if your income grows at 10 percent per year, your income will double in approximately
   a. 700 years.
   b. 70 years.
   c. 10 years.
   d. 7 years.
   e. There is not enough information to answer this question.

7. Using the *rule of 70*, if your parents place $10,000 in a deposit for you on the day you are born, approximately how much will be in the account when you retire at 70 years old if the deposit earns 3 percent per year?
   a. $300
   b. $3,000
   c. $20,000
   d. $70,000
   e. $80,000

8. If people are risk averse, then
   a. they dislike bad things more than they like comparable good things.
   b. their utility functions exhibit the property of diminishing marginal utility of wealth.
   c. the utility they would lose from losing a $50 bet would exceed the utility they would gain from winning a $50 bet.
   d. all of the above are true.
   e. none of the above is true.

9. Which of the following does *not* help reduce the risk that people face?
   a. buying insurance
   b. diversifying their portfolio
   c. increasing the rate of return within their portfolio
   d. All of the above help reduce risk.

10. Which of the following is an example of moral hazard?
    a.   After Joe buys fire insurance, he begins to smoke cigarettes in bed.
    b.   Doug has been feeling poorly lately, so he seeks health insurance.
    c.   Both of Susan's parents lost their teeth due to gum disease, so Susan buys dental insurance.
    d.   All of the above demonstrate moral hazard.
    e.   None of the above demonstrates moral hazard.

11. Firm-specific risk is the
    a.   uncertainty associated with the entire economy.
    b.   uncertainty associated with specific companies.
    c.   risk associated with moral hazard.
    d.   risk associated with adverse selection.

12. Diversification of a portfolio can
    a.   reduce market risk.
    b.   reduce firm-specific risk.
    c.   eliminate all risk.
    d.   increase the standard deviation of the portfolio's return.

13. Compared to a portfolio composed entirely of stock, a portfolio that is 50 percent government bonds and 50 percent stock will have a
    a.   higher return and a higher level of risk.
    b.   higher return and a lower level of risk.
    c.   lower return and a lower level of risk.
    d.   lower return and a higher level of risk.

14. The study of a company's accounting statements and future prospects to determine its value is known as
    a.   diversification.
    b.   risk management.
    c.   information analysis.
    d.   fundamental analysis.

15. If the efficient markets hypothesis is *true*, then
    a.   stocks tend to be overvalued.
    b.   the stock market is informationally efficient, so stock prices should follow a random walk.
    c.   fundamental analysis is a valuable tool for increasing one's stock returns.
    d.   an index fund is a poor investment.
    e.   all of the above are true.

16. Which of the following reduces risk in a portfolio the greatest?
    a.   increasing the number of stocks in the portfolio from 1 to 10
    b.   increasing the number of stocks from 10 to 20
    c.   increasing the number of stocks from 20 to 30
    d.   All of the above provide the same amount of risk reduction.

17. Which of the following should cause the price of a share of stock to rise?
    a.   a reduction in market risk
    b.   an increase in expected dividends
    c.   a reduction in the interest rate
    d.   All of the above should cause the price to rise.
    e.   None of the above should cause the price to rise.

18. Speculative bubbles may occur in the stock market
    a.   when stocks are fairly valued.
    b.   only when people are irrational.
    c.   because rational people may buy an overvalued stock if they think they can sell it to someone for even more at a later date.
    d.   during periods of extreme pessimism because so many stocks become undervalued.

19. Stock prices will follow a random walk if
    a.   people behave irrationally when choosing stock.
    b.   markets reflect all available information in a rational way.
    c.   stocks are undervalued.
    d.   stocks are overvalued.

20. It is difficult for an actively managed mutual fund to outperform an index fund because
    a.   index funds generally do better fundamental analysis.
    b.   stock markets tend to be inefficient.
    c.   actively managed funds trade more often and charge fees for their alleged expertise.
    d.   index funds are able to buy undervalued stocks.
    e.   all of the above are true.

Advanced Critical Thinking

You are a student in the business college at an exclusive private university. The tuition is extremely expensive. Near the end of your senior year, your parents come to visit you in your dorm room. As they enter the room, they see you throwing darts at the stock pages on your bulletin board. You inform them that you received an enormous signing bonus from the company for which you agreed to work after graduation. You are now in the process of picking the stocks in which you plan to invest. Your parents are horrified and they want their money back for your expensive education. Your father says, "There's got to be a better way to choose stocks. I can give you the phone number of my stock analyst or you could at least buy a well-known, well-managed mutual fund."

1. What is the stock valuation method to which your father is referring, and what is its goal?

    _____

    _____

    _____

    _____

    _____

2. Explain the efficient markets hypothesis to your parents. If the efficient markets hypothesis is true, can your father's method for picking stocks achieve its goal?

    _____

    _____

    _____

    _____

    _____

3. If the efficient markets hypothesis is true, what is the only goal of your dart-throwing exercise? Explain.

    _____

    _____

4. If the efficient markets hypothesis is true, which of the following will likely provide the greater return in the long run: your dart-throwing exercise or an actively managed mutual fund? Why?

_____

_____

_____

_____

_____

Solutions

Terms and Definitions

_4_ Finance

_2_ Present value

_9_ Future value

_7_ Compounding

_12_ Risk averse

_10_ Diversification

_6_ Firm-specific risk

_11_ Market risk

_3_ Fundamental analysis

_8_ Efficient markets hypothesis

_1_ Informational efficiency

_5_ Random walk

Practice Problems

1. a. $40,000/1.12 = $35,714.29; $40,000/(1.12)^2 = $31,887.76; $40,000/(1.12)^3 = $28,471.21

   b. No, the cost is $100,000 but the present value of the return is only $96,073.26.

   c. Yes. Although the cost is still $100,000, the present value of the return is now the sum of [$40,000/1.07] + [$40,000/(1.07)^2] + [$40,000/(1.07)^3] = $104,972.65.

   d. Investment is inversely related to the interest rate—lower interest rates stimulate investment.

2. a. 70/2 = 35 years.

   b. $8,000

   c. 70/1 = 70 years.

   d. $4,000

   e. Fastcountry adds $2,000 to its GDP/person in the first 35 years. Growing at the same percent, it adds $4,000 to its GDP over the next 35 years because the same growth rate is now applied to a larger base.

   f. Another 70 years.

3. a. Moral hazard because after she obtains the insurance, she is less careful with her health.

   b. Adverse selection because after he knows that his probability of death is higher than average, he seeks life insurance.

   c. Adverse selection because after he knows that his probability of an accident is higher than average, he seeks more auto insurance.

   d. Moral hazard because after she obtains the insurance, she becomes less careful with fire.

4. a. No. She dislikes bad food more than she likes good food.

   b. Rachel is risk averse because she exhibits diminishing marginal utility of wealth (she dislikes spending, say, $30 on a meal she dislikes more than she enjoys spending $30 on a meal she loves).

   c. She can diversify her risk at a buffet—she does not "put all of her eggs in one basket" at a buffet. This reduces her standard deviation of meals because her meals are always adequate but never terrible or great. A buffet is like a mutual fund of food.

Short-Answer Questions

1. You should prefer $110 one year from today because the PV of $110 one year from today is $110/1.06 = $103.77 and this is greater than $100.

2. After one year: $100(1.08) = $108. After two years: $100(1.08)^2 = $100(1.1664) = $116.64. The account earned $0.64 more interest in the second year because the account earned interest on the first year's interest payment: 0.08($8) = $0.64.

3. The least you should accept is the present value of the future stream of payments which is: $100,000/1.09 + $100,000/(1.09)^2 + $100,000/(1.09)^3 = $91,743.12 + $84,168.00 + $77,218.35 = $253,129.47.

4. 70/5 = 14 years. Your income would double three times in the 42-year period or $40,000(2)^3 = $320,000 per year.

5. Diminishing marginal utility of wealth. Therefore, the increase in utility from a $1 gain is less than the decrease in utility from a $1 loss.

6. Yes. Due to diminishing marginal utility of wealth, the reduction in utility from a lump sum payment to replace a car exceeds the reduction in utility from the payment of 10 premiums of 1/10 of the value of a car.

7. Adverse selection: A high-risk person is more likely to apply for insurance than a low-risk person. Moral hazard: After people buy insurance, they have less incentive to be careful. As a result, the price of insurance is often too high for low-risk people, so they don't buy it.

8. Firm-specific risk—the uncertainty associated with specific companies, and market risk—the uncertainty associated with the entire economy that affects all companies in the stock market. Firm-specific risk can be eliminated with diversification because when one firm does poorly, another unrelated firm may do well reducing the volatility in returns. Market risk cannot be reduced because when the entire economy does poorly, the market portfolio does poorly.

9. Stocks because the standard deviation in the returns to government bonds is zero, while the standard deviation in stock returns is significantly higher. People can vary the proportion they invest in stocks versus risk-free government bonds. Low-risk assets generate low returns, so putting a larger portion of the portfolio in government bonds lowers the return of the portfolio.

10. Buy insurance, diversify a portfolio, and accept a lower return on the portfolio.

11. Determining a company's value by analyzing its accounting statements and future prospects. You can do it yourself, rely on Wall Street analysts, or buy a mutual fund that is actively managed.

True/False Questions

1. F; the present value of $1,000 one year from today is $1,000/1.10 = $909.09.
2. T
3. F; if people's incomes grow at x percent, they double in $70/x$ years.
4. F; $10 the first year, $11 the second year, $12.10 the third year for a total of $33.10.
5. T
6. T
7. F; the utility lost from losing $1,000 is greater.
8. T
9. T
10. F; diversification reduces firm-specific risk.
11. F; diversification of a portfolio from one stock to ten stocks reduces the portfolio's risk to a greater degree.
12. T
13. F; if markets are efficient, stocks are always fairly valued.
14. T
15. T

Multiple-Choice Questions

1. c
2. c
3. b
4. a
5. b
6. d
7. e
8. d
9. c
10. a
11. b
12. b
13. c
14. d
15. b
16. a
17. d
18. c
19. b
20. c

Advanced Critical Thinking

1. Fundamental analysis is the detailed analysis of a firm's accounting statements and future prospects to determine its value. The goal is to choose stocks that are undervalued—those whose stock prices are less than their values.

2. The efficient markets hypothesis argues that the stock market is informationally efficient in that it reflects all available information about the value of the traded stocks. That is, market participants monitor news that affects the value of a stock. Since at any given time the number of buyers of a stock equals the number of sellers, an equal number of people think a stock is undervalued as overvalued. Thus, stock is fairly valued all the time, and its price should follow a random walk. If true, it is not possible to consistently buy undervalued stock.

3. The only thing a person can do is diversify his portfolio to reduce firm-specific risk.

4. If you throw enough darts to remove most of the firm-specific risk (your portfolio starts to resemble the entire market like an index fund) and if you bought and held the stock (you didn't trade often), then it is likely that throwing darts would give you the greater return. This is because active managers of mutual funds tend to trade frequently, incurring trading costs, and they charge fees as compensation for their alleged expertise, yet they cannot reduce market risk.

Chapter 20
Unemployment

Goals
In this chapter you will

- Learn about the data used to measure the amount of unemployment

- Consider how unemployment arises from the process of job search

- Consider how unemployment can result from minimum-wage laws

- See how unemployment can arise from bargaining between firms and unions

- Examine how unemployment results when firms choose to pay efficiency wages

Outcomes
After accomplishing these goals, you should be able to

- Use data on the number of employed, unemployed, and not in the labor force to calculate the unemployment rate and the labor-force participation rate

- Explain why some job search unemployment is inevitable

- Diagram the impact of the minimum wage on high-wage and low-wage sectors

- List the reasons why unions cause unemployment, and alternatively, why unions might increase efficiency in some cases

- Describe the four reasons why firms may choose to pay wages in excess of the competitive wage

Chapter Overview

Context and Purpose

Chapter 20 is the fourth chapter in a four-chapter sequence on the level and growth of output in the long run. In Chapter 17, we learned that capital and labor are among the primary determinants of

317

output and growth. In Chapter 18, we addressed how saving and investment in capital goods affect the production of output. In Chapter 19, we learned about some of the tools people and firms use when choosing capital projects in which to invest. In Chapter 20, we see how full utilization of our labor resources improves the level of production and our standard of living.

The purpose of Chapter 20 is to introduce you to the labor market. We will see how economists measure the performance of the labor market using unemployment statistics. We will also address a number of sources of unemployment and some policies that the government might use to lower certain types of unemployment.

Chapter Review

Introduction   If a country keeps its workers fully employed, it achieves a higher level of GDP than if it leaves many workers idle. In this chapter, we are concerned largely with the *natural rate of unemployment*, which is the amount of unemployment that the economy normally experiences. "Natural" does not mean constant or impervious to economic policy. It means that it is the unemployment that doesn't go away on its own. This chapter addresses the measurement and interpretation of unemployment statistics and some causes and cures for unemployment.

Identifying Unemployment

The Bureau of Labor Statistics (BLS) uses the Current Population Survey to categorize all surveyed adults (age 16 and older) as employed, unemployed, or not in the labor force.

- Employed: worked as paid employees, worked in their own business or family business (full-time or part-time), or had a job but didn't work due to temporary absence.

- Unemployed: not employed but were available for work and looked for work in the last four weeks, or on temporary layoff.

- Not in the labor force: not in previous two categories (student, homemaker, retiree).

BLS then computes:

- Labor force = number of employed + number of unemployed

- Unemployment rate = (number of unemployed/labor force) × 100

- Labor-force participation rate = (labor force/adult pop.) × 100

The labor force is the total number of workers who have made themselves available for work. The unemployment rate is the percent of the labor force that is unemployed. The labor-force participation rate is the percent of the total adult population who are in the labor force. The unemployment rate and the labor-force participation rate vary widely across demographic groups—men, women, black, white, young, old. Prime-age women (25 to 50 years old) have lower labor-force participation rates than men, but once in the labor force, men and women have similar unemployment rates. Prime-age blacks and teenagers have higher unemployment rates than whites and older workers. Female labor-force participation is rising, while male participation is falling.

The normal rate of unemployment around which the unemployment rate fluctuates is the natural rate of unemployment. The deviation in unemployment from the natural rate is known as cyclical unemployment. In 2012, the natural rate of unemployment in the United States was estimated at 5.5 percent. This chapter is concerned with explaining the characteristics and causes of the natural rate.

Because people move into and out of the labor force so often, unemployment is difficult to measure and interpret. For example, over one-third of the unemployed are recent entrants to the labor force, and almost one-half of all spells of unemployment end when the unemployed person leaves the labor force. In addition, unemployment may be inaccurately measured because:

- Some people are counted in the labor force but unemployed even though they are only pretending to look for work so that they can collect government assistance or because they are being paid "under the table." This behavior biases the unemployment statistics upward.

- Some people have had an unsuccessful search for a job and have given up looking for work so they are not counted in the labor force. These individuals are called discouraged workers. This behavior biases the unemployment statistics downward.

Because of these and other problems, the BLS calculates alternative measures of labor underutilization, known as U1 through U6. These statistics attempt to measure the impact on the labor market of long-term unemployment, temporary jobs, discouraged workers, part-time workers, and marginally attached workers.

Knowledge about the duration of unemployment spells may help us design corrective policies for unemployment. Evidence suggests that *most spells are short term, but most unemployment at any given time is long term.* This means that many people are unemployed for short periods, but a few people are unemployed for very long periods. Economists think short-term unemployment is much less of a social problem than long-term unemployment.

In most markets, prices adjust to balance supply and demand. In the ideal labor market, wages would adjust so that there would be no unemployment. However, even when the economy is doing well, the unemployment rate never falls to zero. The following sections address four reasons why the labor market falls short of the ideal market. The first source of unemployment we discuss is due to job search. Frictional unemployment is the unemployment that results from the time it takes for workers to search for the jobs that best suit their tastes and skills. The next three sources of unemployment fall within the category of structural unemployment. Structural unemployment is the unemployment that results because the number of jobs available in some labor markets is insufficient for everyone who wants a job to get one. Structural unemployment occurs because the wage is held above the equilibrium wage. Three possible sources of an excessive wage are minimum-wage laws, unions, and efficiency wages. Frictional unemployment tends to explain shorter spells of unemployment, while structural unemployment tends to explain longer spells of unemployment.

Job Search

Job search is the process of matching workers and jobs. Just as workers differ in their skills and tastes, jobs differ in their attributes. Moreover, information about jobs disseminates slowly. Therefore, it takes time for job candidates and job vacancies to match. *Frictional unemployment* is due to this search time.

Frictional unemployment is inevitable in a dynamic economy. As the demand for products changes, some industries and regions will experience growth while others will contract. These changes in the composition of demand among industries or regions are called *sectoral shifts.* Sectoral shifts cause temporary frictional unemployment as workers in contracting sectors lose their jobs and search for work in the growing sectors.

Frictional unemployment may be reduced by improved information about job openings provided by the Internet. Government may be able to lower frictional unemployment by engaging in activities that shorten the job search time. Two such programs are (1) government-run employment agencies to help match workers and jobs and (2) worker-training programs to retrain workers laid off from contracting sectors. Critics argue that government is ill suited to do these things and that the market does a more efficient job at matching and retraining.

Unemployment insurance pays laid-off workers a portion of their original salaries for a period of time. Unemployment insurance increases frictional unemployment because unemployed workers are more likely to (1) devote less effort to their job search, (2) turn down unattractive job offers, and (3) be less concerned with job security. This does not mean unemployment insurance is bad. Unemployment insurance does provide the worker partial protection against job loss, and it may improve the efficiency of the job market by allowing workers to search longer for the best job match. Overall employment has declined due to food stamps, Social Security disability payments, Pell grants, and extended unemployment benefits.

Minimum-Wage Laws

Structural unemployment results when the number of jobs is insufficient for the number of workers. Minimum-wage laws are one source of structural unemployment. Recall that minimum-wage laws force the wage to remain above the equilibrium wage. This causes the quantity of labor supplied to exceed the quantity of labor demanded. There is a surplus of labor or unemployment. Since the equilibrium wage for most workers exceeds the minimum wage, the minimum wage tends to cause unemployment only for the least skilled and least experienced, such as teenagers. Minimum-wage workers tend to be young, less-educated, part-time workers in food services and drinking establishments. Tips supplement their wages.

Although only a small portion of total unemployment is due to the minimum wage, an analysis of the minimum wage points out a general rule: *If a wage is held above the equilibrium level, the result is unemployment.* The next two sections develop two additional reasons why the wage may be held above the equilibrium level. That is, the next two sections provide two additional sources for structural unemployment.

Note that with frictional unemployment, workers are *searching* for the right job even if the wage is at the competitive equilibrium. In contrast, structural unemployment exists because the wage exceeds the competitive equilibrium wage and workers are *waiting* for jobs to open up.

Unions and Collective Bargaining

A union is a worker association that engages in collective bargaining with employers over wages, benefits, and working conditions. A union is a cartel because it is a group of sellers organized to exert market power. If the union and firm fail to reach an agreement, the union can strike—that is, withdraw its labor services from the firm. Because of the threat of a strike, workers in unions earn about 10 to 20 percent more than nonunion workers. Less-educated workers gain a greater financial advantage from union membership than do better-educated workers.

Unions benefit *insiders* (members) at the expense of *outsiders* (nonmembers). When the union raises the wage above the equilibrium wage, unemployment results. Insiders earn higher wages, and outsiders are either unemployed or must take jobs with nonunion firms. This increases the supply of labor in the nonunion sector and lowers the wage further for nonunion workers.

Most cartels are illegal, but unions are exempt from antitrust legislation. Indeed, legislation, such as the Wagner Act of 1935, promotes the establishment of labor unions. Alternatively, state *right-to-work laws* discourage union membership by making it illegal to require union membership for employment.

There is little agreement about whether unions are good or bad for the economy. Critics argue that unions are cartels that raise the price of labor above the competitive equilibrium. This is inefficient (causes unemployment) and inequitable (insiders gain at the expense of outsiders). Supporters of unions argue that firms have market power and are able to depress the wage, so unions are just a counterbalance to the firm's power. This is most likely to be true in a *company town* where one firm hires most of the workers in the region. Supporters also argue that unions are efficient because firms don't have to bargain with individual workers about salary and benefits. That is, unions may reduce transactions costs.

The Theory of Efficiency Wages

The theory of efficiency wages suggests that firms may intentionally hold wages above the competitive equilibrium because it is efficient for them to do so. Efficiency wages are similar to minimum-wage laws and unions because, in all three cases, unemployment results from wages being held above the equilibrium wage. However, an efficiency wage is unusual in that it is paid voluntarily by the firm. Below, we address four reasons why firms may find it efficient (or profitable) to pay a wage in excess of the competitive equilibrium.

- *Worker health* may be improved by paying a higher wage. Better-paid workers eat a better diet and are more productive. This is more applicable to firms in developing nations and is probably not relevant for firms in the United States.

- *Worker turnover* may be reduced by paying a higher wage because workers will find it difficult to find alternative jobs at the higher wage. Firms may find it profitable to reduce worker turnover because there is a cost associated with hiring and training new workers and because new workers are not as experienced.

- *Worker quality* can be improved by paying a higher wage. Firms cannot perfectly gauge the quality of their job applicants. By paying a wage above the competitive equilibrium, firms have a higher probability of attracting a better pool of high-quality applicants for a job opening.

- *Worker effort* may be increased by paying a higher wage. When a worker's effort cannot be easily monitored, workers may shirk their responsibilities. If caught and fired, a worker earning the competitive equilibrium wage can easily find another job at the same wage. Higher wages make workers eager to keep their jobs and work hard.

Helpful Hints

1. Job search takes time even at the competitive equilibrium wage. Minimum-wage laws, unions, and efficiency wages all create an excess supply of labor (unemployment) by holding the wage above the competitive equilibrium wage. Frictional unemployment, however, exists even at the competitive equilibrium wage because it is inevitable that it takes time for workers and firms to match regardless of the wage. For this reason, structural unemployment resulting from the wage being held above the equilibrium wage can often be thought of as additional unemployment beyond the inherent frictional unemployment.

2. The natural rate of unemployment is persistent, not constant. Changes in minimum-wage laws, unions, and efficiency wages and changes in the job-search process due to the information revolution all have an impact on the natural rate of unemployment. Therefore, the natural rate will change as government policies, institutions, and behaviors change. But since policies, institutions, and behaviors change slowly, so does the natural rate of unemployment.

Terms and Definitions

Choose a definition for each key term.

Key Terms

____ Labor force

____ Unemployment rate

____ Labor-force participation rate

____ Natural rate of unemployment

____ Cyclical unemployment

____ Discouraged workers

____ Frictional unemployment

____ Structural unemployment

____ Job search

____ Sectoral shifts

____ Unemployment insurance

____ Union

____ Collective bargaining

____ Strike

____ Insiders

____ Outsiders

____ Right-to-work laws

____ Efficiency wages

Definitions

1. Workers who stop looking for work due to an unsuccessful search

2. The deviation of the unemployment rate from its natural rate

3. Wages voluntarily paid in excess of the competitive equilibrium wage to increase worker productivity

4. Changes in the composition of demand across industries or regions

5. The process by which workers find appropriate jobs given their tastes and skills

6. Unemployment due to the time it takes for workers to search for the jobs that best suit their tastes and skills

7. Normal rate of unemployment about which the unemployment rate fluctuates

8. Percentage of the adult population in the labor force

9. Legislation that makes it illegal to require union membership for employment

10. An organized withdrawal of labor from the firm

11. Worker association that bargains with employers over wages, benefits, and working conditions

12. Those employed in union jobs

13. A government program that pays laid-off workers a portion of their original salaries

14. The total number of workers, which is the sum of the unemployed and the employed

15. Unemployment that results because the number of jobs available in some labor markets is insufficient for everyone who wants a job to get one

16. Percentage of the labor force that is unemployed

17. The process by which unions and firms agree on labor contracts

18. Those not employed in union jobs

Problems and Short-Answer Questions

Practice Problems

1. Use the following information about Employment Country to answer question 1. Numbers are in millions.

	2012	2013
Population	223.6	226.5
Adult population	168.2	169.5
Number of unemployed	7.4	8.1
Number of employed	105.2	104.2

a. What is the labor force in 2012 and 2013?

_____

_____

b. What is the labor-force participation rate in 2012 and 2013?

_____

_____

c. What is the unemployment rate in 2012 and 2013?

_____

_____

d. From 2012 to 2013, the adult population went up while the labor force went down. Provide a number of explanations why this might have occurred.

_____

_____

_____

e. If the natural rate of unemployment in Employment Country is 6.6 percent, how much is cyclical unemployment in 2012 and 2013? Is Employment Country likely to be experiencing a recession in either of these years?

_____

_____

_____

_____

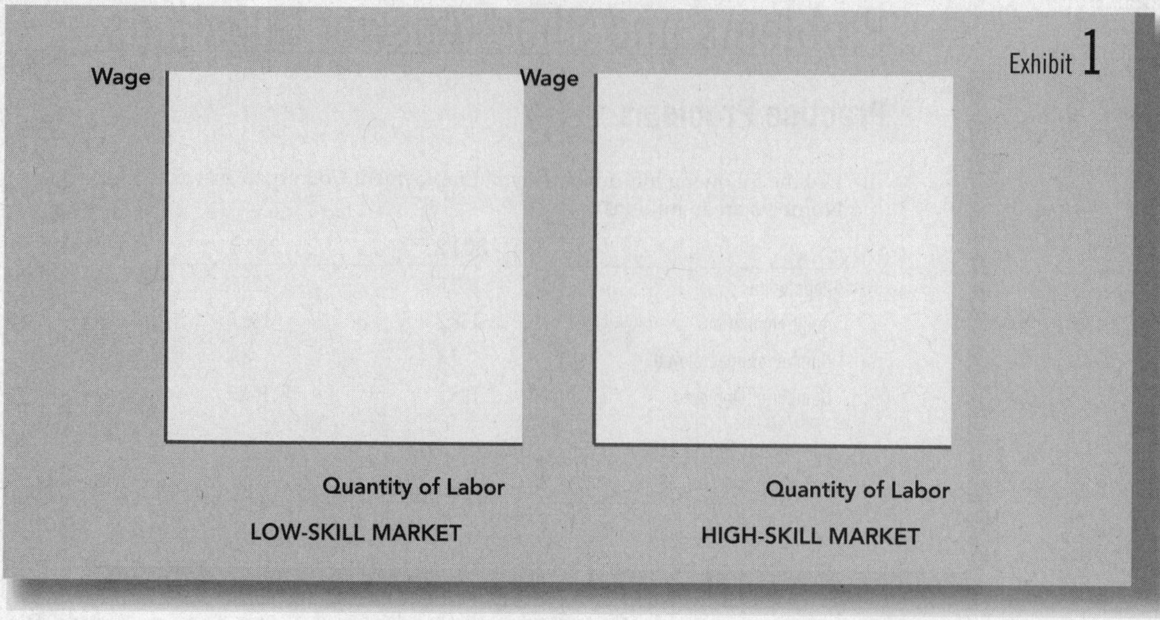

Exhibit 1

Wage | Wage

Quantity of Labor

LOW-SKILL MARKET

Quantity of Labor

HIGH-SKILL MARKET

2. Suppose the labor market is segmented into two distinct markets: the market for low-skill workers and the market for high-skill workers. Furthermore, suppose the competitive equilibrium wage in the low-skill market is $5.00/hour, while the competitive equilibrium wage in the high-skill market is $15.00/hour.

   a.   If the minimum wage is set at $7.00/hour, which market will exhibit the greatest amount of unemployment? Demonstrate it graphically in Exhibit 1.

_____

_____

   b.   Does the minimum wage have any impact on the high-skill market? Why or why not?

_____

_____

   c.   Do your results seem consistent with labor market statistics? Explain.

_____

_____

   d.   Suppose the high-skill market becomes unionized and the new negotiated wage is $18.00/hour. Will this have any effect on the low-skill market? Explain.

_____

_____

_____

3. Answer the following questions about the composition of unemployment.

   a.   What are some of the sources of unemployment?

_____

b. Which type of unemployment is initiated by the firm?

_____

c. Why might a firm pay wages in excess of the competitive equilibrium?

_____

d. Which type of efficiency wage is unlikely to be relevant in the United States? Why or why not?

_____

_____

e. How does frictional unemployment differ from the other sources of unemployment?

_____

_____

Short-Answer Questions

1. Name two reasons why the unemployment rate is an imperfect measure of joblessness.

_____

_____

_____

2. Explain the statement, "Most spells of unemployment are short, and most unemployment observed at any given time is long term."

_____

_____

3. Where would a labor union be more likely to increase efficiency rather than reduce it: a small remote town with one large employer or a major city with many employers? Why?

_____

_____

_____

4. Name two ways that a union increases the disparity in wages between members and nonmembers.

_____

_____

_____

5. Which alternative measure of unemployment attempts to include the impact of discouraged workers in the unemployment statistics? Explain. Is it higher or lower than the official unemployment rate? Explain.

_____

_____

_____

6. Does the minimum wage cause much unemployment in the market for accountants? Why or why not?

_____

_____

_____

7. Which type of unemployment will occur even if the wage is at the competitive equilibrium? Why?

_____

_____

_____

8. How does unemployment insurance increase frictional unemployment?

_____

_____

_____

9. How might the government help reduce frictional unemployment?

_____

_____

_____

10. Which of the following individuals is most likely to be unemployed for the long term: a buggy whip maker who loses his job when automobiles become popular or a waitress who is laid off when a new cafe opens in town? Why?

_____

_____

_____

Self-Test

True/False Questions

_____ 1. The natural rate of unemployment is the amount of unemployment that won't go away on its own, even in the long run.

_____ 2. If the unemployment rate falls, we can be certain that more workers have jobs.

_____ 3. In post–World War II United States, the labor-force participation rate has been rising for women and has been falling for men.

_____ 4. The unemployment rate is about the same for the various demographic groups: men, women, black, white, young, old.

_____ 5. A minimum wage is likely to have a greater impact on the market for skilled workers than on the market for unskilled workers.

_____ 6. The presence of a union tends to raise the wage for insiders and lower the wage for outsiders.

_____ 7. A union is a labor cartel.

_____ 8. Advocates of unions argue that unions may increase efficiency in some circumstances because they decrease the cost of bargaining between labor and management.

_____ 9. An efficiency wage is like a minimum wage in that firms are required by legislation to pay it.

_____ 10. Paying efficiency wages tends to increase worker turnover because workers can get continually higher wages if they "job hop."

_____ 11. Firms may voluntarily pay wages above the level that balances the supply and demand for workers because the higher wage improves the average quality of workers that apply for employment.

_____ 12. If wages were always at the competitive equilibrium, there would be absolutely no unemployment.

_____ 13. Due to the existence of "discouraged workers," the official unemployment rate may overstate true unemployment.

_____ 14. The presence of unemployment insurance tends to decrease the unemployment rate because recipients of unemployment benefits are not counted in the labor force.

_____ 15. Whenever the wage rises above the competitive equilibrium, regardless of the source, the result is additional unemployment.

Multiple-Choice Questions

1. The amount of unemployment that the economy normally experiences is known as
   a. efficiency wage unemployment.
   b. frictional unemployment.
   c. cyclical unemployment.
   d. the natural rate of unemployment.

2. According to the Bureau of Labor Statistics, a husband who chooses to stay home and take care of the household is
   a. unemployed.
   b. employed.
   c. not in the labor force.
   d. a discouraged worker.

Use the following table to answer questions 3 through 5. Numbers are in millions.

Total population	195.4
Adult population	139.7
Number of unemployed	5.7
Number of employed	92.3

3. The labor force is
   a. 92.3 million.
   b. 98.0 million.
   c. 134.0 million.
   d. 139.7 million.
   e. none of the above.

4. The unemployment rate is
   a. 3.2 percent.
   b. 5.7 percent.
   c. 5.8 percent.
   d. 6.2 percent.
   e. Not enough information is available to answer this question.

5. The labor-force participation rate is
   a. 47.1 percent.
   b. 50.2 percent.
   c. 65.9 percent.
   d. 70.2 percent.
   e. none of the above.

6. An accountant with a CPA designation who has been unable to find work for so long that she has stopped looking for work is considered to be
   a. employed.
   b. unemployed.
   c. not in the labor force.
   d. not in the adult population.

7. Which of the following statements is *true*?
   a. Prime-age men and women tend to have similar unemployment rates.
   b. The labor-force participation rate of men is rising.
   c. Blacks have a lower unemployment rate than whites.
   d. Most spells of unemployment are long term, but most unemployment observed at any given time is short term.
   e. All of the above are true.

8. A minimum-wage law tends to
   a. create more unemployment in high-skill job markets than in low-skill job markets.
   b. create more unemployment in low-skill job markets than in high-skill job markets.
   c. have no impact on unemployment as long as it is set above the competitive equilibrium wage.
   d. help all teenagers because they receive a higher wage than they would otherwise.

9. Which one of the following types of unemployment results from the wage being held above the competitive equilibrium wage?
   a. structural unemployment
   b. cyclical unemployment
   c. frictional unemployment
   d. sectoral unemployment
   e. None of the above is correct.

10. If, for any reason, the wage is held above the competitive equilibrium wage,
    a. unions will likely strike, and the wage will fall to equilibrium.
    b. the quality of workers in the applicant pool will tend to fall.
    c. the quantity of labor supplied will exceed the quantity of labor demanded, and there will be unemployment.
    d. the quantity of labor demanded will exceed the quantity of labor supplied, and there will be a labor shortage.

11. Which of the following is *not* a characteristic of minimum-wage workers? They tend to be
    a. young.
    b. less educated.
    c. full time.
    d. in the food service and drinking place industry.

12. Which of the following government policies would fail to lower the unemployment rate?
    a. reduce unemployment benefits
    b. establish employment agencies
    c. establish worker training programs
    d. raise the minimum wage
    e. establish right-to-work laws

13. Sectoral shifts tend to raise which type of unemployment?
    a. frictional unemployment
    b. structural unemployment
    c. unemployment due to unions
    d. unemployment due to efficiency wages

14. Which of the following is an example of a reason why firms might pay efficiency wages?
    a. At equilibrium wages, workers often quit to find better jobs.
    b. At equilibrium wages, workers sleep when the boss is not looking because workers are not deeply concerned about being fired.
    c. At equilibrium wages, only minimally qualified workers apply for the job.
    d. At equilibrium wages, workers cannot afford a healthy diet so they fall asleep at work due to a lack of energy.
    e. All of the above are true.

15. Some frictional unemployment is inevitable because
    a. efficiency wages may hold the wage above the equilibrium wage.
    b. of minimum-wage laws.
    c. there are changes in the demand for labor among different firms.
    d. of unions.
    e. of all of the above.

16. Unions might increase efficiency in the case where they
    a. raise the wage for insiders above the competitive equilibrium.
    b. offset the market power of a large firm in a "company town."
    c. lower the wage of local outsiders.
    d. threaten a strike but don't actually follow through, so there are no lost hours of work.

17. Which of the following statements about efficiency wage theory is *true*?
    a. Firms do not have a choice about whether they pay efficiency wages or not because these wages are determined by law.
    b. Paying the lowest possible wage is always the most efficient (profitable).
    c. Paying above the competitive equilibrium wage tends to cause workers to shirk their responsibilities.
    d. Paying above the competitive equilibrium wage may improve worker health, lower worker turnover, improve worker quality, and increase worker effort.

18. Unions tend to increase the disparity in pay between insiders and outsiders by
    a. increasing the wage in the unionized sector, which may create an increase in the supply of workers in the nonunionized sector.
    b. increasing the wage in the unionized sector, which may create a decrease in the supply of workers in the nonunionized sector.
    c. decreasing the demand for workers in the unionized sector.
    d. increasing the demand for workers in the unionized sector.

19. Which of the following types of unemployment will exist even if the wage is at the competitive equilibrium?
    a. unemployment due to minimum-wage laws
    b. unemployment due to unions
    c. unemployment due to efficiency wages
    d. frictional unemployment

20. If unemployment insurance were so generous that it paid laid-off workers 95 percent of their regular salary,
    a. the official unemployment rate would probably understate true unemployment.
    b. the official unemployment rate would probably overstate true unemployment.
    c. there would be no impact on the official unemployment rate.
    d. frictional unemployment would fall.
    e. none of the above is true.

Advanced Critical Thinking

You are watching the national news with your roommate. The news anchor says, "Unemployment statistics released by the Department of Labor today show an increase in unemployment from 6.1 percent to 6.2 percent. This is the third month in a row where the unemployment rate has increased." Your roommate says, "Every month there are fewer and fewer people with jobs. I don't know how much longer the country can continue like this."

1. Can your roommate's statement be deduced from the unemployment rate statistic? Why or why not?

   _____

   _____

   _____

   _____

   _____

2. What information would you need to determine whether there are really fewer people with jobs?

   _____

   _____

   _____

   _____

   _____

   _____

Solutions

Terms and Definitions

- _14_ Labor force
- _16_ Unemployment rate
- _8_ Labor-force participation rate
- _7_ Natural rate of unemployment
- _2_ Cyclical unemployment
- _1_ Discouraged workers
- _6_ Frictional unemployment
- _15_ Structural unemployment
- _5_ Job search
- _4_ Sectoral shifts
- _13_ Unemployment insurance
- _11_ Union
- _17_ Collective bargaining
- _10_ Strike
- _12_ Insiders
- _18_ Outsiders
- _9_ Right-to-work laws
- _3_ Efficiency wages

Practice Problems

1. a. 2012: 7.4 + 105.2 = 112.6 million
    2013: 8.1 + 104.2 = 112.3 million
    b. 2012: (112.6/168.2) × 100 = 66.9%
    2013: (112.3/169.5) × 100 = 66.3%
    c. 2012: (7.4/112.6) × 100 = 6.6%
    2013: (8.1/112.3) × 100 = 7.2%
    d. Earlier retirements, students staying in college longer, more parents staying at home with children, discouraged workers discontinuing their job search.
    e. 2012: 6.6% − 6.6% = 0%
    2013: 7.2% − 6.6% = 0.6%

In 2012, unemployment is "normal" for Employment Country; therefore, there is no recession. However, in 2013, unemployment is above normal (positive cyclical unemployment), so Employment Country may be in a recession.

2. a. The low-skill market will experience unemployment because there will be an excess supply of labor. (See Exhibit 2.)
    b. No, because the competitive equilibrium wage is above the wage floor.
    c. Yes. We observe a greater amount of unemployment among low-skill workers who are often young and inexperienced.
    d. Yes. The excess supply of skilled workers may cause some skilled workers to move to the unskilled market, increasing the supply of labor in the unskilled market, further reducing the competitive equilibrium wage, and causing even more unemployment there.
3. a. Job search, minimum wage, unions, efficiency wages.
    b. Efficiency wages.
    c. To improve worker health, lower worker turnover, improve worker quality, increase worker effort.
    d. Worker health because in the U.S. workers' wages are significantly above subsistence.
    e. Frictional unemployment exists even when the wage is at a competitive equilibrium.

Short-Answer Questions

1. Some people claim to be looking for work just to collect unemployment benefits, or they are being paid "under the table." Others are discouraged workers and have stopped looking for work due to an unsuccessful search.

2. Many people are unemployed for short periods. A few people are unemployed for very long periods.

Exhibit 2

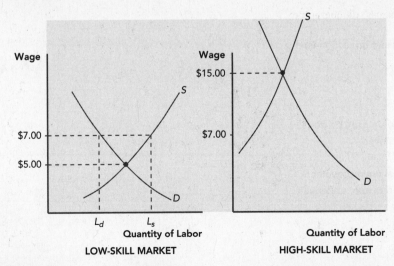

© 2015 Cengage Learning. All Rights Reserved. May not be scanned, copied or duplicated, or posted to a publicly accessible website, in whole or in part.

3. In a small "company" town where a single company has market power that may depress the wage below the competitive equilibrium. This may need to be offset by organized labor.

4. It raises the wage above the competitive equilibrium in the unionized sector. Some of those unemployed in the unionized sector move to the nonunionized sector, increasing the supply of labor and lowering the wage in the nonunion sector.

5. U4. It is total unemployed plus discouraged workers as a percent of the civilian labor force plus discouraged workers. It is a little higher than the official unemployment rate because it includes some nonworking people who have given up looking for work and have fallen out of the labor force.

6. No because the competitive equilibrium wage for accountants exceeds the minimum wage, and hence, the minimum wage is not a binding constraint for accountants.

7. Frictional unemployment because job matching takes time even when the wage is at the competitive equilibrium. Also, continuous sectoral shifts and new entrants into the job market make some frictional unemployment inevitable.

8. Unemployed workers devote less effort to their job search, turn down unattractive job offers, and are less concerned with job security.

9. By establishing employment agencies and worker training programs to retrain workers laid off in the contracting sectors.

10. The buggy whip maker. He will have to retrain because the contraction of the buggy whip business is permanent, while the waitress may just have to relocate, possibly just down the street.

True/False Questions

1. T
2. F; the unemployment rate falls when unemployed workers leave the labor force.
3. T
4. F; unemployment differs across demographic groups.
5. F; a minimum wage has a greater impact on low-wage workers.
6. T
7. T
8. T
9. F; efficiency wages are paid voluntarily by firms.
10. F; efficiency wages reduce turnover.
11. T
12. F; there would still be frictional unemployment.
13. F; the official unemployment rate may understate true unemployment.

14. F; unemployment insurance increases the unemployment rate because it increases frictional unemployment.

15. T

Multiple-Choice Questions

1. d
2. c
3. b
4. c
5. d
6. c
7. a
8. b
9. a
10. c
11. c
12. d
13. a
14. e
15. c
16. b
17. d
18. a
19. d
20. b

Advanced Critical Thinking

1. No. The unemployment rate is the ratio of the number of unemployed to the labor force. If the labor force grows (new graduates, housewives and househusbands entering the labor force) and if few of the new members of the labor force find work, then the unemployment rate will rise but the number of employed could stay the same or rise.

2. The number of employed is a component of the labor force and you can get information on that number directly.

Chapter 21
The Monetary System

Goals
In this chapter you will

- Consider what money is and what functions money has in the economy

- Learn what the Federal Reserve System is

- Examine how the banking system helps determine the supply of money

- See what tools the Federal Reserve uses to alter the supply of money

Outcomes
After accomplishing these goals, you should be able to

- Define money and list the three functions of money

- Explain the role of the Fed in money creation

- Explain the money multiplier in a fractional reserve banking system

- List and explain the tools the Fed uses to change the money supply

Chapter Overview

Context and Purpose

Chapter 21 is the first chapter in a two-chapter sequence dealing with money and prices in the long run. Chapter 21 describes what money is and develops how the Federal Reserve controls the quantity of money. Since the quantity of money influences the rate of inflation in the long run, the following chapter concentrates on the causes and costs of inflation.

The purpose of Chapter 21 is to help you develop an understanding of what money is, what forms money takes, how the banking system helps create money, and how the Federal Reserve controls the quantity of money. An understanding of money is important because the quantity of money affects inflation and interest rates in the long run and production and employment in the short run.

Chapter Review

Introduction   If there were no such thing as money, people would have to rely on barter. *Barter* is when people trade goods and services directly for other goods and services. Barter requires that there be a *double coincidence of wants*. For a trade to take place, each trader has to have what the other one wants—an unlikely event. The existence of money facilitates production and trade, which allow people to specialize in what they do best and raise the standard of living.

The Meaning of Money

Money is the set of assets commonly used to buy goods and services. That is, money is the portion of someone's wealth that is directly spendable or exchangeable for goods and services.

There are three functions of money:

- Money serves as a medium of exchange because money is the most commonly accepted asset when a buyer purchases goods and services from a seller.

- Money serves as a unit of account because money is the yardstick with which people post prices and record debts.

- Money serves as a store of value because people can use money to transfer purchasing power from the present to the future. Other types of wealth—stocks, bonds, rare art—may be a better store of value, but they are not as good at providing liquidity. Liquidity is the ease with which an asset can be converted into a medium of exchange. Money is liquid but loses value when prices rise. The value of rare art tends to rise with inflation, but it is much less liquid.

Money can be divided into two fundamental types—commodity money and fiat money.

- Commodity money is money that has "intrinsic value." That is, it has value independent of its use as money. Gold, silver, and cigarettes in a prisoner-of-war camp are all examples of commodity money. When a country uses gold as money, it is operating under a gold standard.

- Fiat money is money without intrinsic value. It is money by government fiat or declaration. Paper dollars are an example of fiat money.

When we measure the quantity of money, sometimes called the *money stock*, we should clearly include currency (paper bills and coins in the hands of the public) and demand deposits (balances in bank accounts that can be accessed on demand by check or debit card) because these assets are a medium of exchange. Savings balances, however, can easily be transferred into checking; other more restrictive checking accounts, such as money market mutual funds, offer some degree of spendability. In an economy with a complex financial system, it is difficult to draw the line between assets that are money and assets that are not. For this reason, in the United States, we calculate two measures of the money stock, which are shown below:

- M1: Currency, demand deposits, traveler's checks, other checkable deposits
- M2: M1, savings deposits, small time deposits, money market mutual funds, a few minor categories

For our purposes, consider money in the United States to be currency and spendable deposits.

Credit cards are not counted in the stock of money because they are not a method of payment but are instead a method of deferring payment. Debit cards are like an electronic check in that money from the buyer's account is directly transferred to the seller's account. Thus, the value is already captured by the account balance.

In comparison to the size of the U.S. population, there is an unusually large amount of currency in circulation. It is likely that a large portion of this currency is circulating overseas or used by criminal enterprises.

The Federal Reserve System

The Federal Reserve (Fed) is the central bank of the United States. It is designed to oversee the banking system and regulate the quantity of money in the economy.

The Fed was created in 1913 in response to a series of bank failures in 1907. The Fed is run by the Board of Governors, which has seven members appointed by the president and approved by the Senate. The members of the Board of Governors have fourteen-year terms to insulate them from political pressures. One of the seven members of the Board of Governors is appointed by the president to serve as chairman for a four-year term. The Federal Reserve System is composed of the Federal Reserve Board in Washington, D.C., and twelve regional Federal Reserve Banks.

The Fed has two main jobs:

- To regulate the banks and ensure the health of the banking system. The Fed monitors each bank's financial condition and helps clear checks. In a crisis, when banks find themselves short of cash, the Fed may act as the *lender of last resort* to the banks.

- To control the quantity of money in the economy, called the money supply. The Fed's decisions about the money supply are called monetary policy.

The monetary policy branch of the Fed is the *Federal Open Market Committee* (FOMC). There are twelve voting members on the FOMC—the seven members of the Board of Governors plus five of the twelve regional bank presidents. The voting among the regional bank presidents is rotated. The FOMC meets about every six weeks to discuss the condition of the economy and to vote on changes in monetary policy.

The Fed primarily changes the money supply with open-market operations, which are the purchase and sale of U.S. government bonds by the Fed in the open market for debt (thus, the name Federal Open Market Committee).

- To increase the money supply, the Fed creates dollars and uses them to purchase government bonds. After the transaction, additional dollars are in the hands of the public, so the money supply is larger.

- To decrease the money supply, the Fed sells government bonds to the public. After the transaction, fewer dollars are in the hands of the public, so the money supply is smaller.

Changing the money supply changes inflation in the long run and may change employment and output in the short run.

Banks and the Money Supply

Recall that the public can hold its money as currency or demand deposits. Since these deposits are in banks, the behavior of banks affects the money supply. This complicates the Fed's task of controlling the money supply.

The impact that banks have on the money supply can be seen by going through the following three cases:

- Suppose there are *no banks*. Then currency is the only money. If there is $1,000 of currency, there is $1,000 of money.

- Suppose there is *100-percent-reserve banking*. Deposits that are received by a bank but are not loaned out are called reserves. With 100-percent-reserve banking, banks are safe places to store money, but they are not lenders. If the public deposits all $1,000 of its currency in Bank 1, Bank 1's *T-account*, which records changes in the bank's assets and liabilities, would be the following:

Bank 1

Assets	Liabilities
Reserves $1,000	Deposits $1,000

Bank 1 has liabilities of $1,000 because it owes the $1,000 deposit back to the depositor. It has assets of $1,000 because it has cash reserves of $1,000 in its vault. Since currency held by the public has gone down by $1,000 and deposits held by the public have increased by $1,000, the money supply is unaffected. *If banks hold all deposits on reserve, banks do not influence the money supply.*

- Suppose there is fractional-reserve banking. Since few people request the return of their deposit on any given day, Bank 1 need not hold all $1,000 of the deposit as cash reserves. It could lend some of the $1,000 and keep only the remainder on reserve. This is called fractional-reserve banking. The fraction of deposits held as reserves is the reserve ratio. The Fed sets the minimum reserve ratio with a reserve requirement. Suppose Bank 1 has a reserve ratio of 10 percent, which means that it keeps 10 percent of its deposits on reserve and lends out the rest. Its T-account becomes:

Bank 1

Assets		Liabilities	
Reserves	$100	Deposits	$1,000
Loans	$900		

Bank 1 has created money because it still holds a $1,000 deposit, but now a borrower has $900 in currency. *When banks hold only a fraction of deposits as reserves, banks create money.*

This story is not complete. Suppose the borrower of the $900 spends it and the receiver of the $900 deposits it in Bank 2. If Bank 2 also has a reserve ratio of 10 percent, its T-account becomes:

Bank 2

Assets		Liabilities	
Reserves	$ 90	Deposits	$900
Loans	$810		

Bank 2 has created another $810 by its lending activity. Each time money is deposited and a portion of it loaned, more money is created.

If this process continues forever, the total amount of money created by the banking system from the original deposit of $1,000 is $1,000 + $900 + $810 + $729 + . . . = $10,000 (in this case, each loan is 90 percent of the previous loan).

The amount of money the banking system creates from each dollar of reserves is called the money multiplier. The money multiplier is the reciprocal of the reserve ratio. If R is the reserve ratio, then the money multiplier is $1/R$. In the case described here, the money multiplier is $1/.10$ or 10. Thus, $1,000 of new reserves created from the original $1,000 deposit can create a total of $10,000 in deposits. The smaller the reserve ratio, the greater the amount of lending from the same amount of reserves and, hence, the larger the money multiplier. The larger the reserve ratio, the smaller the multiplier.

Fractional-reserve banking does not create net wealth because when a bank loans reserves, which creates money (someone's asset), it also creates an equal value debt contract (someone's liability).

A more detailed bank balance sheet than those shown above show that banks obtain financial resources not only from accepting deposits but also by issuing equity, called *bank capital*, and debt. The value of the owners' equity, or bank capital, is the value of the bank's assets minus the value of the bank's liabilities. Banks are said to employ *leverage* because they use borrowed money to supplement existing funds for investment purposes. The *leverage ratio* is the ratio of the bank's total assets to bank capital. Leverage amplifies the impact of a change in the value of a bank's assets on bank capital. Thus, a small percentage increase in the value of assets can increase bank capital by a much larger percentage. Alternatively, a small percentage decrease in the value of a bank's assets reduces bank capital by a much larger percentage. When the value of assets falls below the value of liabilities, the bank becomes insolvent. To avoid bank failures, regulators impose *capital requirements* on banks. In 2008 and 2009, losses on mortgage loans caused a shortage of bank capital, reducing bank lending, and causing a severe downturn in economic activity.

The Fed's Tools of Monetary Control

The Fed controls the money supply indirectly by influencing the quantity of reserves and the reserve ratio. Recall that the reserve ratio affects the money multiplier.

The Fed influences the quantity of reserves through open market operations and lending directly to banks:

- *Open-market operations:* Recall, when the Fed buys government bonds from the public, the dollars it uses to pay for them increase the dollars in the economy. Each new dollar held as currency increases the money supply one dollar. Each dollar deposited with banks increases bank reserves and, thus, increases the money supply by some multiple. When the Fed sells government securities, dollars are removed from circulation and reserves are reduced at banks. This reduces lending and further reduces the money supply. Open-market operations can easily be used for small or large changes in the money supply. Hence, it is the day-to-day tool of the Fed.

- *Fed lending to banks:* When the Fed lends reserves to banks, the banking system can increase its lending, which creates more money. Traditionally, the Fed influences its lending through the *discount window* by altering the *discount rate*, which is the interest rate the Fed charges when lending to banks. An increase in the discount rate discourages banks from borrowing reserves and decreases the money supply. A decrease in the discount rate increases reserves and the money supply. More recently, the Fed can lend through the Term Auction Facility where the Fed sets the quantity of loans available and the banks set the interest rate by bidding for the loans. Making funds available through the Term Auction Facility increases reserves and the money supply, and it gets funds to the banks in financial need during a financial crisis.

The Fed influences the reserve ratio through reserve requirements and the interest it pays on reserves.

- *Reserve requirements:* Reserve requirements set the minimum reserve ratio for a bank. An increase in the reserve requirement reduces the money multiplier and decreases the money supply. A decrease in the reserve requirement increases the money multiplier and increases the money supply. The Fed rarely changes reserve requirements because changes in reserve requirements disrupt the business of banking. For example, an increase in reserve requirements immediately restricts bank loans. Alternatively, it could be ineffective when banks are holding excess reserves.

- *Paying interest on reserves:* When the Fed increases the interest rate it pays on banks' reserve deposits at the Fed, banks hold more reserves, increasing the reserve ratio reducing the money multiplier, and decreasing the money supply. This tool is new (2008), so it is not clear how important it will become.

The Fed's control of the money supply is not precise because:

- The Fed does not control the amount of money people choose to hold as deposits versus currency. When the public deposits a greater amount of their currency, bank reserves increase, and the money supply increases.

- The Fed does not control the amount of reserves that the banks lend. The reserve requirement sets the minimum reserve ratio, but banks can hold *excess reserves*— reserves in excess of those required. If banks increase their excess reserves, lending decreases, and the money supply decreases.

In times prior to the existence of deposit insurance, if depositors feared that a bank had made unsound loans with their deposits and that the bank might become bankrupt, they would "run" to the bank to remove their deposit. This is known as a "bank run." With fractional reserves, only a few depositors can immediately get their money back. This behavior causes a decrease in the money supply for two reasons. First, people increase their holdings of currency by withdrawing deposits from banks. This reduces reserves, bank lending, and the money supply. Second, banks, fearing deposit withdrawal, hold excess reserves and further decrease lending and the money supply. This is no longer a major problem due to the Federal Deposit Insurance Corporation (FDIC). Also, the Fed collects weekly data on reserves and deposits, so it can detect changes in depositor and bank behavior.

The federal funds rate is the interest rate banks charge each other for short-term loans. When the Fed lowers the target for the federal funds rate, it buys bonds with open-market operations supplying more bank reserves, and the money supply increases. When the Fed raises the federal funds target, the money supply decreases.

Helpful Hints

1. Fiat money maintains value due to artificial scarcity. Gold has value because people desire it for its intrinsic value and because it is naturally scarce (alchemists have never been able to create gold). However, fiat money is cheap and easy to produce. Therefore, fiat money maintains its value only because of self-restraint on the part of the producer. If U.S. dollars are a quality store of value, it is because the dollar is difficult to counterfeit, and the Fed shows self-restraint in the production of dollars.

2. Paper dollars are considered "currency" only when in the hands of the nonbank public. When economists use the word currency, we mean "currency in the hands of the nonbank public." When you deposit currency in the bank, you now own a deposit, and your paper dollars are now the "reserves" of the bank. Currency in the hands of the nonbank public has decreased while deposits have increased by an equal amount. At this point, the money supply is unaltered because money is the sum of currency (in the hands of the nonbank public) and deposits.

3. The money multiplier is most easily understood in words. If we state the relationship among reserves, deposits, and the multiplier in words, it clarifies the relationship. Since a fractional reserve system implies that "reserves are some percent of deposits," it follows that "deposits are some multiple of reserves." For example, if reserves are 1/5 (or 20 percent) of deposits, then deposits are five times (or 1/.20) reserves. Since deposit expansion actually takes place due to banks' lending some of their reserves, it is most useful to us to think in terms of "deposits are some multiple of reserves."

4. It is easy to remember the impact of open-market operations by asking yourself, "Who pays?" When the Fed buys a government bond from the public, the Fed pays with "new dollars" and the money supply expands. When the Fed sells government bonds, the public pays with dollars and the Fed "retires" the dollars. That is, the dollars cease to exist when the Fed receives payment. Note that when the Fed sells bonds, it is not "issuing" bonds. It is selling existing bonds that were previously issued by the U.S. government.

Terms and Definitions

Choose a definition for each key term.

Key Terms

____ Money

____ Medium of exchange

____ Unit of account

____ Store of value

____ Liquidity

____ Commodity money

____ Fiat money

____ Currency

____ Demand deposits

____ Federal Reserve (Fed)

____ Central bank

____ Money supply

____ Monetary policy

____ Reserves

____ Fractional-reserve banking

____ Reserve ratio

____ Money multiplier

____ Bank capital

____ Leverage

____ Leverage ratio

____ Capital requirement

____ Open-market operations

____ Reserve requirements

____ Discount rate

____ Federal funds rate

Definitions

1. A banking system in which banks hold only a fraction of deposits as reserves
2. Paper bills and coins in the hands of the public
3. The function of money when used to transfer purchasing power to the future
4. The interest rate the Fed charges on loans to banks
5. The ratio of assets to bank capital
6. The function of money when used as a yardstick to post prices and record debts
7. Money in the form of a commodity with intrinsic value
8. The central bank of the United States
9. The set of assets generally accepted in trade for goods and services
10. The fraction of deposits held as reserves
11. The interest rate at which banks make overnight loans to one another
12. The quantity of money in the economy
13. Money without intrinsic value
14. The function of money when used to purchase goods and services
15. The purchase and sale of U.S. government bonds by the Fed
16. Deposits that banks have received but have not lent out
17. The minimum legal percent of deposits that banks must hold as reserves
18. Decisions by the central bank concerning the money supply
19. Balances in bank accounts that can be accessed on demand by check
20. The amount of money the banking system generates from each dollar of reserves
21. The use of borrowed money to supplement existing funds for purposes of investment
22. An institution designed to regulate the banking system and money supply
23. The ease with which an asset can be converted into the economy's medium of exchange
24. The resources a bank's owners have put into the institution
25. A government regulation specifying a minimum amount of bank capital

Problems and Short-Answer Questions

Practice Problems

1. Suppose the Federal Reserve purchases a U.S. government bond from you for $10,000.
   a. What is the name of the Fed's action?

   _____

   b. Suppose you deposit the $10,000 in First Student Bank. Show this transaction on First Student Bank's T-account.

   First Student Bank

Assets	Liabilities

   c. Suppose the reserve requirement is 20 percent. Show First Student Bank's T-account if they loan out as much as they can.

   First Student Bank

Assets	Liabilities

   d. At this point, how much money has been created from the Fed's policy action?

   _____

   e. What is the value of the money multiplier?

   _____

   f. After infinite rounds of depositing and lending, how much money could be created from the Fed's policy action?

   _____

   g. If during the rounds of depositing and lending, some people keep extra currency and fail to deposit all of their receipts, will there be more or less money created from the Fed's policy action than you found in part *f*? Why?

   _____

   _____

   _____

   h. If during the rounds of depositing and lending, some banks fail to loan the maximum amount of reserves allowed but instead keep excess reserves, will there be more or less money created from the Fed's policy action than you found in part *f*? Why?

   _____

   _____

   _____

2. Suppose the entire economy contains $1,000 worth of one-dollar bills.

   a. If people fail to deposit any of the dollars but instead hold all $1,000 as currency, how large is the money supply? Explain.

   _____

   _____

   b. If people deposit the entire $1,000 worth of bills in banks that are required to observe a 100 percent reserve requirement, how large is the money supply? Explain.

   _____

   _____

   c. If people deposit the entire $1,000 worth of bills in banks that are required to observe a 20 percent reserve requirement, how large could the money supply become? Explain.

   _____

   _____

   d. In part c, what portion of the money supply was created due to the banks? (Hint: $1,000 of bills already existed.)

   _____

   _____

   e. If people deposit the entire $1,000 worth of bills in banks that are required to observe a 10 percent reserve requirement, how large could the money supply become?

   _____

   f. Compare your answer in part e to part c. Explain why they are different.

   _____

   _____

   g. If people deposit the entire $1,000 worth of bills in banks that are required to observe a 10 percent reserve requirement, but they choose to hold another 10 percent as excess reserves, how large could the money supply become?

   _____

   h. Compare your answer in part c to part g. Are these answers the same? Why or why not?

   _____

   _____

   _____

Short-Answer Questions

1. What is barter, and why does it limit trade?

   _____

   _____

   _____

2. What are the three functions of money?

   _____

   _____

   _____

3. What are the two basic kinds of money?

   _____

4. What two main assets are clearly money in the United States, and how do they differ from all other assets? (i.e., define money)

   _____

   _____

   _____

5. What are the two main jobs of the Federal Reserve?

   _____

   _____

   _____

6. What are the monetary policy tools of the Fed?

   _____

   _____

   _____

7. If the Fed wished to expand the money supply, how should they adjust each of their policy instruments that underlie the tools described in question 6 above?

   _____

   _____

8. If the Fed buys $1,000 of government bonds from you and you hold all of the payment as currency at home, by how much does the money supply rise?

   _____

9. If the Fed buys $1,000 of government bonds from you, you deposit the entire $1,000 in a demand deposit at your bank, and banks observe a 10 percent reserve requirement, by how much could the money supply increase?

   _____

10. Suppose the reserve ratio is 20 percent. If you write a check on your account at Bank 1 to buy a $1,000 government bond from your roommate, and your roommate deposits the $1,000 in her account at Bank 2, by how much will the money supply change?

_____

_____

_____

11. Suppose there is no deposit insurance. Suppose rumors circulate that banks have made many bad loans and may be unable to repay their depositors. What would you expect depositors and banks to do, and what would their behavior do to the money supply?

_____

_____

_____

12. What must the Fed do with open-market operations and the money supply if it wishes to reduce the federal funds rate?

_____

_____

_____

Self-Test

True/False Questions

_____ 1. Money and wealth are the same thing.

_____ 2. Fiat money is money that is used in Italy.

_____ 3. Commodity money has value independent of its use as money.

_____ 4. The M1 money supply is composed of currency, demand deposits, traveler's checks, and other checkable deposits.

_____ 5. When you are willing to go to sleep tonight with $100 in your wallet and you have complete confidence that you can spend it tomorrow and receive the same amount of goods as you would have received had you spent it today, money has demonstrated its function as a medium of exchange.

_____ 6. Money has three functions: It acts as a medium of exchange, a unit of account, and a protection against inflation.

_____ 7. Credit cards are part of the M2 money supply and are valued at the maximum credit limit of the cardholder.

_____ 8. The Federal Reserve is the central bank of the United States and is run by the seven members of the Board of Governors.

_____ 9. The Federal Open Market Committee (FOMC) meets about every six weeks and discusses the condition of the economy and votes on changes in monetary policy.

_____ 10. If there is 100 percent reserve banking, the money supply is unaffected by the proportion of the dollars that the public chooses to hold as currency versus deposits.

_____ 11. If the Fed purchases $100,000 of government bonds, and the reserve requirement is 10 percent, the maximum increase in the money supply is $10,000.

_____ 12. If the Fed desires to contract the money supply, it could do any of the following: sell government bonds, increase the discount rate, increase the reserve requirement, and increase the interest rate paid on reserves.

_____ 13. If the Fed sells $1,000 of government bonds, and the reserve requirement is 10 percent, deposits could fall by as much as $10,000.

_____ 14. An increase in the reserve requirement increases the money multiplier and increases the money supply.

_____ 15. If banks choose to hold excess reserves, lending decreases, and the money supply decreases.

Multiple-Choice Questions

1. Which of the following is _not_ a function of money?
   a. unit of account
   b. store of value
   c. protection against inflation
   d. medium of exchange

2. The M1 money supply is composed of
   a. currency, demand deposits, traveler's checks, and other checkable accounts.
   b. currency, demand deposits, savings deposits, money market mutual funds, and small time deposits.
   c. currency, government bonds, gold certificates, and coins.
   d. currency, NOW accounts, savings accounts, and government bonds.
   e. none of the above.

3. An example of fiat money is
   a. gold.
   b. paper dollars.
   c. solid silver coins.
   d. cigarettes in a prisoner-of-war camp.

4. The Board of Governors of the Federal Reserve System consists of
   a. seven members appointed by Congress and seven appointed by the president.
   b. seven members elected by the Federal Reserve Banks.
   c. twelve members appointed by Congress.
   d. seven members appointed by the president.
   e. five members appointed by the president and seven rotating presidents of the Federal Reserve Banks.

5. Commodity money
   a. has no intrinsic value.
   b. has intrinsic value.
   c. is used exclusively in the United States.
   d. is used as reserves to back fiat money.

6. To insulate the Federal Reserve from political pressure,
   a. the Board of Governors are elected by the public.
   b. the Board of Governors have lifetime tenure.
   c. the Board of Governors are supervised by the House Banking Committee.
   d. the Board of Governors are appointed to fourteen-year terms.

7. Which of the following statements is *true*?
   a. The FOMC meets once per year to discuss monetary policy.
   b. The Federal Reserve was created in 1871 in response to the Civil War.
   c. When the Fed sells government bonds, the money supply decreases.
   d. The primary tool of monetary policy is the reserve requirement.

8. Required reserves of banks are a fixed percentage of their
   a. loans.
   b. assets.
   c. deposits.
   d. government bonds.

9. If the reserve ratio is 25 percent, the value of the money multiplier is
   a. 0.25.
   b. 4.
   c. 5.
   d. 25.
   e. none of the above.

10. Which of the following policy actions by the Fed is likely to increase the money supply?
    a. reducing reserve requirements
    b. selling government bonds
    c. increasing the discount rate
    d. increasing interest on reserves
    e. All of these will increase the money supply.

11. Suppose Joe changes his $1,000 demand deposit from Bank A to Bank B. If the reserve requirement is 10 percent, what is the potential change in demand deposits as a result of Joe's action?
    a. $1,000
    b. $9,000
    c. $10,000
    d. $0

12. A decrease in the reserve requirement causes
    a. reserves to rise.
    b. reserves to fall.
    c. the money multiplier to rise.
    d. the money multiplier to fall.
    e. none of the above.

13. The discount rate is
    a. the interest rate the Fed pays on reserves.
    b. the interest rate the Fed charges on loans to banks.
    c. the interest rate banks pay on the public's deposits.
    d. the interest rate the public pays when borrowing from banks.
    e. the interest rate paid by banks at the Term Auction Facility.

14. Which of the following policy combinations would consistently work to increase the money supply?
    a. sell government bonds, decrease reserve requirements, decrease the discount rate
    b. sell government bonds, increase reserve requirements, increase the discount rate
    c. buy government bonds, increase reserve requirements, decrease the discount rate
    d. buy government bonds, decrease reserve requirements, decrease the discount rate
    e. none of the above

15. Suppose the Fed purchases a $1,000 government bond from you. If you deposit the entire $1,000 in your bank, what is the total potential change in the money supply as a result of the Fed's action if reserve requirements are 20 percent?
    a. $1,000
    b. $4,000
    c. $5,000
    d. $0

16. Suppose all banks maintain a 100 percent reserve ratio. If an individual deposits $1,000 of currency in a bank,
    a. the money supply is unaffected.
    b. the money supply increases by more than $1,000.
    c. the money supply increases by less than $1,000.
    d. the money supply decreases by more than $1,000.
    e. the money supply decreases by less than $1,000.

17. If the Fed engages in an open-market purchase, and at the same time, it raises reserve requirements,
    a. the money supply should rise.
    b. the money supply should fall.
    c. the money supply should remain unchanged.
    d. we cannot be certain what will happen to the money supply.

18. Which of the following statements about a bank's balance sheet is true?
    a. An increase in a bank's capital increases its leverage ratio.
    b. Assets minus liabilities equals owner's equity or capital.
    c. The largest liability on the bank's balance sheet is its loans.
    d. Because a bank is highly leveraged, a large change in the value of its assets has little impact on its capital.
    e. None of the above is correct.

19. The Fed's tools of monetary control are
    a. government expenditures, taxation, reserve requirements, and interest rates.
    b. the money supply, government purchases, and taxation.
    c. coin, currency, demand deposits, and commodity money.
    d. open-market operations, lending to banks, reserve requirements, and paying interest on reserves.
    e. fiat, commodity, and deposit money.

20. If banks increase their holdings of excess reserves,
    a. the money multiplier and the money supply decrease.
    b. the money multiplier and the money supply increase.
    c. the money multiplier decreases, and the money supply increases.
    d. the money multiplier increases, and the money supply decreases.

Advanced Critical Thinking

Suppose you are a personal friend of Ben Bernanke (the chairman of the Board of Governors of the Federal Reserve System on the date of publication of this Study Guide). He comes over to your house for lunch and notices your couch. Mr. Bernanke is so struck by the beauty of your couch that he simply must have it for his office. Mr. Bernanke buys it from you for $1,000 and, since it is for his office, pays you with a check drawn on the Federal Reserve Bank of New York.

1. Are there more dollars in the economy than before? Why or why not?

   _____

   _____

   _____

   _____

   _____

2. Why do you suppose that the Fed doesn't buy and sell couches, real estate, and so on instead of government bonds when they desire to change the money supply?

   _____

   _____

   _____

   _____

   _____

3. If the Fed doesn't want the money supply to rise when it purchases new furniture, what might it do to offset the purchase?

   _____

   _____

Solutions

Terms and Definitions

 _9_ Money
_14_ Medium of exchange
 _6_ Unit of account
 _3_ Store of value
_23_ Liquidity
 _7_ Commodity money
_13_ Fiat money
 _2_ Currency
_19_ Demand deposits
 _8_ Federal Reserve (Fed)
_22_ Central bank
_12_ Money supply
_18_ Monetary policy
_16_ Reserves
 _1_ Fractional-reserve banking
_10_ Reserve ratio
_20_ Money multiplier
_24_ Bank capital
_21_ Leverage
 _5_ Leverage ratio
_25_ Capital requirement
_15_ Open-market operations
_17_ Reserve requirements
 _4_ Discount rate
_11_ Federal funds rate

Practice Problems

1. a. Open-market operations
   b.

First Student Bank

Assets		Liabilities	
Reserves	$10,000	Deposits	$10,000

   c.

First Student Bank

Assets		Liabilities	
Reserves	$2,000	Deposits	$10,000
Loans	$8,000		

   d. $10,000 + $8,000 = $18,000
   e. $1/.20 = 5$
   f. $10,000 × 5 = $50,000$
   g. Less because a smaller amount of each loan gets redeposited to be available to be loaned again.
   h. Less because a smaller amount of each deposit gets loaned out to be available to be deposited again.
2. a. $1,000 because there is $1,000 of currency and $0 of deposits.

b. $1,000 because there is now $0 of currency and $1,000 of deposits.
c. $1,000 × (1/.20) = $5,000$ because $1,000 of new reserves can support $5,000 worth of deposits.
d. The total potential increase is $5,000, but $1,000 was currency already in the system. Thus, an additional $4,000 was created by the banks.
e. $1,000 × (1/.10) = $10,000.$
f. Banks can create more money from the same amount of new reserves when reserve requirements are lower because they can lend a larger portion of each new deposit.
g. $1,000 × 1/(.10 + .10) = $5,000.$
h. Yes, they are the same. With regard to deposit creation, it doesn't matter why banks hold reserves. It only matters how much they hold.

Short-Answer Questions

1. Barter is trading goods and services directly for other goods and services. It requires a double coincidence of wants.
2. Medium of exchange, unit of account, store of value.
3. Commodity money, fiat money.
4. Currency and demand deposits. They are the assets that are directly spendable and are commonly accepted in trade for goods and services.
5. Regulate banks to ensure the health of the banking system, and control the quantity of money in the economy.
6. Open-market operations, Fed lending to banks, reserve requirements, and the Fed paying interest on bank reserves.
7. Buy U.S. government bonds, loan more reserves to banks by lowering the discount rate and/or increasing loans available at the Term Action Facility, lower the reserve requirement, and decrease interest paid on reserves.
8. $1,000
9. $1,000 × (1/.10) = $10,000$
10. The money supply will not change at all. In this case, reserves are only moved from one bank to another.
11. Depositors will withdraw their deposits reducing bank reserves. Banks will try to hold excess reserves to prepare for the deposit withdrawal. Both will reduce bank lending and the money supply.
12. It must buy bonds, which injects reserves into the banking system and increases the money supply.

True/False Questions

1. F; money is the spendable portion of one's wealth.
2. F; fiat money is money without intrinsic value.

3. T
4. T
5. F; money demonstrated its function as a store of value.
6. F; store of value, not a hedge against inflation.
7. F; credit cards are not included in the money supply.
8. T
9. T
10. T
11. F; the maximum increase in the money supply is $100,000 \times (1/0.10) = \$1,000,000$.
12. T
13. T
14. F; an increase in the reserve requirement decreases the money multiplier, which decreases the money supply.
15. T

Multiple-Choice Questions

1. c
2. a
3. b
4. d
5. b
6. d
7. c
8. c
9. b
10. a
11. d
12. c
13. b
14. d
15. c
16. a
17. d
18. b
19. d
20. a

Advanced Critical Thinking

1. Yes. When the Fed purchases anything, it pays with newly created dollars, and there are more dollars in the economy.
2. The transaction costs and storage costs would be staggering. Also, the value of the inventory of "items" would never be certain. The open market for government bonds is much more efficient.
3. The Fed could sell government bonds of equal value to offset other purchases.

Chapter 22

Money Growth and Inflation

Chapter Overview

Context and Purpose

Chapter 22 is the second chapter in a two-chapter sequence dealing with money and prices in the long run. Chapter 21 explained what money is and how the Federal Reserve controls the quantity of money. Chapter 22 establishes the relationship between the rate of growth of money and the inflation rate.

The purpose of this chapter is to acquaint you with the causes and costs of inflation. You will find that, in the long run, there is a strong relationship between the growth rate of money and inflation. You will also find that there are numerous costs to the economy from high inflation but that there is not a consensus on the importance of these costs when inflation is moderate.

Chapter Review

Introduction   *Inflation* is an increase in the overall level of prices. *Deflation* is a decrease in the overall level of prices. *Hyperinflation* is extraordinarily high inflation. There is great variation in inflation over time and across countries. In this chapter, we address two questions: What causes inflation, and why is inflation a problem? The answer to the first question is that inflation is caused when the government prints too much money. The answer to the second question requires more thought and will be the focus of the second half of this chapter.

The Classical Theory of Inflation

This section develops and employs the quantity theory of money as an explanation of the price level and inflation.

When prices rise, it is rarely because products are more valuable but rather because the money used to buy them is less valuable. Thus, *inflation is more about the value of money than about the value of goods*. An increase in the overall price level is equivalent to a proportionate fall in the value of money. If P is the price level (the value of goods and services measured in money), then $1/P$ is the value of money measured in terms of goods and services. If prices double, the value of money has fallen to $1/2$ its prior value.

The value of money is determined by the supply and demand for money. If we ignore the banking system, the Fed controls the money supply. Money demand reflects how much wealth people want to hold in liquid form. While money demand has many determinants, in the long run, one is dominant—the price level. People hold money because it is a medium of exchange. If prices are higher, more money is needed for the same transaction, and the quantity of money demanded is higher.

Money supply and money demand need to balance for there to be monetary equilibrium. Monetary equilibrium is shown in Exhibit 1 for money supply MS_1 at point A. Recall that the value of money measured in goods and services is $1/P$. When the value of money is high, the price level is low, and the quantity of money demanded is low. Therefore, the money demand curve slopes negatively in the graph. Since the Fed fixes the quantity of money, the money supply curve is vertical. In the long run, the overall level of prices adjusts to equate the quantity of money demanded to the quantity of money supplied.

Suppose the Fed doubles the quantity of money in the economy from MS_1 to MS_2. There is now an excess supply of money at the original price level. Since people now are holding more money than they desire, they will rid themselves of the excess supply of money by buying things—goods and services or bonds. Even if people buy bonds (lend money), the bond issuer (borrower) will take the money and buy goods and services. Either way, an injection of money increases the demand for goods and services. Since the ability of the economy to produce goods and services has not changed, an increase in the demand for goods and services raises the price level. The price level will continue to rise (and the value of money will fall) until the quantity of money demanded is raised to the level of the quantity of money supplied (point B). That is, the price level adjusts to equate money supply and money demand. Thus, the conclusions of the *quantity theory of money* are: (1) The quantity of money in the economy determines the price level (and the value of money), and (2) an increase in the money supply increases the price level, which means that growth in the money supply causes inflation.

The classical dichotomy suggests that economic variables can be divided into two groups—nominal variables (those measured in monetary units) and real variables (those measured in physical units). Although prices are nominal variables, relative prices are real variables. For example, the ratio of your earnings per hour to the price of candy

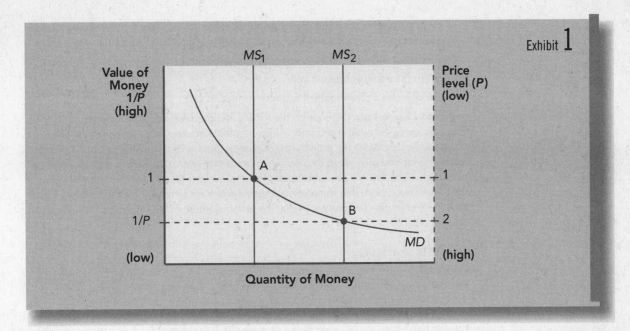

Exhibit 1

bars is a real variable measured in candy bars per hour. Changes in the money supply affect nominal variables but not real variables. Real output is determined by productivity and factor supplies, and not by the quantity of money. However, the value of nominal variables is determined by and is *proportional* to the quantity of money. For example, if the money supply doubles, prices double, wages double, and all dollar values double, but real output, employment, real interest rates, and real wages remain unchanged. This result is known as monetary neutrality. Money is unlikely to be neutral in the short run, but it is likely to be neutral in the long run.

The classical dichotomy and monetary neutrality can be demonstrated with the quantity equation. To begin, we define the velocity of money as the speed of circulation of money. Then $V = (P \times Y)/M$ where V is the velocity of money, P is the price of output, and Y is the amount of real output (and $P \times Y$ = nominal GDP), and M is the quantity of money. If nominal output is $500 (500 items at $1 each) and M is $100, then $V = 5$. That is, in order for $100 to accommodate $500 of purchases and sales, each dollar must be spent, on average, five times.

Rearranged, we get the quantity equation: $M \times V = P \times Y$. If the quantity of money increases, P or Y must rise, or V must fall. Our theory of inflation takes five steps:

- V is relatively stable in the long run.

- Therefore, changes in M cause proportional changes in nominal output ($P \times Y$).

- Real output (Y) is determined by productivity and factor supplies in the long run and is not affected by changes in M.

- If Y is fixed, an increase in M causes proportional changes in P.

- Thus, inflation results from rapid growth in the money supply.

Hyperinflation is sometimes defined as inflation that exceeds 50 percent per month. In those cases, the data show that there is a close link between money growth and inflation. This supports the conclusions of the quantity theory.

Why do countries print too much money if they know it causes inflation? Governments do it to pay for expenditures. When governments spend, they get the money by taxing, borrowing, or printing more money. Countries that have high spending, inadequate tax revenue, and limited ability to borrow may turn to printing money. When a government raises revenue by printing money, it has engaged in an inflation tax. When the government prints money and prices rise, the value of the existing money held by people falls. An inflation tax is a tax on people who hold money.

If money is neutral, changes in money will have no effect on the *real interest rate*. Recall the relationship between the real interest rate, *nominal interest rate*, and inflation:

real interest rate = nominal interest rate – inflation rate

Solving for the nominal interest rate:

nominal interest rate = real interest rate + inflation rate

The real interest rate depends on the supply and demand for loanable funds. In the long run, money is neutral and only affects nominal variables, not real variables. Thus, when the Fed increases the growth rate of money, there is an increase in the inflation rate and a one-for-one increase in the nominal interest rate while the real interest rate remains unchanged. The one-for-one adjustment of the nominal interest rate to inflation is called the Fisher effect. Note that the nominal interest rate is set when the loan is first made, and thus, the Fisher effect actually says that the nominal interest rate adjusts one-for-one with *expected inflation*.

The Costs of Inflation

People often argue that inflation is a serious economic problem because when prices rise, their incomes can't buy as many goods and services. Thus, they believe that inflation directly lowers their standard of living. This argument, however, has a fallacy. Since people earn incomes by selling services, such as labor, inflation in nominal incomes goes hand in hand with inflation in prices. Therefore, inflation generally does not directly affect people's real purchasing power.

There are, however, a number of more subtle costs of inflation:

- *Shoeleather costs:* Recall, inflation is a tax on people who hold money. To avoid the tax, people hold less money and keep more invested in interest-bearing assets when inflation is high than they do when inflation is low. As a result, people have to go to the bank and withdraw money more often than they would if there were no inflation. These costs are sometimes metaphorically called shoeleather costs (since your shoes are worn out from all those trips to the bank). The actual cost of holding less cash is wasted time and inconvenience. At high rates of inflation, this cost is more than trivial.

- *Menu costs:* There are numerous costs associated with changing prices—the cost of printing new menus, price lists, and catalogs; mailing costs to distribute them; the cost of advertising new prices; and the cost of deciding the new prices themselves.

- *Relative-price variability and the misallocation of resources:* Since it is costly to change prices, firms change prices as rarely as possible. When there is inflation, the relative price of goods whose price is held constant for a period of time is falling with respect to the average price level. This misallocates resources because economic decisions are based on relative prices. A good whose price is changed only once per year is artificially expensive at the beginning of the year and artificially inexpensive by the end of the year.

- *Inflation-induced tax distortions:* Inflation raises the tax burden on income earned from saving and, thus, discourages saving and growth. Inflation affects two types of taxes on saving:

  (1) *Capital gains* are the profits made from selling an asset for more than its purchase price. Nominal capital gains are subject to taxation. Suppose you buy a stock for $20 and sell it for $50. Also suppose the price level doubles while you owned the stock. You only have a $10 real gain (because you would need to sell the stock for $40 just to break even), yet you must pay taxes on the $30 nominal capital gain because the tax code does not account for inflation.

  (2) *Nominal interest* is taxed even though part of the nominal interest rate is to compensate for inflation. When government takes a fixed percent of the nominal interest rate as taxes, the after-tax real return grows smaller as inflation increases. This is because the nominal interest rate rises one-for-one with inflation and taxes increase with the nominal interest rate, yet the pretax real return is unaffected by inflation. Therefore, the after-tax real return falls.

Because there are taxes on nominal capital gains and nominal interest, inflation lowers the after-tax real return on saving, and thus, inflation discourages saving and growth. This problem can be solved by eliminating inflation or by indexing the tax system so that taxes are assessed only on real gains.

- *Confusion and inconvenience:* Money serves as the unit of account, which means that the dollar is the yardstick by which we measure economic values. When the Fed increases the money supply and causes inflation, it decreases the value of money and shrinks the size of the economic measuring stick. This makes accounting for firms' profits more difficult and, thus, makes choosing investments more complicated. It also makes daily transactions more confusing.

- *A special cost of unexpected inflation—arbitrary redistribution of wealth:* The costs of inflation previously described exist even if inflation is stable and predictable. Inflation has an additional cost to the economy, however, if it is unexpected because it arbitrarily redistributes wealth. For example, the terms of a loan are generally expressed in nominal values based on a certain amount of expected inflation (see the Fisher effect equation). However, if inflation becomes higher than expected, borrowers are allowed to repay the loan with dollars that purchase less than expected. Borrowers gain at the expense of lenders. The opposite is true when inflation is less than expected. If inflation were perfectly predictable, regardless of its size, this redistribution would not take place. However, high inflation is never stable. Therefore, low inflation is preferred because it is more stable and predictable.

- *Deflation:* The Friedman rule argues that small and predictable deflation equal to the real interest rate could be desirable because it would drive nominal interest rates to near zero, reducing shoe leather costs. Alternatively, the costs of deflation can mirror the other costs of inflation. In addition, deflation is usually a sign of broader economic problems.

Helpful Hints

1. The price of money is $1/P$. Since we measure the price of goods and services in terms of money, we measure the price of money in terms of the quantity of goods and services for which money can be exchanged. For example, if a basket of goods and services costs $5, then $P = \$5$. The price of a dollar is then $1/P$ or $1/5$ of the basket of goods. That is, one dollar exchanges for $1/5$ of the basket of goods. If the price of the basket of goods doubles so that it now sells for $10, the price of money has fallen to one-half its original value. Numerically, since the price of the basket is now $10, or $P = \$10$, the price of money has fallen to $1/P$ or $1/10$ of the basket of goods. To summarize, when the price of a basket of goods and services doubles from $5 to $10, the price of money falls by half from $1/5$ to $1/10$ of the basket of goods.

2. When dealing with the quantity theory, imagine you are at an auction. At the end of the auction, we can calculate the number of items sold and the average price of each item sold. Suppose we repeat the auction, only now the doorman doubles the money each buyer takes into the auction—if you had $20, you now have $40, and so on. If all participants spend the same percent of their money as at the prior auction (equivalent to a constant velocity) and if the items available to buy are unchanged (equivalent to a constant real output), what must happen to the average price of goods sold at the auction? Prices at the auction will precisely double, showing that prices are proportional to the quantity of money.

3. Unexpected inflation works like a tax on future receipts. We know that unexpected inflation redistributes wealth. Although it can be difficult to remember who wins and who loses on nominal contracts through time, you can always keep things straight if you remember that *unexpected inflation works like a tax on future receipts and a subsidy to future payments.* Therefore, when inflation turns out to be higher than we thought it would be when a loan contract was written, the recipient of the future payments is worse off because they receive dollars with less purchasing power than they had bargained for. The person who borrowed is better off because they were able to use

the money when it had greater value, yet they were allowed to repay the loan with money of lower value. Therefore, when inflation is higher than expected, wealth is redistributed from lenders to borrowers. Alternatively, when inflation is less than expected, winners and losers are reversed.

This concept can be applied to any contract that extends through time. Consider a labor contract. Recall, when inflation is greater than we expected, those who receive money in the future are harmed, and those who pay are helped. Therefore, firms gain at the expense of workers when inflation is greater than anticipated. When inflation is less than expected, winners and losers are reversed.

Terms and Definitions

Choose a definition for each key term.

Key Terms	Definitions
____ Inflation	1. Resources wasted when inflation causes people to economize on money holdings
____ Deflation	2. The practice of a government raising revenue by printing money
____ Hyperinflation	3. The theory that the quantity of money determines prices and the growth rate of money determines inflation
____ Quantity theory of money	
____ Nominal variables	4. Variables measured in physical units
____ Real variables	5. The costs associated with changing prices
____ Classical dichotomy	6. Interest rate uncorrected for inflation
____ Monetary neutrality	7. Profits made from selling an asset for greater than the purchase price
____ Velocity of money	8. The one-to-one adjustment of the nominal interest rate to inflation
____ Quantity equation	9. An increase in the overall level of prices
____ Inflation tax	10. Extraordinarily high inflation
____ Nominal interest rate	11. $M \times V = P \times Y$
____ Real interest rate	12. The theoretical separation of nominal and real variables
____ Fisher effect	13. Interest rate corrected for inflation
____ Shoeleather costs	14. Variables measured in monetary units
____ Menu costs	15. Rate at which money circulates
____ Capital gains	16. A decrease in the overall level of prices
	17. The property that changes in the money supply affect nominal variables but not real variables

Problems and Short-Answer Questions

Practice Problems

1. Use the quantity equation for this problem. Suppose the money supply is $200, real output is 1,000 units, and the price per unit of output is $1.
   a. What is the value of velocity?

b. If velocity is fixed at the value you solved for in part *a*, what does the quantity theory of money suggest will happen if the money supply is increased to $400?

_____

_____

c. Is your answer in part *b* consistent with the classical dichotomy? Explain.

_____

_____

d. Suppose that when the money supply is doubled from $200 to $400, real output grows a small amount (say 2 percent). Now what will happen to prices? Do prices more than double, less than double, or exactly double? Why?

_____

_____

e. When inflation gets very high, people do not like to hold money because it is losing value quickly. Therefore, they spend it faster. If when the money supply is doubled, people spend money more quickly, what happens to prices? Do prices more than double, less than double, or exactly double? Why?

_____

_____

f. Suppose the money supply at the beginning of this problem refers to M1. That is, the M1 money supply is $200. What would the M2 quantity equation look like if the M2 money supply were $500 (and all other values were as stated at the beginning of the problem)?

_____

_____

_____

2. The following questions are related to the Fisher effect.
    a. To demonstrate your understanding of the Fisher effect, complete the following table.

Real Interest Rate	Nominal Interest Rate	Inflation Rate
3%	10%	_____
_____	6	2%
5	_____	3

The following questions about the Fisher effect are unrelated to the table above.

b. Suppose people expect inflation to be 3 percent, and suppose the desired real interest rate is 4 percent. What is the nominal rate?

_____

c. Suppose inflation turns out to be 6 percent. What is the actual real interest rate on loans that were signed based on the expectations in part *b*?

_____

_____

d. Was wealth redistributed to the lender from the borrower or to the borrower from the lender when inflation was expected to be 3 percent but, in fact, turned out to be 6 percent?

_____

_____

    e. What would have happened had inflation turned out to be only 1 percent?

_____

_____

3. Income taxes treat nominal interest earned on savings as income even though much of the nominal interest is simply to compensate for inflation.

    a. To see what this does to the incentive to save, complete the following table for both the low-inflation and high-inflation country.

	Low-Inflation Country	High-Inflation Country
Real interest rate	5%	5%
Inflation rate	3	11
Nominal interest rate	_____	_____
Reduced interest rate due to a 25% tax	_____	_____
After-tax nominal interest rate	_____	_____
After-tax real interest rate	_____	_____

    b. In which country is there a greater incentive to save? Why?

_____

_____

    c. What could the government do to eliminate this problem?

_____

_____

Short-Answer Questions

1. If the money supply doubles, what must happen in the long run to the quantity of money demanded and the price level?

_____

_____

_____

2. Explain the classical dichotomy.

_____

_____

_____

3. Within the framework of the classical dichotomy, which type of variable is affected by changes in money and which type is not? What phrase do we use to capture this effect?

_____

_____

_____

4. Is money more likely to be neutral in the long run or the short run? Why?

_____

_____

_____

5. Suppose the money supply were to increase by 10 percent. Explain what would happen to each variable in the quantity equation.

_____

_____

_____

6. What are the three sources of revenue a government can use to support its expenditures? Which method causes inflation, and who bears the burden of this method of raising revenue?

_____

_____

_____

7. In the long run, what does an increase in the growth rate of the money supply do to real and nominal interest rates?

_____

_____

_____

8. Does inflation erode the value of our income and, thereby, lower our standard of living? Explain.

_____

_____

_____

9. What are the costs of inflation when inflation is perfectly anticipated?

_____

_____

_____

10. Suppose inflation turns out to be lower than we had expected. Who is likely to gain: borrowers or lenders? union workers or firms? Why?

_____

_____

_____

11. What is the inconsistency in the following statement? "When inflation is high but stable and predictable, inflation does not redistribute wealth."

_____

_____

_____

12. Does inflation (if correctly anticipated) make borrowers worse off and lenders better off when it raises nominal interest rates? Why or why not?

_____

_____

_____

Self-Test

True/False Questions

_____ 1. An increase in the price level is the same as a decrease in the value of money.

_____ 2. The quantity theory of money suggests that an increase in the money supply increases real output proportionately.

_____ 3. If the price level were to double, the quantity of money demanded would double because people would need twice as much money to cover the same transactions.

_____ 4. In the long run, an increase in the money supply tends to have an effect on real variables but no effect on nominal variables.

_____ 5. If the money supply is $500, real output is 2,500 units, and the average price of a unit of real output is $2, the velocity of money is 10.

_____ 6. The Fisher effect suggests that, in the long run, if the rate of inflation rises from 3 percent to 7 percent, the nominal interest rate should increase 4 percentage points, and the real interest rate should remain unchanged.

_____ 7. An inflation tax is "paid" by those who hold money because inflation reduces the value of their money holdings.

_____ 8. Monetary neutrality means that a change in the money supply doesn't cause a change in anything at all.

_____ 9. Inflation erodes the value of people's wages and reduces their standard of living.

_____ 10. Inflation reduces the relative price of goods whose prices have been temporarily held constant to avoid the costs associated with changing prices.

_____ 11. The shoeleather costs of inflation should be approximately the same for a medical doctor and for an unemployed worker.

_____ 12. Inflation tends to stimulate saving because it raises the after-tax real return to saving.

_____ 13. Countries that spend more money than they can collect from taxing or borrowing tend to print too much money, which causes inflation.

_____ 14. If inflation turns out to be higher than people expected, wealth is redistributed to lenders from borrowers.

_____ 15. If the nominal interest rate is 7 percent and the inflation rate is 5 percent, the real interest rate is 12 percent.

Multiple-Choice Questions

1. In the long run, inflation is caused by
   a. banks that have market power and refuse to lend money.
   b. governments that raise taxes so high that it increases the cost of doing business and, hence, raises prices.
   c. governments that print too much money.
   d. increases in the price of inputs, such as labor and oil.
   e. none of the above.

2. When prices rise at an extraordinarily high rate, it is called
   a. inflation.
   b. hyperinflation.
   c. deflation.
   d. hypoinflation.
   e. disinflation.

3. If the price level doubles,
   a. the quantity demanded of money falls by half.
   b. the money supply has been cut by half.
   c. nominal income is unaffected.
   d. the value of money has been cut by half.
   e. none of the above is true.

4. In the long run, the demand for money is most dependent upon
   a. the level of prices.
   b. the availability of credit cards.
   c. the availability of banking outlets.
   d. the interest rate.

5. The quantity theory of money concludes that an increase in the money supply causes
   a. a proportional increase in velocity.
   b. a proportional increase in prices.
   c. a proportional increase in real output.
   d. a proportional decrease in velocity.
   e. a proportional decrease in prices.

6. An example of a real variable is
   a. the nominal interest rate.
   b. the ratio of the value of wages to the price of soda.
   c. the price of corn.
   d. the dollar wage.
   e. none of the above.

7. The quantity equation states that
   a. money × price level = velocity × real output.
   b. money × real output = velocity × price level.
   c. money × velocity = price level × real output.
   d. none of the above is true.

8. If money is neutral,
    a. an increase in the money supply does nothing.
    b. the money supply cannot be changed because it is tied to a commodity such as gold.
    c. a change in the money supply only affects real variables such as real output.
    d. a change in the money supply only affects nominal variables such as prices and dollar wages.
    e. a change in the money supply reduces velocity proportionately; therefore, there is no effect on either prices or real output.

9. If the money supply grows 5 percent and real output grows 2 percent, prices should rise by
    a. 5 percent.
    b. less than 5 percent.
    c. more than 5 percent.
    d. none of the above.

10. Velocity is
    a. the annual rate of turnover of the money supply.
    b. the annual rate of turnover of output.
    c. the annual rate of turnover of business inventories.
    d. highly unstable.
    e. impossible to measure.

11. Countries that employ an inflation tax do so because
    a. the government doesn't understand the causes and consequences of inflation.
    b. the government has a balanced budget.
    c. government expenditures are high and the government has inadequate tax collections and difficulty borrowing.
    d. an inflation tax is the most equitable of all taxes.
    e. an inflation tax is the most progressive (paid by the rich) of all taxes.

12. An inflation tax is
    a. an explicit tax paid quarterly by businesses based on the amount of increase in the prices of their products.
    b. a tax on people who hold money.
    c. a tax on people who hold interest-bearing savings accounts.
    d. usually employed by governments with balanced budgets.
    e. none of the above.

13. Suppose the nominal interest rate is 7 percent while the money supply is growing at a rate of 5 percent per year. Assuming real output remains fixed, if the government increases the growth rate of the money supply from 5 percent to 9 percent, the Fisher effect suggests that, in the long run, the nominal interest rate should become
    a. 4 percent.
    b. 9 percent.
    c. 11 percent.
    d. 12 percent.
    e. 16 percent.

14. If the nominal interest rate is 6 percent and the inflation rate is 3 percent, the real interest rate is
    a. 3 percent.
    b. 6 percent.
    c. 9 percent.
    d. 18 percent.
    e. none of the above.

15. If actual inflation turns out to be greater than people had expected, then
    a. wealth was redistributed to lenders from borrowers.
    b. wealth was redistributed to borrowers from lenders.
    c. no redistribution occurred.
    d. the real interest rate is unaffected.

16. Which of the following costs of inflation does *not* occur when inflation is constant and predictable?
    a.   shoeleather costs
    b.   menu costs
    c.   costs due to inflation-induced tax distortions
    d.   arbitrary redistributions of wealth
    e.   costs due to confusion and inconvenience

17. Suppose that, because of inflation, a business in Russia must calculate, print, and mail a new price list to its customers each month. This is an example of
    a.   shoeleather costs.
    b.   menu costs.
    c.   costs due to inflation-induced tax distortions.
    d.   arbitrary redistributions of wealth.
    e.   the Friedman rule.

18. Suppose that, because of inflation, people in Brazil economize on currency and go to the bank each day to withdraw their daily currency needs. This is an example of
    a.   shoeleather costs.
    b.   menu costs.
    c.   costs due to inflation-induced tax distortions.
    d.   costs due to inflation-induced relative price variability, which misallocates resources.
    e.   costs due to confusion and inconvenience.

19. If the real interest rate is 4 percent, the inflation rate is 6 percent, and the tax rate is 20 percent, what is the after-tax real interest rate?
    a.   1 percent
    b.   2 percent
    c.   3 percent
    d.   4 percent
    e.   5 percent

20. Which of the following statements about inflation is *not* true?
    a.   Unanticipated inflation redistributes wealth.
    b.   An increase in inflation increases nominal interest rates.
    c.   If there is inflation, taxing nominal interest income reduces the return to saving and reduces the rate of economic growth.
    d.   Inflation reduces people's real purchasing power because it raises the cost of the things people buy.

Advanced Critical Thinking

Suppose you explain the concept of an "inflation tax" to a friend. You correctly tell them, "When a government prints money to cover its expenditures instead of taxing or borrowing, it causes inflation. An inflation tax is simply the erosion of the value of money from this inflation. Therefore, the burden of the tax lands on those who hold money." Your friend responds, "What's so bad about that? Rich people have all the money, so an inflation tax seems fair to me. Maybe the government should finance all of its expenditures by printing money."

1.   Is it true that rich people hold more money than poor people do?

    _____

    _____

    _____

2. Do rich people hold a higher percentage of their income as money than poor people do?

_____

_____

_____

3. Compared to an income tax, does an inflation tax place a greater or lesser burden on the poor? Explain.

_____

_____

_____

_____

_____

4. Are there any other reasons why engaging in an inflation tax is not good policy?

_____

_____

_____

_____

Solutions

Terms and Definitions

<u>9</u> Inflation

<u>16</u> Deflation

<u>10</u> Hyperinflation

<u>3</u> Quantity theory of money

<u>14</u> Nominal variables

<u>4</u> Real variables

<u>12</u> Classical dichotomy

<u>17</u> Monetary neutrality

<u>15</u> Velocity of money

<u>11</u> Quantity equation

<u>2</u> Inflation tax

<u>6</u> Nominal interest rate

<u>13</u> Real interest rate

<u>8</u> Fisher effect

<u>1</u> Shoeleather costs

<u>5</u> Menu costs

<u>7</u> Capital gains

Practice Problems

1. a. $(1{,}000 \times \$1)/\$200 = 5$

   b. $\$400 \times 5 = \$2 \times 1{,}000$, prices will double from \$1 to \$2

   c. Yes. The classical dichotomy divides economic variables into real and nominal. Money affects nominal variables proportionately and has no impact on real variables. In part *b*, prices double, but real output remains constant.

   d. The quantity equation says that nominal output must change in proportion to money. Prices will still rise, but since real output is larger, prices will less than double.

   e. Money has a proportional impact on nominal output if V is constant. If V grows, a doubling of M will cause P to more than double.

   f. $\$500 \times 2 = \$1 \times 1{,}000$, M2 velocity is 2.

2. a.

Real Interest Rate	Nominal Interest Rate	Inflation Rate
3%	10%	7%
4	6	2
5	8	3

   b. $3\% + 4\% = 7\%$

   c. People would have signed loan contracts for 7 percent nominal interest. Therefore, $7\% - 6\% = 1\%$.

   d. People expected a real interest rate of 4 percent, but the actual real interest rate turned out to be 1 percent. Wealth was redistributed to the borrower from the lender.

   e. The original loan contract would be the same. Thus $7\% - 1\% = 6\%$. The actual real rate is 6 percent

instead of 4 percent, so wealth is redistributed to lenders from borrowers.

3. a.

	Low-Inflation Country	High-Inflation Country
Real interest rate	5%	5%
Inflation rate	3	11
Nominal interest rate	8	16
Reduced interest rate due to a 25% tax	2	4
After-tax nominal interest rate	6	12
After-tax real interest rate	3	1

   b. In the low-inflation country, because the after-tax real interest rate is larger.

   c. They could eliminate inflation or tax only real interest income.

Short-Answer Questions

1. The quantity of money demanded must double to maintain monetary equilibrium because spending will double on the same amount of goods causing prices to double and the value of money to fall by half.

2. The view that macroeconomic variables can be divided into two groups: real (measured in physical units) and nominal (measured in monetary units).

3. Nominal are affected. Real are not. Monetary neutrality.

4. In the long run because it takes time for people and markets to adjust prices in response to a change in the money supply. In the short run, mistakes are likely to be made.

5. V remains constant. Y remains constant. M rises by 10 percent, and P rises by 10 percent.

6. Taxes, borrowing, and printing money. Printing money. Those who hold money because its value decreases.

7. No impact on the real interest rate. Raises the nominal interest rate one-to-one with the increase in the growth rate of money and prices.

8. No. Income is a result of selling labor services, the value of which rises along with other prices during an inflation.

9. Shoeleather costs; menu costs; costs due to relative-price variability, which misallocates resources; tax distortions; confusion; and inconvenience.

10. Lenders and workers. Those who receive dollars in the future on contract receive dollars of greater value than they bargained for.

11. When inflation is high, it is always unstable and difficult to predict.

12. No. The nominal interest rate adjusts one-to-one with the rise in inflation so that the real rate is unaffected. Neither the borrower nor lender gains.

True/False Questions

1. T
2. F; it increases price proportionately.
3. T
4. F; the money supply tends to have an effect on nominal variables but not real variables.
5. T
6. T
7. T
8. F; it doesn't cause a change in real variables.
9. F; inflation in incomes goes hand in hand with inflation in prices.
10. T
11. F; the opportunity costs of trips to the bank are greater for a medical doctor.
12. F; inflation tends to reduce the after-tax return to saving.
13. T
14. F; wealth is redistributed to borrowers from lenders.
15. F; the real interest rate is 2 percent because 7% − 5% = 2%.

Multiple-Choice Questions

1. c
2. b
3. d
4. a
5. b
6. b
7. c
8. d
9. b
10. a
11. c
12. b
13. c
14. a
15. b
16. d
17. b
18. a
19. b
20. d

Advanced Critical Thinking

1. Yes, rich people probably hold more dollars than poor people do.
2. No, by a wide margin, the poor hold a larger percentage of their income as money. In fact, the poor may have no other financial asset at all.
3. An inflation tax places a far greater burden on the poor than on the rich. The rich are able to keep most of their assets in inflation-adjusted, interest-bearing assets. We observed this in Brazil and Argentina during periods of high inflation.
4. Inflation imposes many other costs on the economy besides the inflation tax: shoeleather costs, menu costs, tax distortions, confusion, etc.

Chapter 23

Aggregate Demand and Aggregate Supply

Goals
In this chapter you will

- Learn three key facts about short-run fluctuations
- Consider how the economy in the short run differs from the economy in the long run
- Use the model of aggregate demand and aggregate supply to explain economic fluctuations
- See how shifts in either aggregate demand or aggregate supply can cause booms and recessions

Outcomes
After accomplishing these goals, you should be able to

- Explain why the term "business cycle" is misleading
- Explain why money is unlikely to be neutral in the short run
- List three reasons why the aggregate-demand curve is downward sloping
- Demonstrate the short-run and long-run effects of an oil price shock on the economy

Chapter Overview

Context and Purpose

To this point, our study of macroeconomic theory has concentrated on the behavior of the economy in the long run. Chapters 23 and 24 now focus on short-run fluctuations in the economy around its long-term trend. Chapter 23 introduces aggregate demand and aggregate supply and shows how shifts in these curves can cause recessions. Chapter 24 focuses on how policymakers use the tools of monetary and fiscal policy to influence aggregate demand.

The purpose of Chapter 23 is to develop the model economists use to analyze the economy's short-run fluctuations—the model

367

of aggregate demand and aggregate supply. We will learn about some of the sources for shifts in the aggregate-demand curve and the aggregate-supply curve and how these shifts can cause recessions. We will also introduce actions policymakers might undertake to offset recessions.

Chapter Review

Introduction   Over the last 50 years, U.S. real GDP has grown about 3 percent per year. However, in some years, GDP has experienced a contraction. A period when output and incomes fall, and unemployment rises, is known as a recession when it is mild and a depression when it is severe. The U.S. economy experienced a deep recession from late 2007 to early 2009. This chapter focuses on the economy's short-run fluctuations around its long-term trend. To do this, we employ the model of aggregate demand and aggregate supply.

Three Key Facts about Economic Fluctuations

- *Economic fluctuations are irregular and unpredictable:* Although economic fluctuations are often termed *the business cycle*, the term "business cycle" is misleading because it suggests that economic fluctuations follow a regular, predictable pattern. In reality, economic fluctuations are irregular and unpredictable.

- *Most macroeconomic quantities fluctuate together:* Although real GDP is usually used to monitor short-run changes in the economy, it really doesn't matter which measure of economic activity is used because most macroeconomic variables that measure income, spending, or production move in the same direction, though by different amounts. Investment is one type of expenditure that is particularly volatile across the business cycle.

- *As output falls, unemployment rises:* When real GDP declines, the rate of unemployment rises because when firms produce fewer goods and services, they lay off workers.

Explaining Short-Run Economic Fluctuations

Classical theory is based on the classical dichotomy and monetary neutrality. Recall, the classical dichotomy is the separation of economic variables into real and nominal, while monetary neutrality is the property that changes in the money supply only affect nominal variables, not real variables. Most economists believe these classical assumptions are an accurate description of the economy in the long run but not in the short run. That is, over a period of a number of years, changes in the money supply should affect prices but should have no impact on real variables such as real GDP, unemployment, real wages, and so on. However, in the short run, from year to year, changes in nominal variables such as money and prices are likely to have an impact on real variables. That is, in the short run, nominal and real variables are not independent. As a result, in the short run, changes in money can temporarily move real GDP away from its long-run trend.

We use the model of aggregate supply and aggregate demand to explain economic fluctuations. This model can be graphed with the price level, measured by the CPI or the GDP deflator on the vertical axis and real GDP on the horizontal axis. The aggregate-demand curve shows the quantity of goods and services households, firms, the government, and customers abroad wish to buy at each price level. It slopes negatively. The aggregate-supply curve shows the quantity of goods and services that firms produce and sell at each price level. It slopes positively (in the short run). The price level and output adjust to balance aggregate supply and demand. This model looks like an ordinary microeconomic supply-and-demand model. However, the reasons for the slopes and the sources of the shifts in the aggregate-supply and -demand curves differ from those for the microeconomic model.

Exhibit 1

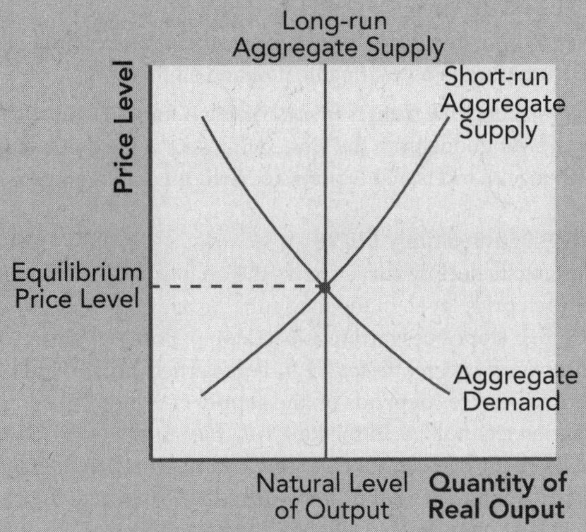

The Aggregate-Demand Curve

Exhibit 1 illustrates the model of aggregate supply and aggregate demand.

The aggregate-demand curve shows the quantity of goods and services demanded at each price level. Recall, GDP = $C + I + G + NX$. To address why aggregate demand slopes downward, we address the impact of the price level on consumption (C), investment (I), and net exports (NX). (We ignore government spending [G] because it is a fixed policy variable.) A decrease in the price level increases consumption, investment, and net exports for the following reasons:

- The price level and consumption: *the wealth effect*. At a lower price level, the fixed amount of nominal money in consumers' pockets increases in value. Consumers feel wealthier and spend more, increasing the consumption component of aggregate demand.

- The price level and investment: *the interest-rate effect*. At a lower price level, households need to hold less money to buy the same products. They lend some money by buying bonds or depositing in banks, either of which lowers interest rates and stimulates the investment component of aggregate demand. (Lower interest rates may also stimulate spending on consumer durables.)

- The price level and net exports: *the exchange-rate effect*. Since, as described earlier, a lower price level causes lower interest rates, some U.S. investors will invest abroad, increasing the supply of dollars in the foreign-currency exchange market. This act causes the real exchange rate of the dollar to depreciate, reduces the relative price of domestic goods compared to foreign goods, and increases the net exports component of aggregate demand.

The three effects described here also work in reverse. All three explanations of the downward slope of the aggregate-demand curve assume that the money supply is fixed.

When something causes a change in the quantity of output demanded at each price level, it causes a shift in the aggregate-demand curve. The following events and policies cause shifts in aggregate demand:

- *Shifts arising from changes in consumption:* If consumers save more, if stock prices fall so that consumers feel poorer, or if taxes are increased, consumers spend less and aggregate demand shifts left.

- *Shifts arising from changes in investment:* If firms become optimistic about the future and decide to buy new equipment, if an investment tax credit increases investment, or if the

Fed increases the money supply, which reduces interest rates and increases investment, aggregate demand shifts right.

- *Shifts arising from changes in government purchases:* If federal, state, or local governments increase purchases, aggregate demand shifts right.

- *Shifts arising from changes in net exports:* If foreign countries have a recession and buy fewer goods from the United States or if the value of the dollar rises on foreign exchange markets, net exports are reduced and aggregate demand shifts left.

The Aggregate-Supply Curve

The aggregate-supply curve shows the quantity of goods and services firms produce and sell at each price level. In the long run, the aggregate-supply curve is vertical while in the short run, it slopes upward (positive slope). Both can be seen in Exhibit 1.

The *long-run aggregate-supply curve* is vertical because, in the long run, the supply of goods and services depends on the supply of capital, labor, and natural resources, and on production technology. In the long run, the supply of goods and services is independent of the level of prices. It is the graphical representation of the classical dichotomy and monetary neutrality. That is, if the price level rises and all prices rise together, there should be no impact on output or any other real variable.

The long-run aggregate-supply curve shows the level of production that is sometimes called *potential output* or *full-employment output*. Since in the short run output can be temporarily above or below this level, a better name is the natural level of output because it is the amount of output produced when unemployment is at its natural, or normal, rate. Anything that alters the natural level of output shifts the long-run aggregate-supply curve to the right or left. Since in the long run, output depends on labor, capital, natural resources, and technological knowledge, we group the sources of the shifts in long-run aggregate supply into these categories:

- *Shifts arising from changes in labor:* If there is immigration from abroad or a reduction in the natural rate of unemployment from a reduction in the minimum wage, long-run aggregate supply shifts right.

- *Shifts arising from changes in capital:* If there is an increase in physical or human capital, productivity rises and long-run aggregate supply shifts right.

- *Shifts arising from changes in natural resources:* If there is a discovery of new resources, or a favorable change in weather patterns, long-run aggregate supply shifts right.

- *Shifts arising from changes in technical knowledge:* If new inventions are employed, or international trade opens up, long-run aggregate supply shifts right.

Long-run growth and inflation may be depicted as a rightward shift in the long-run aggregate-supply curve (from the events described above) and an even larger rightward shift in the aggregate-demand curve due to increases in the money supply. Thus, over time, output grows and prices rise.

The *short-run aggregate-supply curve* slopes upward (positively) because a change in the price level causes output to deviate from its long-run level for a short period of time, say, a year or two. There are three theories that explain why the short-run aggregate-supply curve slopes upward, and they all share a common theme: Output rises above the natural level when the actual price level exceeds the expected price level. The three theories are:

- *The sticky-wage theory:* Suppose firms and workers agree on a nominal wage contract based on what they expect the price level to be. If the price level falls below what was expected, firms pay the same wage but receive lower prices for their output. This reduces profits, causing the firm to hire less labor and reduce the quantity of goods and services supplied.

- *The sticky-price theory:* Because there is a cost to firms for changing prices, termed *menu costs*, some firms will resist reducing their prices when the price level unexpectedly falls. Thus, their prices are "too high" and their sales decline, causing the quantity of goods and services supplied to fall.

- *The misperceptions theory:* When the price level unexpectedly falls, suppliers only notice that the price of their particular product has fallen. Hence, they mistakenly believe that there has been a fall in the *relative price* of their product, causing them to reduce the quantity of goods and services supplied.

The three effects described above also work in reverse.

Note two features of the explanations above: (1) In each case, the quantity of output supplied changed because actual prices deviated from expected prices, and (2) the effect will be temporary because people will adjust their expectations over time. We can express aggregate supply mathematically with the following equation:

$$\text{Quantity of Output Supplied} = \text{Natural Level of Output} + a(\text{Actual Price Level} - \text{Expected Price Level})$$

where a is a number that determines how much output responds to unexpected changes in the price level.

Events that shift the long-run aggregate-supply curve also tend to shift the short-run aggregate-supply curve in the same direction. However, the short-run aggregate-supply curve can shift while the long-run aggregate-supply curve remains stationary. In the short run, the quantity of goods and services supplied depends on perceptions, wages, and prices, all of which were set based on the expected price level. If people and firms expect higher prices, they set wages higher, reducing the profitability of production and reducing the quantity supplied of goods and services at each price level. Thus, the short-run aggregate-supply curve shifts left. A lower expected price level shifts the short-run aggregate-supply curve to the right. In general, things that cause an increase in the cost of production (an increase in wages or oil prices) cause the short-run aggregate-supply curve to shift left while a decrease in the cost of production causes the short-run aggregate-supply curve to shift right.

Two Causes of Economic Fluctuations

Exhibit 1 shows the model of aggregate supply and aggregate demand in long-run equilibrium. That is, the level of output is at the long-run natural level where aggregate demand and long-run aggregate supply intersect, and perceptions, wages, and prices have fully adjusted to the actual price level as demonstrated by short-run aggregate supply intersecting at the same point.

There are two basic causes of a recession: a leftward shift in aggregate demand and a leftward shift in aggregate supply.

- **A Shift in Aggregate Demand** We use a four-step approach: (1) Determine which curve the event affects. (2) Determine which way the curve moves. (3) Determine the new short-run equilibrium. (4) Determine the transition from the short-run equilibrium to the long-run equilibrium.

Suppose households cut back on their spending because they are pessimistic or nervous about the future. Consumers spend less at each price level so aggregate demand shifts left in Exhibit 2. In the short run, the economy moves to point B because the drop in the price level was unexpected. When prices fall below expectations, sticky wages, sticky prices, and misperceptions about relative prices cause firms to cut back on production. We can see that the economy is in a recession at P_2, Y_2 because output is below the natural level. The recession will remedy itself or self-correct over time. Since actual prices are below prior expectations, price expectations will be reduced over time and wages and prices will fall to levels commensurate with P_3. In particular, the sticky-wage theory suggests that once workers and firms expect lower prices, they will negotiate lower wages. This encourages production, the short-run aggregate-supply curve shifts right, and the economy arrives at point C. Policymakers could try to eliminate the recession by increasing aggregate demand with an increase in government spending or an increase in the money supply. If properly done, the government moves the economy back to point A. To summarize, in the short run, shifts in aggregate demand cause fluctuations in output. In the long run, shifts in aggregate demand only cause changes in prices. Policymakers can potentially mitigate the severity of economic fluctuations.

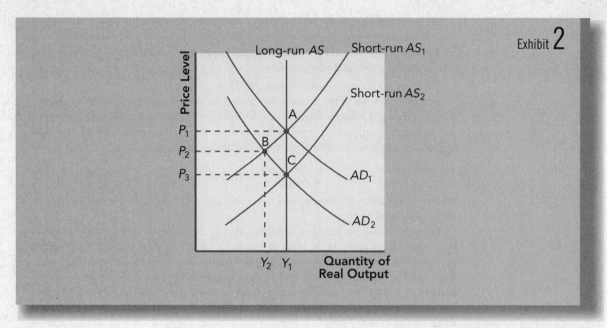

Exhibit 2

Exhibit 2 can be used to demonstrate that money matters in the short run, but money is neutral in the long run. Starting at point A, if the Fed reduces the money supply, the economy moves to point B and experiences a recession. Since output falls, we say that money matters. In the long run, price expectations and wages are reduced, and the economy moves to point C. Output returns to the natural level and prices have fallen; therefore, money is neutral in the long run.

The two biggest shocks to aggregate demand in the United States were the leftward shift during the Great Depression and the rightward shift during World War II. The recession of 2008–2009 caused a significant reduction in aggregate demand. Housing prices started to fall in 2006 causing borrowers to default on their loans. Banks foreclosed and sold the homes causing spending on new home construction to collapse. Financial institutions that owned mortgage-backed securities suffered losses and reduced their lending. All of these events caused aggregate demand to shift left. The government attempted to shift aggregate demand back to the right. The Fed lowered interest rates, Congress rescued the financial system, and the government increased its spending.

- **A Shift in Aggregate Supply**   Use the same four-step method described above. Suppose OPEC raises the price of oil, which raises the cost of production for many firms. This reduces profitability, firms produce less at each price level, and short-run aggregate supply shifts to the left in Exhibit 3. In the short run, prices rise, reducing the quantity demanded along the aggregate-demand curve and the economy arrives at point B. Since output has fallen (stagnation) and the price level has risen (inflation), the economy has experienced stagflation. Higher prices may temporarily cause workers to demand higher wages, further shifting short-run aggregate supply to the left and temporarily causing a *wage-price spiral*. However, in the long run, the unemployment at Y_2 will, in time, put downward pressure on workers' wages, will increase profitability, and will shift aggregate supply back to its original position, and the economy returns to point A. Alternatively, policymakers could increase aggregate demand and move the economy to point C, avoiding point B altogether. Here, policymakers *accommodate* the shift in aggregate supply by allowing the increase in costs to raise prices permanently. Output is returned to long-run equilibrium, but prices are higher. To summarize, a reduction in short-run aggregate supply causes stagflation. If policymakers shift aggregate demand in a manner to increase output, it causes more inflation.

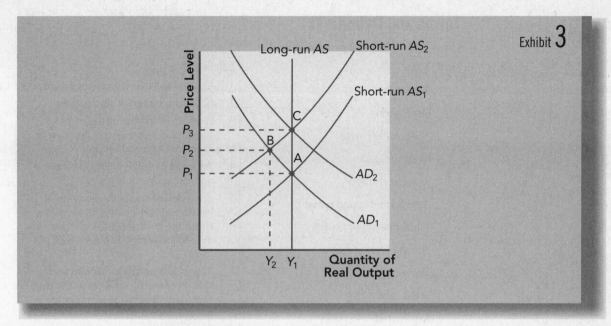

Helpful Hints

1. There are no changes in real variables along the long-run aggregate-supply curve. When all prices change equally, no real variables have changed. A vertical long-run aggregate-supply curve simply demonstrates this classical lesson. Pick any point on the long-run aggregate-supply curve. Now double the price level and all nominal values such as wages. Although the price level has doubled, relative prices have remained constant including the real wage, W/P. There has been no change in anyone's incentive to produce and, thus, no change in output. It follows that if the economy is temporarily producing a level of output other than the long-run natural level, then at least some wages or prices have failed to adjust to the long-run equilibrium price level. This causes at least some relative prices to change, which stimulates or discourages production. This is, in fact, what is happening along a short-run aggregate-supply curve.

2. Output can fluctuate to levels both above and below the natural level of output. The examples of economic fluctuations in the text tend to focus on recessions. That is, the examples deal with periods when output is less than the natural level. Note, however, that output can be above the natural level temporarily because unemployment can be below its natural rate. This economic condition is known as a boom. A boom will occur when there is a positive aggregate-demand shock—for example, if there is an increase in the money supply, an increase in domestic investment, or an increase in government purchases. A boom will also occur if there is a positive aggregate-supply shock—for example, if the price of oil were to fall or union wage demands were to decrease. To help you, these cases are addressed in the problems that follow.

3. You may shift the short-run aggregate-supply curve left and right or upward and downward. Suppose there is an increase in the wage of workers. We have suggested that the rise in the wage will increase the cost of production, decrease profitability at each price level, and decrease production at each price level. That is, it will shift the short-run aggregate-supply curve to the left. However, we could have suggested that the increase in the wage will increase the cost of production, requiring firms to charge a higher price in order to continue the same level of production. That is, it shifts the short-run aggregate-supply curve upward on the graph. In the first case, we lowered the quantity supplied at each price. In the second case, we raised the price at each quantity supplied. The resulting shift is the same.

Terms and Definitions

Choose a definition for each key term.

Key Terms	Definitions

Key Terms

____ Recession

____ Depression

____ The business cycle

____ Model of aggregate demand and

   aggregate supply

____ Aggregate-demand curve

____ Aggregate-supply curve

____ Natural level of output

____ Menu costs

____ Stagflation

____ Accommodative policy

Definitions

1. Costs associated with changing prices
2. Short-run economic fluctuations
3. A policy of increasing aggregate demand in response to a decrease in short-run aggregate supply
4. A period of mildly falling incomes and rising unemployment
5. A curve that shows the quantity of goods and services that households, firms, the government, and customers abroad are willing to buy at each price level
6. The production of goods and services that an economy achieves in the long run when unemployment is at its natural or normal rate
7. A period of falling output and rising prices
8. A period of unusually severe falling incomes and rising unemployment
9. A curve that shows the quantity of goods and services that firms are willing to produce at each price level
10. The model most economists use to explain short-run fluctuations in the economy around its long-run trend

Problems and Short-Answer Questions

When necessary, draw a graph of the model of aggregate demand and aggregate supply on scratch paper to help you answer the following problems and questions.

Practice Problems

1. For the following four cases, trace the impact of each shock in the aggregate-demand and aggregate-supply model by answering the following three questions for each: What happens to prices and output in the short run? What happens to prices and output in the long run if the economy is allowed to adjust to long-run equilibrium on its own? If policymakers had intervened to move output back to the natural level instead of allowing the economy to self-correct, in which direction should they have moved aggregate demand?
   a. aggregate demand shifts left

   _____

   _____

   _____

b.   aggregate demand shifts right

_____

_____

_____

c.   short-run aggregate supply shifts left

_____

_____

_____

d.   short-run aggregate supply shifts right

_____

_____

_____

2.   The following events have their *initial impact* on which of the following: aggregate demand, short-run aggregate supply, long-run aggregate supply, or both short-run and long-run aggregate supply? Do the curves shift to the right or left?

a.   The government repairs aging roads and bridges.

_____

b.   OPEC raises oil prices.

_____

c.   The government raises unemployment benefits, which raises the natural rate of unemployment.

_____

d.   Americans feel more secure in their jobs and become more optimistic.

_____

_____

e.   A technological advance takes place in the application of computers to the manufacturing of steel.

_____

f.   The government increases the minimum wage.

_____

g.   Because price expectations are reduced, wage demands of new college graduates fall.

_____

h.   The Federal Reserve decreases the money supply.

_____

i.   A drought destroys much of the Midwest corn crop.

_____

3. Suppose the economy is in long-run equilibrium. Then, suppose the Federal Reserve suddenly increases the money supply.
    a. Describe the initial impact of this event in the model of aggregate demand and aggregate supply by explaining which curve shifts which way.

    _____

    b. What happens to the price level and real output in the short run?

    _____

    c. If the economy is allowed to adjust to the increase in the money supply, what happens to the price level and real output in the long run when compared to their original levels? What name do economists attach to the long-run impact of a change in the money supply on the economy?

    _____

    d. Does an increase in the money supply move output above the natural level indefinitely? Why or why not?

    _____

    _____

4. Suppose the economy is in long-run equilibrium. Then, suppose workers and firms suddenly expect higher prices in the future and agree to an increase in wages.
    a. Describe the initial impact of this event in the model of aggregate demand and aggregate supply by explaining which curve shifts which way.

    _____

    b. What happens to the price level and real output in the short run?

    _____

    c. What name do we have for this combination of movements in output and prices?

    _____

    d. If policymakers wanted to move output back to the natural level of output, what should they do?

    _____

    e. If policymakers were able to move output back to the natural level of output, what would the policy do to prices?

    _____

    f. If policymakers had done nothing at all, what would have happened to the wage rate as the economy self-corrected or adjusted back to the natural level of output on its own?

    _____

    _____

    _____

    g. Is it likely that an increase in price expectations and wages *alone* can cause a permanent increase in the price level? Why or why not?

    _____

    _____

    _____

5. Suppose the economy is at a point such as point B in Exhibit 2. That is, aggregate demand has decreased, and the economy is in a recession. Describe the adjustment process necessary for the economy to adjust on its own to point C for each of the three theoretical short-run aggregate-supply curves.

    a.   the sticky-wage theory

    _____

    _____

    _____

    b.   the sticky-price theory

    _____

    _____

    _____

    c.   the misperceptions theory

    _____

    _____

    _____

    d.   Do you think the type of adjustments described above would take place more quickly from a recession or from a period when output was above the long-run natural level? Why or why not?

    _____

    _____

    _____

Short-Answer Questions

1. Name the three key facts about economic fluctuations.

    _____

    _____

    _____

2. What are the three reasons the aggregate-demand curve slopes downward? Explain them.

    _____

    _____

    _____

    _____

3. Explain the slope of the short-run aggregate-supply curve using the sticky-wage theory.

    _____

    _____

    _____

    _____

4. Does a shift in aggregate demand alter output in the short run? Why or why not?

    _____

    _____

    _____

    _____

5. Does a shift in aggregate demand alter output in the long run? Why or why not?

    _____

    _____

    _____

    _____

6. If the economy is in a recession, why might policymakers choose to adjust aggregate demand to eliminate the recession rather than let the economy adjust, or self-correct, on its own?

    _____

    _____

    _____

    _____

7. Which component of aggregate demand is most volatile over the business cycle?

    _____

8. Why is a decrease in the money supply unlikely to be neutral in the short run?

    _____

    _____

    _____

    _____

9. Suppose OPEC breaks apart and oil prices fall substantially. Initially, which curve shifts in the aggregate-supply and aggregate-demand model? In what direction does it shift? What happens to the price level and real output?

    _____

    _____

10. What causes both short-run and long-run aggregate supply to shift together? What causes only the short-run aggregate supply to shift while the long-run aggregate supply remains stationary?

_____

_____

_____

_____

Self-Test

True/False Questions

_____ 1. Over the last 50 years, U.S. real GDP has grown at about 5 percent per year.

_____ 2. Investment is a particularly volatile component of spending across the business cycle.

_____ 3. An increase in price expectations shifts the long-run aggregate-supply curve to the left.

_____ 4. If the classical dichotomy and monetary neutrality hold in the long run, then the long-run aggregate-supply curve should be vertical.

_____ 5. Economists refer to fluctuations in output as the "business cycle" because movements in output are regular and predictable.

_____ 6. One reason aggregate demand slopes downward is the wealth effect: A decrease in the price level increases the value of money holdings and consumer spending rises.

_____ 7. If the Federal Reserve increases the money supply, the aggregate-demand curve shifts to the left.

_____ 8. The misperceptions theory explains why the long-run aggregate-supply curve is downward sloping.

_____ 9. A rise in price expectations that causes wages to rise causes the short-run aggregate-supply curve to shift left.

_____ 10. If the economy is in a recession, the economy will adjust to long-run equilibrium on its own as wages and price expectations rise.

_____ 11. In the short run, if the government cuts back spending to balance its budget, it will likely cause a recession.

_____ 12. The short-run effect of an increase in aggregate demand is an increase in output and an increase in the price level.

_____ 13. A rise in the price of oil tends to cause stagflation.

_____ 14. In the long run, an increase in government spending tends to increase output and prices.

_____ 15. If policymakers choose to try to move the economy out of a recession, they should use their policy tools to decrease aggregate demand.

Multiple-Choice Questions

1. Which of the following statements about economic fluctuations is *true*?
    a. A recession is when output rises above the natural level of output.
    b. A depression is a mild recession.
    c. Economic fluctuations have been termed the "business cycle" because the movements in output are regular and predictable.
    d. A variety of spending, income, and output measures can be used to measure economic fluctuations because most macroeconomic quantities tend to fluctuate together.
    e. None of the above is true.

2. According to the interest-rate effect, aggregate demand slopes downward (negatively) because
    a. lower prices increase the value of money holdings and consumer spending increases.
    b. lower prices decrease the value of money holdings and consumer spending decreases.
    c. lower prices reduce money holdings, increase lending, interest rates fall, and investment spending increases.
    d. lower prices increase money holdings, decrease lending, interest rates rise, and investment spending falls.

3. Which of the following would *not* cause a shift in the long-run aggregate-supply curve?
    a. an increase in the available labor
    b. an increase in the available capital
    c. an increase in the available technology
    d. an increase in price expectations
    e. All of the above shift the long-run aggregate-supply curve.

4. Which of the following is *not* a reason why the aggregate-demand curve slopes downward?
    a. the wealth effect
    b. the interest-rate effect
    c. the classical dichotomy/monetary neutrality effects
    d. the exchange-rate effect
    e. All of the above are reasons why the aggregate-demand curve slopes downward.

5. In the model of aggregate demand and aggregate supply, the initial impact of an increase in consumer optimism is to
    a. shift short-run aggregate supply to the right.
    b. shift short-run aggregate supply to the left.
    c. shift aggregate demand to the right.
    d. shift aggregate demand to the left.
    e. shift long-run aggregate supply to the left.

6. Which of the following statements is *true* regarding the long-run aggregate-supply curve? The long-run aggregate-supply curve
    a. shifts left when the natural rate of unemployment falls.
    b. is vertical because an equal change in all prices and wages leaves output unaffected.
    c. is positively sloped because price expectations and wages tend to be fixed in the long run.
    d. shifts right when the government raises the minimum wage.

7. According to the wealth effect, aggregate demand slopes downward (negatively) because
   a. lower prices increase the value of money holdings and consumer spending increases.
   b. lower prices decrease the value of money holdings and consumer spending decreases.
   c. lower prices reduce money holdings, increase lending, interest rates fall, and investment spending increases.
   d. lower prices increase money holdings, decrease lending, interest rates rise, and investment spending falls.

8. The natural level of output is the amount of real GDP produced
   a. when there is no unemployment.
   b. when the economy is at the natural level of investment.
   c. when the economy is at the natural level of aggregate demand.
   d. when the economy is at the natural rate of unemployment.

9. Suppose the price level falls. Because of fixed nominal wage contracts, firms become less profitable, and they cut back on production. This is a demonstration of the
   a. sticky-wage theory of the short-run aggregate-supply curve.
   b. sticky-price theory of the short-run aggregate-supply curve.
   c. misperceptions theory of the short-run aggregate-supply curve.
   d. classical dichotomy theory of the short-run aggregate-supply curve.

10. Suppose the price level falls but suppliers only notice that the price of their particular product has fallen. Thinking there has been a fall in the relative price of their product, they cut back on production. This is a demonstration of the
    a. sticky-wage theory of the short-run aggregate-supply curve.
    b. sticky-price theory of the short-run aggregate-supply curve.
    c. misperceptions theory of the short-run aggregate-supply curve.
    d. classical dichotomy theory of the short-run aggregate-supply curve.

11. Suppose the economy is initially in long-run equilibrium. Then suppose there is a reduction in military spending due to the end of the Cold War. According to the model of aggregate demand and aggregate supply, what happens to prices and output in the *short run?*
    a. Prices rise; output rises.
    b. Prices rise; output falls.
    c. Prices fall; output falls.
    d. Prices fall; output rises.

12. Suppose the economy is initially in long-run equilibrium. Then suppose there is a reduction in military spending due to the end of the Cold War. According to the model of aggregate demand and aggregate supply, what happens to prices and output in the *long run?*
    a. Prices rise; output is unchanged from its initial value.
    b. Prices fall; output is unchanged from its initial value.
    c. Output rises; prices are unchanged from the initial value.
    d. Output falls; prices are unchanged from the initial value.
    e. Output and the price level are unchanged from their initial values.

13. Suppose the economy is initially in long-run equilibrium. Then suppose there is a drought that destroys much of the wheat crop. According to the model of aggregate demand and aggregate supply, what happens to prices and output in the *short run?*
    a. Prices rise; output rises.
    b. Prices rise; output falls.
    c. Prices fall; output falls.
    d. Prices fall; output rises.

14. Suppose the economy is initially in long-run equilibrium. Then suppose there is a drought that destroys much of the wheat crop. If policymakers allow the economy to adjust to long-run equilibrium on its own, according to the model of aggregate demand and aggregate supply, what happens to prices and output in the *long run*?
    a. Prices rise; output is unchanged from its initial value.
    b. Prices fall; output is unchanged from its initial value.
    c. Output rises; prices are unchanged from the initial value.
    d. Output falls; prices are unchanged from the initial value.
    e. Output and the price level are unchanged from their initial values.

15. Stagflation occurs when the economy experiences
    a. falling prices and falling output.
    b. falling prices and rising output.
    c. rising prices and rising output.
    d. rising prices and falling output.

16. Which of the following events shifts the short-run aggregate-supply curve to the right?
    a. an increase in government spending on military equipment
    b. an increase in price expectations
    c. a drop in oil prices
    d. a decrease in the money supply
    e. none of the above

Use Exhibit 4 to answer questions 17 and 18.

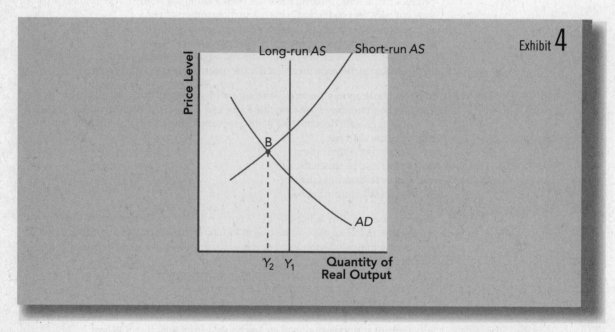

17. Suppose the economy is operating in a recession such as point B in Exhibit 4. If policymakers wished to move output to its long-run natural level, they should attempt to
    a. shift aggregate demand to the right.
    b. shift aggregate demand to the left.
    c. shift short-run aggregate supply to the right.
    d. shift short-run aggregate supply to the left.

18. Suppose the economy is operating in a recession such as point B in Exhibit 4. If policymakers allow the economy to adjust to the long-run natural level on its own,
    a. people will raise their price expectations, and the short-run aggregate supply will shift left.
    b. people will reduce their price expectations, and the short-run aggregate supply will shift right.
    c. people will raise their price expectations, and aggregate demand will shift left.
    d. people will reduce their price expectations, and aggregate demand will shift right.

19. According to the model of aggregate supply and aggregate demand, in the long run, an increase in the money supply should cause
    a. prices to rise and output to rise.
    b. prices to fall and output to fall.
    c. prices to rise and output to remain unchanged.
    d. prices to fall and output to remain unchanged.

20. Policymakers are said to "accommodate" an adverse supply shock if they
    a. respond to the adverse supply shock by increasing aggregate demand, which further raises prices.
    b. respond to the adverse supply shock by decreasing aggregate demand, which lowers prices.
    c. respond to the adverse supply shock by decreasing short-run aggregate supply.
    d. fail to respond to the adverse supply shock and allow the economy to adjust on its own.

Advanced Critical Thinking

You are watching the evening news on television. The news anchor reports that union wage demands are much higher this year because the workers anticipate an increase in the rate of inflation. Your roommate says, "Inflation is a self-fulfilling prophecy. If workers think there are going to be higher prices, they demand higher wages. This increases the cost of production, and firms raise their prices. Expecting higher prices simply causes higher prices."

1. Is this true in the short run? Explain.

   _____

   _____

   _____

2. If policymakers do nothing and allow the economy to adjust to the natural level of output on its own, does expecting higher prices cause higher prices in the long run? Explain.

   _____

   _____

   _____

3. If policymakers accommodate the adverse supply shock, does the expectation of higher prices cause higher prices in the long run? Explain.

   _____

   _____

   _____

Solutions

Terms and Definitions

_4_ Recession

_8_ Depression

_2_ The business cycle

_10_ Model of aggregate supply and demand

_5_ Aggregate-demand curve

_9_ Aggregate-supply curve

_6_ Natural rate of output

_1_ Menu costs

_7_ Stagflation

_3_ Accommodative policy

Practice Problems

1. a. Prices fall; output falls. Prices fall; output returns to the natural level. Shift aggregate demand to the right.

   b. Prices rise; output rises. Prices rise; output returns to the natural level. Shift aggregate demand to the left.

   c. Prices rise; output falls. Price level returns to original value; output returns to the natural level. Shift aggregate demand to the right.

   d. Prices fall; output rises. Price level returns to original value; output returns to the natural level. Shift aggregate demand to the left.

2. a. aggregate demand, right

   b. short-run aggregate supply, left

   c. both short-run and long-run aggregate supply, left

   d. aggregate demand, right

   e. both short-run and long-run aggregate supply, right

   f. both short-run and long-run aggregate supply, left

   g. short-run aggregate supply, right

   h. aggregate demand, left

   i. short-run aggregate supply, left

3. a. Aggregate demand shifts to the right.

   b. Price level rises, and real output rises.

   c. Price level rises, and real output stays the same. Money neutrality.

   d. No. Over time, people and firms adjust to the new higher amount of spending by raising their prices and wages.

4. a. Short-run aggregate supply shifts left.

   b. Prices rise, and output falls.

   c. Stagflation.

   d. Shift aggregate demand to the right.

   e. Prices would rise more and remain there.

   f. The high unemployment at the low level of output would put pressure on the wage to fall back to its original value shifting short-run aggregate supply back to its original position.

g. No. Increases in the cost of production need to be "accommodated" by government policy to permanently raise prices.

5. a. At point B, prices have fallen, but nominal wages are stuck at a high level based on a higher price expectation. Firms are less profitable, and they cut back on production. As workers and firms recognize the fall in the price level (learn to expect P_3), new contracts will have a lower nominal wage. The reduction in labor costs causes firms to increase production at each price level shifting the short-run aggregate supply to the right.

   b. At point B, some firms have not reduced their prices because of menu costs. Their products are relatively more expensive, and sales fall. When they realize the lower price level is permanent (learn to expect P_3), they lower their prices and output rises at each price level, shifting the short-run aggregate supply to the right.

   c. At point B, some firms mistakenly believe that only the price of their product has fallen and they have cut back on production. As they realize that all prices are falling (learn to expect P_3), they will increase production at each price, which will shift short-run aggregate supply to the right.

   d. More slowly from a recession because it requires prices to be reduced, and prices are usually more sticky downward. The adjustment when output is above normal requires prices and wages to rise.

Short-Answer Questions

1. Economic fluctuations are irregular and unpredictable; most macroeconomic quantities fluctuate together; and when output falls, unemployment rises.

2. Wealth effect: Lower prices increase the value of money holdings and consumer spending increases. Interest-rate effect: Lower prices reduce the quantity of money held, some is loaned, interest rates fall, and investment spending increases. Exchange-rate effect: Lower prices decrease interest rates, the dollar depreciates, and net exports increase.

3. In the short run, nominal wages are fixed based on fixed-price expectations. If actual prices unexpectedly fall while nominal wages remain fixed, firms are less profitable, and they cut back on production.

4. Yes. Changes in aggregate demand cause actual prices to deviate from expected prices. Due to sticky wages, sticky prices, and misperceptions about relative prices, firms respond by changing output.

5. No. In the long run, output is determined by factor supplies and technology (long-run aggregate supply). Changes in aggregate demand only affect prices in the long run.

6. Because they think they can get the economy back to the long-run natural level of output more quickly or, in the case of a negative supply shock, because they are more concerned with output than inflation.

7. Investment.

8. Because a decrease in aggregate demand from a decrease in the money supply may reduce the price level unexpectedly. In the short run, some prices and wages are stuck, and some producers have misperceptions regarding relative prices causing output to fall.

9. Short-run aggregate supply shifts right. Prices fall, and output rises.

10. Changes in the available factors (labor, capital, natural resources) and technology shift both long-run and short-run aggregate supply. Changes in price expectations that may be associated with wage demands and oil prices only shift short-run aggregate supply.

True/False Questions

1. F; the U.S. economy has grown at about 3 percent per year.
2. T
3. F; changes in price expectations shift the short-run aggregate-supply curve.
4. T
5. F; fluctuations in output are irregular.
6. T
7. F; aggregate demand shifts to the right.
8. F; it explains why the short-run aggregate-supply curve is upward sloping.
9. T
10. F; in a recession, the economy adjusts to long-run equilibrium as wages and prices fall.
11. T
12. T
13. T
14. F; in the long run, it tends to increase prices, but it has no impact on output.
15. F; policymakers should increase aggregate demand.

Multiple-Choice Questions

1. d
2. c
3. d
4. c
5. c
6. b
7. a
8. d
9. a
10. c
11. c
12. b
13. b
14. e
15. d
16. c
17. a
18. b
19. c
20. a

Advanced Critical Thinking

1. Yes. An increase in price expectations shifts the short-run aggregate-supply curve to the left and prices rise.

2. No. In the long run, the increase in unemployment will cause wages and price expectations to fall back to their prior levels.

3. Yes. If policymakers accommodate the adverse supply shock with an increase in aggregate demand, the price level will rise permanently.

Chapter 24

The Influence of Monetary and Fiscal Policy on Aggregate Demand

Goals
In this chapter you will

- Learn the theory of liquidity preference as a short-run theory of the interest rate

- Analyze how monetary policy affects interest rates and aggregate demand

- Analyze how fiscal policy affects interest rates and aggregate demand

- Discuss the debate over whether policymakers should try to stabilize the economy

Outcomes
After accomplishing these goals, you should be able to

- Show what an increase in the money supply does to the interest rate in the short run

- Illustrate what an increase in the money supply does to aggregate demand

- Explain crowding out

- Describe the lags in fiscal and monetary policy

Chapter Overview

Context and Purpose

Chapter 24 is the second chapter in a three-chapter sequence that concentrates on short-run fluctuations in the economy around its long-term trend. In Chapter 23, we introduced the model of aggregate supply and aggregate demand. In Chapter 24, we see how the government's monetary and fiscal policies affect aggregate demand.

387

The purpose of Chapter 24 is to address the short-run effects of monetary and fiscal policies. In Chapter 23, we found that when aggregate demand or short-run aggregate supply shifts, it causes fluctuations in output. As a result, policymakers sometimes try to offset these shifts by shifting aggregate demand with monetary and fiscal policy. Chapter 24 addresses the theory behind these policies and some of the shortcomings of *stabilization policy*.

Chapter Review

Introduction   Chapters 17 through 22 demonstrated the impact of fiscal and monetary policy on saving, investment, and long-term growth. Chapter 23 demonstrated that shifts in aggregate demand and short-run aggregate supply cause short-run fluctuations in the economy around its long-term trend and how monetary and fiscal policymakers might shift aggregate demand to stabilize the economy. In this chapter, we address the theory behind stabilization policies and some of the shortcomings of stabilization policy.

How Monetary Policy Influences Aggregate Demand

The aggregate-demand curve shows the quantity of goods and services demanded at each price level. Recall from Chapter 23 that aggregate demand slopes downward due to the wealth effect, the interest-rate effect, and the exchange-rate effect. Since money is a small part of total wealth and since the international sector is a small part of the U.S. economy, the most important reason for the downward slope of U.S. aggregate demand is the interest-rate effect.

The interest rate is a key determinant of aggregate demand. To see how monetary policy affects aggregate demand, we develop Keynes's theory of interest rate determination called the theory of liquidity preference. This theory suggests that the interest rate is determined by the supply and demand for money. Note that the interest rate being determined is both the nominal and the real interest rate because, in the short run, expected inflation is unchanging so changes in the nominal rate equal changes in the real rate.

Recall, the money supply is determined by the Fed and can be fixed at whatever level the Fed chooses. Therefore, the money supply is unaffected by the interest rate and is a vertical line in Exhibit 1. People have a demand for money because money, as the economy's most liquid asset, is a medium of exchange. Hence, people have a demand for it even though it has no rate of return because it can be used to buy things. The interest rate is the opportunity cost of holding money. When the interest rate is high, people hold more wealth in interest-bearing bonds and economize on their money holdings. Thus, the quantity of money demanded is reduced. This is shown in Exhibit 1. The equilibrium interest rate is determined by the intersection of money supply and money demand.

Note that, in the long run, the interest rate is determined by the supply and demand for loanable funds. In the short run, the interest rate is determined by the supply and demand for money. This poses no conflict.

- In the long run, output is fixed by factor supplies and technology, the interest rate adjusts to balance the supply and demand for loanable funds, and the price level adjusts to balance the supply and demand for money.

- In the short run, the price level is sticky and cannot adjust. For any given price level, the interest rate adjusts to balance the supply and demand for money. The interest rate influences aggregate demand and thus output.

Each theory highlights the behavior of interest rates over a different time horizon.

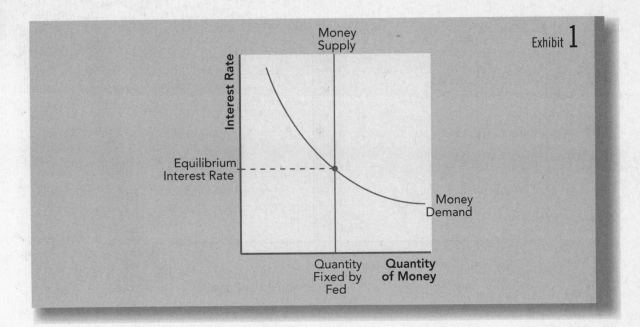

We can use the theory of liquidity preference to add precision to our explanation of the negative slope of the aggregate-demand curve. Recall from previous chapters, the demand for money is positively related to the price level because at higher prices, people need more money to buy the same quantity of goods. Thus, a higher price level shifts money demand to the right, as shown in Exhibit 2, panel (a). With a fixed money supply, a larger money demand raises the interest rate. A higher interest rate reduces investment expenditures and causes the quantity demanded of goods and services to fall in Exhibit 2, panel (b).

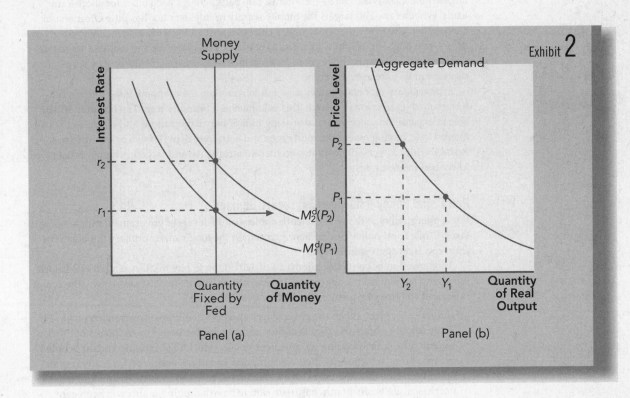

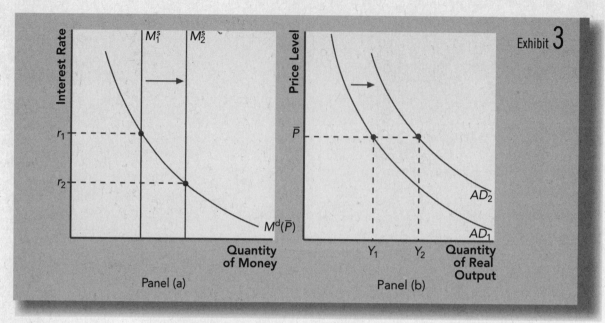

Returning to the point of this section: How does monetary policy influence aggregate demand? Suppose the Fed buys government bonds shifting the money supply to the right, as in Exhibit 3, panel (a). The interest rate falls, reducing the cost of borrowing for investment. Hence, the quantity of goods and services demanded at each price level increases, shifting aggregate demand to the right in Exhibit 3, panel (b).

The Fed can implement monetary policy by targeting the money supply or interest rates. In recent years, the Fed has targeted the interest rate because the money supply is hard to measure and because money demand fluctuates, causing fluctuations in interest rates, aggregate demand, and output for a given money supply. In particular, the Fed has targeted the *federal funds rate*—the interest rate banks charge each other for short-term loans. Whether the Fed targets the money supply or interest rates has little effect on our analysis because every monetary policy can be described in terms of the money supply or the interest rate. For example, the monetary policy expansion used to increase aggregate demand in the example above could be described as an increase in the money supply or a decrease in the interest rate target.

Expansionary monetary policy may fail to stimulate the economy if the interest rate has reached its zero lower bound. This is known as a liquidity trap. The Fed may still be able to expand the economy by increasing inflationary expectations and reducing the real interest rate, buying assets like mortgages and corporate debt (known as quantitative easing), which lowers interest rates on those instruments, and targeting higher inflation to lower real interest rates.

How Fiscal Policy Influences Aggregate Demand

Fiscal policy refers to the government's choices of the levels of government purchases and taxes. While fiscal policy can influence growth in the long run, its primary impact in the short run is on aggregate demand.

An increase in government purchases of $20 billion to buy military aircraft is reflected in a rightward shift in the aggregate-demand curve. There are two reasons why the actual rightward shift may be greater than or less than $20 billion:

- *The multiplier effect:* When the government spends $20 billion on aircraft, incomes rise in the form of wages and profits of the aircraft manufacturer. The recipients of the new income raise their spending on consumer goods, which raises the incomes of people in other firms, which raises their consumption spending, and so on for many rounds. Since aggregate demand may rise by much more than the increase in government purchases, government purchases are said to have a multiplier effect on aggregate demand. There is a formula for the size of the multiplier effect. It says that for every dollar the government spends, aggregate demand shifts to the right by $1/(1 - MPC)$, where MPC stands for the *marginal propensity to consume*—the fraction of extra income that a household spends on consumption. For example, if the MPC is 0.75, the multiplier is $1/(1 - 0.75) = 1/0.25 = 4$, which means that \$1 of government spending shifts aggregate demand to the right by a total of \$4. An increase in the MPC increases the multiplier.

In addition to the multiplier, the increase in purchases may cause firms to increase their investment expenditures on new equipment, further increasing the response of aggregate demand to the initial increase in government purchases. This is known as the *investment accelerator*.

Thus, the aggregate-demand curve may shift by more than the change in government purchases.

The logic of the multiplier effect applies to other changes in spending besides government purchases. For example, shocks to consumption, investment, and net exports may have a multiplier effect on aggregate demand.

- *The crowding-out effect:* The crowding-out effect works in the opposite direction of the multiplier. An increase in government purchases (as in the case above) raises incomes, which shifts the demand for money to the right. This raises the interest rate, which lowers investment. Thus, an increase in government purchases increases the interest rate and reduces, or crowds out, private investment. Due to crowding out, the aggregate-demand curve may shift right by less than the increase in government purchases.

Whether the final shift in the aggregate-demand curve is greater than or less than the original change in government spending depends on which is larger: the multiplier effect or the crowding-out effect.

The other half of fiscal policy is taxation. A reduction in taxes increases households' take-home pay and, hence, increases their consumption. Thus, a decrease in taxes shifts aggregate demand to the right while an increase shifts aggregate demand to the left. The size of the shift in aggregate demand depends on the relative size of the multiplier and crowding-out effects described above. In addition, a reduction in taxes that is perceived by households to be permanent improves the financial condition of the household a great amount and increases aggregate demand substantially. A change in taxes that is perceived to be temporary has a much smaller effect on aggregate demand.

The sizes of fiscal policy mulipliers are very difficult to predict.

Finally, fiscal policy might have an effect on aggregate supply for two reasons. First, a reduction in taxes might increase the incentive to work and cause aggregate supply to shift right. *Supply-siders* believe this effect could be so large that tax revenue could increase. Most economists do not believe this is the normal case. Second, government purchases of capital, such as roads and bridges, may increase the amount of goods supplied at each price level and shift the aggregate-supply curve to the right. This effect is more likely to be important in the long run.

Using Policy to Stabilize the Economy

Keynes (and his followers) argued that the government should actively use monetary and fiscal policies to stabilize aggregate demand and, as a result, output and employment.

The Employment Act of 1946 holds the federal government responsible for promoting full employment and production. The act has two implications: (1) The government should not be the cause of fluctuations, so it should avoid sudden changes in fiscal and monetary policy; and (2) the government should respond to changes in the private economy in order to stabilize it. For example, if consumer pessimism reduces aggregate demand, the proper amount of expansionary monetary or fiscal policy could stimulate aggregate demand to its original level, thereby avoiding a recession. Alternatively, if excessive optimism increases aggregate demand, contractionary monetary or fiscal policy could dampen aggregate demand to its original level, thereby avoiding inflationary pressures. Failure to actively stabilize the economy may allow for unnecessary fluctuations in output and employment.

Some economists argue that the government should not use monetary and fiscal policy to try to stabilize short-run fluctuations in the economy. While they agree that, in theory, activist policy can stabilize the economy, they feel that, in practice, monetary and fiscal policy affect the economy with a substantial lag. The lag for monetary policy is at least six months, so it may be hard for the Fed to "fine-tune" the economy. Fiscal policy has a long political lag because it takes months or years to pass spending and taxation legislation. These lags mean that activist policy could be destabilizing because expansionary policy could accidentally increase aggregate demand during periods of excessive private aggregate demand, and contractionary policy could accidentally decrease aggregate demand during periods of deficient private aggregate demand.

Automatic stabilizers are changes in fiscal policy that automatically stimulate aggregate demand in a recession so that policymakers do not have to take deliberate action. The tax system automatically lowers tax collections during a recession when incomes and profits fall. Government spending automatically rises during a recession because unemployment benefits and welfare payments rise. Hence, both the tax and government spending systems increase aggregate demand during a recession. A strict balanced budget rule would eliminate automatic stabilizers because the government would have to raise taxes or lower expenditures during a recession.

Helpful Hints

1. The multiplier can be derived in a variety of different ways. Your text shows you that the value of the multiplier is $1/(1 - MPC)$. However, it doesn't show you how this number is generated. Below, you will find one of the many different ways that the value of the multiplier can be derived for the case of an increase in government spending:

   $$\Delta\text{output demanded} = \Delta\text{spending on output,}$$

   which says that the change in output demanded equals the change in spending on output. Denoting Y as output demanded, G as government spending, and noting that output equals income, then

   $$\Delta Y = \Delta G + [(MPC) \times \Delta Y],$$

   which says that the change in output demanded is equal to the change in total spending where total spending is composed of the change in government spending plus the change in consumption spending induced by the increase in income (say 0.75 of the change in income).

   Solving for ΔY, we get

   $$\Delta Y - [(MPC) \times \Delta Y] = \Delta G$$

   $$\Delta Y \times (1 - MPC) = \Delta G$$

   $$\Delta Y = 1/(1 - MPC) \times \Delta G,$$

   which says that a $1 increase in government spending causes an increase in aggregate demand of $1/(1 - MPC) \times \$1$. If the MPC equals 0.75, then $1/(1 - 0.75) = 4$ and a $1 increase in government spending shifts aggregate demand to the right by $4.

2. An increase in the MPC increases the multiplier. If the MPC were 0.80, suggesting that people spend 80 percent of an increase in income on consumption goods, the multiplier would become $1/(1 - 0.80) = 5$. This is larger than the multiplier generated above from an MPC of 0.75. There is an intuitive appeal to this result. If people spend a higher percentage of an increase in income on consumption goods, any new government purchase will have an even larger multiplier effect and shift the aggregate-demand curve further to the right.

3. The multiplier works in both directions. If the government reduces purchases, the multiplier effect suggests that the aggregate-demand curve will shift to the left by a greater amount than the initial reduction in government purchases. When the government reduces purchases, wages and profits of people are reduced, and they reduce their consumption expenditures, and so on, creating a multiple contraction in aggregate demand.

4. Activist stabilization policy has many descriptive names. Activist stabilization policy is the use of discretionary monetary and fiscal policies to manage aggregate demand in such a way as to minimize the fluctuations in output and to maintain output at the long-run natural level. As such, activist stabilization policy is sometimes called *discretionary policy* to distinguish it from automatic stabilizers. It is also called *aggregate demand management* because monetary and fiscal policies are used to adjust or manage total spending in the economy. Finally, since policymakers attempt to counter the business cycle by reducing aggregate demand when it is too high and by increasing aggregate demand when it is too low, stabilization policy is sometimes referred to as *countercyclical policy*.

5. Activist stabilization policy can be used to move output toward the long-run natural level from levels of output that are either above or below the natural level of output. As in the previous chapter, most of the examples of stabilization policy in the text assume the economy is in a recession—a period when output is below the long-run natural level. However, activist stabilization policy can be used to reduce aggregate demand and output in periods when output exceeds the long-run natural level. When output exceeds the natural level, we sometimes say that the economy is in a boom, an expansion, or that the economy is overheating. When the economy's output is above the natural level, the economy is said to be overheating because, left alone, the economy will adjust to a higher level of expected prices and wages, and output will fall to the natural level (short-run aggregate supply shifts left). Most economists believe that the Federal Reserve needs political independence to combat an overheating economy. This is because the activist policy prescription for an overheating economy is a reduction in aggregate demand, which usually faces political opposition. That is, "taking away the punch bowl just as the party gets going" is not likely to be politically popular.

Terms and Definitions

Choose a definition for each key term.

Key Terms

____ Theory of liquidity preference

____ Liquidity

____ Federal funds rate

____ Fiscal policy

____ Multiplier effect

____ Investment accelerator

____ Marginal propensity to consume, or MPC

____ Crowding-out effect

____ Stabilization policy

____ Automatic stabilizers

Definitions

1. The dampening of the shift in aggregate demand from expansionary fiscal policy, which raises the interest rate and reduces investment spending

2. The interest rate banks charge one another for short-term loans

3. The amplification of the shift in aggregate demand from expansionary fiscal policy, which raises investment expenditures

4. Keynes's theory that the interest rate is determined by the supply and demand for money in the short run

5. Changes in fiscal policy that do not require deliberate action on the part of policymakers

6. The use of fiscal and monetary policies to reduce fluctuations in the economy

7. The amplification of the shift in aggregate demand from expansionary fiscal policy, which raises incomes and further increases consumption expenditures

8. The ease with which an asset is converted into a medium of exchange

9. The fraction of extra income that a household spends on consumption

10. The setting of the level of government spending and taxation by government policymakers

Problems and Short-Answer Questions

Practice Problems

1. If the Federal Reserve were to engage in activist stabilization policy, in which direction should they move the *money supply* in response to the following events?
    a. A wave of optimism boosts business investment and household consumption.

    _____

    b. To balance its budget, the federal government raises taxes and reduces expenditures.

    _____

    c. OPEC raises the price of crude oil.

    _____

    d. Foreigners experience a reduction in their taste for U.S.-produced Ford automobiles.

    _____

e. The stock market falls.

_____

2. If the Federal Reserve were to engage in activist stabilization policy, in which direction should they move *interest rates* in response to the same events listed in problem 1?
    a. A wave of optimism boosts business investment and household consumption.

    _____

    b. To balance its budget, the federal government raises taxes and reduces expenditures.

    _____

    c. OPEC raises the price of crude oil.

    _____

    d. Foreigners experience a reduction in their taste for U.S.-produced Ford automobiles.

    _____

    e. The stock market falls.

    _____

    f. Explain the relationship between Fed policy in terms of the money supply and policy in terms of the interest rate.

    _____

    _____

    _____

3. If policymakers were to use fiscal policy to actively stabilize the economy, in which direction should they move government spending and taxes?
    a. A wave of pessimism reduces business investment and household consumption.

    _____

    b. An increase in price expectations causes unions to demand higher wages.

    _____

    c. Foreigners increase their taste for domestically produced Ford automobiles.

    _____

    d. OPEC raises the price of crude oil.

    _____

4. Suppose the economy is in a recession. Policymakers estimate that aggregate demand is $100 billion short of the amount necessary to generate the long-run natural level of output. That is, if aggregate demand were shifted to the right by $100 billion, the economy would be in long-run equilibrium.
    a. If the federal government chooses to use fiscal policy to stabilize the economy, by how much should they increase government spending if the marginal propensity to consume (*MPC*) is 0.75 and there is no crowding out?

    _____

    _____

b. If the federal government chooses to use fiscal policy to stabilize the economy, by how much should they increase government spending if the marginal propensity to consume (*MPC*) is 0.80 and there is no crowding out?

_____

_____

c. If there is crowding out, will the government need to spend more or less than the amounts you found in *a* and *b* above? Why?

_____

_____

d. If investment is very sensitive to changes in the interest rate, is crowding out more of a problem or less of a problem? Why?

_____

_____

e. If policymakers discover that the lag for fiscal policy is two years, should that make them more likely to employ fiscal policy as a stabilization tool or more likely to allow the economy to adjust on its own? Why?

_____

_____

5. a. What does an increase in the money supply do to interest rates in the short run? Explain.

_____

_____

_____

b. What does an increase in the money supply do to interest rates in the long run? Explain.

_____

_____

_____

c. Are these results inconsistent? Explain.

_____

_____

_____

Short-Answer Questions

1. Why is the money supply curve vertical when it is drawn on a graph with the interest rate on the vertical axis and the quantity of money on the horizontal axis?

   _____

   _____

   _____

2. Why does the money demand curve slope negatively when it is drawn on a graph with the interest rate on the vertical axis and the quantity of money on the horizontal axis?

   _____

   _____

   _____

3. Why does an increase in the price level reduce the quantity demanded of real output? (Use the interest-rate effect to explain the slope of the aggregate-demand curve.)

   _____

   _____

   _____

   _____

4. Explain how an increase in the money supply shifts the aggregate-demand curve.

   _____

   _____

   _____

   _____

5. Explain the intuition of the multiplier effect resulting from an increase in government spending. Why should a bigger *MPC* make the multiplier effect larger?

   _____

   _____

   _____

   _____

6. Explain how an increase in government spending may lead to crowding out.

   _____

   _____

   _____

7. Suppose the government spends $10 billion on a public works program in order to stimulate aggregate demand. If the crowding-out effect exceeds the multiplier effect, will the aggregate-demand curve shift to the right by more or less than $10 billion? Why?

_____

_____

_____

_____

8. How does a cut in taxes affect aggregate supply?

_____

_____

_____

9. Which is likely to have a greater impact on aggregate demand: a temporary reduction in taxes or a permanent reduction in taxes? Why?

_____

_____

_____

10. Explain why taxes and government spending may act as automatic stabilizers. What would a strict balanced-budget rule cause policymakers to do during a recession? Would this make the recession more or less severe?

_____

_____

_____

Self-Test

True/False Questions

_____ 1. An increase in the interest rate increases the quantity demanded of money because it increases the rate of return on money.

_____ 2. When money demand is drawn on a graph with the interest rate on the vertical axis and the quantity of money on the horizontal axis, an increase in the price level shifts money demand to the right.

_____ 3. Keynes's theory of liquidity preference suggests that the interest rate is determined by the supply and demand for money.

_____ 4. The interest-rate effect suggests that aggregate demand slopes downward because an increase in the price level shifts money demand to the right, increases the interest rate, and reduces investment.

_____ 5. An increase in the money supply shifts the money supply curve to the right, increases the interest rate, decreases investment, and shifts the aggregate-demand curve to the left.

_____ 6. Suppose investors and consumers become pessimistic about the future and cut back on expenditures. If the Fed engages in activist stabilization policy, the policy response should be to decrease the money supply.

_____ 7. In the short run, a decision by the Fed to increase the money supply is essentially the same as a decision to decrease the interest rate target.

_____ 8. Because of the multiplier effect, an increase in government spending of $40 billion will shift the aggregate-demand curve to the right by more than $40 billion (assuming there is no crowding out).

_____ 9. If the *MPC* (marginal propensity to consume) is 0.80, then the value of the multiplier is 8.

_____ 10. Crowding out occurs when an increase in government spending increases incomes, shifts money demand to the right, raises the interest rate, and reduces private investment.

_____ 11. Suppose the government increases its expenditure by $10 billion. If the crowding-out effect exceeds the multiplier effect, then the aggregate-demand curve shifts to the right by more than $10 billion.

_____ 12. Suppose investors and consumers become pessimistic about the future and cut back on expenditures. If fiscal policymakers engage in activist stabilization policy, the policy response should be to decrease government spending and increase taxes.

_____ 13. Many economists prefer automatic stabilizers because they affect the economy with a shorter lag than activist stabilization policies.

_____ 14. In the short run, the interest rate is determined by the loanable-funds market, while in the long run, the interest rate is determined by money demand and money supply.

_____ 15. Unemployment benefits are an example of an automatic stabilizer because when incomes fall, unemployment benefits rise.

Multiple-Choice Questions

1. Keynes's liquidity preference theory of the interest rate suggests that the interest rate is determined by
    a. the supply and demand for loanable funds.
    b. the supply and demand for money.
    c. the supply and demand for labor.
    d. aggregate supply and aggregate demand.

2. When money demand is expressed in a graph with the interest rate on the vertical axis and the quantity of money on the horizontal axis, an increase in the interest rate
    a. increases the quantity demanded of money.
    b. increases the demand for money.
    c. decreases the quantity demanded of money.
    d. decreases the demand for money.
    e. does none of the above.

3. When the supply and demand for money are expressed in a graph with the interest rate on the vertical axis and the quantity of money on the horizontal axis, an increase in the price level
    a. shifts money demand to the right and increases the interest rate.
    b. shifts money demand to the left and increases the interest rate.
    c. shifts money demand to the right and decreases the interest rate.
    d. shifts money demand to the left and decreases the interest rate.
    e. does none of the above.

4. For the United States, the most important source of the downward slope of the aggregate-demand curve is
   a. the exchange-rate effect.
   b. the wealth effect.
   c. the fiscal effect.
   d. the interest-rate effect.
   e. none of the above.

5. In the market for real output, the initial effect of an increase in the money supply is to
   a. shift aggregate demand to the right.
   b. shift aggregate demand to the left.
   c. shift aggregate supply to the right.
   d. shift aggregate supply to the left.

6. The initial effect of an increase in the money supply is to
   a. increase the price level.
   b. decrease the price level.
   c. increase the interest rate.
   d. decrease the interest rate.

7. The long-run effect of an increase in the money supply is to
   a. increase the price level.
   b. decrease the price level.
   c. increase the interest rate.
   d. decrease the interest rate.

8. Suppose a wave of investor and consumer pessimism causes a reduction in spending. If the Federal Reserve chooses to engage in activist stabilization policy, it should
   a. increase government spending and decrease taxes.
   b. decrease government spending and increase taxes.
   c. increase the money supply and decrease interest rates.
   d. decrease the money supply and increase interest rates.

9. The initial impact of an increase in government spending is to shift
   a. aggregate supply to the right.
   b. aggregate supply to the left.
   c. aggregate demand to the right.
   d. aggregate demand to the left.

10. If the marginal propensity to consume (MPC) is 0.75, the value of the multiplier is
    a. 0.75.
    b. 4.
    c. 5.
    d. 7.5.
    e. none of the above.

11. An increase in the marginal propensity to consume (MPC)
    a. raises the value of the multiplier.
    b. lowers the value of the multiplier.
    c. has no impact on the value of the multiplier.
    d. rarely occurs because the MPC is set by congressional legislation.

12. Suppose a wave of investor and consumer optimism has increased spending so that the current level of output exceeds the long-run natural rate. If policymakers choose to engage in activist stabilization policy, they should
    a. decrease taxes, which shifts aggregate demand to the right.
    b. decrease taxes, which shifts aggregate demand to the left.
    c. decrease government spending, which shifts aggregate demand to the right.
    d. decrease government spending, which shifts aggregate demand to the left.

13. When an increase in government purchases raises incomes, shifts money demand to the right, raises the interest rate, and lowers investment, we have seen a demonstration of
    a. the multiplier effect.
    b. the investment accelerator.
    c. the crowding-out effect.
    d. supply-side economics.
    e. the liquidity trap.

14. Which of the following statements regarding taxes is correct?
    a. Most economists believe that, in the short run, the greatest impact of a change in taxes is on aggregate supply, not aggregate demand.
    b. A permanent change in taxes has a greater effect on aggregate demand than a temporary change in taxes.
    c. An increase in taxes shifts the aggregate-demand curve to the right.
    d. A decrease in taxes shifts the aggregate-supply curve to the left.

15. Suppose the government increases its purchases by $16 billion. If the multiplier effect exceeds the crowding-out effect, then
    a. the aggregate-supply curve shifts to the right by more than $16 billion.
    b. the aggregate-supply curve shifts to the left by more than $16 billion.
    c. the aggregate-demand curve shifts to the right by more than $16 billion.
    d. the aggregate-demand curve shifts to the left by more than $16 billion.

16. When an increase in government purchases increases the income of some people, and those people spend some of that increase in income on additional consumer goods, we have seen a demonstration of
    a. the multiplier effect.
    b. the investment accelerator.
    c. the crowding-out effect.
    d. supply-side economics.
    e. none of the above.

17. When an increase in government purchases causes firms to purchase additional plant and equipment, we have seen a demonstration of
    a. the multiplier effect.
    b. the investment accelerator.
    c. the crowding-out effect.
    d. supply-side economics.
    e. none of the above.

18. Which of the following is an automatic stabilizer?
    a. military spending
    b. spending on public schools
    c. unemployment benefits
    d. spending on the space shuttle
    e. All of the above are automatic stabilizers.

19. Which of the following statements about stabilization policy is *true*?
    a. In the short run, a decision by the Fed to increase the targeted money supply is essentially the same as a decision to increase the targeted interest rate.
    b. Congress has veto power over the monetary policy decisions of the Fed.
    c. Long lags enhance the ability of policymakers to "fine-tune" the economy.
    d. Many economists prefer automatic stabilizers because they affect the economy with a shorter lag than activist stabilization policy.
    e. All of the above are true.

20. Which of the following best describes how an increase in the money supply shifts aggregate demand?
    a. The money supply shifts right, the interest rate rises, investment decreases, and aggregate demand shifts left.
    b. The money supply shifts right, the interest rate falls, investment increases, and aggregate demand shifts right.
    c. The money supply shifts right, prices rise, spending falls, and aggregate demand shifts left.
    d. The money supply shifts right, prices fall, spending increases, and aggregate demand shifts right.

Advanced Critical Thinking

You are watching a nightly network news broadcast. The opening report is a story about today's meeting of the Fed's Federal Open Market Committee. The business correspondent reports that the Fed raised interest rates by a quarter of a percent today to head off future inflation. The report then moves to interviews with prominent politicians. The response of a member of Congress to the Fed's move is negative. She says, "The Consumer Price Index has not increased, yet the Fed is restricting growth in the economy, supposedly to fight inflation. My constituents will want to know why they are going to have to pay more when they get a loan, and I don't have a good answer. I think this is an outrage, and I think Congress should have hearings on the Fed's policymaking powers."

1. What interest rate did the Fed raise?

   _____

   _____

2. State the Fed's policy in terms of the money supply.

   _____

   _____

3. Why might the Fed raise interest rates before the CPI starts to rise?

   _____

   _____

   _____

   _____

4. Many economists believe that the Fed needs to be independent of politics. Use the congresswoman's statement to explain why so many economists argue for Fed independence.

   _____

   _____

   _____

   _____

   _____

   _____

Solutions

Terms and Definitions

_4_   Theory of liquidity preference

_8_   Liquidity

_2_   Federal funds rate

_10_ Fiscal policy

_7_   Multiplier effect

_3_   Investment accelerator

_9_   Marginal propensity to consume, or MPC

_1_   Crowding-out effect

_6_   Stabilization policy

_5_   Automatic stabilizers

Practice Problems

1. a. Decrease the money supply

   b. Increase the money supply

   c. Increase the money supply

   d. Increase the money supply

   e. Increase the money supply

2. a. Increase interest rates

   b. Decrease interest rates

   c. Decrease interest rates

   d. Decrease interest rates

   e. Decrease interest rates

   f. In the short run, with prices sticky or fixed, an increase in the money supply implies a reduction in interest rates and a decrease in the money supply implies an increase in interest rates.

3. a. Increase spending, decrease taxes

   b. Increase spending, decrease taxes

   c. Decrease spending, increase taxes

   d. Increase spending, decrease taxes

4. a. Multiplier = $1/(1 - 0.75) = 4$; $100/4 = \$25$ billion.

   b. Multiplier = $1/(1 - 0.80) = 5$; $100/5 = \$20$ billion.

   c. More, because as the government spends more, investors spend less so aggregate demand won't increase by as much as the multiplier suggests.

   d. More of a problem. Government spending raises interest rates. The more sensitive investment is to the interest rate, the more it is reduced or crowded out by government spending.

   e. More likely to allow the economy to adjust on its own because if the economy adjusts before the impact of the fiscal policy is felt, the fiscal policy will be destabilizing.

5. a. It lowers interest rates because, in the short run, with prices sticky or fixed, money demand is unchanging. Thus, an increase in the money supply requires a decrease in interest rates to induce people to hold the additional money.

   b. It has no effect because, in the long run, the increase in spending causes a proportional increase in prices, output is fixed at the natural level, money

is neutral, and interest rates are determined by the supply and demand for loanable funds, which have not changed.

   c. No. Prices are likely to be sticky in the short run and flexible in the long run.

Short-Answer Questions

1. Because the quantity of money is fixed at whatever value the Fed chooses and this quantity is not dependent on the interest rate.

2. The interest rate is the opportunity cost of money since money earns no rate of return. Thus, an increase in the interest rate causes people to economize on cash balances and hold more wealth in interest-bearing bonds.

3. An increase in the price level shifts money demand to the right, increases the interest rate, and decreases investment.

4. The money supply shifts right, the interest rate decreases, investment increases at each price level, which is a rightward shift in the aggregate-demand curve.

5. When the government purchases goods, it causes an increase in the incomes of the sellers. They spend some percent of their new higher income on goods and services, raising others' incomes, and so on. The higher the *MPC*, the greater the percent of new income spent in each round.

6. An increase in government spending raises incomes, shifts money demand right, raises the interest rate, and reduces investment.

7. By less than $10 billion because the crowding-out effect, which reduces the shift in aggregate demand, more than offsets the multiplier effect, which amplifies the shift.

8. It causes an increase in aggregate supply by increasing the incentive to work.

9. Permanent because it improves the financial condition of the household more, and thus, they spend more.

10. Income tax collections fall during a recession, and government spending on welfare and unemployment benefits rises. It would cause the government to raise other taxes and lower other spending. More severe.

True/False Questions

1. F; an increase in the interest rate decreases the quantity demanded of money because it raises the opportunity cost of holding money.

2. T

3. T

4. T

5. F; an increase in the money supply decreases the interest rate, increases investment, and shifts aggregate demand to the right.
6. F; the Fed should increase the money supply.
7. T
8. T
9. F; the value of the multiplier is 5.
10. T
11. F; the aggregate-demand curve shifts to the right by less than $10 billion.
12. F; policymakers should increase government spending and decrease taxes.
13. T
14. F; in the short run, the interest rate is determined by money demand and money supply, while in the long run, it is determined by the loanable-funds market.
15. T

Multiple-Choice Questions

1. b
2. c
3. a
4. d
5. a
6. d
7. a
8. c
9. c
10. b
11. a
12. d
13. c
14. b
15. c
16. a
17. b
18. c
19. d
20. b

Advanced Critical Thinking

1. The federal funds rate.
2. They decreased the money supply (or lowered its growth rate).
3. Because monetary policy acts on the economy with a lag. If the Fed waits until inflation has arrived, the effect of its policy will arrive too late. Thus, the Fed may wish to respond to its forecast of inflation.
4. Politicians must be responsive to the short-term needs of voters. Monetary policy must take a long-term view and make politically painful decisions when the economy is overheating (when output is above the long-run natural rate). In this case, there

is pressure for prices to rise in the future so the standard policy response is to contract aggregate demand now. It is unpopular to "take the punch bowl away just as the party gets going."